CARL

The C ... he general edit‹
the dea... of the S... ... publi... books about C
economics, geography, history, politics, society, and related subjects. It includes ir
new works as well as reprints of classics in the fields. The editorial committee v
manuscripts and suggestions, which should be sent to the dean of the School of C
Studies and Research, Carleton University.

LAND OF THE MIDNIGHT SUN

A HISTORY OF THE YUKON

KEN S. COATES WILLIAM R. MORRISON

CARLETON LIBRARY SERIES 202

McGILL-QUEEN'S UNIVERSITY PRESS   Montreal & Kingston • London
UNIVERSITY OF WASHINGTON PRESS   Seattle

© McGill-Queen's University Press 2005

ISBN 0-7735-2756-7 (cloth)
ISBN 0-7735-2757-5 (paper)

Legal deposit second quarter 2005
Bibliothèque nationale du Québec

Printed in Canada on acid-free paper that is 100% ancient forest free (100% post-consumer recycled), processed chlorine free

McGill-Queen's University Press acknowledges the support of the Canada Council for the Arts for our publishing program. We also acknowledge the financial support of the Government of Canada through the Book Publishing Industry Development Program (BPIDP) for our publishing activities.

Library and Archives Canada Cataloguing in Publication Data

Coates, Kenneth, 1956–
Land of the midnight sun : a history of the Yukon / Ken S. Coates,
William R. Morrison. – 2nd ed.

(Carleton Library; 202)
Includes bibliographical references and index.
ISBN 0-7735-2756-7 (cloth)
ISBN 0-7735-2757-5 (pbk)

1. Yukon Territory – History. I. Morrison, William R. (William Robert), 1942– II. Title.

FC4011.C62 2005   971.9'1   C2004-904638-1

Library of Congress Cataloging-in-Publication Data

Coates, Kenneth, 1956–
Land of the midnight sun : a history of the Yukon / Ken S. Coates, William R. Morrison.– [2nd ed.] p. cm.

Includes bibliographical references and index.
ISBN 0-295-98475-9 (UWP pbk. : acid-free paper)

1. Yukon Territory – History. I. Morrison, William R. (William Robert), 1942– II. Title.

F1091.C6 2005   971.9'1-DC22   2004021052

Designed and typeset by studio oneonone in 10/12 Sabon

CONTENTS

ILLUSTRATIONS

MAPS

PREFACE

When this book was first published in 1988, it was the collaboration of two historians of quite different ages, personalities, interests, and backgrounds. We were and are a disparate team. One of us was raised in the Yukon, the other in Ontario. One was drawn to the study of Yukon history by the absence of historical analysis about a region he viewed as his homeland; to the other, the Yukon provided an opportunity to study the evolution of Canadian attitudes and policies towards the North, stemming from an early interest in the RCMP. The book represented a union of these approaches – an attempt to see the North from both the inside and the outside.

In the first edition, we tried to incorporate the entire Yukon into our investigation. We believed then, and we still do, that in the past the activities of newcomers to the Yukon – explorers, traders, miners, and government officials – had attracted most of the attention from researchers and writers. The First Nations people, until thirty years ago, were wrongly relegated to the background. The irony of this is obvious, for the aboriginal people of the Yukon have persisted in occupying their corner of the world, while non-aboriginals, as a group, demonstrated in the past surprisingly little commitment to the territory, moving in and out as the seasons and business cycles dictated. The history of the Yukon should be the history of both groups and of the relationship between them. We have tried to bring these often separate strands of Yukon history together in the hope that aboriginals and whites will recognize how their histories – and their futures – are very much intertwined.

This book also reflects our belief that the history of the Yukon Territory is far more than the experience of the Klondike gold rush and the building of the Alaska Highway. In the past, these dramatic events drew most of the attention given to the Yukon, to the detriment of our understanding of the complexities of its history. While giving them their rightful due, we have covered the full range of the Yukon experience. It is in this larger picture that the major themes of Yukon history become particularly evident: aboriginal persistence, the transiency of the white population, formal and informal processes of racial segregation, the boom-and-bust cycles of the economy, the debilitating effects of colonial status, and the Yukon's inability to control its own destiny.

This study is dominated by our understanding of the Yukon Territory as one of Canada's colonies. The political, cultural, and economic realities of being a colony within Canada had a major impact on the territory's evolution during the last century. Rooted deep in the past, the struggle to shed the bonds of colonialism and to gain a full measure of local autonomy dominates contemporary politics and government in the Yukon.

Much has changed since we completed the first edition of this book. The writing project began when we were colleagues at Brandon University – a fortuitous circumstance that started a long friendship and professional collaboration. *Land of the Midnight Sun* was the first book we wrote together. *Strange Things Done: Murder in Yukon History*, recently published by McGill-Queen's University Press, will be our tenth.

A great deal of professional and personal water has flowed under our respective bridges since that first collaboration. Ken was recruited to the University of Victoria, where he lived and worked in southern comfort, all the while maintaining extensive contact with the Yukon Territory. Bill moved to the Centre for Northern Studies at Lakehead University, where he became the director of the centre and worked on the promotion of northern Canadian history. We were both fanatics about a new invention called the Internet, which allowed us to send entire files of draft chapters back and forth across the country. We wrote *Land of the Midnight Sun* as an e-collaboration, often passing multiple drafts of sections back and forth each day and enjoying the convenience and interactivity of the new technology. Still living a long way from each other, we hardly ever meet, but e-mail makes it seem as though we have offices next door to each other.

We were pleased with the results of the first edition of this book, save for the unfortunate mistake of leaving Faro off the map of the modern Yukon, an omission that (deservedly) earned us a full-page rebuke in a Whitehorse newspaper. The book enjoyed reasonable sales and was generally well reviewed. But writers are their own strongest critics, and from the very beginning we knew that there were things we wanted to correct, should the opportunity arise again. In recent years, new works of scholarship have emerged, written by established experts such as Julie Cruikshank and new academics such as Charlene Porschild, Barbara Kelcey, and Kathryn Morse. Territorial debates have changed greatly, with the land claims substantially

resolved, self-government negotiations underway, and the Yukon's autonomy movement set in new directions. Yet old issues, such as the Alaska
Highway natural-gas pipeline and the proper commemoration of Klondike
history, have remained alive and controversial. It was clear to us that the
ideas with which we concluded the first edition were beginning to sound a
little hollow and outdated.

Our careers have changed as well. We both had the good luck of being
able to work on the founding of the University of Northern British Columbia, the first degree-granting institution in Canada created with an explicit-
ly northern focus. It remains a crowning achievement in both our careers. Ken
left UNBC after it opened, and worked in New Zealand, New Brunswick,
Japan, and Saskatchewan. In 2004 he returned to the West Coast as one of
the founding academic leaders at a new university in Squamish. Bill completed his term as dean of graduate studies and research and returned to
teaching and research, enjoying two semesters as a visiting professor at
Duke University.

The collaboration that started in Brandon has continued to serve us very
well. It seemed only natural, then, to return to *Land of the Midnight Sun*,
and we were delighted when McGill-Queen's and the Carleton Library Series asked us to prepare a second edition. We are very attached to the arguments and concept of this book and have thoroughly enjoyed the opportunity to update and expand our earlier work. The is the first time we have
brought out a revised second edition of one of our books, and it was interesting to see what needed to be changed after fifteen years. In the 1988 edition, the terms "First Nations" and "aboriginal" were never used; they were
just beginning to come into use, and we used the word "Indians" throughout the book. Most of these references have been changed in this edition to
reflect modern usage. The references to distance have been changed to include the metric system, as well as the imperial, except where the result seems
historically inappropriate. We have, however, retained the nomenclature
"The Yukon," instead of "Yukon," which became popular in official territorial circles in the late 1980s. It is true that "The" in the territory's name
is anomalous (none of the provinces or other territories have it), but we have
decided to stick with the common usage. More importantly, we have written a new final chapter to reflect the important changes that have taken place
in the Yukon since the first edition was published.

Our efforts have, as in the past, been supported and encouraged by others. Aurèle Parisien at MQUP is a superb editor and even better friend. His
ready wit, sharp pen, and keen editorial eye keep us on our toes. The press's
editorial staff, particularly Joan McGilvray, have done an excellent job of
bringing this book into print. We have been supported, as well, by our respective institutions. The University of Northern British Columbia and the
University of Saskatchewan provided grants in aid of publication; their

support for our scholarly activities is acknowledged with gratitude. We have drawn continual inspiration from our friends and scholarly colleagues in history, northern history, and northern studies, including Robin Fisher, Greg Poelzer, Jim Miller, Bill Waiser, Jon Swainger, Ted Binnema, Dave DeBrou, Mary-Ellen Kelm, Shelagh Grant, and Kerry Abel. We are grateful for their example, for their solid works of scholarship, and for their encouragement of our careers.

Our families, of course, have stood behind us throughout our careers. Ken has had the unique pleasure of watching his brother Colin receive an appointment as a Canadian research chair in history at Glendon College, York University. Bradley, Ken's oldest son, has taken the first big steps towards a graduate degree in history and may represent yet another sacrifice on the altar of Clio. Mark has opted for graduate studies in psychology; watching his academic progress is a delight. Laura's fascination with classical Rome and Greece is likely to turn into further studies in the field. Marlon and Hana, too young to face the forces of what seems to be the family trade, know not what awaits them. Their joyous vitality and enthusiasm for life are an inspiration and a great antidote to aging. The past year has been difficult for Carin. She has faced grave challenges with remarkable spirit and determination and has emerged with her smile intact and her optimism firmly in place. She makes it possible for me – Ken – to write; it is impossible to describe properly the love and admiration I have for her. Bill, as the elder partner in this long collaboration, is an empty nester, with Catherine, John, Claire, and Ruth standing on their own feet as fine young adults. Graeme and Ella, much-welcomed grandchildren, continue to be sources of delight, and Linda a cheerful and tolerant source of strength and support.

We want *Land of the Midnight Sun* to resonate both with the people who live in the Yukon and with those who visit this remarkable land. We take enormous pleasure from learning that Yukoners have used this history to understand the complexities of territorial history and to address the challenges of the present better. We are thrilled when we hear from travellers who have found that the book increased their appreciation for the Yukon, which remains one of the most beautiful and inspirational places on this earth. Finally, we are humbled by the task of trying, in a small number of pages, to make sense of the complex and multifaceted history of the Yukon Territory. Our historical work on the North, like the region itself, remains a work in progress. We have much still to do.

KEN COATES, University of Saskatchewan
BILL MORRISON, University of Northern British Columbia

LAND

OF THE

MIDNIGHT

SUN

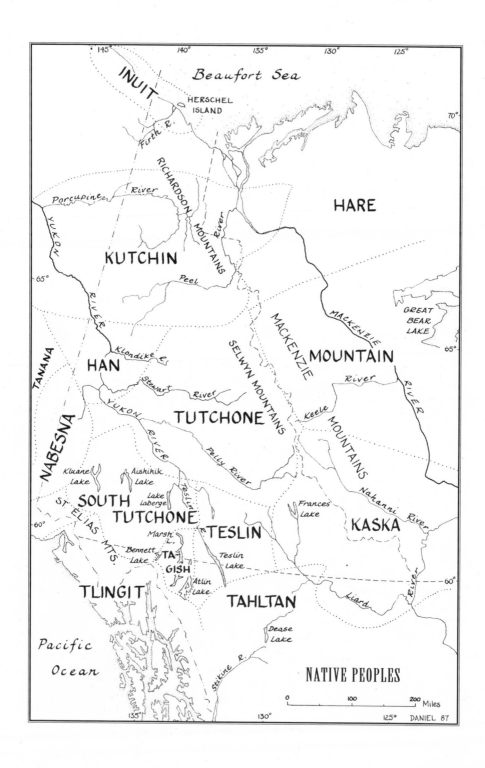

Beaufort Sea

INUIT

HERSCHEL
ISLAND

Firth R.

HARE

Porcupine River

RICHARDSON MOUNTAINS

KUTCHIN

River

Peel

MACKENZIE

GREAT
BEAR
LAKE

YUKON RIVER

Klondike C.

HAN

Stewart River

SELWYN MOUNTAINS

MACKENZIE

MOUNTAIN

River

Keele

RIVER

TANANA

YUKON RIVER

TUTCHONE

Pelly River

MOUNTAINS

Nahanni River

NABESNA

Kluane
Lake

Aishihik
Lake

Lake
Laberge

Teslin

Frances
Lake

KASKA

ST. ELIAS MTS.

SOUTH
TUTCHONE

Marsh
L.

Bennett
Lake

TA-
GISH

TESLIN

Teslin
Lake

RIVER

Atlin
Lake

TLINGIT

TAHLTAN

Liard

Pacific
Ocean

Dease
Lake

Stikine R.

NATIVE PEOPLES

0   100   200 Miles

DANIEL 87

ONE

The Natives' Yukon

Yukon – what a vivid image the word evokes in the minds of people all over the world: miners and gold, snow and hardship, Mounties and Dangerous Dan McGrew. But these things, while rooted in fact, reflect only a single dramatic episode that occurred over a few years of the long and generally little-known history of the region. An irony of a land rich in historical irony is that the Yukon, one of the youngest parts of North America as far as European civilization is concerned, was almost certainly the first part of the continent to bear the footprint of humankind. It is a young land, yet at the same time almost unimaginably old.

Non-Canadians sometimes have vague and confused notions about the Yukon. Many Americans, for instance, believe that the territory is part of Alaska and, lumping the Klondike gold rush with the later one in Nome, think of the two as one large northern gold frontier. But Canadians should not be smug about this; as modern-day Yukoners will attest, they too are often pretty vague about the territory, thinking of it, along with the North-west Territories and Nunavut, as a kind of undefined "North." Indeed, outsiders' ignorance and neglect of their homeland is one of the main complaints that Yukoners have about their treatment by the rest of the country.

The neglect may seem strange, for Canada is a northern country. The North – the "True North, strong and free" of our national anthem – is the symbol of our identity and our future. Our national myth is that the North has given a special quality to our character. Leading nineteenth-century Canadian thinkers claimed that the future belonged to northern peoples, arguing that the country's character rested in the hardiness, fortitude, and inventiveness demanded by the winter climate.[1]

Such ideas may have been fodder for academics and the occasional politician, but they do not reflect the realities of Canadian life. Even during periods of national navel gazing, when Canadians have agonized about the alleged lack of a national identity, little public attention has been devoted to
the northern nature of this identity. Has the North in fact shaped the Canadian character? Is it truly a part of Canada, in the sense that it is part of a
Canadian homeland? Or is it a place to exploit, a national treasure house,
where people can seek their fortunes in order to return with their wealth to
southern places? The North means different things to different people. To
some it is a place to be pillaged. To its aboriginal inhabitants it is and for
millennia has been simply a homeland – a fact that should be obvious but
seemed to surprise the nation when it received wide publicity during the
Mackenzie Valley pipeline hearings in the mid 1970s.[2] To Yukoners, southern Canada is "the outside" and its residents are "outsiders." But perhaps
"outsiders" equally well describes how Yukoners see themselves in their relations with the rest of their country.

This book is a history of a northern region that has been created by geography and by legislative fiat. The borders of the Yukon Territory are partly natural (its southern three-quarters consisting of the upper Yukon River
valley and most of its drainage basin) and partly artificial (its western border at the 141st meridian reflecting nothing more than European power politics of a century and a half ago).

There are several explanations of the origin of the territory's name. John
Bell, the first European to stand on the banks of the upper Yukon River, said
that the Indians called it *Youcon*, or white water river. It has subsequently
been suggested that the term derives from the Kutchin word *Yu-kun-ah*,
meaning great river. The Hudson's Bay Company wrote the name of its river
and its fort as John Bell had done, but when the company withdrew in 1869,
the Americans opted for the more concise spelling that remains in common
usage. Most of the other geographic features of the Yukon, however, bear
not their original names but those given to them by European explorers.[3]

The Yukon Territory covers 186,100 square miles (482,000 km²), of
which about 1 per cent is inland water and more than half is wooded. Its
elevation varies from sea level on the northern coast to 19,850 feet (6,050 m)
at the top of Mount Logan, the highest point in Canada. Much of the territory is mountainous, the chains running from the northwest to the southeast. The highest peaks, including Mount Logan, are in the spectacular
Kluane region of the Yukon's extreme southwest corner, and it is these
mountains that effectively cut the territory off from the Pacific. Whitehorse,
although only 100 miles (160 km) from tidewater, has a climate very different from that of the Alaskan coastal settlements of Skagway and Haines.
A geographical oddity worth a question in Trivial Pursuit is that the entire
territory lies farther west than Vancouver. Beaver Creek, a highway com-

It is not easy to depict cold in a photograph, but this view of a Dawson City street, shrouded in ice fog, taken at -60°F (-51°C), is a fairly successful attempt (National Archives of Canada [NA]).

munity near the Alaskan border, has the distinction of being Canada's most westerly community.

Despite the proximity of the ocean, the climate is continental. The brilliant, intense summer months are warm, with temperatures occasionally recorded in the mid-thirties Celsius, but the winters can be paralysingly cold; the lowest temperature ever recorded in Canada was in February 1947 at Snag, northwest of Kluane Lake, when the mercury plummeted to -81°F (-63°C). In the southern parts of the territory, the winters are often broken by chinooks, gusts of warm Pacific air that push across the mountains, raising the temperature (and the spirits of the residents) dramatically in a matter of hours. Yukoners find some solace in the fact that their periods of extreme cold, unlike those in the Eastern Arctic, are generally not accompanied by bone-jarring winds. The semi-arid climate keeps rainfall to a minimum and helped to create the "world's smallest desert" just outside Carcross. Permafrost is present everywhere north of the Porcupine River and also occurs here and there throughout the territory.

The Yukon possesses a striking geographic diversity. Along the southern border, a series of major lakes, tucked neatly among the mountain valleys, dominates the landscape. For many centuries, the Native people have inhabited the shores of Kluane, Aishihik, Dezadeash, Kushwa, Bennett, Tagish, Marsh, Laberge, and Teslin lakes. In the extreme north, the Arctic coastal plain slopes gently down from the mountains to the Beaufort Sea. Just off the coast is Herschel Island, the northernmost part of the Yukon. At some almost unimaginable time in the past, when this part of North America was closer to the equator, great deciduous forests covered the land that now lies under the Beaufort Sea waters. Over countless centuries these were turned into the oil that has for some years past been the target of numerous exploration companies.

Different natural forces gave the Yukon its other treasures. Rich lodes of silver, lead, copper, and other ores lay locked in the mineral-rich hills of the Yukon River valley. At some distant geological period, gold was deposited in the rocks not far from present-day Dawson City. Later, water eroded these rocks, ripped the gold from them, and glacial creeks carried sand, gravel, and finely ground gold away from the original location – the mother lode – and deposited them in creek beds. Since that part of the Yukon – the Klondike district – was never glaciated, the gold stayed in the creeks where it fell; otherwise, it would have been torn from the bedrock and deposited many miles to the south, and there would have been no Klondike gold rush. Over thousands of years the creeks shifted in their beds, and more sand and muck buried the gold. There it lay until Europeans and North Americans, who valued gold almost more than life itself, came to search for it.

In its primeval state, the Yukon was well stocked with wildlife – moose and caribou, mountain sheep and goats, bears, and animals that later supported the commercial fur trade, such as marten, beaver, and fox. A variety of fish, including Pacific salmon migrating from the Bering Strait, grayling, lake trout (char), whitefish, and northern pike could be found in the Yukon's many rivers and lakes.

Much of the Yukon is well treed, though not densely, with spruce, poplar, and lodgepole pine being the most common species. In areas where the ground thaws deeply in summer, the spruce can grow as tall as 120 feet (36.5 m). In the parts of the territory that escaped glaciation there are plants that occur nowhere else in the Canadian North. It comes as a surprise to the non-botanist – who might think that the Yukon's official wildflower, the ubiquitous fireweed, is the only flower in evidence – that the territory contains at least a dozen species of wild orchids.

The most notable feature of the territory is the great river that gives the region its name. The southern three-quarters of the Yukon Territory, part of British Columbia, and much of Alaska – an area of 325,500 square miles (841,000 km²) – is drained by this broad and mighty but fairly placid river, as it flows from its source, less than 20 miles (32 km) from salt water at the Lynn Canal, over 2,000 miles (3,200 km) to its mouth near St Michael on the Bering Strait. The fact that it is easily navigable from its mouth almost to its source has been a great advantage to the region. Like the other great northern river, the Mackenzie, the Yukon has provided a ready (though long and slow) avenue of transportation into the interior. Unlike the St Lawrence, the Yukon River has no great rapids in its lower reaches to hamper commerce and travel, though navigation on it was never trouble free; Miles Canyon and the nearby Whitehorse Rapids blocked river steamers from travelling the entire route. There were also several smaller impediments. Five Finger Rapids and the Rink Rapids and the constantly shifting sandbars in the river presented major difficulties for all but the most shallow-draft vessels.

The Yukon together with Alaska is the oldest continuously inhabited part of North America. It is almost universally accepted that humankind, in some distant past, came to this continent across a land bridge from Asia. Therefore, people first entered the hemisphere through western Alaska and migrated via the Yukon into the rest of North America. This may have taken place before the beginning of the last ice age, about twenty thousand years ago. Thus, human habitation of what is now Canada began not just in the Yukon but in one of the most northerly parts of the territory – the Old Crow basin. Through an irony of geography and climate, during the last ice age, while much of the rest of what is now North America was weighed down by a heavy layer of glacial ice, the Old Crow basin was free of ice in the summers, probably because the snowfall was too scanty to breed glaciers.

There is a great deal of uncertainty about when the first Alaskans and Yukoners arrived. Most North American archaeologists accept that these people first reached the regions south of the ice sheet in significant numbers about 11,000 BC, though some would put the date very much earlier than that. There is considerable controversy over when people first reached this continent and how long they stayed in the Northwest before spreading south.[4] The traditional view was that they came south through what is now the central Yukon and British Columbia, but more recent theory suggests a coastal route, stopping and camping at locations that are now submerged by coastal waters.

Some of the most interesting and controversial Canadian archaeological finds have been made in the valley of the Old Crow River. The excitement started with the discovery in 1966 of a caribou bone that had been worked by hand into a flesher – a tool to scrape hides – as well as other bones that had evidently been altered by humans. Radio carbon dating gave a date for the flesher of 25,000 BC. This was a find of sensational dimensions. To uncover in the northwesternmost part of Canada evidence of humankind's activities in North America thousands of years older than any other accepted find – such a discovery would revolutionize the understanding of the prehistory of North America. Even as the debate started, scientists, particularly teams led by Richard Harrington and William H. Irving, returned to the field, hoping to find further confirmation of the existence of early humans in the Yukon.

But there were two difficulties with this discovery, neither of which has yet been resolved. First, although it was obvious that the flesher was of human origin, there was no way to tell whether the work had been done on a bone from a freshly killed animal or on one perhaps thousands of years old, picked up somewhere already fossilized. As for the other bones that had seemingly been worked by human hands, it was suggested that they had been cracked by large carnivores or by freezing and thawing, or perhaps they too were tools made from fossilized bones. None of these artifacts had been found in the locations where they had originally been dropped; they had all been carried in some way, probably by water, from their point of origin to where they were found, so geological dating was of no use. (The shifting sands of the Old Crow flats are geologically unstable, meaning that the location of a particular item at a specific depth cannot be readily tied to a specific era.) Many experiments were done with caribou bones – throwing them to lions, freezing them, and breaking them in various ways. While those who believed that the flesher was indeed 27,000 years old were convinced that the results of these experiments proved their theory, others were skeptical. Their doubts were justified in 1985, when more sophisticated radiocarbon tests indicated that the flesher and some or the other bones dated from about AD 1000, though others were indeed much older. What was needed was further proof, perhaps indisputable evidence of a campsite, fire, or human dwelling.

In 1975 a number of limestone caves were discovered in the Old Crow region. In them were deposits of dust, bones, pollen, and debris which, when deciphered by paleontologists, gave a record of the natural history of the region for the past 20,000 years. At the beginning of that period, the rock flow of the caves had begun to fill with loess – fine wind-blown dust. This accumulated at the rate of less than a millimetre per year for about 10,000 years. Analysis revealed that at first the land was tundra, inhabited by horses, mammoths, caribou, muskoxen, bison, mountain sheep, elk, wolves, and bears. About 14,000 years ago the climate warmed appreciably, permitting shrubs and small trees to grow. The pollen in the layers of dust in the caves showed that about 10,000 years ago the area became forested with spruce trees. Then the loess stopped blowing as vegetation covered the northern Yukon, and the large animals disappeared from the region.

Unfortunately, nothing in the caves suggested a human presence. The oldest incontrovertible traces of humans are some flint artifacts dating to about 10,000 BC. There are a few suggestions of human activity in the form of flint flakes dating to 14,000 BC, as well as a massive number of bones, which simply seem too numerous to have been brought to the caves by any animal other than man. But there are no traces of fire from the 16,000 BC level of the caves, nor are there any tools – the things that are necessary to convince the doubters. The search continues, and the Old Crow region remains a hotbed of archaeological research.

A glimpse into Yukon prehistory over several millennia is provided by Catherine McClellan's sensitive and evocative vignettes of Native life at different periods. The earliest one, titled "late winter on a branch of the Porcupine River, 11,000 years ago," describes a people engaged in a hunter-gatherer way of life. The chief difference between their lives and those of later generations is the lack of tree cover and thus firewood in that era. Nonetheless, they were successful in hunting caribou and bison (and the occasional mammoth, though these were disappearing from the country), from which they obtained food and clothing:

Bison meat is rare at this season of the year. In summer, everybody in camp can help to drive a herd over a cliff or up a narrow canyon by setting fires in the grass and then running and shouting behind to scare the animals. The dogs help in the drive too. Bison that break their bones as they fall over the cliff, or bunch up at the head of a canyon, can be quite easily killed by the hunters. In winter it is not so easy. The hunters had to follow the herd on foot for many miles before they had a chance to make this kill, but it was a specially good one. Butchering the cow, the hunters found an unborn calf in her – just the kind of food to give to the two wise but nearly toothless older men on whose knowledge the welfare of the group depends.[5]

The more recent prehistory of the Yukon is better known. Sites have been investigated in the northern part of the territory which indicate that the prehistory of the last few millennia is that of Inuit rather than Indian peoples, for the artifacts dating from that period are common to the Inuit of antiquity. A caribou antler punch found near Dawson City has been dated to 21,900 BC, but the same questions arise about it as about the flesher found near Old Crow. The southern part of the Yukon, on the other hand, was almost completely covered by glaciers during the last ice age; thus the earliest traces of human occupation, found at a site along the Alaska Highway near the Aishihik River, date to about 5,200 BC.

In more recent times there have been a number of distinct but related Native peoples in the Yukon. Inland Tlingit, related to the Tlingit people of the Pacific northwest coast, lived in the area of the southern lakes. To the far north, the Inuit occupied the Arctic slope and Herschel Island. The

Athapaskan peoples covered much of the territory. They are racially, and in some cases linguistically, akin to Native people living to the west of them in Alaska and to the east and southeast of them in the Mackenzie Valley. It is not possible to link these people with those who were in the Yukon during the glacial period, but it does seem that their direct ancestors were living in the Yukon by at least 8,000 BC.[6]

Some of the history of the precontact Athapaskans – or Dene – particularly the migration of different subgroups, can be deduced from a study of linguistics. The linguistic history of the Dene suggests that as late as about 700 BC they were a single, closely related group of people with a homeland in east-central Alaska and the adjacent part of the Yukon. After this date the Dene began to disperse, a movement into the present groupings that was not completed until about AD 1400. The First Nations of the Yukon are thus part of a large, widely dispersed indigenous people. Because they traditionally did not observe rigid geographical boundaries, and because their languages shade into one another through various dialects, attempts to divide them into distinct tribes or bands are arbitrary. Most of the names given to them are the creations of Europeans, but in recent years they have revived traditional names and now insist on indigenous usage.

The First Nations were hunters and gatherers, their lives governed by the natural environment and the changing seasons. The Gwich'in people's lives were centred around the hunting of large game animals, particularly caribou. Winter hunting was done on foot, and snowshoes were an important item of manufacture. The mainstay of the hunt, the Porcupine River caribou herd, was hunted intensely during the fall migration. The technique of the hunt was to construct two long rows of wooden sticks in the path of the animals, thus funnelling them into an enclosure, or surround, made of branches. Snares made of hide were set, and when the animals followed the path of sticks or were frightened into it, they ran into the snares and were killed with bows and arrows. Sometimes the caribou were driven into a lake and then speared. Both techniques were highly effective, and if the migration occurred when and where it was expected, it produced an abundance of food and useful animal products. Although other animals, including moose, bear, hare, and ptarmigan, were hunted, the caribou was to the Gwich'in what the seal was to the Inuit – food, clothing, and a host of other necessities. They thus had to live, at least in certain seasons, where the caribou lived. In particular, they had to wait for them at river crossings and other likely places during the fall migration, when the animals were at their fattest and their hides were in the best condition. They also ate fish, which they speared or trapped in weirs. The Tron'dëk Hwëch'in (formerly called the Han), who inhabited the west-central Yukon, were particularly adept at this, developing the Klondike fishing grounds into the mainstay of their seasonal round. People supplemented their diet with berries, rose hips, and other wild plants.

The harvesting of large animals, particularly moose and caribou, provided the basis of native life in the upper Yukon River basin (Yukon Government photo).

In each area of the Yukon, the indigenous people adapted their eating habits, seasonal movements, and lifestyle to make the best use of the available food resources. These groups, therefore, differed quite markedly. In the Alsek River drainage, in the Yukon's southwest corner, people maintained regular contact with the coastal First Nations and built their life around the abundant salmon stocks. The Kaska Dena of the southeast, on the other hand, relied primarily on non-migratory fish and the hunting of large game animals. In all cases, poor fish stocks, a decline in the number of large animals, exceptionally cold winters or wet summers, or unpredictable changes in animal migratory habits could bring suffering and even starvation. In such instances there was usually recourse to smaller game – squirrels and rabbits – or berries, roots, and other plants to sustain life until the returns from the hunt improved.

The aboriginal peoples of the Yukon pursued a way of life that has been described as "restricted wandering." Such people identify a particular territory as their own and take measures to restrict the access of others to its resource. As the seasons passed, they moved about freely, according to no rigid pattern, in pursuit of food. The largest social unit was the local group or band – either a single extended family or a small number of related or

"A Co-Yukon Deer Corral," drawn by Frederick Whymper in 1865, clearly shows the traditional aboriginal technique of driving caribou into a "surround." The two rows of branches funnel the animals to the enclosure where they are easily killed (authors' collection).

friendly families. At certain times of the year, perhaps when a seasonal fish run or caribou migration ensured that food supplies were plentiful, a larger number of families might live and hunt in one location. An intense social round of activities followed, including games, ceremonies, and even the launching of raids and attacks on neighbouring First Nations groups. Such sites were found along all the major rivers and lakes, and, logically, many later became the sites of fur trading posts and aboriginal villages. The social structure of these people was egalitarian. There were few differences in status, and although there were men who were recognized as leaders, their leadership was informal and largely advisory in nature; they had no means of enforcing their wishes.

The Native people were intensely spiritual, though not in a way that Christian missionaries would readily acknowledge. They had few public religious forms except for shamans, who had a particular relationship with the supernatural that enabled them to cure illness, place spells on enemies, and bring good luck in the hunt. The First Nations' world view, however, was

Top: Gwich'in people dancing, from Alexander Hunter Murray's journal of 1847–48 (Murray, *Journal of the Yukon*)

Bottom: Gwich'in winter dwelling of caribou hide, half-banked with snow and protected by a windbreak of trees, drawn by Alexander Hunter Murray (Murray, *Journal of the Yukon*)

Murray's drawing of an adult
Gwich'in man with facial
tattooing, wearing typical
ornaments and beads, probably
of European manufacture
(Murray, *Journal of the Yukon*)

filled with spirits – they suffused all animate and inanimate objects – and
much of their behaviour was rooted in a strong awareness of the presence of
spiritual forces.

The Inuit living on the Yukon's Arctic slope followed a very different
lifestyle. The Arctic had been inhabited in a series of waves separated by
many generations as the people adapted to changing environmental conditions and the development of new technology. Partly because these people
lived in treeless regions, making their campsites and artifacts easier to find
than those of people who lived in the forest, their prehistory can be more
readily traced. The Inuit of the Western Arctic, unlike their relatives of inland Alaska, lived largely off the resources of the sea, which provided a rich
foundation for their adaptation to a harsh and unforgiving environment.
Theirs was a unique society. Europeans would marvel at its simplicity yet
wonder at its complexity, for the Inuit were able to live well in a land that
white men found most inhospitable.[7]

Long before the first European actually set foot in the Yukon River valley or along the Arctic slope, the Native peoples had learned of the existence of white men. The various Native groups – coastal Tlingit, Tagish, Tutchone, Kaska, Han, Kutchin (to give them the names the Europeans originally gave them) and Inuit – had for centuries been regular traders among themselves, bartering surplus goods from their own region for supplies not otherwise available. When Europeans – Russian in the 1740s and British in the 1770s – arrived along the Pacific northwest coast, news of their appearance travelled inland quickly.

Local desire for the new trade goods, especially such products as knives, axes, and pots, ensured an enthusiastic response to the advance of Europeans along the coast and down the Mackenzie River. The Dene people of central Alaska shifted significantly to the east, to exploit the trading opportunities better. Long-established intertribal trading networks were abandoned or were altered, or expanded to carry manufactured goods into the Yukon and furs out to the Europeans.

The newcomers made their presence felt, even though they had not yet advanced beyond the periphery. The trading First Nations people unwittingly carried European diseases into the interior, killing an untold number of people who had yet to see a European face-to-face. T.H. Canham, an Anglican missionary who worked in the Yukon in the late nineteenth century, was told by his congregation that the "great diminution during the past century in the number of native inhabitants" was due to "the ravages of smallpox communicated from the southern indians soon after the date of the earliest explorations."[8] The Yukon First Nations, who numbered between seven and eight thousand before the Europeans arrived, declined rapidly in subsequent years; the loss of many elders to the devastating diseases was an incalculable loss to a society that relied on oral traditions.

By the 1830s, the upper Yukon River valley was one of the few blank spots on the European maps of North America, sharing that status with parts of the Eastern Arctic and the Arctic Archipelago. Such gaps could not be tolerated, particularly when the unknown lands might hold commercial opportunities. It was therefore only a matter of time before European traders and explorers breached the mountain barriers and entered the Yukon basin. The indigenous people of the interior, dependent on other Natives for manufactured goods, eagerly awaited the fur traders' advance. The written history of the Yukon was about to begin.

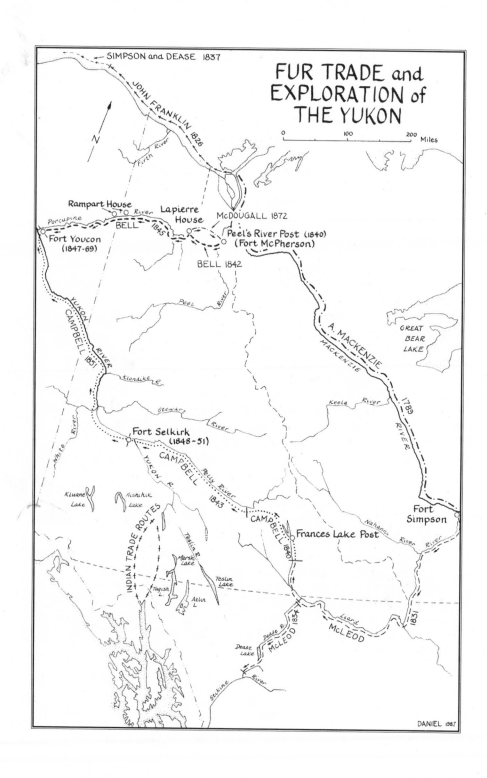

FUR TRADE and
EXPLORATION of
THE YUKON

SIMPSON and DEASE 1837

JOHN FRANKLIN 1826

Firth River

N

0   100   200 Miles

Rampart House   Lapierre
                        House   McDOUGALL 1872
Porcupine   River
BELL   1845   Peel's River Post (1840)
Fort Youcon   (Fort McPherson)
(1847-69)
                        BELL 1842

Peel   River

YUKON   A. MACKENZIE
                                              GREAT
CAMPBELL   BEAR
         RIVER   LAKE
                                    MACKENZIE
              Klondike R.

White River   Stewart   River   Keele   River   1789

Fort Selkirk   RIVER
(1848-51)
              CAMPBELL
Kluane   Aishihik   YUKON R. 1843
Lake   Lake   Pelly River

                    CAMPBELL   Fort
INDIAN TRADE ROUTES   1840   Frances Lake Post   Simpson
                   Teslin R.   Nahanni
                                                River   River
         Marsh
         Lake   1831
    Tagish   Teslin
           Atlin   Lake   Liard
           L.   Dease R.   McLEOD
                           McLEOD 1854
                     Dease
                     Lake
                           River

                                              DANIEL 1987

TWO

The Fur Trade

The European advance into the Yukon was surprisingly slow, given the voracious appetite of the fur trade companies for new areas to develop. First Nations peoples from the Mackenzie River valley, the Lynn Canal region, and the lower Yukon had passed along stories of the area's riches and urged traders on the periphery to expand their operations farther inland, hoping that the establishment of trading posts would break their reliance on other First Nations for their European supplies. But the economic realities of the North American fur trade slowed the European commercial powers as they moved towards the far Northwest.

The Russians established a tenuous base on the lower Yukon River, but they could not afford to mount a major expedition inland, and the British advance across North America was stalled by battles between competitive traders. The wintering partners of the North West Company, creators and protectors of a proud tradition that stressed strength, daring, and success at any cost, led the trade across the continent. In 1789 Alexander Mackenzie, searching for a navigable passage to the Pacific Ocean, followed the river that now bears his name, but it turned north, not west, and he called it the River of Disappointment, since the vast underpopulated lands draining into the river seemed to hold little prospect of profit. Faced with competition to the south, however, the North West Company decided early in the nineteenth century to test the value of Mackenzie's discoveries. Posts were established at Fort Liard and Fort Good Hope, and they provided good returns to the company.[1]

The expansion did not solve the North West Company's many financial woes. Company traders often treated the indigenous people badly, forcing

them to trade at their posts, misusing alcohol, and disrupting aboriginal settlements. On occasion the Native people struck back, burning company
posts. More often they simply avoided them. Yet the returns came in,
swelling the North West Company's domination of European markets. But
volume did not mean profit, for the company's trade lines, stretching from
Montreal to the Mackenzie, were seriously overextended, while the rival
Hudson's Bay Company, firmly based in its posts, had expanded less aggressively, surrendering much of the trade to the Montreal traders. Since
neither company seemed to be winning the cut-throat and increasingly violent competition, economic logic and the strong urging of the British Colonial Office dictated an end to the rivalry and a consolidation of the fur trade
enterprise. Lengthy negotiations followed – complicated by the intense personal animosities that remained from the years of competition – and in
1821 resulted in the merger of the North West Company and the Hudson's
Bay Company.[2]

The task of coordinating the unwieldy fur trade of the Northwest now
fell to George Simpson, governor of the Northern District of the Hudson's
Bay Company. Armed with an authoritarian outlook – Peter C. Newman
calls him "a bastard by birth, and by persuasion" – an acerbic pen, and a re-
lentless determination to improve the firm's profits, Simpson moved quickly
to rationalize the fur trade.[3] Years of competition had swept much of Rupert's Land barren of furs, forcing the company to look elsewhere for the
pelts needed to supply European markets. The recently opened Mackenzie
Valley offered just such a prospect, and Governor Simpson was determined
not to miss the opportunity. Simpson ordered the re-establishment of abandoned North West Company posts and the opening of new establishments
along the Mackenzie and its major tributary, the Liard.

In 1825, Russian and British diplomats negotiated a boundary line separating their North American territories. Both sides accepted the 141st
meridian, plus the "panhandle" – a vaguely defined strip of land extending
southward along the coast to 54°40′ north latitude – seemingly settling a
long-standing dispute over economic jurisdiction in the region. This line, set
by uncaring diplomats half a world away, became the permanent boundary
between the Yukon Territory and Alaska. At the time it was drawn, no one
(except, of course, the few inhabitants) knew anything about the land the
line bisected. In later years, when Canadian and American governments gave
substance to the political division, the First Nations of the Yukon River valley were forced to choose a national allegiance. Meanwhile, the 1825 boundary was simply a European convention, of no importance in the North.[4]

The Russian American Fur Company maintained a series of posts along
the Alaskan coast and on the islands of the panhandle. To augment the declining returns from the depleted coastal fur stocks, the Russians encouraged
their Tlingit trading partners to maintain and extend their trading contacts

with Native people in the interior. The coastal Tlingit did so with enthusiasm and skill, for the middleman trade brought considerable profit and allowed them to extend their domination over inland peoples. By the early 1820s, the Russian-Tlingit trade reached far inland, drawing thousands of pelts annually from British territory in what is now northern British Columbia and the Yukon. The Hudson's Bay Company's discovery of this trade angered Governor Simpson, who demanded immediate retaliation.

Under the 1825 treaty, British subjects had the right to travel on rivers originated on British soil and passed through Russian territory to the sea. In 1833, Simpson sent Peter Skene Ogden aboard the *Dryad* to exploit one such river. Ogden was to sail up the Stikine River and establish a trading post, Fort Drew, on British territory. The fort would, Simpson believed, prevent the coastal peoples from "raiding" British territory and would protect the returns from the Mackenzie River district. The Russians, however, ignored the terms of the treaty and refused to let Ogden pass upstream, touching off a diplomatic furor that soured British-Russian relations for much of the decade.[5]

Simpson then sought another means of penetrating the Russian trading zone. Fortunately for the Hudson's Bay Company, explorations undertaken earlier by Murdoch McPherson and John McLeod had pioneered a practical route. McPherson had travelled along the mid-Liard River basin in 1824, reaching as far as the Beaver River. The company had moved slowly to exploit the discovery, establishing Fort Halkett on the Nelson River in 1829.

John McLeod's voyages proved even more crucial. In 1831 he had been commissioned to "to get some information on the sources of the West Branch of the Liard River." He and his party left Fort Simpson and the Mackenzie River on 28 June 1831. Their journey covered more than 500 miles (800 km) through land previously unknown to Europeans, along one of the most treacherous rivers in North America. McLeod's exploration ended at Lake Simpson, slightly west of the Frances River in what is now the southern Yukon. The diary of his journey and the accompanying maps were forwarded to Simpson, who confidently declared that the territory was "perhaps the richest Beaver country in America." McLeod was more cautious than his superior, emphasizing the formidable difficulties of travelling the Liard and the great distances involved in reaching the district.[6]

The combination of McLeod's discoveries and continuing Russian encroachments on company trade spurred Simpson on. He ordered further exploration of the Liard basin, hoping to find a route to the northwest coast. McLeod returned to the field in 1834, unknowingly travelling on the heels of Ogden's failed attempt to break through the Russian blockade on the Stikine. Again, McLeod's efforts were successful, for he ascended the Dease River, crossed Dease Lake, and portaged into the Stikine River watershed. He learned that the end point of his journey, along the Tuya River, was the principal meeting place between the coastal and interior First Nations. Upon his return, he once more dispatched a full report of his journey to Simpson.

Simpson reacted with enthusiasm to the discovery that the company could strike back overland at the Russian traders. The journey would be hard, and transportation costs would eat up much of the profit from any post established in the area, but the company believed that a small post would gather considerable trade from the "poor timid Indians of the Interior."

The task of establishing the post fell in 1836 to John Hutchinson, then stationed at Fort Halkett. Four days out of his home post, Hutchinson learned from his aboriginal companions that the Nahanni people intended to attack the brigade. He beat a hasty retreat, only to suffer a blistering attack from the pen of Simpson. "The Governor and Committee consider it a stain upon the character of the concern that the Russians should so long be allowed to drain the country of its riches," Simpson wrote, "while we remained paralyzed by terror in Mackenzie's [District] through the childish reports of a nervous creature who was never calculated for the enterprising life of an Indian trader."[7]

Simpson passed the vital duty of westward expansion to Robert Campbell, a dour God-fearing Scot. Campbell was one of that legion of ambitious fur traders who did so much to make the world aware of the interior of British North America. Born in Perthshire in 1808, his interest in the fur trade was sparked by tales told by his cousin, a chief factor with the Hudson's Bay Company. Hired by the company at the age of twenty-two, Campbell was employed at the experimental farm at Red River. He found supervising cabbages and sheep uninteresting and petitioned the company to send him north as a fur trader. When a position was finally offered, Campbell leapt at the chance for adventure, fuelled by dreams of glory and fame as a North American explorer. In 1837 he reached Dease Lake, where he built a small post and settled in for the winter. The antagonism of the local indigenous people, a harsh winter, and a lack of supplies brought on near starvation and forced Campbell to retreat in the spring. Ever stubborn, he demanded permission to return to Dease Lake the following year.[8]

However, following the *Dryad* affair, Hudson's Bay Company and Russian American Fur Company officials, aided by their countries' diplomats, had sought a negotiated settlement. An agreement was reached in February 1839, permitting the Hudson's Bay Company to lease the Alaskan panhandle for an annual payment of two thousand land-otter pelts and other benefits. Company ships and coastal posts could now collect the furs from the northwest coast, rendering further expansion inland along the Liard totally unnecessary. Robert Campbell and his crew were effectively rendered superfluous and faced absorption into the regular trading corps.

As exploration in one direction ended, a new avenue developed. In 1837 two HBC explorers, Thomas Simpson and Peter Warren Dease, seconded to scientific surveys in the Arctic, had been sent to chart the coastline west of the Mackenzie River district. Officially undertaken for "the acquisition of scientific knowledge and information, and unconnected with a view towards advantage from Trade,"[9] the Simpson and Dease expedition was in fact carefully calculated to enhance the Hudson's Bay Company's image before an increasingly critical British public. In covering the distance left unexplored after the expedition of John Franklin a decade earlier, Thomas Simpson casually observed: "The Colville [River] separates the Franklin and Pelly Mountains, the last seen by us; and probably flows in a long course through a rich fur country, and unknown tribes in the west side of the Rocky Mountains."[10]

The discovery was a revelation to the always alert Governor Simpson. He quickly ordered a two-pronged expedition towards the Colville River. John Bell, then stationed at Fort Good Hope, was sent in 1839 to explore the Peel River, discovered earlier by John Franklin. He returned the following year and established Peel's River Post (Fort McPherson) to tap the lower Mackenzie fur trade and as a base for explorations to the westward. Bell's initial attempts to cross the mountains were thwarted by the eastern Gwich'ins' unwillingness to share the secrets of access to the west. Even after he had successfully crossed the Richardson Mountains in 1842, descending perhaps as far as the Porcupine River, his aboriginal guide abandoned him, forcing Bell to retreat to the security of his post. The Peel River Gwich'in dominated the trade with western Native people, not allowing them to visit the HBC post for the purpose of trade. Reluctant to surrender their profitable position as middlemen, the Gwich'in interfered with Bell's progress whenever possible. However, First Nations people from the west – travelling without furs – did visit the post, thus encouraging Bell to continue his efforts to reach across the mountains and holding out the promise of bountiful fur returns if the explorations proved successful.[11]

The conscientious but cautious John Bell was reluctant to proceed alone into unknown districts, where all but local guides had consistently proved unreliable, but he could not ignore Governor Simpson's repeated demands to continue the search. He set out again in 1845, this time taking Native guides from the mid-Mackenzie River basin. In August of that year he was able to report to Simpson: "I have great pleasure in informing you that I have at length after much trouble and difficulties succeeded in reaching the 'Youcon,' or White Water River, so named by the natives from the pale colour of its water." Like McLeod before him, Bell cautioned that transportation difficulties would impede the trade, but he also reported that the Yukon appeared to be a rich fur trade district. If further incentive was required – and Simpson's excited reaction to Bell's discovery suggested that it was not – Bell also learned from the local First Nations that Russian trade goods had reached well up into the interior.[12]

John Bell was not left alone to carry on the search to the Colville River. Robert Campbell, recently freed from the Dease Lake trade, was delegated to follow John McLeod's early exploration along the west branch of the Liard, hoping to find the "Toucho" or Great Water River reported by the Natives. Campbell set out in the early summer of 1840, accompanied by several of the men who had travelled with McLeod almost a decade before. Upon reaching the Frances River, Campbell continued past McLeod's farthest point – the junction of the Simpson River – and on 19 July reached Frances Lake. Leaving most of his men to build a small cabin, Campbell proceeded with the exploration. After crossing the Finlayson Lakes, he reached the banks of a large river, which he named the Pelly.[13] Unlike McLeod and Bell before him, Campbell wrote enthusiastically about the prospects for trade in the new district. "Few places," he wrote, "present a more favourable appearance for establishing a post than Frances Lake." Although Campbell would later regret his sanguine analysis, the Hudson's Bay Company now had two routes into the as-yet-unknown valley of the "Colville."[14]

One further effort was made to identify a quick access to the river valley to the west of the Mackenzie River. Chief Trader Lewes dispatched Andrew McBeath in 1843 from Fort Norman to explore the headwaters of the Gravel (later the Keele) River and to locate a pass through the mountains. McBeath, like Bell, encountered trouble with his local guides, who abandoned him several days' journey into the hills. He attempted to press on alone but reluctantly admitted defeat after several days of fruitless effort. This exploratory thrust, undertaken without Simpson's approval, marked the limits of Hudson's Bay Company interest in westward exploration. The company had two routes into the new district; the time had come to exploit the opening.[15]

Robert Campbell set out first to expand the company's trade. From the beginning the trade was hampered by difficulties with navigation along the Liard River, by the animosity of the local First Nations, and by a shocking lack of country provisions in the area. A shortage of men in the Mackenzie River district stalled the construction of a post at Frances Lake until 1842. Campbell had standing orders to continue his explorations, but several times the near starvation of his men forced him to cancel his plans. Nevertheless, he did descend the Pelly to its junction with the Lewes (Yukon) River in 1843. Simpson had arranged with the Russian American Fur Company to receive Campbell if he was able to continue his exploration farther into Alaska, but when Campbell learned from his guides that First Nations on the lower river planned to attack his expedition, he called off the more extensive exploration and returned to Frances Lake. Simpson was disappointed with Campbell's reluctance to proceed – rumours of violent tribes downstream were commonplace when Native guides did not wish their employers to continue – but he authorized Campbell to establish a trade at the junction of the Lewes and Pelly. The achievement of that goal would wait another five years.[16]

The push west from Peel River was more successful. In 1846, one year after Bell's final exploration to the "Youcon," the company opened Lapierre House on the Bell River. The factor, Alexander Hunter Murray, was accompanied by his new bride, the first European woman to enter the Yukon. The following summer, Mrs Murray, due to deliver her first baby, remained behind at Lapierre House when Murray led an expedition to the junction of the Yukon and Porcupine rivers and, two miles upstream, erected Fort Youcon, the largest and most important post in the new district. That the new post was probably inside Russian territory, and hence in direct violation of an 1839 undertaking to the Russian American Fur Company, occurred to company officials but did not deter them.[17]

Much of the Yukon River valley still remained unknown to Europeans, but the Hudson's Bay Company had little interest in further discoveries. Robert Campbell, reluctant to settle down to the business of trading furs, requested permission to explore towards the Pacific Ocean. But Simpson, after initially authorizing the journey, recognized the dangers inherent in such an exploration: "If we obtained our supplies from thence, we should be opening a communication to the most valuable part of the Northern Department by which strangers might find their way thither, and with our supplies we should be obliged to introduce the extravagant tariff of the N.W. Coast."[18]

The prospect of exploring the lower Yukon River similarly held little attraction. Shortly after arriving at Fort Youcon, Alexander Hunter Murray learned from the First Nations that the Russians were but a short distance

Lapierre House, opened in 1846, was the first Hudson's Bay Company post west of the Richardson Mountains. It was abandoned when the company retreated from the Yukon River trade in 1893 (Yukon Archives [YA]).

downstream. Recognizing the possible diplomatic and legal ramifications of further encroachment into Russian territory, Simpson postponed fur explorations in that direction. With Fort Youcon established and Campbell's men advancing along the Pelly, the company could now develop the local fur trade.[19]

Murray soon received further confirmation of Russian designs on the trade of the middle Yukon basin. Beginning in 1847 and continuing annually thereafter, the Native people kept him apprised of his competitors' movements along the river. In 1849 Natives travelling downstream laden with British trading supplies reported to Vasilii Deryabin, manager of the Nulato post, who was travelling upstream at the time, that rival traders had established a post to the east. Deryabin dispatched a note to Alexander Murray and returned downstream to report the British advance to his superiors. Murray could not read the Russian script and passed the message on to Fort Simpson. From there it went to Governor Simpson. After more than a year, during which time the HBC men braced for the imminent arrival of the Russians and a forced retreat from their post, Simpson wrote to Murray that translators in London had deciphered the poorly written message. The note, which may have been an identifying jacket covering a longer letter that Murray never received, simply identified the writer and contained no threats or warnings. The HBC men could rest easy. If the Russians were coming, they were not likely to be belligerent.[20]

With the threat of immediate expulsion settled, the Fort Youcon trade soon proved to be a most profitable addition to the corporate empire. The same could not be said of Robert Campbell's effort to the south. The Frances Lake Pelly River trade proved a major disappointment from the very beginning. In the first year, the lack of food near Frances Lake forced Campbell to break up his establishment, sending three men to winter at Fort Simpson and a fourth to Fort Halkett. The men returned the following spring, permitting Campbell to make his foray down the Pelly. Simpson was most anxious that a post be established at the junction of the Pelly and Lewes, and sent a major expeditionary force in 1845 to assist Campbell. Like so many of the company's plans in the southern Yukon, this one failed. Campbell had trouble getting his supplies up the wild and dangerous Liard River, and the Fort Frances area did not generate enough country produce – fish and wild animals – to support even a few men. Once more, Campbell sent a number of his men to Mackenzie River posts – placing unanticipated demands on posts already struggling to meet their own food needs. Unsure of the prospects of expanding the trade, Campbell called off the expedition to the Pelly and Lewes, declaring that the Indians from that area would bring their furs to Frances Lake.[21]

Simpson, however, ordered Campbell to continue his expansion, and he arranged for the necessary men and supplies. Campbell stalled once more and proceeded to Fort Simpson to secure further aid for his expedition. Murdoch McPherson, in charge of the Mackenzie District, was perturbed by Campbell's unauthorized appearance and wrote to Simpson that the man "has a strong reluctance to go down the Pelly, which he has manifested all along, but did not act sufficiently candid in that respect." With some sympathy, McPherson noted that earlier attempts had failed because of the explorer's "groundless dread of the Indians and of starvation, which unfortunately had taken a strong possession of Mr. Campbell's mind and which is more to be pitied than blamed."[22]

Nonetheless, Campbell set out for a third time, and this time he succeeded. In September 1848 he reached the confluence of the Yukon and Pelly rivers and built a post, which he named Fort Selkirk. With his enthusiasm for adventure boosted by this accomplishment, Campbell now sought permission to continue his explorations, but Simpson was more interested in the successful establishment of the trade and ordered the trader to stay where he was. Doing so was not easy. Difficulties of supply continued to plague the Frances Lake Pelly River trade. In both 1849 and 1850 the annual outfit did not arrive intact, and James Stewart, Campbell's able and dedicated assistant, made a series of difficult journeys in an attempt to bring supplies to Fort Selkirk.

The receipt of trading goods did not ensure success. Year after year, the Chilkat Nation (a subgroup of the Tlingit) from the Lynn Canal region entered the Fort Selkirk trading zone and carried away most of the prime furs that otherwise would have gone to the Hudson's Bay Company. The Tlingit were trading with the company's SS *Beaver*, which paid the higher tariff of the northwest coast rather than the lower one of the interior.

In 1850 Robert Campbell was directed to descend the Lewes to Fort Youcon, exploring the region between his post and Fort Youcon, in order to permit the Fort Selkirk traders to bring their supplies in through that route and allow the abandonment of the Liard River system. The journey, conducted in June 1851, proved an easy one. Little new was discovered, for Natives had earlier informed the company traders of the course of the river; Campbell had corresponded regularly with Murray at Fort Youcon via First Nations travellers. Fort Selkirk was, all believed, about to be put on a more secure foundation. The enthusiasm was misplaced.

The Tlingit returned en masse in 1851 and once more swept the region clean of prime furs, leaving only poor quality pelts for the Fort Selkirk traders. To Campbell's horror, several Mackenzie District officers were arguing for the closure of the unprofitable southern Yukon trade. The issue was resolved the following year. On 21 August 1852, when Campbell had unwisely dispatched almost all of his men on supply and provisioning work, a group of Tlingit ransacked Fort Selkirk, forcing him to flee for his life.[23]

Leaving several of his men with his trusted associate James Stewart, Campbell raced down the river to Fort Youcon and then on to Fort Simpson. There he hoped to convince James Anderson, who was now in charge of the Mackenzie District, to provide the men and arms necessary to punish

Robert Campbell (1808–94), one of the first Hudson's
Bay Company traders in the region, came to the southern
Yukon in 1840 and spent a dozen difficult years there
(Glenbow Archives, NA 1010-15).

the Tlingit. Anderson refused. Unwilling to accept the ignominious loss of
"his" district, Campbell set off on an epic snowshoe trek from Fort Simpson
to Crow Wing, Minnesota, and on to Governor Simpson's headquarters at
Lachine, near Montreal – a journey of more than three thousand miles. But
Simpson rejected his pleas for assistance and sent him on furlough to England. Robert Campbell's Yukon career was over.

Although Campbell's time in the Yukon was scarcely filled with glory, his
name is firmly entrenched in its history. He is remembered while John
McLeod is largely ignored – because Campbell publicized his activities, especially in his memoirs.[24] (One account of his explorations in the Yukon was
published in the elementary school textbook, the *Fifth Royal Reader.*) Campbell's account, which emphasizes his role, damns his critics, and paints a picture of commitment, courage, and accomplishment, has been widely accepted as the standard interpretation of events. But the contemporary records
portrayed him in a less favourable light. He complained constantly about

others within the Hudson's Bay Company's service, claiming many times that they were deliberately interfering with his efforts. Also, he assumed, mistakenly, that he had been specially selected for higher service within the company and had a particular claim to the attention of Governor Simpson. Responding to Campbell's incessant complaints, Simpson finally wrote with more than a hint of exasperation: "You appear somewhat to have misunderstood the scope of authority I gave you for carrying out your discoveries ... I have never hinted that your charge was to be considered separate and independent."[25]

Campbell never reconciled himself to subordinate status within the company. Faced with difficulties and questions about his efforts, he threatened to resign his commission on several occasions. When, to his surprise, Simpson once agreed to his request, he withdrew it. Over time, Campbell became obsessed with the prospects of the Frances Lake and Fort Selkirk trade, in spite of all the difficulties and in spite of his hesitations about the local aboriginal people, and even after evidence mounted against the trade ever being profitable. As James Anderson wrote, "Campbell is a zealous, enterprising man & a really estimable character I understand – but he is mad when he touches on the prospects of Selkirk."[26] Perhaps most surprisingly, Campbell heartily disliked the southern Yukon, an opinion he omitted from his memoirs. His journals and letters written at the trading post are filled with caustic comments about the weather and the loneliness. He spent little time with the indigenous people who lived near the post, but pined for companionship, literate discussion, and freedom from the fear of starvation. Although he was ambitious and had great plans for his district, he hated and feared the North, as the bad poetry committed to his journal reveals:

O Solitude, where are the charms
That sages have seen in thy face?
Better dwell in the midst of alarms
Than reign in this horrible place.[27]

Campbell was particularly anguished when his good friend James Stewart was away from the post, and he found solace in the Bible, his constant companion. He did not, to use the language of later adventurers into the unknown, have the "right stuff."

With the destruction of Fort Selkirk, the Hudson's Bay Company's hopes for a profitable return rested entirely on the success of the Fort Youcon enterprise. Fortunately for the HBC, this post, unlike Fort Selkirk, exceeded even its most optimistic projections. The value of the new post lay, ironically, in a change in the long-established fur trade. Beaver had long been the industry standard, supplying a relatively stable felt-hat trade. The introduction and popularity of the inexpensive silk hat in the mid-1840s thoroughly disrupted the beaver markets, forcing the Hudson's Bay Company to sell off huge stocks of beaver pelts at rock-bottom prices. As the beaver trade declined, markets for luxury furs – mink, fox, and especially marten – improved significantly. Fort Youcon, the company was pleased to discover, sat in the centre of one of North America's richest marten areas. For more than twenty years it became one of the company's most valuable producers of the prime marten pelts so highly prized in Europe.[28]

The Fort Youcon trade was slow to develop, largely because the traders did not have enough trade goods to purchase all the pelts that the Native people brought to the post. As news of the fur wealth of the Yukon filtered back to Governor Simpson, the annual indent (the annual order for trade goods) was enlarged. Not all company officers supported this initiative into what they knew to be Russian territory. James Anderson, for example, cut back the Fort Youcon staff in 1852, arguing that in the aftermath of the attack on Fort Selkirk the transmountain trade should be cut altogether. The Native trade networks quickly reformed around the new post, with the local Gwich'in regulating access to the traders. The post was even free of the problem of food supplies that faced the other Mackenzie District forts. Aboriginal hunters and company servants harvested the abundant local resources, including salmon and whitefish, moose, caribou, small game, and the produce from a small garden, ensuring that Fort Youcon remained the envy of other posts.[29]

Trade goods were brought to the Yukon by a route so long and circuitous that it hardly seems possible that the trade it supported could have yielded the Hudson's Bay Company any profit. A glance at a map of Canada shows the staggering logistical feat of bringing goods to the Yukon and taking the furs back to market. Every summer, ships brought trade goods from Britain to York Factory, on the west coast of Hudson Bay. From there they were shipped upriver to Lake Winnipeg and the Red River Settlement, the hub of the western fur trade, in what is now Manitoba. From there the goods went west along the North Saskatchewan River, then over the Methye Portage to the Athabasca River; down that river to Lake Athabasca; across the lake to the Slave River; down the Slave to Great Slave Lake; across that lake to the Mackenzie River; down that river to Peel River; up the Peel to Peel's River Post; across the mountains, a long and arduous journey, to the Bell River; and finally down the Bell and Porcupine rivers to the Yukon and Fort Youcon. It sounds – and was – remarkable, especially when it is remembered that except for some sailing on Lake Winnipeg, it was all done with the muscle power of Native, Métis, and British labourers.

Because of this enormously long and complicated trade route, the Yukon trade operated on a seven-year cycle. This meant that from the time when trade goods were bought from the manufacturers in England until the furs arrived at auction in England to pay for them, seven years had elapsed. It is a mark of the profitability of the Yukon marten trade that the post was main-

Frederick Whymper drew this scene at Fort Youcon in 1865, four years before the Americans arrived to order the Hudson's Bay Company out of what had become United States territory (authors' collection).

tained in the face of these impressive logistical and financial difficulties. Until the company was forced to abandon the post in 1869, Fort Youcon served as the centre of European activity in the upper Yukon basin.

The indigenous people of the Yukon River basin welcomed the advance of the fur traders, especially as it freed them from dependence on the Gwich'in bands east of the Richardson mountains, and they moved quickly to exploit the opportunities now available. Displaying a sophisticated understanding of the nuances of European trading systems, they sought at every opportunity to exploit the Hudson's Bay Company's concern about Russian expansion. Those who traded at Fort Youcon repeatedly informed the company traders about Russian plans, prices, and promises, and the company's men had no means of judging the accuracy of the reports. Most often they assumed that they were true and made their plans accordingly.

Behind the vague and uncertain Native reports lay an attempt by the Russian American Fur Company to defend its trading interests in the area. Although poorly financed and chronically short of men and boats along the lower Yukon, the Russian traders travelled with some regularity to the Lake Mintokh area at the western end of the Yukon flats. Efforts to expand beyond this point had stalled after the communication between Deryabin and Alexander Murray. In 1851 Natives from the Koyukuk River attacked the Nulato post, the Russian company's main establishment in the area, killing

Deryabin and several of his employees. The post was immediately re-established, but plans to push upriver had to be postponed. The Russians' inability to challenge the Hudson's Bay Company directly left Fort Youcon secure and profitable.[30]

Frequent Native reports about Russian trade served to alert the HBC traders to the possibility that competition could swiftly alter the commercial balance in the Yukon basin. Consequently, they sought other means of controlling aboriginal trading and trapping activities, for instance, by trading only through the "principal men," who were showered with generous gifts in anticipation of their enduring support. But the Native people were difficult to control. If the terms of trade were not sufficiently attractive, they simply withheld their furs, traded only low-quality pelts, or took their furs downstream to the Russians. The trading chiefs lacked permanent authority within their bands, and their advice was ignored if the negotiated conditions were deemed unacceptable.

The fact that the Native people responded so cautiously to the Fort Youcon fur trade underscores their conservative response to European trade goods. Many items – knives, pots, and axes – had been in use among them for years before direct contact. They knew in advance which goods they wanted and, like other aboriginal people across the country, did not succumb to a "furs for trinkets" exchange. Initially, they traded primarily for only a few select items, particularly guns, ammunition, tobacco, and beads, which they used as currency. These items were accepted only if they fitted within very rigid specifications; on one occasion, they rejected an entire shipment of beads because they were the wrong colour. Other goods, such as blankets, were "tried out" first. If found to be a useful addition to indigenous material culture, a process that usually required several years' use, the goods were adopted on a more widespread basis. It was once thought that within a few years, perhaps a generation, of contact with white traders, the First Nations lost their traditional skills and became more or less dependent on the traders. More recent research has dispelled this ethnocentric view. Certainly, the history of the Yukon First Nations shows that they took from the trade only what they wanted; the trade was a supplement to their way of life and did not control it. Conversely, the First Nations exerted considerable influence over the pace and direction of the trade.

The Native people did their best to get the most favourable terms possible from the HBC traders. The officers had to follow an official price list, or tariff, established for the entire Mackenzie River district. The Yukon tariff compared unfavourably with the prices offered along the northwest coast, but the company refused aboriginal demands to raise it. The Hudson's Bay Company really had little choice. If the Fort Youcon tariff was enriched, the company traders believed, the Peel River First Nations would carry their furs to the Youcon to trade, forcing the company to transport them back again.

Faced with intransigence on price, the Native people nonetheless kept the pressure on, demanding goods on credit, expecting more generous "presents" (economically part of the overall exchange), and paying careful attention to the quality of the trade goods. The threat of a boycott was a powerful tool. In 1865 they used this tactic against Strachan Jones, a company officer who was unbending in his refusal to respond to Native requests; their refusal to trade while he remained at the post led to his removal.

The Native people were also very aware of the Europeans' vulnerability. There never were more than a dozen or so company men at Fort Youcon, an island of British influence surrounded by a much larger number of indigenous people. From time to time, the Natives were not above hinting that they might attack the post unless conditions of trade improved – a threat that took on a new urgency after the destruction of Fort Selkirk. The best the company could do was to point out to them that to destroy Fort Youcon would hurt them economically.

The non-appearance of Russian traders and the Natives' failure to attack the post gradually convinced the HBC traders that the threats need not be taken too seriously. At no point, however, did the traders feel confident that they could reject the threats or warnings out of hand. The vulnerability of Fort Youcon and the comparative power of the aboriginal people ensured at least partial attention to their requests. When in the early 1860s the First Nations commented that the Russians were again planning an expedition upstream, the Fort Youcon traders sought their superiors' permission to challenge the Russians on the lower Yukon, thus ensuring the company continued access to the vaunted mid-Yukon marten-producing areas. Their request was initially rejected.

The aboriginal warnings of impending trouble were finally borne out in 1862. After a decade of inactivity in the field of exploration, Ivan Furuhjelm, chief manager of Russia's colonies, demanded greater initiative from the officers of the fur trade. In an attempt to expand business in the Yukon, Ivan Lukin was ordered to travel secretly to Fort Youcon and report on the HBC operations. Lukin arrived unannounced, stayed for a few days, and returned downriver. This visit provided concrete proof that the Native reports, only partially believed over the years, had considerable substance. The Russians were coming.[31]

Now that the Russians knew the location of the post, the Hudson's Bay Company could legitimately be expelled at any moment. Faced with the imminent loss of the valuable Yukon River trade, the company decided in 1864 to take the offensive. Boats were dispatched downstream, bypassing middlemen and carrying competition deeper into Russian territory. A Protestant missionary from Alaska later described the episode: "Long before any steamboats plied these waters, the Hudson Bay voyageurs from Fort Yukon came down through the rapids in large flat-bottomed boats loaded with trade

Tanana man, 1865, drawn by Frederick Whymper, who said that these people reminded him "of the ideal North American Indian I had read of but never seen" (authors' collection)

goods, and returned with furs for which these were bartered. Old natives at Tanana still tell with admiration of the Batteaux with six pairs of oars which brought them guns and blankets and powder and shot and tea and tobacco, and gave them better terms than the Russians from Nulato gave."[32]

The Fort Youcon Gwich'in, who had so carefully sown the seeds of competition, unexpectedly found themselves done out of a valuable trading position. While there is no question that the Native people welcomed the advance of the fur trade, certain aspects of the arrival of Europeans carried serious long-term costs. Particularly devastating was the importation of European disease. North American First Nations had been biologically separate from Europe and consequently had had no exposure to many common diseases, including measles, influenza, chicken pox, smallpox, and whooping cough. The fatal effects of these diseases were felt even before European Company explorers reached the Yukon River valley, for the illnesses had been passed inland via Native trading networks. Now, with Europeans in their midst, the opportunities for exposure increased. Although the HBC officers helped out whenever possible, the First Nations had no means of treating the new diseases. Illnesses of the type now being experienced had traditionally been blamed on the sorcery of enemies; shamans, or spiritual leaders, were believed to have great powers to cast spells of this kind. Nothing of this magnitude had ever before been visited upon the Yukon First Nations, and traditional explanations seemed less than adequate in the face of repeated "virgin soil" epidemics. Anthropologist Shepherd Krech III has estimated that over the first fifty years of contact, close to five-sixths of the Gwich'in Nation perished from the many illnesses.[33]

Few outbreaks matched the severity of the 1865 scarlet fever epidemic. Boat crews carrying supplies for the Mackenzie River district contracted the disease and carried it with them into the northland. With no replacements available in the district, the company felt it had no choice but to send them on their way. The infected boat crews continued downstream to Peel's River Post. The disease, which ravaged many bands along the Mackenzie, passed over the mountains with the Fort Youcon supply expedition. Native people died by the dozen; whole families were wiped out in a matter of days. Many of the stricken people, panicking in the face of the unknown, fled from the trading post, seeking the security of the bush. Unwittingly, they carried the deadly germs to other people throughout the Yukon basin. HBC officers calculated that between 170 and 200 of Fort Youcon's Native people perished, as did countless others far from the view of the traders.[34]

The pattern was repeated many times in the fur trade period, albeit on a smaller scale. It is difficult to assess its demographic consequences. In harsh biological terms, the loss of the elderly and the very young – the most likely victims of any outbreak – was less serious than the death of men and women in their reproductive years. Even so, the population loss was staggering. More difficult to comprehend are the cultural implications of this systematic devastation. The repeated thinning of the population carried away many of the bands' elders, destroying at the same time much of the oral tradition, local knowledge, and traditional skill so essential to the cultural survival of First Nations people. The Natives were, if anything, adaptable, but they had to struggle very hard to overcome the personal and communal losses attending the spread of European diseases.

The Native people had to deal with more Europeans than just the fur traders. This period also brought the first missionaries and other adventurers interested in unlocking the many mysteries of the upper Yukon River valley. The Church of England and the Roman Catholic Church had raced each other across the Northwest, hoping to be the first to place their mark on the "heathens" of the north. By 1858, the Anglicans' Church Missionary Society (CMS) and the Catholic Oblates of Mary Immaculate (OMI) had reached the lower Mackenzie. The Reverend William West Kirkby made the first move into the Yukon River valley in 1861. Leaving his post at Fort Simpson for three years, he travelled with the HBC fur brigades to Fort

Youcon, capitalizing on the company's bias in favour of the Protestant missionary effort. Buoyed by what he felt was an enthusiastic response, Kirkby vowed to return.[35]

When he did, in 1862, his competition followed. Father Seguin of the OMI had been assigned to the Fort Youcon area and had also accompanied the fur traders across the divide. But the HBC officers spurned Seguin, offering only minimal courtesies and encouraging the Native people to remain loyal to Kirkby and the CMS. If Kirkby was pleased with the traders' response, he was distressed by the apparent indifference of the local Gwich'in. The excitement attending Kirkby's first visit had faded, raising doubts in the missionary's mind about the chances for success in this isolated charge. But the CMS was not easily dissuaded from pursuing a promising field, particularly with the Catholics so close on their heels. Counting on the HBC-CMS alliance to block the OMI from the Yukon, Kirkby directed his efforts towards recruiting a missionary for the area.[36]

Kirkby's call for assistance was heard by Robert McDonald, a mixed-blood volunteer from Red River. Experienced in Native missions and blessed with a facility for indigenous languages, McDonald left for Fort Youcon in the summer of 1862. He worked quickly to gain the allegiance of the local aboriginal people, placing particular importance upon learning their language and translating the Bible and other religious documents. The unassuming missionary was perfectly suited for his northern service. He respected Native lifeways and sought to integrate Christian teachings into indigenous culture, rather than demanding an immediate end to age-old traditions. Unfortunately, these promising beginnings faltered in 1864, when the usually robust missionary fell ill with influenza and, for a time, lay near death. He petitioned for permission to abandon his post and asked his superiors to secure a replacement.[37]

The CMS, always hard pressed to find acceptable candidates for service anywhere in Rupert's Land, reluctantly turned to the task of finding another northern missionary. In 1865 William Carpenter Bompas answered the call. Already thirty-four and serving as a curate in a small English parish, Bompas was an unlikely missionary. He had attempted several times to secure a place overseas with the CMS but had been turned down because of his unimpressive academic accomplishments and his comparatively advanced years. While the CMS would not have sent a man of Bompas's qualifications to such a vital field as China or Africa, the organization agreed to dispatch him to replace McDonald at Fort Youcon.[38]

Bompas – single, uncomfortable in the structured society of England, and desperately anxious to start his work in the North – left almost immediately for his northern posting. On Christmas Day 1865 he arrived at Fort Simpson, where to his surprise and consternation he found that McDonald had made an unexpectedly complete recovery from his illness and was ready to

William Carpenter Bompas (1834–1906), first bishop of the Diocese of Selkirk (later, Diocese of Yukon) in an idealized portrait. Bompas was a driven, zealous man, notable for his devotion to his indigenous charges and for his inability to get along with his fellow whites in the North (Anglican Church Archives).

return to Fort Youcon. Kirkby was most anxious that the North not lose the eager Bompas. Thus it was agreed that Bompas would work as an itinerant preacher, travelling through the Mackenzie and Yukon regions as need dictated, while McDonald would return to Fort Youcon, thus ensuring that the upper Yukon would remain a Church of England preserve, free from Catholic interference. It was a modest beginning for the missionary enterprise in the Yukon, but the foundations of a much broader effort had clearly been set.

Only later would the missionaries actively publicize their northern adventures outside the confines of the church. For the time being, public knowledge of the Northwest rested on the scanty reports of the fur traders, Robert Campbell's contributions being the most noticeable. In the 1860s, however, a small band of American scientist-adventurers began a more thorough exploration of the Yukon River valley, at the same time going out of their way to promote their discoveries, publishing popular travelogues as well as scientific articles describing one of North America's last unknown frontiers.

One of the first, and most intriguing, of these adventurers was the young Robert Kennicott. The New Orleans-born Kennicott had become a scientist of some note by the age of twenty. After a short term as the natural history curator at Northwestern University museum, he was recruited by Spencer Fullerton Baird of the Smithsonian Institution to undertake an extended zoological examination of the subarctic. Kennicott's application was well received by HBC Governor George Simpson, who offered transportation with the fur brigades and access to the Mackenzie River and Yukon basin posts. Kennicot set out in the summer of 1860, travelling from Red River to Fort Resolution. In August he pushed on to Fort Youcon, where he passed the winter. For more than a year he travelled back and forth between Fort Youcon and Peel's River Post, collecting hundreds of specimens of the flora and fauna of the district. When during a visit to Fort Simpson in 1862 he heard that his father lay near death, he hurriedly departed for Chicago.[39]

Kennicott left a striking legacy in the scientific world, one that extended far beyond his short stay in the North. He was, by all accounts, a remarkable man, blessed with scientific intuition and a gregarious nature. He made many friends among the fur traders, firing their interest in scientific collecting. The HBC officer corps offered excellent material for the Smithsonian's scientific interests. These men were, in the main, educated and literate people, often suffering from intellectual starvation in their isolated northern postings. Naturalist William Dall described Kennicott's impact on the traders: "The advent of Kennicott, young, joyous, full of news of the outside world, ready to engage in any of their expeditions or activities and to take hardships without grumbling was an event in their lives. When he taught them how to make birdskins and collect Natural History objects and showed them how, by means of their collections, their names would become known in the civilized world and even printed in books, they seized on the project with enthusiasm."⁴⁰

Kennicott clearly had the HBC traders on side. At Fort Youcon he asked James Lockhart to collect animals and birds and requested that Strachan Jones gather fish and insects. James Flett of Lapierre House – an "unadorned brick," according to the scientist – supported the work enthusiastically. However, not leaving matters to chance, Kennicott asked Spencer Baird of the Smithsonian: "Please write to him and set him up a little – not failing to compliment his stepson William for his bird skinning as Flett is pleased with his being noticed ... Only please remember to write within Flett's comprehension – he is a brick, but, as I've said, an unpolished one and is quite uneducated." The careful cultivation of the traders worked. Lockhart was so anxious to get to collecting that as soon as the spring fur boat departed he rushed into the field. Even before Kennicot left the North, he could write confidently to Baird: "The operations in zoology here are getting quite in earnest and we can now turn the crank and keep the wheels ... going from the Smithsonian." For decades to come, Kennicott's many northern friends inundated the Smithsonian Institution and other museums with natural history items, aboriginal artifacts, reports on northern life, and descriptions of Native society.

A later observer noted that Kennicott had "by his travels and collections added directly and indirectly perhaps more than any other to the riches of the Smithsonian collection." His efforts succeeded primarily because of his ability to mobilize the considerable talents and enthusiasms of the fur traders. By demonstrating how men isolated by distance from the comforts and stimulation of European culture could earn respect and admiration in the best intellectual and social circles, Kennicott earned the continued support of dozens of company officers.

Kennicott's interest in the Yukon basin had not been satiated, and when in 1864 Perry McDonough Collins offered him a chance to return, he leapt at the opportunity. Collins had made his fortune in the California gold rush and, excited about the prospects for investments in Russia, had secured an appointment as American commercial agent on the Amur River in Siberia. When he returned from this post in 1857, he proposed an overland telegraph line to link the United States with Siberia. After many unsuccessful attempts, he sold the idea to the Western Union Telegraph Company, which had just finished a line across the United States. The project was, for its time, of staggering proportions. The line had to cover hundreds of miles of unsurveyed and almost unpopulated territory. The success of the venture would also rely on the Russians' ability to build a connecting line from the Amur to St. Petersburg, no mean feat in itself. Late in 1864 the Overland Telegraph

Company – formally organized and with the requisite rights-of-way across the United States, British North America, and Alaska in hand – was ready to start work.⁴¹

The task of organizing this project fell to Charles Bulkley, a military engineer, and Captain Charles Scammon. Bulkley sought out the highly regarded Robert Kennicott, the only American (and one of the few men outside the employ of the Hudson's Bay Company) who knew anything of the far Northwest, to command the exploration work on the Yukon River section of the survey. Kennicott was quick to quit his job at the Smithsonian on the condition that he be permitted to combine scientific collecting with his exploratory work for the telegraph company. Bulkley agreed and named Kennicot director of the Scientific Corps in addition to his other duties. Kennicott signed on a number of scientists, including the youthful William Dall, a doctor by training and a naturalist by avocation, to accompany the expedition. He also recruited the Victoria artist Frederick Whymper to record the progress of the surveys. Crews set out from San Francisco in the spring of 1865, but even as Bulkley's men headed for the Northwest, the telegraph project was perilously close to disaster. Other men were at the same time attempting the equally difficult task of laying a telegraph line along the floor of the Atlantic Ocean. When that remarkable exercise succeeded in July 1866, plans for the Overland Telegraph collapsed immediately. However, teams in the field did not learn of this disaster for another year, so the surveys pushed on.

For Robert Kennicott, the assignment answered his fondest wish. Ever since leaving the North three years before, he had longed to return, and now, with the necessary financial backing, he could. By May 1865 Kennicott – along with Frank Ketchum and Michael Lebarge, two Canadians who were to oversee construction of the telegraph line through the mid-Yukon River valley, had reached Nulato. Here, tragedy struck. Never a healthy man, Kennicott had suffered a mild stroke before leaving the United States. Still bothered by the affliction, he seemed to have lost the spark and enthusiasm that had so marked his personality. One morning he could not be found in camp. His colleagues set out in search and found his body on the bank of the nearby Yukon River. Kennicott's death sent a shock wave through the fur trade posts of the Northwest. The HBC officers had lost a treasured friend, and the scientific community had lost a man of great potential, only partially realized.

William Dall, who had been scheduled to journey to Siberia, took over Kennicott's scientific duties and remained in the Yukon, while Ketchum and Lebarge assumed responsibility for supervising the surveys and directing the preliminary work on the telegraph. While Dall and Whymper passed the winter at Nulato, Ketchum and Lebarge, accompanied by the Russian American Fur Company trader Ivan Lukin (who had first visited Fort Youcon in

1862) journeyed to the Hudson's Bay Company post. After a return trip down the Yukon to secure provisions for further exploration, Ketchum and Lebarge returned to Fort Youcon. Pushing on overland, they reached as far as Fort Selkirk, the site of Robert Campbell's ill-fated trading post, before turning back once more. Dall and Whymper, meanwhile, had journeyed up to Fort Youcon, where they were reunited with their colleagues. The telegraph crews' preliminary explorations completed, they now departed – Dall's notebooks filled with observations and his bags bulging with specimens of the region's natural history. Whymper also had been active, sketching numerous pictures of the human and physical landscape.

Arrival at Nulato brought unwelcome news of the successful laying of the transatlantic cable and the collapse of Perry Collins's dream of a northern link to Europe. Yet the ambitious telegraph scheme had contributed, in ways few had imagined to the opening of the northland. Dall and Whymper produced lavishly illustrated travelogues of their journeys, awakening many North Americans to the possibilities of the Yukon River valley. Ketchum, Lebarge, and several other employees had been struck by the potential of the North and returned to it in the wake of the American purchase of Alaska. Long a private preserve of the Hudson's Bay Company and the Russian American Fur Company, the Yukon basin had now been exposed to the world.

As long as the land west of the 141st meridian was still in Russian hands, little had been done to develop the region. The Russian government had at times urged its fur company to expand its activities in the Alaskan interior and had supported Collins's telegraph project, but in fact it had done little to exploit the potential of its North American holdings. The United States had long shown an interest in the Russian territories. Alaska held resource riches and was strategically placed in the North Pacific. In the passionate era of Manifest Destiny and dreams of a democratic empire spanning the continent, the thought of America leapfrogging across British North America to gain a foothold in the far Northwest was attractive in some quarters. Russia, for its part, was anxious to dispense with a disappointing colony.

Negotiations picked up in the wake of the American Civil War. Late in March 1867, Russian and American negotiators, the latter led by Secretary of State William Seward, concluded a deal. The Americans paid $7.2 million for what American critics immediately labelled "Seward's Icebox." The Americans, waiting in anticipation of an announcement, moved in quickly. Hutchinson, Kohl and Company of San Francisco purchased the assets of the Russian American Fur Company and moved into the Yukon River trade. Free traders, a few American missionaries, and a small number of government officials followed the commercial migration into the newly acquired territories.

Increased American activity, first noticeable in the lower reaches of the Yukon, threatened to transform life in the Yukon even more substantially.

The Hudson's Bay Company soon lost the lower Yukon trade. The annual boat excursions continued, but in 1868 HBC officers met American traders at the mouth of the Tanana River, the usual centre of exchange for the middle Yukon basin. The Americans demanded an immediate end to British trading on American soil and petitioned their government to intercede. The British and the HBC officials feigned ignorance, claiming that they had no confirmation that Fort Youcon was actually on United States territory and promising to abandon the post if scientific evidence was provided that it lay outside Canada. This was a useful tactic, but it did not prevent the HBC from preparing for the inevitable evacuation of Fort Youcon. James McDougall, who was in charge of the post and had been warned to expect American orders to vacate, was uneasy with the company's cautious approach and argued that a new post should be opened farther downstream to head off any American advance. He was overruled.[42]

American representations at the diplomatic level carried the day. In midsummer 1869, Governor McTavish of the Hudson's Bay Company sent word that Fort Youcon was to be abandoned forthwith. The men and supplies were to be moved to a new post, to be built at the ramparts along the Porcupine River, a site erroneously believed to be in British territory. Hoping to prevent any advantage to the advancing Americans, McDougall was ordered to "set fire to the Fort and destroy everything that he cannot bring away with him." It seemed that an ignoble end awaited a successful fur-trading venture. But Fort Youcon was not destined to go up in flames.[43]

In late July of that year, Captain Charles Raymond of the U.S. Navy, travelling aboard the steamer *Yukon*, arrived at Fort Youcon before the instructions to destroy the establishment had reached McDougall. After ascertaining that the site was on American soil, Raymond immediately occupied the post on behalf of the American government, installed American traders, and ordered the Hudson's Bay Company to cease all trading activities. Because of the lateness of the season, the HBC men did not have time to move up the Porcupine, so decided to pass the winter at Fort Youcon. McDougall could purchase food supplies from the Native people but had to turn away all proffered furs.[44]

Despite repeated protestations of friendship and cooperation, the American traders (Captain Raymond having left) and the HBC men passed an uneasy winter. Barred by the Americans from trading furs to the HBC men, the Natives people retaliated by refusing to sell food to the Yankees. The American flag, run up the Fort Youcon flagpole, disappeared mysteriously one night. The indigenous people of the region, who had enjoyed generally favourable relations with the British, resented the intrusion of the Americans into their trading zone and promised McDougall that they would remain loyal to the HBC, even after it retreated up the Porcupine.

There was no glory in the company's abandonment of Fort Youcon. When the ice set in the fall, McDougall sent several men up the Porcupine to establish a small post at the foot of the upper ramparts. The rest of the establishment followed the next spring. By this time the Company's head office had decided to sell the buildings at the old post to Hutchinson, Kohl and Company of San Francisco, and McDougall was ordered to return to Fort Youcon in the summer of 1870 to meet representatives of the American firm and negotiate the final terms. He arrived early in July and waited in vain until 3 September, when he learned that Hutchinson, Kohl and Company had no intention of purchasing the property and did not even plan to use the fort that year. McDougall removed some supplies that had been left behind during the spring evacuation and returned to Rampart House. Eventually, American traders took over the abandoned post.

The forced removal from Fort Youcon marked the end of an era, for the Americans carried a new level of competitive exchange into the trade, altering the economic balance in the region. They also brought the values of the American frontier, including an unsympathetic attitude towards the First Nations and a determination to broaden the economic base into other, non-fur, trade sectors. The Hudson's Bay Company was in full retreat and would never again have such a presence in the Yukon.[45]

The twenty years between 1847 and 1867 had given the Yukon a place on the maps of the world, but much about this vast, diverse land remained unknown, except to the Native people, who shared their secrets reluctantly. They had been brought into the nexus of European commerce and had proved themselves adept at dealing with the new economic and social forces. An even greater change lay in the offing.

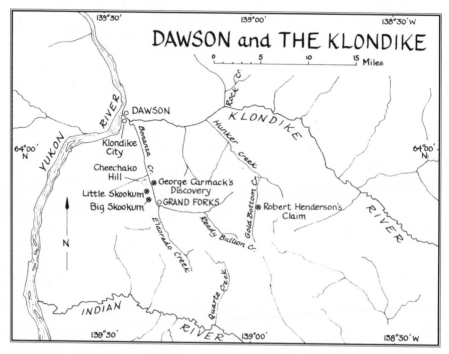

DAWSON and THE KLONDIKE

139°30' 139°00' 138°30'W

0   5   10   15 Miles

YUKON RIVER

DAWSON

KLONDIKE

Rock Cr.

Hunker creek

64°00' N

Klondike City

Bonanza Cr.

Cheechako Hill

George Carmack's Discovery

Little Skookum

Big Skookum

GRAND FORKS

Gold Bottom Cr.

Robert Henderson's Claim

RIVER

64°00' N

Eldorado Creek

Ready Bullion Cr.

N

Quartz Creek

INDIAN RIVER

139°30' 139°00' 138°30'W

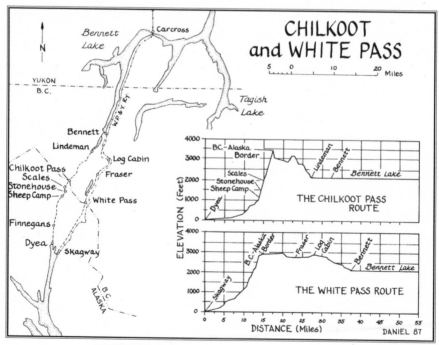

CHILKOOT and WHITE PASS

N

Bennett Lake

Carcross

5   0   10   20 Miles

YUKON
B.C.

W.P. & Y. RY.

Tagish Lake

Bennett

Lindeman

Log Cabin

Chilkoot Pass
Scales

Fraser

Stonehouse
Sheep Camp

White Pass

Finnegans

Dyea

Skagway

B.C.
ALASKA

4000
3000
2000
1000
0

ELEVATION (Feet)

BC - Alaska Border

Scales
Stonehouse
Sheep Camp

Dyea

Lindeman

Bennett

Bennett Lake

THE CHILKOOT PASS ROUTE

4000
3000
2000
1000
0

B.C. Alaska Border

Fraser

Log Cabin

Bennett

Bennett Lake

Skagway

THE WHITE PASS ROUTE

0   5   10   15   20   25   30   35   40   45   50   55

DISTANCE (Miles)

DANIEL 87

THREE

The Search for Bonanza
1870–1896

The unceremonious ejection of the Hudson's Bay Company from Fort Youcon signalled a dramatic shift in the region's fortunes. With American traders now established in the old British post, the contours of the Yukon basin fur trade had been thrown into disarray. The company now faced a difficult choice – to stay in the Porcupine River basin and fight for the remnants of a once profitable trade or to withdraw to the security of the company's one remaining monopoly zone, the Mackenzie River valley. The decision was not easily arrived at, for factions within the HBC held very different visions of the firm's future in the North.

The company was fortunate in its officer in the Yukon. James McDougall was a man of ability, admired in the trade and destined for a long and successful career with the HBC. Perhaps more important at this juncture, McDougall was well liked by the local Native people, who respected his honesty, his easygoing manner, and his openness. They were genuinely distressed when McDougall informed them of the forced evacuation, and they spoke earnestly of their determination not to trade with the Americans. This was more than mere speechifying, though their loyalty was directed more to McDougall than to the Hudson's Bay Company.

Shortly after the Americans arrived, McDougall started construction of a small post at Howling Dog (or Rampart House), below the ramparts on the Porcupine River. But even as the post was being occupied, the company decided to abandon the location and reorient the Yukon trade around the small outpost at Lapierre House. The mistake of the previous year – leaving Fort Youcon standing for the Americans to occupy – was not repeated. McDougall was ordered to burn down the building before he left.

Lapierre House proved to be too isolated to serve the Yukon basin trade properly, and in 1872 the company move to re-establish Rampart House, this time at the upper end of the ramparts, a point believed to be well within Canadian territory. The manoeuvre served two purposes, offering Yukon Natives an opportunity to continue trading with the HBC and keeping American traders in the Yukon River basin out of the lucrative trade of the Mackenzie River district.[1]

To northern officers, the Yukon fur trade was far from a dead issue. In 1871, the Canadian, British, and united States governments negotiated the Treaty of Washington. Among its many terms was a small and seemingly inconsequential provision permitting Canadians freedom of navigation along the Yukon, Porcupine, and Stikine rivers. This concession had been won largely through the intervention of Donald A. Smith, chief commissioner of the Hudson's Bay Company, but its importance was not immediately evident. For the company, the right of free navigation held great promise for the northern trade. Until then, supplies for the Mackenzie and Yukon districts had always come overland from Red River, a long and costly journey. Some within the firm believed the transportation system could be turned on its head. Supplies, they argued, could be brought in by way of the Yukon and Porcupine rivers, carried overland to the Mackenzie River basin, and from there dispersed to the northern posts. Because this system would use steamers rather than canoes, it promised faster, cheaper, and more efficient transportation. It also held out the opportunity to re-establish a company presence throughout the Yukon River basin.

Not all in the company supported the initiative. The venerable firm had undergone major changes in the 1860s, selling its stock publicly, surrendering its monopoly and land rights to the Canadian government in 1869-70, and undergoing massive internal reorganization. The death of Governor George Simpson in 1860 had resulted in control passing to more cautious administrators.[2] In the midst of the reorganization of the Yukon trade, William Hardisty, chief of the Mackenzie River district, ordered James McDougall to find an easier route across the Richardson Mountains. The pass then in use, across Stony Creek, was long, arduous, and inefficient. A better route was required if the HBC was to have any hope of reorienting its transportation route.

McDougall succeeded beyond all expectations. In the summer of 1872 he examined the area north of Peel's River Post and found a low, level pass of some 35 miles (56 km), half the length of the pass currently in use. McDougall was ecstatic about the prospects of the new route; with a little work – some swampy land had to be filled, a few hills levelled, and a couple of bridges built – McDougall Pass could be converted into a usable passage, joining the East Rat River to the Bell.[3] William Hardisty was similarly excited about the prospects: "The advantages of the new route discovered by

Mr. McDougall are so apparent as to justify us also I think, in looking forward to a bright future for the old District which has labored so long under the disadvantages, which its isolation and other obstacles have thrown in the way of thorough development of its resources."[4]

Their excitement soon dissolved in the face of corporate intransigence. To purchase the steamers required for the Yukon River and to invest in the road across McDougall Pass required a strong commitment to the northern fur trade. The new Hudson's Bay Company, interested in selling its massive prairie landholdings and moving into the southern retail trade, would make no such commitment. McDougall's Pass sat unused and remained so until the Klondike gold rush. For Hardisty, McDougall, and other northern traders, the decision not to proceed was a slap in the face. Having lost the chance to expand and modernize the trade, the northern officers could only do their best to hold on to a shrinking company presence in the Northwest.

The discovery of McDougall's Pass raises an interesting question, one that seems not to have occurred to the company's officers in the 1870s. The new pass was not that far from the HBC posts and trails. The eastern Gwich'in bands regularly travelled through the area, especially when hunting caribou, yet the traders had never been told of the existence of this route. That this knowledge was kept from the HBC men, thus ensuring that the longer Stony Creek Pass remained in use, points once more to the willingness and ability of the First Nations to influence the direction of the fur trade. The company routinely hired aboriginal people to pack supplies over the mountains, a distance of some 70 miles (110 km). Had the packers told of the easier route, they would have been doing themselves out of work and income. Besides, the Hudson's Bay Company never seems to have asked them if there was an easier way.

The decision not to develop the new pass left the Porcupine River trade on a very tenuous footing. Americans were making major inroads into the company trade. Native protestations of loyalty dissolved with the discovery that the American traders paid more for furs and made a greater variety of trade goods available than the HBC did. Yet the company continued to believe that "a considerable quantity of Furs will fall into our hands from Indians lower down the Yukon river, who will be induced by the superiority of our goods to continue our traffic with the Indians."[5] The optimism was not entirely misplaced. The company's tobacco and blankets remained much in demand throughout the Yukon River basin, and Natives along the Yukon River either travelled to Rampart House to trade or secured the goods through intertribal exchange.

Beyond this modest success, however, the company's trade had fallen on hard times. The Americans proved to be intense competitors, sending aboriginal assistants to establish temporary trading posts across the river from Rampart House, escalating prices, and offering generous gifts to those who agreed to trade at their stations. The company tried to entice these Native traders back, offering employment to particularly talented hunters, providing goods on credit, and trying to match the Americans' gift giving. John Firth, a trader destined for a long career along the Porcupine and later at Fort McPherson, even walked to the Arctic coast in an attempt to convince Native people north of the fort to bring their furs to the HBC post. But returns continued to plummet. In 1866 Fort Youcon had attracted more than £6,000 worth of furs, fully one-third of the returns for the entire Mackenzie River district. By the 1880s Rampart House was bringing in between £425 and £900, representing a scant 2 to 4 per cent of the Mackenzie River take. Yet the company held on, if only to protect the Mackenzie River district from American advances.[6]

To make matters worse, Rampart House now faced a new challenge. In 1888 Robert McConnell of the Geological Survey of Canada made a brief foray through the Porcupine River valley. McConnell had planned to survey the Rampart House site but decided instead to push on to Fort Youcon, where he hoped to meet up with a river steamer. He missed the boat, but his decision to leave without making a survey, believing it was "no object for delay," was about to come back to haunt the Hudson's Bay Company.[7]

The next year a small American survey team led by J. Henry Turner arrived to locate the Canada-U.S. boundary along the Porcupine River. A quick examination of the area proved – to Turner's surprise and the Hudson's Bay Company's dismay – that Rampart House was a full 33 miles (53 km) within American territory. Turner stayed two winters at Camp Colonna, his station near the border, since inclement weather through 1889–90 prevented accurate observations. He made a side trip to the Arctic Ocean, accompanied by John Firth, the HBC trader who earlier had walked to the Arctic coast, and there Turner he again took sightings of the Canada-U.S. boundary before leaving in the spring of 1891.[8]

John Firth, incidentally, symbolized the new northern Yukon fur trade. When the trade had had a higher profile and more profitable returns, the company had sent its best, upwardly mobile traders to the post – Murray, Hardisty, and McDougall. These men were talented and aggressive, and used their northern service as a launching pad for their careers. Firth lacked the formal qualifications of the others. He did not write as well, had few contacts in the company, and lacked the ambition of his predecessors. But in other ways he was perfectly suited for northern service. A gentle manner and quiet demeanour masked his often-noted physical power. He respected the Native people, and in turn they thought highly of him. He married a local First Nations woman and settled permanently in the area. Firth spent more than fifty years in the region, most of it at Rampart House and Fort McPherson, showing a dedication to the people and the land that exceeded that of his employer.

The discovery that its post was on American territory gave the company pause. Was the expense of moving justified? Staying was no option, for the Americans had repeatedly refused to permit foreigners to operate on their soil. With some reluctance, stakes were pulled up once more and a new Rampart House – the third – was built, this time on the Canadian side of the border. Almost immediately, the company doubted the wisdom of the move.

As Turner was surveying the region, American whalers were arriving at Herschel Island, off the Yukon's Arctic coast. Although primarily interested in the whales, the ships' officers immediately recognized the potential of additional profits through the fur trade. The whalers ignored the standard conventions of the interior trade, offering repeating rifles, alcohol, and a variety of other goods that were not available from either the American traders or the Hudson's Bay Company. The First Nations from Porcupine quickly learned of these new opportunities and reoriented their trade around Herschel Island. John Firth, who had fought for years to prop up Rampart House's declining trade, threw up his hands in resignation. As his superior reported, Firth did "not so much mind the opposition from down the River, but it is difficult to oppose the trade from the coast, as they are giving higher prices than ever."[9]

The resignation spread. By 1890–91, company officials freely admitted that Rampart House was nothing more than a frontier post, designed to keep the Americans at bay and not expected to turn a profit. With the arrival of free traders in the southern Mackenzie and the escalating costs at Rampart House, even this logic seemed indefensible. After giving the Porcupine First Nations several months' notice of its plan to quit the area, the Hudson's Bay Company abandoned both Rampart House and Lapierre House in the summer of 1893.

The departure of the HBC marked an inglorious end to a trade that had lasted for almost half a century. All the men who had opened the district – Alexander Hunter Murray, John Bell, and Robert Campbell – were now dead. The once dynamic trading empire had contracted its fur operations while moving on into new, southern directions. The fur trade continued – and would even enjoy a major revival in the twentieth century – but the company that had spread the European presence across much of the continent was in retreat.

The HBC left in the Yukon a First Nations population that was very different from the one it had encountered half a century earlier. The population had been severely depleted by a seemingly endless series of epidemics. Native society had undergone substantial change, based on the new European technology and the commercial imperatives of the fur trade. The aboriginal people had held their own against everything but disease, from which there was little protection. They had participated eagerly in the fur trade and had influenced the nature of the exchange. The HBC, which had started it all, was now gone from the Yukon, but the fur trade continued, sustained by Native harvesting and the arrival of new traders. For now, however, the Porcupine River district looked deserted, without a substantial European presence and with the First Nations pulled to Herschel Island, Fort McPherson, or the Yukon River for their trade.

The situation along the Yukon River was very different, for as economic and social activities declined along the Porcupine River, they expanded rapidly upriver from Fort Youcon. Americans had discovered the Yukon. Before the purchase, although the Yukon had been the preserve of its Native inhabitants, the British and Russian fur traders, and a few missionaries, it had been almost totally ignored by the rest of the world. The American purchase of Alaska had changed all that, though people still knew precious little about the Northwest. Because the international boundary was unmarked (and had been almost irrelevant in the Russian era) and because the entire valley tended to be a single geographical and economic unit, the awakening of interest in Alaska spilled over into the Yukon. The telegraph expedition that had preceded the purchase had led to several books about the region being published in the United States, where people were curious about this huge and apparently useless land, which was now theirs. Robert Kennicott's journals were published in the *Transactions of the Chicago Academy of Sciences* (1869), William Dall wrote a book entitled *Alaska and Its Resources* (1870), and Frederick Whymper published *Travels in America and on the Yukon* (1869).

Americans lost no time in seizing the commercial opportunities of the Yukon Valley, which the Russians had neglected. As soon as the transfer took place, an American trading company, the Pioneer Company, was formed, made up of former HBC men, Americans who had worked for the telegraph expedition, and even a Russian or two who wanted to stay in the country.[10] The company was not successful, but the Alaska Commercial Company, which took it over in 1869, had better luck. Two French Canadian brothers, François and Moise Mercier, former HBC employees, provided the energy and enterprise that led to the Alaska Commercial Company's early success. While Moise Mercier took over the trade at Fort Youcon, his brother worked out of St Michael to establish a trading network that eventually reached into Canadian territory along the river. Another founder of the company was Michael Lebarge, who had been with Kennicott on the telegraph expedition. For many years this company dominated the commercial life, Canadian as well as American, of the entire valley.

These first American commercial ventures sought to replace the Hudson's Bay Company and to reproduce its fur-trading successes. This they did admirably, fuelling even greater interest in the business future of the Yukon River basin. At the same time, the advance guard of the North American mining frontier arrived on the scene, setting the Yukon on a markedly different course.

Although the first whites to penetrate the Yukon – the explorers, fur traders, and missionaries – had left their mark on the country, it was a gentle and largely unobtrusive one (save for the impact of disease), for they amended but did not radically alter its economy, appearance, or cultural balance. It was the miners who changed the face of the land irrevocably, bringing it firmly into the orbit of the modern world of development and technology. Perhaps nothing in the history of the Western Hemisphere has been so disruptive to aboriginal societies or has acted as so powerful a magnet to lure men into new and strange territory as the possibility of a gold strike. So it was with Mexico in the early sixteenth century and with California in the 1840s, and so it was, to a comparable degree, in late-nineteenth-century Yukon.

The great discovery of gold in the Yukon that happen in 1896 did not occur in a vacuum. It seems simplistic to say so, but gold discoveries are rarely serendipitous; people do not stumble over gold while out for a walk. For gold to be found, there must be people looking for it. Like the discoveries in California in 1849 and later in British Columbia, gold was discovered in the Yukon because miners knew or had good reason to believe it was there and had spent years looking for it. If there was gold in the southern and central parts of the western mountain chain, why should there not be gold in the north as well?[11]

In 1872 three men came to explore the mineral possibilities of the upper Yukon Valley: Leroy Napoleon McQuesten (who understandably preferred the nickname Jack), Arthur Harper, and Alfred Mayo. McQueston was a farm boy from New England who had participated in the California gold rush and had later prospected on the Fraser and Finlay rivers in British Columbia.[12] For a time he had worked in the north for the Hudson's Bay Company, learning survival and trading skills that were to serve him well in the Yukon. A good-natured, generous man, he later came to be called the Father of the Yukon. Harper had emigrated from northern Ireland as a teenager in 1832 and had followed gold rushes in North America for two decades. It was he who reasoned that there ought to be gold in the northern part of the Rockies, since there had been plenty of it in the south. Mayo, a slight wiry man, was a former circus acrobat from Kentucky who enjoyed practical jokes. Like the other two, he was driven by a hunger for discovery and adventure.

While still in the South, the three heard from a man who had worked at Fort Youcon that there were rumours in the North about gold. Since the 1850s, stories had been circulating among the fur traders that there was gold in the tributaries of the Yukon River. One of the employees of the Hudson's Bay Company had written home in 1864 that gold had been found upriver in good quantities, but for some reason he had not investigated this story.[13] Thus, when McQuesten, Harper, and Mayo came into the Yukon in 1872

by way of the Bell and Porcupine rivers, the smell of gold was in the air. Mc-
Questen later related a story he had heard about an early find:

One of the officers [of the Hudson's Bay Company] that came up on the steamer washed out of a jar of dirt near Fort Yukon and he had about a teaspoonful
of something yellow in the pan and the officer threw it away remarking that it
would not do to let the men see it as they would all leave the steamer ... by the
way the officer acted trying to hide it from the other men he supposed it must
be gold.[14]

In 1873, while Harper searched for gold in the Tanana region of Alaska,
McQuesten and Mayo took jobs with Moise Mercier of the Alaska Commercial Company, and in the summer of 1874 Mercier and McQuesten travelled from St Michael aboard the company's steamboat *Yukon,* upstream
past the company's posts on the river and into the Canadian part of the valley. Six miles downstream from the confluence of the Klondike and Yukon
rivers, near the aboriginal village of Nuklako, the men built Fort Reliance,
the first settlement in what would become the gold country. The purpose of
the post was to shorten the journey that the Tron'dëk Hwëch'in people had
to make to trade at the posts on the lower Yukon. McQuesten and an assistant, Frank Bonfield, hired the local people to carry logs for the post and to
hunt and dry meat for the winter. A crude drawing made by a local artist in
1884 shows the buildings – six in all – huddled near the riverbank, their log
roofs covered with shingles made of birchbark.

Fort Reliance was an instant success. The traders had plenty of meat, they
lived in secure quarters, and before the spring of 1875 they had traded all
their goods for furs. That year Mayo joined them, and they took over the
trade of the upper Yukon Valley on behalf of the Alaska Commercial Company, operating it on a commission basis. They eventually established other
posts in the region, but Fort Reliance became the centre of activity in the area
and the point from which distances to later communities would be reckoned;
Fortymile was forty miles downstream, and Sixtymile River was sixty miles
upstream.

But McQuesten, Bonfield, Harper, and Mayo were primarily miners who
had turned to trading for a living, and when rumours of gold reached them,
they listened eagerly. Although they had not found gold themselves, they had
put in place the support network that would sustain the miners who were to
come. A main feature of this system was the "grubstake," a system in which
the traders gave prospectors supplies and equipment for a season's work on
credit. The trust involved in this arrangement was an essential feature of
Yukon society in this era.

Their relations with the indigenous people were generally good, but an
incident in 1877 shows the problems that could arise and the rough-and-

ready way in which they were solved. In the store at Fort Reliance, Mayo had mixed arsenic with grease and put it out to kill mice. Some Native people broke into the store, and three women ate the grease and died. Their friends and relatives were furious, and the future of the trade was in question. Jack McQuesten settled the matter:

I told them that the poison was put in the store to destroy mice and it was out of the way of children and the old people ought to know better and the people that died it was their own fault for breaking into the store and taking things that didn't belong to them. There was one blind girl about sixteen years old that got poisoned – her father said that she was a great help to her mother and he had taken one of our dogs to replace the girl, but if I would pay for the girl he would return the dog. I told him I would think the matter over and let them know later on. Finally I told him the girl's Mother could keep the dog, so that settled the matter and that was the last I ever heard about the poison.[15]

All through the early 1870s tantalizing traces of gold appeared in the Yukon Valley, and stories about gold finds circulated among the men in the region. McQuesten reported that "Harper & Co. ... had done considerable prospecting ... found Gold in all of the streams ... but nothing that would pay." Again, "Mr. Rob Bear had about thirty dollars in coarse gold that an Indian by the name of Larieson gave him." In the fall of 1878, McQuesten went to Sixtymile River and "found Gold on all the bars in small quantities." He noted that in one place "a man could make $6.00 to $8.00 per day but not extensive enough to put on a string of sluices."[16]

The first man who actually found enough gold in the Yukon to cause a degree of interest outside the country was probably George Holt, who in 1878 also had the distinction of being, with his party, the first white man to cross either the Chilkoot Pass or the White Pass – it is uncertain which route he took.[17] Such a feat required some courage as well as stamina, for the Tlingit (Chilkat) people of the region were jealous of their territorial rights; having made a good living for years acting as middlemen between coastal traders and the people of the interior, they were not keen to see outsiders exploring their trading routes. But somehow Holt got past them and reached the headwaters of the Yukon River.

The route over the passes became known as the "poor man's route," for it was far shorter, and thus cheaper, than the long steamboat ride upriver from St Michael or the route over the mountains from Fort McPherson. Beginning with Holt's journey, a small number of men began to use the passes each spring, many of them prospecting in the Yukon Valley only for the summer before drifting on down the river to the outside world. Some, however, did spend more than a summer in the North; it has been estimated that by 1882 about fifty white people were wintering in the region.

In that year another party of miners reached Fort Reliance via the Chilkoot Pass. This one included a French Canadian named Joseph Ladue, who later played a large role in the gold rush. Ladue and his partners spent the winter of 1882–83 at Fort Reliance and, to keep themselves busy during the winter, experimented with a new mining technique. During the winter it was impossible to see whether the ground was gold bearing or not, since it was frozen solid. Ladue and the others tried building fires on the ground and scooping out the mud when it thawed. This worked well at first, but after spending three days on a ten-foot hole which promptly filled with water, they gave up.

The little party of miners spent most of their evenings in the store at Fort Reliance, talking and playing cards with Jack McQuesten. At one point, they decided that since there was sure to be a gold rush sooner or later, and since there was no formal authority in the district, they had better make some laws of their own to keep order when the rush occurred. Borrowing from the traditions established in California and elsewhere, they drew up a set of mining laws establishing the size of claims, the rules for staking them, and other matters of interest to miners. McQuesten was selected as the first mining recorder.[18]

The pivotal year in the early mining era was 1885, for in that year a party of prospectors on the Stewart River found a small but tantalizing amount of gold – several thousand dollars' worth – enough to stimulate interest in the region. The technique they used was "bar" mining – panning the sandbars in the river and creeks. Within a year there were two hundred men wintering in the upper Yukon Valley. In the summer of 1885 Jack McQuesten, convinced that there was more money to be made supplying the miners than catering to the traditional fur trade, went to San Francisco to convince the directors of the Alaska Commercial Company to change their retailing policy from trading for furs with the Native people to supplying the miners. He returned to Fort Reliance that fall with fifty tons of mining supplies. In the next year he and Harper moved their post from Fort Reliance to Fort Nelson, on the Stewart River. Now the trade with aboriginal people was rapidly supplanted by commercial activity revolving around the search for gold; the trading frontier was being pushed into the background, and the mining frontier was beginning to unfold.

After 1885 the number of men searching for gold in the Yukon Valley steadily increased. There were a few white women too, for some of the miners brought their wives. The two hundred of 1885 grew to about a thousand by 1894, three years before most North Americans had even heard of the place. A majority of these men were veteran miners – men who had gone to earlier rushes in California, Nevada, or Colorado, or to the Fraser River and the Cariboo in British Columbia. They were not greenhorns or idealists, and they did not take foolish chances if they could avoid doing so; very few travelled in the winter months, and they wintered close to a trading post whenever possible, to avoid the risk of starvation. Life in the North was not easy, and the chance of gaining real wealth was slight, but life in the factories of the nineteenth-century American industrial revolution was not much easier, and there the chance of gaining real wealth was virtually non-existent. For many of these men, therefore, gold mining was an alternative to low-paid wage labour and thus provided an escape from the factories – just as pioneering in the West did for others, with the difference that gold miners sometimes struck it rich, whereas farmers rarely did.

These were not the wild-eyed, almost crazed goldseekers of the later Klondike rush but pragmatic men and women, weighing their chances, looking out for opportunities, and working patiently while awaiting the arrival of the big strike. They made up a highly mobile population. Since they owned nothing but their mining equipment and their personal effects, they could easily move from one location to another. Walter H. Pierce was a typical example. He had worked in the goldfields of Colorado, Idaho, and the Cassiar district of British Columbia before crossing the Chilkoot Pass in 1884. He and his partners built a boat at the headwaters of the Yukon, then spent the summer floating down the river, panning the sandbars at the mouths of the creeks that fed the river. In some places they made as much as twenty-five dollars a day, more than ten times the average industrial wage in that era. In other places they found only traces. In any case, the gold in the sandbars soon gave out, since there was never much in any one place, and the miners were thus constantly on the move. In the fall they retraced their journey and wintered in Juneau.

The next year Pierce and his partners came again, this time with enough supplies for eighteen months. Again they spent the summer on the Yukon and its tributaries, testing "favourable looking streams, sometimes staying a week in one place."[19] Where necessary they built canoes or rafts, and went up likely tributaries. They travelled light, living off the land, finding traces of gold almost everywhere but no substantial amount. They had a hard winter in 1885–86 – two of the party died of scurvy – and in the spring Pierce and the other survivors went south. One of the early pioneers of the region, Pierce met the fate of a number of men who led the free and irregular life of the miner; back in Juneau in the fall of 1886 he was charged with the murder of a dance-hall girl. He was acquitted but died four years later of tuberculosis, still in his thirties.[20]

In 1886 the first substantial discovery of gold was made in the region. Harry Madison and Howard Franklin, two of Joe Ladue's original partners of 1882, went down the Yukon River 40 miles (64 km) from Fort Reliance to the mouth of the Fortymile River, then poled their boat 23 miles (37 km) upstream. This took them westward across the 141st meridian into Alaska, though they likely neither knew nor cared that by doing so they had entered the United States. After some searching, they found a rich deposit of coarse placer gold. As a result, the traders – McQuesten, Harper, and Mayo again moved their operations, this time from the Stewart River to the mouth of the Fortymile. Although the Stewart post was kept open, the main activity now shifted to the new settlement of Fortymile, which happened to be in Canada though the strike upstream was in the United States. Fortymile became the first fairly permanent town in the Canadian part of the Yukon Valley and remained a centre of activity until the strike of 1896, when it was largely abandoned.

News of the strike in the Fortymile district brought more miners to the Yukon, and by the winter of 1886–87 there were perhaps five hundred men wintering there, mostly in the vicinity of the new discovery. It was in this period that sympathetic observers (mostly the local missionaries) began to see what the mining frontier held in store for the aboriginal people of the region. At first the arrival of the miners brought a kind of prosperity to some First Nations people, for a few were hired as packers or day-labourers. But the long-term impact on them was almost entirely bad.[21] The Hudson's Bay Company had always banned liquor as an item of trade in the area. But the miners wanted alcohol and either imported it or made their own. Moreover, they had no objection to teaching the distillers' art to the Native people.

Probably the worst result of the mining activity was that fur trading ceased to be the major economic activity in the region. This had an effect that did not occur to observers at the time: it tended to make the Yukon First Nations powerless outsiders in the economic life of their own country. The fur trade could not be carried on successfully without the support of aboriginal people, and because the fur traders were dependent on them for success, the First Nations were able to shape the nature and flow of the trade to a degree that is only now being recognized. But on the mining frontier the Natives played no role apart from doing a bit of casual day labour and supplying a little food. Thus they had no control whatever over the mining activities, which proceeded as though they did not exist.

Although it is arguable to what degree the miners "corrupted" the Natives (missionaries had many arguments with others on this point), there is no question that the indigenous people were relegated to the periphery of the mining activity. Certainly, they could sell their meat and fish to the miners, as they had done to the Hudson's Bay Company, but even if they had wanted to leave their traditional pursuits in favour of full-time wage labour, they could not have done so. Most mining operations, then and for some years to come, were small and did not require a large workforce. Furthermore, many of the miners were infected with racial prejudice, believing that aboriginal people were lazy and unreliable, incapable of a day's work. As the mining frontier developed in the late 1880s, the pressing need for day labour meant that some Native people did find jobs, but they were hired reluctantly and paid less than whites.²² At one point, white workers formed a "combination" to exclude Native workers from the goldfields.²³ When Natives did find work they could earn as much as eight dollars a day²⁴ – much more than they could make from trapping fur though less, of course, than a white man was paid for doing the same job – but they had to live close to the mining region to get the work.²⁵

Another aspect of the problem was that after 1885 the trading posts were located with a view to serving the miners' needs rather than those of the Natives. The First Nations were seriously inconvenienced when their trading posts were shifted suddenly and almost without warning. When Fort Reliance was abandoned in 1887, the people who had traded there were compelled to travel the much greater distance to Fortymile. Worse still, there were occasions when whites entered into direct competition with the aboriginal people: prospectors down on their luck in this early period sometimes tried a bit of trapping or even trading for furs.

It was thus the early gold-mining activities that introduced the industrial sector to the economy of the Yukon region. In the fur trade era little pressure had been put on the Yukon's natural resources, and the skills of the Native people had been an integral part of its economy. With the arrival of the miners, new economic priorities appeared. Now aboriginal skills were increasingly seen as irrelevant, and the focus of economic activity turned to the exploitation of nonrenewable resources. Now the skills of the hunter took second or third place to the skills of the geologist and the prospector. Also, the men who worked for the Hudson's Bay Company had come north for years at a time and had often become deeply committed to the long-term development and prosperity of the region. By contrast, most of the miners were transients, who sought only to strike it rich and make enough money to leave the region forever. For them, and for many others who followed them to the North, the Yukon was not a home but an opportunity.

Faced with prejudice and the disruption of their way of life, most Yukon First Nations avoided the mining communities as much as possible, preferring to live in areas distant from the mines. They continued to hunt and trap and to trade with the Hudson's Bay Company and the American traders, even if doing so meant making long journeys. In the late 1880s the Gwich'in of the Porcupine River region discovered a new outlet for their furs and their meat in the whaling community which grew up at Herschel Island, off the Yukon's Arctic coast. But this new trade also proved disruptive. The whalers were far more ruthless traders than the Hudson's Bay Company or the Americans; they would do anything to attract the Natives to Herschel Island and were quite prepared to use alcohol and repeating rifles as lures, both of which had been banned for trade by the Canadian government.²⁶ The social carnival that came to characterize trade at Herschel contrasted with the sober commercialism of the Hudson's Bay Company in the interior, and the company saw its trade at Rampart House fall off dramatically – a process that further disrupted the existing social and economic structure.

There was innovation as well as disruption in the Yukon in the late 1880s, for it was in this period that the techniques of mining in permafrost were developed. Joe Ladue had experimented with them at Fort Reliance during the winter of 1882–83, and they were perfected five years later during the rush to the Fortymile district. The gold that lay beneath the ground in the Yukon Valley was locked in the soil for all or part of the year by permafrost. Near the surface the ground thawed in summer, releasing the gold, but farther down the dirt and the gold within it were permanently frozen. If the miners were to work their claims for more than a few months each year, they would have to find a way to free from the frozen soil the flakes and small nuggets that made up the placer gold. In the early days the technique employed was called "skim digging." This involved working during the summer on the top two feet or so – about a metre – of the surface gravel along the creek beds. Below this depth either water was encountered, which made the work impossible, or permafrost, which made it too difficult to be profitable.[27]

When coarse gold was discovered in the Fortymile district, however, the miners began to look for ways to mine the soil down to bedrock. They assumed that because gold was heavy, the greatest concentrations would be found in the gravels that lay just above the bedrock. This was not always the case, as the history of the Klondike discoveries later showed, but there was a bigger problem – how to deal with the permafrost.

In 1887–88, when William Ogilvie of the Geological Survey of Canada was wintering near Fortymile, he suggested to the miners a technique he had seen used in Ottawa to reach broken water mains during the winter. Fires, he said, should be built to thaw the soil, which could be scraped off; then a new fire should be built, and so on down to bedrock. The thawed soil could be piled beside the shaft until spring freed the creek water that was needed to wash the gold from the dirt. This suggestion was immediately adopted (some miners, like Joe Ladue, had already experimented with it), and it became the pattern for the early stage of mining in the district. Thus, most of the actual mining – the digging – took place in the winter. An advantage of this technique was that no timbering was needed in the mining shafts, which often ran horizontally as well as vertically under the ground. The permafrost was as hard as granite and would not collapse, unless weakened by fire or an early thaw.

The payoff occurred after the spring thaw when the gold, if there was any, was washed from the dirt. This was originally done in a shallow metal pan, which looked like a cross between a pie tin and a washbasin or a Chinese wok, with a smallish flat bottom and gradually sloping sides. Dirt and water were put in the pan, then the pan was moved in a circular manner so that the water and some of the dirt swished around and then slopped over the side. The water, being lightest, ran over the side first, then the lighter soil, then the sand and gravel; the gold flakes and dust, being much heavier, stayed at the bottom. After this had been done several times, nothing was left but whatever gold the dirt had contained. Tourists in the Yukon are still invited to try their hands at this simple technique.

Panning was simple and cheap but not very efficient; inevitably, a certain amount of gold escaped with the water and dirt. It was also time consuming and thus came to be used mostly for initial testing of the value of paydirt, or on claims where the dirt was so rich that some loss did not matter. More efficient was the rocker box, which looked like a turn-of-the-century washing machine and separated the gold from the dirt by vigorous agitation.

The third method used in the Fortymile district and later in the Klondike was the sluice box. This was a wooden trough, typically 6 to 10 feet (1.8 to 3 m) long, with little wooden crosspieces about half an inch (1.3 cm) in height, called "riffles," nailed at intervals to the bottom. The sluice box was fixed at an incline, and water was run in at the higher end. When gold-bearing dirt was shovelled in with the water, the water washed the dirt out of the lower end, while the heavier gold sank to the bottom and was caught by the riffles. Every so often the water was diverted from the box, and the gold scraped from the riffles. Sluice boxes were much more efficient than pans or rockers, but they needed a good supply of water – easy enough to come by in the early days, but more difficult later in the Klondike when hundreds of miners were competing for the flow of one small creek.

There was an alternative method that used much less labour and enabled winter mining to be avoided altogether. This was hydraulic mining, which was developed in California and reached the Yukon Valley in 1890. It involved directing high-pressure hoses at the banks and beds of creeks. Because the creeks were made up of a loose aggregate of rocks, soil, and gravel, the material was easily broken up by these hoses, and the resulting slurry was directed into sluice boxes. The pressure was created by flumes from neighbouring creeks directed downhill in the manner of a small hydroelectric plant. The first one on the Fortymile, built by Frank Buteau, George Matlock, and their partners, developed 24 feet of pressure and ate the ground away in giant bites.[28] This technique was developed further in the Klondike.

Because of the 1886 discovery of gold, it was Fortymile, not Dawson City, that was the first gold-mining community in the Yukon and the first settlement that was more than a trading post.[29] Even though many of the claims were across the border in Alaska, the community itself, located strategically at the confluence of the Fortymile and Yukon rivers, was in Canada, and its residents would have been subject to Canadian law had there been any in the vicinity. But there was no formal law in Fortymile. Not until 1894, eight years after its founding, did the first Mounted Policeman arrived at the community to enforce Canadian law.

Fortymile in its early days was incredibly isolated, dependent for its supplies on wholesalers in San Francisco, thousands of miles to the south. Two small steamboats linked the community with St Michael, 1,900 miles (3,000 km) down the Yukon, but if the ships failed to make the trip upriver, as happened in 1889, the community was threatened with starvation. At its largest, Fortymile had about 150 buildings clustered around the store. There was a blacksmith shop, an Anglican mission, a school (some of the miners had their families with them), and ten saloons. Because of the expense and difficulty of getting supplies in, the miners there in its early days had to resort to improvisation: "They made stoves and chimneys out of rocks and mud, using flat rocks for the tops of the stoves. For windows they cut clear pieces of Yukon River ice slightly larger than the window openings and fastened them in place with wooden buttons."[30]

Fortymile reached its zenith in the summer of 1894, when close to a thousand people lived in or near it. That year produced a rival, for down the Yukon River another strike had been made in the Birch Creek district of Alaska by Sergi Gologoff Chernosky – a Creole[31] interpreter working for Mercier and Harper – and his brother-in-law Pitka Pavaloff. A new town was founded by Jack McQuesten to supply the miners there. It was on the Yukon River flats, just across the American side of the 141st meridian, and was named Circle City because of its location on the Arctic Circle.

Circle City, like Fortymile, depended entirely on the success of the local miners. The Birch Creek strike was a rich one, even better than Fortymile, and it too spawned a store, saloons (twenty-eight of them), theatres, and even a library. With seven hundred people actually living in the town by 1896, and more in the district, it drained most of the population from its rival and was described as the largest log-cabin city in the world.[32]

Thus the gold-mining community in the Yukon basin before the great discovery of 1896 was an international one, revolving around the communities of Fortymile in the Yukon and Circle City in Alaska. The fact that the mining districts were split by an international boundary was of no importance to anyone who lived in the region. Miners whose property lay close to the 141st meridian often did not know in which country they were working. The merchants moved their operations across the border from one community to another without a thought – because it hardly mattered. Until the mid-1890s, the miners were living in a society virtually of their own making. For a number of years there were no government officials on either side of the border. The miners paid no taxes, nor did they pay royalties on the gold they found, and those on the Canadian side paid no customs duty on the goods they brought in from San Francisco. The only laws the miners obeyed were those they drafted for themselves.

This was the essential difference between the Yukon in the pre- and post-gold-rush periods. Before the arrival of the North-West Mounted Police, the Yukon was an isolated society of miners – a "community of hermits whose one common bond was their mutual isolation," as Pierre Berton has put it.[33] There were, of course, the colourful characters who seemed to gravitate to gold-mining communities, their nicknames reading like a list of characters from a boys' novel: Salt Water Jack, Big Dick, Squaw Cameron, Jimmy the Pirate, Buckskin Miller, Pete the Pig.[34] But many others were sober citizens (or reasonably so) who were not fleeing from civilization but had made a conscious decision to come north for a chance at real prosperity, believing that the streets of Fortymile were more likely to be paved with gold than those of the factory cities to the south.

In a sense, the miners' society was one of the freest in the hemisphere.[35] The men came and went as they pleased, made their own laws, and depended only on themselves and their partners for survival. The partnerships were highly flexible and informal. Men came together to prospect or work a certain property; if one man decided that the effort was not worthwhile, the partnership broke up with no hard feelings, and each man went his own way to seek his fortune as he saw best. Everyone sought gold, but each as an individual in his own way, joining with others only as it suited him: "For much of his time in the territory a miner never knew whom he might end up associating with, and many of those to whom he became linked in some common enterprise were likely to be strangers to him."[36]

The mobile, casual, almost ephemeral nature of the miners' society is illustrated by the career of a man named Chris Sonnikson, who crossed the coastal mountains in the spring of 1886 with his partners Charley Braises and Old Solomon.[37] They built a boat at the headwaters of the Yukon and planned to go downriver to the Stewart. But on the way they learned that a veteran miner named Densmore was prospecting the upper Yukon, so they changed their plans and joined five other men working in the region.

The new party of eight worked the sandbars of the upper Yukon, some of them prospecting while the others worked the bars where traces of gold had been found. They took turns watching the Densmore party to see if anything valuable turned up there. After a few weeks the Yukon River rose, flooding the most likely sandbars. Sonnikson and Braises then decided to go to the Salmon River, where the water had fallen, while Old Solomon chose to stay with the others on the Yukon and wait for its water to fall. The two men prospecting on the Salmon River split up after a while; Braises went back to the Yukon, while Sonnikson joined a man they had met in another party and went with him to prospect the Hootalinqua for a time, after which he went back to join Braises on the Yukon River. Then Sonnikson and Braises went back to where they had left Old Solomon but discovered that he and the others had staked the whole sandbar for themselves as soon as the water had fallen. The two then left for another sandbar, but they soon broke up, Braises selling his share in the bar to Sonnikson and leaving for the winter, while Sonnikson joined yet another party.

All this coming and going, joining and rejoining, took place in the five months between April and September 1886, and it shows the remarkably fluid and individualistic nature of mining society in the Yukon in the early days. Each miner, although operating on his own, did so by means of a "personal community" of other miners whom he could join or leave as his interests dictated.

As the Yukon mining frontier developed in the late 1880s, the trading and transportation network that held the fragile community together and linked it to the "outside" also became more sophisticated. In 1893 a powerful force appeared at Fortymile to challenge the McQuesten-Harper-Ladue partnership. John J. Healy had been a trader, miner, and sheriff in the goldfields of Idaho and Montana. In 1886, sensing that a rush was due in the North, he moved to Alaska. He was astute enough to realize that the Chilkoot Pass would someday see heavy traffic, so he opened a store athwart the "poor man's route" to the Yukon, at the head of the Lynn Canal. This store became the nucleus of the town of Dyea. He then persuaded three Chicago financiers to back him in a new trading company that would challenge the Alaska Commercial Company, and in 1892 the North American Trading and Transportation Company was formed. By the fall of that year Healy had steamed up the Yukon River in the *Porteus B. Weare*, a vessel named after one of his backers. In 1893 he arrived at Fortymile, where he built a store called Fort Cudahy (named for another of his backers, a Chicago meat packer) across the Fortymile River from the town, and entered into competition with McQuesten's store.

Healy's prices were attractive, but unlike McQuesten he would not grubstake the miners; for this reason and because of his abrasive personality, the miners disliked him. When a woman who worked for him brought a trivial charge against him to a miners' meeting, the miners happily awarded her a year's wages and passage home. Healy paid, but his resentment against the ad hoc legality of the proceedings moved him to complain to an old friend from his Montana days – Sam Steele of the North-West Mounted Police. The gist of his letter was that Fortymile needed some British justice. This was to have important consequences for the mining community.

The miners' meeting, which had so infuriated Healy, was the basic unit of government in the mining communities before the arrival of the Canadian authorities. During this period the miners' society was, in a sense, one of the most democratic in the world. The miners' meetings, which were attended by all the miners in an area, meetings began as early as 1885, as soon as there were enough miners to justify them, and continued until just after the arrival of the North-west Mounted Police detachment in 1895. A meeting could be called by anyone to hear criminal cases, mining disputes, or personal grievances and quarrels, and it then delivered a verdict by a majority vote – often banishment from the community – which was binding on all parties. It could also pass bylaws to regulate any aspect of the community. A witness to these meetings wrote a description of them:

The powers of the miners' meeting are threefold – legislative, judicial, and executive. No provision is made for a governing officer, the whole fabric resting on the great American principle, "majority rules." Universal suffrage is given, and all have an equal vote. The method of procedure is as follows: If a man has a grievance, he posts a notice to that effect and calls a meeting for a certain date. At the appointed time the miners of the locality assemble, generally in the open air, and a moderator from their number is appointed. Then the prosecutor presents his case; the defendant answers. There is a cross-questioning, speeches pro and con are made, and in the end someone puts a motion, which is either carried or defeated. If carried, the penalty is imposed without delay.[38]

The miners' meeting was more than just a community court, however; it was the basic regulator of mining society, governing not only its legal but also to a large extent its social relationships. Mining society was so fragmented and individualistic that some means had to be found not only to enforce laws but also to regulate personal behaviour for the good of the community. This was done by applying various sanctions to people whose behaviour fell too far outside community norms.

Miners in the Yukon lived in a community where each person might have to depend for his success or even his survival on the goodwill or reliability of a stranger. For instance, it was essential that travellers in the country be sure that they could call on anyone at any time for food and shelter; to refuse aid to a stranger in need was unthinkable. Similarly, in a country without police, banks, or secure storage facilities, it was necessary that people be able to leave their goods and property untended for long periods without fear of pilferage; thus, petty theft was viewed as a serious crime. The selfish man, the loner, the man who pursued his own interests in disregard of others' rights and interests was more than a nuisance; he was a threat to the whole community. For this reason, the miners' meeting judged not only offences but also the character of the accused; not only his past deeds, but what he was likely to do in the future – delivering what has been called "forward-looking justice."[39]

Other societies have had similar views of behaviour. A Canadian example is Inuit society. The Inuit in the pre-contact period put a high value on good nature, sharing, and helpfulness, qualities that were essential for their survival in a harsh environment. People who were bad tempered and abusive, if only in words, were sometimes killed before they could express themselves in actions, since an unreliable person was a danger to everyone.[40] The miners' meeting worked on the same principle, though actions rather than words were necessary as proof of guilt, and the punishment was generally banishment rather than death.

The case of Frank Leslie shows the process in action. In 1886 he persuaded four experienced miners in Seattle that he had knowledge of a rich deposit of gold on the Stewart River. The men came up with a grubstake, and the party went over the Chilkoot Pass to the Stewart. It soon proved that the story was a lie, and during the winter of 1886–87, while the men were wintering on the Stewart, the four dupes discussed lynching Leslie. Fearing for his life, he waited until it was his week to cook, then dosed a dish of fried beans with powdered arsenic that was kept to poison wild animals. But he misjudged the dose and only made his partners sick. He then tried to shoot them while they slept but was overpowered. The partners took him downriver to the Stewart River post, where a miners' meeting was convened. Leslie's defence was that he had originally acted in good faith, believing the story about the gold to be true, and that he had poisoned and then tried to shoot his partners in self-defence. The meeting accepted his story. Nevertheless,

he was considered an undesirable citizen, and after much discussion it was decided to banish him, so he was furnished with a sled, provisions enough to get out if he could, was ordered to move up-river at least one hundred and fifty miles from that camp, and assured that if ever he was seen within that distance of it, any one then present would be justified in shooting him on sight. He left to make his way unaided up the Yukon, to and over the Dyea [Chilkoot] Pass, more than five hundred miles, in the inclement weather and spring months, and he succeeded so well that he reached Haines Mission ... It was thought he richly deserved punishment, but as they had no prison in which to confine him, nor any way to detain him for any length of time, all they could do was hang him or banish him. His death they did not wish to be directly responsible for, though many of them felt they were condemning him to death in agreeing to the sentence imposed.[41]

The miners' system of justice is further illustrated by the case of a miner on the trail who broke into a cache belonging to another man and took the supplies he needed, an action that no one would have objected to in the Yukon. But he left the rest of the cache unprotected, and animals got at it and destroyed it. When he reached Circle City he told no one what he had done, so when the owner returned to the cache, it was empty. Without supplies he almost died before getting to town. He had identified the thief by following his trail to town, and after waiting a few days for the man to confess on his own, he called a miners' meeting. The thief confessed and was banished from the country. It is significant that the punishment for this offence was the same as for the previous one. Indeed, permitting a cache to be destroyed was a form of attempted murder, and in this case the miners likely delivered a fairer justice than a formal court would have done.

In both these instances the mining community exercised a notable degree of restraint. The purpose of the meetings was not only to dispense justice but to prevent conflict. When individuals failed to exercise restraint, the miners' meeting was often able to command it. At Fortymile in the winter of 1893–94, two miners named Wickham and Matlock got into a drunken argument. Wickham stabbed Matlock in the back, but Matlock was able to go to his cabin, get a gun, and return to shoot Wickham through his cabin window. Both men survived, but at a miners' meeting that was called to handle the incident, they were told that if there was further trouble between them, both would be banished. Eventually they became good friends. On another occasion, at Circle City in 1896, the meeting ruled in the case of two men who had shot at each other that if one killed the other, or even if one died in suspicious circumstances, the other would be hanged without trial.[42]

It is significant that there is very little evidence of homicide on the early mining frontier in the Yukon Valley. There were one or two killings. For instance, in Circle City in 1896 a miner tried to shoot a bartender and was himself shot; the bartender then called a miners' meeting, which ruled he had acted in self-defence. There may have been some unrecorded incidents. But the essential fact is that the miners' meetings and the whole social organization of the mining community militated against violence and were remarkable successful in preventing it.[43]

Considering that the majority of these miners were Americans, it is perhaps surprising that disputes in the Yukon were not generally settled by private rather than public means. Why were there no duels or vendettas in the Yukon? Certainly there were quarrels, and every man in the district had a gun, so both the motivation and the means for private violence were there. It has been suggested that one reason is that the miners never really thought of themselves as residents of the Yukon. Even those who had been there for years were only transients – men who had come north to strike it rich.[44] They expected some day to return to a home in the south and were conscious of the reputation they would have there. It would not do for a man who had struck it rich and wished to establish a comfortable bourgeois life to return home marked as a murderer or desperado. In other words, the Yukon mining frontier was not like Australia had been early in the century – a place that people could never hope to leave, where they could therefore behave as they pleased. It was a temporary place from which they hoped to return with a good reputation as well as wealth. Most men did not want to be criminals, nor did they want to be vigilantes. The miners' meeting, by shifting responsibility for punishment to the community as a whole, absolved the individual miners; none of them could be held individually accountable for the community's actions.

The miners did not publicize their northern adventures a great deal and in fact did little to attract attention to the area. There were others, however, drawn by the mystique of the unknown, who came to investigate the human and physical secrets of the upper Yukon River basin. Among the first of these was a pair of German explorers, Aurel and Arthur Krause, who had previously studied the Siberian Chukotsk Peninsula. They came to the Yukon in 1881 on behalf of the Geographical Society of Bremen. After spending a winter at the head of the Lynn Canal, Arthur Krause crossed the Chilkoot Pass to Lake Lindeman, becoming the first scientist to map the route. His brother remained on the coast to study the Tlingit.

Americans, drawn by the great debates in the United States about the value of Secretary of State Seward's purchase of the territory, were understandably interested in the upper Yukon River basin. Their interest, however, was not limited to the American side of the border. The Frederick Schwatka expedition of 1883 was the result of the American army's desire to find out about Alaska in case it should be called upon to defend the place. In particular, General Nelson A. Miles, whose idea the expedition was, wanted to determine what the attitude of the local Native people would be to the arrival of the Americans. Schwatka, a lieutenant in the U.S. Cavalry, was thirty-four when he went to Alaska. He was chosen because of his previous experience in the North; in 1879 he had led an expedition to the central Canadian Arctic to look for traces of the lost Franklin expedition. He had also found time during his military service to earn a medical degree and to study enough law to be admitted to the Nebraska bar. Like Robert Peary, a more famous explorer of a generation later, Schwatka was a military man who did not do much soldiering. He spent most of his career either studying or exploring.

There were eight men in the party that left Portland in May 1883, including a doctor, a topographer, a photographer, and an artist – all military men – as well as a miner named J.B. Mitchell, who had prospected in the Yukon Valley and presumably knew the country. The expedition steamed north past the settlements on the Lynn Canal – by 1883 salmon canneries had been established there – and landed at the future site of Dyea. On 11 June 1883 the men crossed the Chilkoot Pass: Schwatka's description of the journey, which was aided by Native packers who charged him from ten to twelve dollars for the trip, is the earliest complete account of the route to have been written in English and circulated widely:

About five o'clock [a.m.] we commenced the toilsome ascent of this coast range pass ... Up banks almost perpendicular they scrambled on their hands and knees, helping themselves by every projecting rock and clump of juniper and dwarf spruce, not even refusing to use their teeth on them at the worst places. Along the steep snow banks and the icy fronts of glaciers steps were cut with knives, while rough alpenstocks from the valley helped them to maintain their footing. In some such places the incline was so steep that those having boxes on their backs cut scratches in the icy crust with the corners as they passed along ... In some of these places a single mis-step, or the caving in of a foothold would have sent the unfortunate traveller many hundred feet headlong to certain destruction. Yet not the slightest accident happened, and about ten o'clock, almost exhausted, we stood on top of the pass.[45]

Schwatka, like most successful explorers, had a strong ego, and he gave names to dozens of the topographical features he passed, ignoring the fact that they already had names that had been given them by indigenous people, and in many cases by whites as well. His attempt to rename the Chilkoot Pass after a French geographer failed, but some of his names stuck. These included Lake Lindeman, after the secretary of the Geographical Society of Bremen; Lake Bennett, after the editor of the New York *Herald*, who was a patron of exploration; and Marsh Lake (the miners had called it Mud Lake), after an American paleontologist. One of his names gave rise to later controversy. He decided that the river which the Hudson's Bay Company men had called the Lewes was actually the upper part of the Yukon, and he marked it so on his map. Later, the Canadian government changed the name back to Lewes, but the name did not stick. Despite local support for the original non-Native appellation, the name for the entire river system from Marsh Lake to the lower river was changed back to Yukon in the 1950s. Having left his stamp on the maps of northwestern Canada, Schwatka floated down the Yukon, past the future site of Dawson City, and into American territory.

The American expeditions finally forced a Canadian response. News of the Schwatka expedition roused Ottawa from its total indifference to the Yukon, and seventeen years after it had acquired the region the Canadian government was moved to send a party north to see what was there. In charge of this party was George M. Dawson, assistant director (later director) of the Geological Survey of Canada. The survey, founded in 1842, was one of Canada's oldest and most useful government agencies. Originally designed to assist the mining industry by studying and reporting on the geology of Canada, it also became involved in "economic geology," particularly in providing information that aided the government in its awarding of railway land grants. The GSC was thus the logical agency to report on the potential riches of the Yukon.

Dawson had been born in Pictou, Nova Scotia, in 1849, son of Sir John William Dawson, a geologist and naturalist who later became principal of McGill University. An illness in his youth had left George Dawson dwarfed, with a twisted back, but he had studied geology and natural science in Edinburgh and London, graduating with high honours. When he came to the Yukon he had already done extensive mapping in British Columbia and had written a comprehensive report on the Haida Nation. He had also served with the International Boundary Commission of 1873, which had marked the 49th parallel on the prairies. The two other main members of the party were Richard G. McConnell, another geologist, and William Ogilvie, a dominion land surveyor for the government who had played a leading part in the original survey of the prairie prairies.[46]

The party left for the North in April 1887 and reached the Yukon by different routes, Dawson and McConnell travelling by way of the Stikine River and the old telegraph trail, while Ogilvie went over the Chilkoot Pass. At the end of June 1887, Dawson and his party entered the southern Yukon by way of the Liard River and Frances Lake. They then portaged to the upper Pelly River, canoed down it, and by early August had reached the site of Fort Selkirk. On the way, Dawson panned in places for gold and discovered that "Small 'colours' [might] be found in almost any suitable locality along the river, and 'heavy colours' in a considerable number."[47] He interviewed the miners he met in order to be able to assess as accurately as possible the region's mining potential. One man, Thomas Boswell, told Dawson that he had worked a bar on the Ross River that paid eighteen dollars a per day. There were only two men working the entire Pelly, and they had made just ten to twenty dollars a day when they found a good location.

Dawson formed an opinion of regions he did not have time to visit by talking to miners who knew the country. From a man named John McCormack he got information on the Big Salmon River, and Thomas Boswell helped him with facts about Teslin Lake and the Nisutlin River. All this material was published as part of the annual report of the Geological Survey of Canada for 1887–88 and was reissued ten years later at the height of the gold rush to satisfy the public demand for information about the Yukon. Dawson also patriotically changed some of Schwatka's names back to their originals, leading to some later confusion in the maps of the Yukon.[48]

Ogilvie's trip into the Yukon over the Chilkoot Pass was an enterprise involving 120 aboriginal packers, for he brought seven tons of supplies and equipment with him – even then civil servants did not travel light, and the surveys he had been ordered to make required that he to carry a number of instruments. On the way he met three men who were soon to become famous in the Yukon as well as outside: George Carmack, Skookum Jim, and Dawson (sometimes Tagish) Charlie. Skookum ("strong") Jim and Dawson Charlie were working as packers, and Skookum Jim carried 156 pounds of bacon over the pass for Ogilvie. Carmack (Ogilvie spells it "Carmac") was living with the Tagish people, doing nothing in particular. These three were to make the famous discovery of 1896. Accompanying Ogilvie was William Moore, a man who had made and lost a fortune in the Cassiar goldfield. While Ogilvie went over the Chilkoot Pass, Moore persuaded a Chilkoot man named Jim to breach the traditional Native secrecy about these routes and guide him over a parallel pass, which he named after Thomas White, minister of the interior.[49] When Moore met Ogilvie again he was full of the possibilities of this new route: "Every night during the two months [Moore] remained with us he would picture the tons of yellow dust yet to be found in the Yukon valley. He decided then and there that Skagway would be the entry port to the golden fields of the Yukon, and the pass would reverberate with the rumble of railway trains."[50]

While Dawson and McConnell mapped the Yukon country and made scientific observations, Ogilvie spent most of his time talking to the miners in the Fortymile region. Since he was an official representative of the Canadian government, the miners were anxious to know what Ottawa had in mind for the Yukon. In particular, they wanted to know what mining laws were likely to be enforced if Ottawa ever asserted its authority in the mining district. Ogilvie informed them that since the Yukon was unique, there being no placer gold mines anywhere under federal jurisdiction in Canada, no regulations applicable to the Yukon had ever been drawn up, and they should abide by the British Columbia rules, which limited placer claims to 100 feet (30.5 m) of frontage. When the miners complained that this was far too small for permafrost country, Ogilvie agreed that a 500-foot (152.5 m) frontage running from the base of the hills on one side of the creek to the base of the hills on the other would be fairer, and this was eventually adopted by Ottawa. The effect of this ruling, of course, was to limit the paydirt to fewer lucky people.

More disturbing to the miners was Ogilvie's news that the Canadian government's policy was to collect a 2.5 per cent royalty on gold taken from crown land. This the miners "universally condemned."[51] The reason they generally gave for their condemnation was the expense of mining in the North, but underlying it was the feeling that since the government provided them with absolutely nothing in the way of services, it had no right to tax them, certainly not without "representation." Such an action was simple theft. These men were mining in a virtual no man's land as far as constituted authority was concerned, so they felt they had the right to keep what they could find. In any case, since Ogilvie was not there to collect taxes, the issue was theoretical.

Ogilvie and his party spent the winter of 1887–88 at Fortymile. Over the winter he made a number of astronomical observations to determine the longitude of the settlement and to ascertain where the 141st meridian crossed the Fortymile River. He was compelled to adapt his techniques to northern conditions. First, he needed to find a base for the astronomical transit, because the tripod (which weighed more than 400 pounds) had been left at the foot of the passes. A tree stump 22 inches (55 cm) in diameter had to be found as a substitute, and since trees that size were not plentiful in the central Yukon, the search took three days. Observations were taken in temperatures ranging from -30°F to -50°F (-35°C to -46°C). Ogilvie was able to make twenty-two observations between November and February. He marked the position of Fortymile and was able to determine the location of the 141st meridian with a small degree of error – when he returned in 1895 to check his work, he found that his line was 109 feet (33 m) too far east, perhaps because, as he reported, his tree stump tended to rise and fall slightly with the changes in temperature.

Meanwhile, Richard McConnell was leading a separate expedition by way of Fort McPherson, the Bell River, and Lapierre House. He found this post as well as Rampart House to be in decline – the latter was kept open "as a protection against the encroachment of traders from the west."[52] He went on to Fort Youcon and then up the river to Fortymile, where he witnessed a minor stampede:

A report was brought up by the men on the steamer that a miner had boarded the boat at the mouth of Beaver River, and after talking in a hurried manner to the captain, had suddenly departed, and in his haste had left his purse behind him. The miners reasoned that nothing but a rich find could cause such an excitement, and immediately loaded their boats and started on a wild goose chase down the river only to meet with disappointment at the end of their journey. A few received a passage up again on the steamer, but the greater number drifted on down towards St. Michael's, and left the mining country altogether.[53]

McConnell continued up the Yukon River and left the country in September 1888 by way of the Chilkoot Pass.

When Ogilvie returned to Ottawa in January 1889 he reported at length to A.M. Burgess, deputy minister of the interior. The gist of his recommendations was that the time was not ripe for Ottawa to assert its authority in the Yukon:

I advised him that ... until such times as there were more and better means of transport it would be unwise in us to interfere with the affairs of the region ... that to attempt to collect customs ... would likely endanger prospecting in our country. Generally my advice was that, as the country was in a very unsettled state, and our mining laws, so far as known, unsatisfactory to the miners, even of our own nationality, any attempt to take charge of affairs on our side of the line would hinder prospecting- to the American side, and they would stay there till something very rich was discovered in Canada.[54]

This was welcome news to the deputy minister, for the government was looking for an excuse to do nothing in the Yukon in order to avoid the expense of establishing an administration there. So Ogilvie's advice was accepted.

After the Dawson expedition, events in the Yukon accelerated towards the great discovery that in retrospect seems inevitable. The more people there were in the country looking for the gold that lay in such tremendous quantities in the river's tributaries, the more likely it was to be discovered. By 1890 the Yukon's potential was beginning to attract the attention of the international press. In that year an American periodical, *Frank Leslie's Illustrated News*, sent a party into the region. It was headed by E.J. Glave, an English journalist and explorer – an associate in Africa of the famous Henry M. Stanley of "Dr. Livingstone, I presume?" fame. But the member of this party who became most famous was a forty-five-year-old Oklahoma-born cowboy and logger named Jack Dalton. The party explored the region between Dezadeash Lake and the Pacific Ocean and travelled over the Chilkat Pass – roughly the route of the modern Haines Highway. Dalton returned to Haines Mission in 1894 and built a hotel and a trading post. By 1896 he had blazed the packtrail that bore his name, and he was making a fair living from supplying prospectors who used his route.

Schwatka returned to the North in 1891, this time working for a group of newspapers that were anxious to supply their public with colourful news of Alaska. He went north from Juneau and explored extensively in the almost unknown region of the Taku and Teslin rivers.[55] In 1895 Ogilvie also returned to the Yukon, this time to mark the international boundary from the Yukon River south though the middle of what was then the richest gold country. He stayed in the North during the winter of 1895–96 and was on hand when the great discovery took place. He was thus able to play a tremendously useful role in sorting out much of the early confusion about boundaries and claims that accompanied the rush.

While the federal government, represented by Dawson and Ogilvie, paid scant attention to the Yukon, the Anglican Church continued its struggle to bring the Christian gospel to the aboriginal people of the Yukon. The Anglican missionaries had never had an easy time in the Yukon Valley. Problems with money, supply, and particularly manpower had plagued the church from the beginning of its service in the region. The work itself was extremely difficult, for the Natives were widely scattered through the region and seldom altered their nomadic habits to suit the needs of northern clergy. Moreover, the First Nations were not initially receptive to the Anglicans' message; W.W. Kirkby referred to them as "treacherous, savage and cruel." William C. Bompas, though he dedicated his life to what he viewed as the spiritual advancement of the Yukon First Nations, commented, "These mountain Loucheux seem the 'lowest of all people' but I cannot help hoping they are a 'chosen race.'"[56]

Bompas, made bishop of Athabaska in 1874 and then in 1891 appointed bishop of the new Diocese of Selkirk – later, Diocese of the Yukon – worked hard to find funds and competent missionaries for northern service. Throughout his long incumbency, he was never able really to succeed on either count, partly because of his irascible and combative personality and his unwillingness to perform that most vital part of the missionary enterprise – returning to settled areas on speaking and fundraising tours. The Church Missionary Society in London was more interested in supporting mission fields in Africa and Asia than in Canada, and it was to these places that the bright and ambitious young clergy wanted to go. The Canadian North had to be content with the leftovers. The sad truth, as Bompas himself admitted, was that first-rate men would not come to the Yukon, and second-raters, or those from the lower middle class for whom even the Yukon would be a step up, had to be sought: "It is best not to try to send gentlefolks hither whether male or female, simply because these gentlefolks who undertake pioneer life in the far west, have to come down a peg in their position which is mostly painful to themselves and to those about them. Those of an inferior grade in going to the far west generally rise a peg which is mostly pleasant to themselves and to their neighbours. It is less consequence to me whether he passed a College course or not."[57] The result was that the Canadian Northwest received missionaries who were "tough but uncultivated ... suitable for Rupert's Land although not for the more sophisticated fields in Asia."[58]

Men who chose to stay and make a career in the northern mission field had to be physically hardy, for ministering to the First Nations of the Yukon Valley involved travelling from place to place continually – covering a huge area and meeting the different Native groups. Robert McDonald, once he recovered from his illness, began to serve the entire Yukon basin from a base at Fort McPherson, crossing the Richardson Mountains every year to visit individual bands. These journeys took him to Fort Youcon and two or three hundred miles past it down the valley, and easily totalled more than a thousand miles of travelling a year. Another missionary, V.C. Sim, who had been recruited to serve in the northern Yukon and had reopened the mission at Rampart House, travelled constantly, attempting to meet each band in his charge at least once a year. Sim's health suffered from the rigours of his long and arduous travels, and he died at Rampart House in 1885 after four years' service.[59] Bishop Bompas, who preferred ministering to indigenous people rather than whites, spent weeks travelling along the Porcupine and Yukon rivers, and in 1872 he crossed overland from the Porcupine and spent several days at an Inuit camp along the Yukon's Arctic coast.

The arrival of the miners represented a new challenge for the missionaries, who had hoped to bring Christianity to the Native people before the society was fouled by the advance of the frontier. The miners brought alcohol and a seemingly insatiable appetite for Native women, and the missionaries were sure that the First Nations would be debauched and demoralized through such contact. Bompas moved into the middle of the mining field, establishing Buxton Mission at Fortymile in 1892 in an attempt to head off what he feared was the impending corruption of his aboriginal charges.

The missionaries enjoyed varying degrees of success in their attempts to win the hearts of the Native people and the miners. Missionaries who were conscious of their lower-middle-class status might overcompensate for it by putting on airs before the miners, and the class-consciousness of late-Victorian society which these men reflected was bound to clash with the rough egalitarianism of the miners' society. J.W. Ellington, who served as a missionary in the region in the 1880s, was so unpopular with the miners that they played pranks on him "and made his life such a burden, that mind and body both gave way and he had to be taken back to England, where he died in 1892."[60] Others, such as T.H. Canham, remained with the aboriginal congregations and had comparatively little contact with the incoming white population.

Bompas and the other missionaries recoiled at the changes wrought by the miners. But they were comparatively powerless to influence either the First Nations or the miners. The former bent somewhat to the moral pleas of the earnest but pedantic Bompas, whose wife Selina joined him at Fortymile after a five-year separation, but they generally followed their own desires in their dealings with whites. The miners wrote off the Anglican missionaries and their wives as whiners and killjoys, people who did not understand the traditions and realities of the North American frontier.

When Native people came to visit Fortymile to trade or just to visit, Bompas took charge of them as much as he could and gave them a few hours of religious instruction. In winter, when the miners had plenty of free time, there were many moral snares in Fortymile for the Natives. As Bompas's wife later wrote of the miners, "We have every reason to fear that their goings on will be very sad and distressing, and to the ruin of our poor Indians."[61]

Unable by their own efforts to alter the behaviour of the Natives or the miners, the missionaries looked south for help. Bompas wrote letters to the Church Missionary Society, to temperance organizations in Canada and England, to the Department of Indian Affairs, the North-West Mounted Police, and the Department of the Interior, demanding attention to the Yukon. In 1893 he wrote on two occasions to Thomas Mayne Daly, superintendent general of Indian affairs, complaining that the flow of liquor in Fortymile district was debauching the Indians and endangering relations between the races: "I think it right to inform you of the danger to which the Indians of the neighbourhood are now exposed for want of any police restraint upon the free and open manufacture and sale of intoxicating liquor among them. About 210 miners have passed the present winter in this vicinity, in British Territory. The Indians have learned from them to make whiskey for themselves, but there has been drunkenness of whites and Indians together with much danger of the use of fire arms."[62] The following year, he noted: "My own interest lies principally in the preservation of the Indians who I fear will be finished in a few years unless Government protection is afforded them. Some of them manufacture liquor and it is supplied to them by Whites, and especially to the Indian women for the purposes of debauchery."[63]

The complaints took on an increasingly anguished tone, for Bompas truly believed that the introduction of alcohol and the increase in sexual contact between Natives and whites would mark the end of the spiritually and culturally innocent Yukon First Nations. He made no apologies for his strident and public appeals: "Where the life of an Indian is concerned there appears less occasion to stand upon ceremony." Though at first his warnings made little impression on southern officials, his appeals could not be ignored forever.[64]

These urgings, combined with those of businessman John Healy and William Ogilvie, who also were pressing the government to move into the Yukon, finally met with success. In 1894 two members of the North-West Mounted Police were ordered north on a reconnaissance mission. The government's purpose in finally asserting itself in the Yukon was twofold: "In the interests of the peace and good government of that portion of Canada, in the interest also of the public revenue, it is highly desirable that immediate provision be made for the regulation and control of the traffic in intoxicating liquor, for the administration of lands containing the precious metals, for the collection of customs duties upon the extensive imports being made into that section of Canada from the United States ... for the protection of the Indians, and for the administration of justice generally."[65]

Leading this two-man expedition was Inspector Charles Constantine; his companion was Staff Sergeant Charles Brown. Born in England in 1849, Constantine had emigrated to Canada with his family as a boy of five. He had served with the Wolseley expedition to Red River in 1870, been appointed chief of the Manitoba Provincial Police in 1880, and in 1886 had joined the NWMP.[66] The two men climbed the Chilkoot Pass and arrived at Fortymile, where they spent the season investigating local conditions. Constantine made an important demonstration of Canada's sovereignty over the Yukon by collecting $3,200 in customs duties from the miners on the Canadian side of the 141st meridian. He reported that there was some grumbling over the matter but that "better counsels prevailed," and the money was collected without trouble – showing once more that the miners were not disposed to violence.[67] In October he returned south to plan for a larger expedition.

The next year, 1895, the government sent Constantine back to the Yukon, this time in charge of a party of twenty police. Travelling by steamer via St Michael, the men reached Fortymile in late July and immediately built a post, Fort Constantine, near Healy's Fort Cudahy, across the river from Fortymile. When the post was finished, Constantine was able to report proudly to Ottawa that he was writing from "the most northerly military or semi-military post in the British Empire."[68]

Constantine's reports to his superiors give an interesting picture of the Yukon in the last years of its pre-gold-rush history. He found to his surprise that, contrary to the opinion of Bishop Bompas, there was little drunkenness among the miners. "Many of the miners do not drink at all," he wrote, "and but a few to excess ... When they come in from the mines for winter they have a general carouse ... [then] the camp settles down ... and is ... quiet."[69] Some miners wanted substantial economic development in the Yukon, particularly in mining, and thought that this could best be accomplished by improving navigation on the Yukon River. Others wanted to keep Yukon society closed to outsiders to prevent an influx of thieves, gamblers, and rival miners.

OLD STION N.W.M.P. FORTYMILE YUKON   1901

The North-West Mounted Police came to the Yukon in 1894, when Inspector Charles Constantine arrived on a reconnaissance mission. His report convinced his superiors of the need for a permanent station in the Fortymile district. This photograph was taken in 1901, five years after the police had moved their operations to Dawson City (authors' collection).

Constantine had been asked by the government to report on the aboriginal people of the region and to act as an Indian agent for the district. At the same time, he was told to spend as little money as possible on them, since the government had no intention of negotiating a treaty with them. Official policy was to extend the Indian treaties only to areas where long-term economic development and a large white population were expected. Since Ottawa believed that the Yukon was a flash in the pan, no treaty was required with the First Nations there. Constantine viewed the Natives he met with a marked lack of compassion. They were, he said, "a lazy, shiftless lot and are content to hang around the mining camps. They suffer much from chest trouble, and die young."[70] For Bompas, who continued to express his concern for the Natives, Constantine had nothing but contempt:

Bishop Bompas is a disturbing element. He has no use for any person unless he is an Indian. Has the utmost contempt for the whites generally and myself in particular ...The Indians are chiefly American ones ... living on the miners through the prostitution of the squaws. There is a comfortable living for them if they would work which they will not do, preferring to take what they can get so long as they do not starve. During the fish and game season they could procure sufficient of both to keep them comfortably during the winter, but no, they must have a feast and gorge themselves so long as any food lasts.[71]

His main concern, and the government's, was that the Native people should not cause any trouble or interfere with the development of the mining industry. If they presented no danger, they could safely be ignored. What Constantine did not realize or did not care to know was that the people he described were only a small minority, not typical of the First Nations population of the region. The few who seemed always to be hanging around Fortymile were the people who had been incapacitated by disease and alcohol, and could not survive in the bush as the majority of their people continued to do.

The Canadian government had invested Constantine with a wide range of powers. Not only was he in charge of the police, but he was also the region's magistrate, which made him arresting officer, judge, and jailer in all but the most serious criminal cases. He was also the land agent, the gold commissioner, and the collector of customs. On 26 July 1895 the Canadian government created a new District of Yukon, setting the region apart as a distinct district of the North-West Territories, and giving official recognition to its special character.[72]

A case a year later adjudicated by Constantine marked the change that was taking place in the area's legal system. No longer could the miners regulate themselves; law and order was now dictated by Ottawa and on Ottawa's terms. Two men who owned a claim on Glacier Creek leased it to a third man, who hired labourers to work it, then defaulted on the payments and left the country. The aggrieved workers called a miners' meeting, which voted to seize the claim, sell it, and give the proceeds to the workers. But when the new owner came to the police post (which was also the recording office for claims) to register his claim, he was refused registration because the miners' actions were contrary to Canadian law. The man left "breathing defiance." Constantine realized that this was the issue on which his authority would stand or fall: "This was the turning-point, and should I give them their way or recognize them in any manner, trouble would never cease." He immediately sent Inspector D'Arcy Strickland, his second-in-command, to the disputed claim with ten men, telling him to act circumspectly but firmly, and he sent a note to the miners' leaders warning them to clear off the claim, which they did. One of those men who went to Glacier Creek to evict the miners described what happened there:

Thereupon a party of twelve of us, armed with Lee-Metfords and prepared for all possible contingencies (for no one could tell how the matter would end, or in what spirit we should be received) went up Forty Mile River in boats and marched across country from Forty Mile to Glacier. I suppose we presented a formidable appearance with our rank and file and our magazine rifles, or perhaps the wrongdoers were beginning to realize that their action had been unjustifiable, for we experienced no resistance of any kind. We warned those in possession off the claim under penalty, and formally handed it to the original owner. We had not to make a single arrest, and after informing every one at the creek that such a proceeding was not legal and must not occur again, we simply marched back to head-quarters, and thus the whole business, which might easily have grown to

Inspector Charles Constantine, second row, fourth from left, and the NWMP detachment at Fort Constantine, Fortymile, in the winter of 1895–96 (Glenbow Archives, NA 919-15)

alarming proportions, closed peacefully and satisfactorily ... No ill-will was born us for our share in the proceedings, and I think that every one was in his heart glad to feel that there was a force in the land that would protect his individual rights and those of others.[73]

Thus ended the most serious and practically the only challenge to police and government authority in the Yukon ever posed by an organized group.[74]

It might be wondered why the miners so easily surrendered their authority to the police. The miners' solution to this problem might have been fairer than the solution decreed by the police, for apparently the workers were never paid. It was certainly the kind of decision that a miners' meeting was accustomed to making. But as has been pointed out, the miners were disposed to accept and obey law and order, albeit with grumbling.[75]

This incident – combined with Constantine's recommendation that the police force in the Yukon be strengthened, together with Bompas's pleas, and the bright prospects for the region outlined by Dawson and Ogilvie – eventually persuaded Ottawa that something important was about to happen in the Yukon. An extra twenty men were dispatched there, doubling the number of police in the area. By February 1896 the Yukon boasted forty policemen. This timely show of authority was fortunate for the Yukon and for Canadian interests there, for the event that would make the Yukon world famous was about to take place.

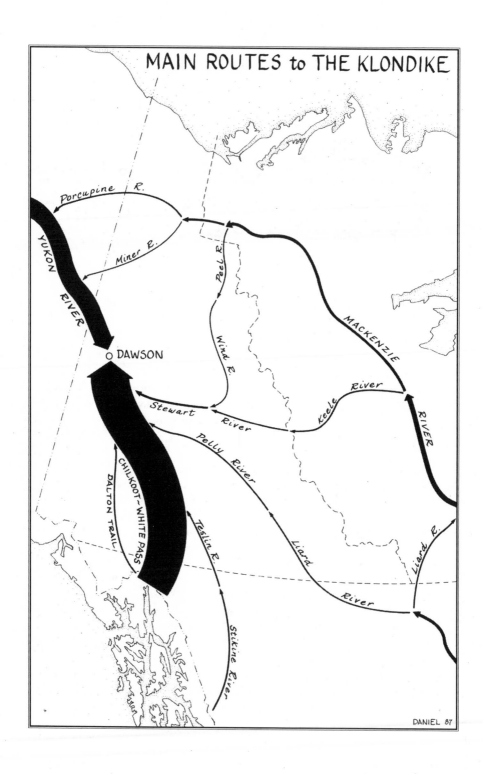

MAIN ROUTES to THE KLONDIKE

Porcupine R.

YUKON RIVER

Miner R.

Peel R.

MACKENZIE

o DAWSON

Wind R.

Keele River

RIVER

Stewart River

Pelly River

CHILKOOT–WHITE PASS

DALTON TRAIL

Teslin R.

Liard River

Liard R.

River

Stikine River

DANIEL 87

FOUR

The Gold Rush
1896–1900

The Yukon, or Klondike, gold rush is one of the few events in Canadian history – perhaps the only one – that has entered into the collective memory of the entire world. The period contained many elements of dime-novel fiction: danger, hardship, harsh climate, challenge, greed, triumph, and despair. It also had to do with wealth and sudden riches, themes of perennial fascination. So absorbed have non-Canadians been by the gold rush that some have actually attempted to appropriate it into the history of their own country. Americans in particular have tended to confuse the Yukon rush with the smaller one in Alaska that followed it; books have appeared that depict the Yukon as part of the American mining frontier, and there is even a "family entertainment park" outside San Francisco that features the Yukon among five "historic American areas."

The timing of the gold rush was perfect. It was the climax of a series of gold discoveries in western North America which began in California in 1849. The first gold rush in Canada's Pacific region took place on the Queen Charlotte Islands in 1842, and it was followed by a major rush on the Fraser River in 1858. About twenty-five thousand people came to British Columbia during this episode, many of them American veterans of the California gold rush. Two years later gold was found near Cariboo Lake, and in 1861 more gold was discovered on the Stikine River. The trail of gold stretched even farther north when in 1871 there was a rush to the Cassiar district of northern British Columbia. This path, laid out in successive rushes over fifty years, was like an arrow pointing directly at the basin of the Yukon River.[1]

And the world, particularly the United States, was psychologically ready for a new rush. The American census of 1890 had revealed that although there was still some free land left in the United States, there was no longer a "frontier" of steadily advancing settlement. This was seen as a turning point in American history, because for the first time since the Pilgrims landed in 1620 it seemed that America had reached its limits. True, there was still space on the Canadian prairies, but homesteading in this region did not appeal to everyone. Where else was a man to go to earn his fortune by the sweat of his brow, away from cities and settled areas? Where could he go for a fresh start, a last chance to make his fortune? The Yukon seemed to offer one last opportunity.

Even economics, that "dismal science," heightened the importance of the gold rush, particularly in the United States. The generation that went to the Yukon had been nurtured on an economic controversy that seems strange to modern ears: an argument over the amount of specie (money in the form of coins rather than paper) that ought to be in circulation. The argument about what was called "free silver" was like the economic program of the Canadian Social Credit Party in that it was so complex that although many people believed in it with the devotion of zealots, few understood how it was supposed to work. At its root was the struggle between tight money and inflation – between the capitalists, who wanted the amount of money in circulation strictly controlled, and the debtors, who wanted it increased so that their debts would be easier to pay off and money for investment and expansion would be easier to come by.

The ferocity of the fight between these factions in the United States, which reached its peak in the election of 1896 – just a few months after the great discovery of gold in the Yukon – was made worse by the fact that there was an economic depression that year which was for a time much worse than that of the 1930s, though it did not last as long. This helps explain why the news of the discovery of gold was greeted with such joy and relief in North America and elsewhere. It was an event the world wanted to happen.

A trivial episode that occurred sixty years after the rush shows how deeply the event penetrated the North American consciousness. In 1955 the Quaker Oats Company, sponsors of a radio show featuring the exploits of Sergeant Preston of the Mounted Police and his dog King, dreamed up a promotional gimmick. The company's advertising agency bought nineteen acres of land near Dawson City, printed elaborate deeds to pieces of it, and announced that for a "limited time only," each box of Puffed Wheat would contain a certificate to one square inch of the romantic Klondike gold fields. It proved to be "one of the most successful sales promotions in North American business history."[2] Within a few weeks twenty-one million boxes containing deeds were sold. Although the millions of kids who acquired these certificates actually owned nothing, since the deeds were never registered, and although the government repossessed the land for non-payment of taxes in 1965, the promotional stunt had tapped a deep vein of advertising gold – one of the most pervasive of North American folk memories.

These memories had been kindled by the rush itself, but they were kept alive by writers of popular fiction – several of Jack London's grippingly realistic stories are set in the gold rush Yukon – and particularly by the poetry of Robert Service. Generations of schoolchildren recited "The Cremation of Sam McGee" and his other ballads. It says much for the power of the Yukon legend that Service, though a secondary talent at best, is arguably the best known of all Canadian poets, and probably the one whose verse has made the most money.

What, then, was this gold rush that so fascinated its own and later generations? In the first place, despite the suddenness with which it occurred, it was not an accident. The men (and women – for a few men brought their wives into the country) who had been prospecting the Yukon River valley since the 1880s were confident that there would be a big strike eventually. Of course, miners always think that, but in this case there was evidence. Small amounts of gold had been found on the Stewart River in 1885, and soon afterwards more had been found near Fortymile. Not enough was found to make anyone rich, but there was enough to lure several hundred men into the country each summer, enough to keep two or three trading posts in business. Because the gold was alluvial, found in flecks and grains and small nuggets in the stream beds, it was evident that at some earlier time it had been washed down from somewhere. Where was that somewhere, that mother lode – on a hill or up another creek? Given the example of California in 1849 and British Columbia a decade later, there were bound to be rich diggings in the Yukon. It was not a question of whether gold would be found in quantity, but when and where.

The gold was indeed there, and in huge quantities, waiting to be discovered. Because the discovery of August 1896 was, in retrospect, inevitable – since men knew of the gold and were searching for it everywhere – it hardly seems important who made the great discovery. Yet people care passionately about such things (as the story of the discovery of insulin, another Canadian legend, has shown) for to be first is to be famous as well as merely rich. There is still controversy about who deserves the honour for the Yukon gold rush, but the basic facts are clear enough.

Four men were involved in the discovery, all veterans of the North. George Washington Carmack was an American. Born in California, he had prospected in Alaska for a dozen years before coming to the Yukon. His partners were two Tagish brothers, Skookum Jim and Dawson Charlie.[3] Carmack was unusual among the miners in that he was free of racial prejudice against Native people. In fact, he was married to his partners' sister Kate, and he got along with the Native people so well that the miners called him Siwash George. This was an insult; Siwash was a derogatory term for an aboriginal person, and Carmack was generally considered to be a "squaw man." The fourth protagonist of the drama was Robert Henderson of Nova Scotia, another experienced miner.

None of these men was a greenhorn, or "cheechako," to use the northern epithet. The two First Nations men had been born in the country, and the white men had been mining for years – Henderson had been seeking gold in one place or another for twenty-four years by 1896. They were tough, too; Henderson had once fallen off a log while cutting trees to bridge a stream and had impaled his calf on the stump of a sapling; he had hung upside down "like a quarter of beef" for four or five minutes, then freed himself, and crawled to his tent, and was back at work within two weeks.[4]

In July 1896 Carmack, his family, and his two partners were at the site of what would soon become Dawson City, at the junction of the Klondike and Yukon rivers. They were fishing for salmon and drying it for dog food when Henderson appeared. He had been prospecting with some other men on the small creeks that fed the Klondike River, and, as the unwritten code of the miners required him to do, he told Carmack that he had found promising traces of gold on Gold Bottom Creek. Carmack asked if there would be a chance for him to stake a claim and get in on the prospects, and Henderson replied that Carmack was welcome but not his brothers-in-law; there was no place at Gold Bottom for any "damned Siwashes." His prejudice was to cost him dearly, for the brothers heard the remark and resented it.

In early August Carmack, Skookum Jim, and Dawson Charlie poled their boat up the Klondike River for a mile or two, then made their way up Rabbit Creek, through the sand, mud, and fallen stumps that marked its mouth, panning in the shallows as they went. It was perfect weather, the height of a late Yukon summer. Pierre Berton described the scene: "They were struck by the splendour of the scene that lay spread out before them like an intricate Persian carpet: the little streams tumbling down the flanks of the great mountain, the hills crimson, purple, and emerald-green in the warm August sunlight (for already the early frosts were tinting trees and shrubs), the cranberry and salmonberry bushes forming a foreground fringe to the natural tapestry."[5] Passing a fork where an even smaller creek (or "pup," in miners' parlance) flowed into Rabbit Creek from the south, they went over the "dome" – a large hill that separated the creeks – and paid a visit to Henderson's camp at Gold Bottom Creek. Carmack later claimed that he had asked Henderson to join them at Rabbit Creek but Henderson had refused. Henderson denied this and said that Carmack had promised to tell him if he found anything worthwhile. Again Henderson insulted the Natives, this time by refusing to sell them tobacco. "His obstinacy," wrote Carmack late in life, "cost him a fortune."

Keish, or Skookum Jim (1855–1916), a member of the Tagish Nation, was one of the men who made the great discovery on Bonanza Creek. As a young man, he had worked as a packer over the coastal mountains. Skookum means "strong" in the Chinook jargon (NA, PA 44683).

George Washington Carmack (1860–1922), Skookum Jim's partner and brother-in-law, staked Discovery Claim on Bonanza Creek. He later repudiated his aboriginal wife and married a white woman (NA, C 25638).

Back went Carmack and his companions to Rabbit Creek, and there, on 16 August 1896, they became the stuff of legend. Panning up and down the stream, they found encouraging traces of gold. Then, in a place where the bedrock was exposed, one of them found a nugget about the size of a dime. They turned over loose pieces of the rock and saw more gold lying in the cracks, "thick between the flaky slabs, like cheese sandwiches," Carmack related. Whooping for joy, they danced about for a few minutes and then quickly panned enough gold to fill an empty shotgun shell, and made camp for the night.

The next morning Carmack blazed a tree with his axe, and wrote out his notice of claim:

To Whom it May Concern:
I do this day, locate and claim, by right of discovery, five hundred feet, running up stream from this notice. Located this 17th day of August, 1896.

G.W. Carmack.

Under the mining regulations then in force in the Yukon, claims made in creeks were 500 feet (152.5 m) wide, running from "rim-rock to rim-rock" of the creek. Carmack, as official discoverer, could make two claims, and his partners one each. With a tape measure the men staked these out: one for Dawson Charlie, one for Skookum Jim, and another for Carmack. The claims were numbered, as on all Klondike creeks, "One Above [upstream from] Discovery," "One Below Discovery," and so on. (Later, when the three men were no longer friends and Carmack had deserted his Native wife for the respectability of Dawson society, Skookum Jim said that it was he who had made the discovery but Carmack had persuaded him to put the extra claim in Carmack's name, since the white miners would not recognize him as a legitimate discoverer. Given the racial attitudes of the time, this is not an implausible story.) After the four claims were measured and staked, Carmack ripped a piece of bark from a birch tree and used it to make a sign on his discovery stake: "I name this creek Bonanza. George Carmack." Thus, Rabbit Creek changed its name and became world famous.

The three men broke camp and headed down the Yukon River to Fortymile to register their claims. On the way they met a number of prospectors and told them the good news. They had no reason to keep it a secret, since they had staked all the claims they were legally entitled to. But they did not walk back over the dome to tell Robert Henderson. The men they met on their way downriver thought that their story was just more prospectors' hot air – Carmack had a reputation for stretching the truth – but when Carmack showed them the shotgun shell full of gold, they took off in a hurry for Bonanza Creek. When the discoverers reached Fortymile to register their claims they were again laughed at, but the shell full of gold spoke for itself.

It was not the kind of gold that had been found on other creeks – experienced miners could tell where gold came from by its appearance. Men soon began to leave Fortymile for Bonanza Creek, and within a day or two the settlement was all but deserted.

It seemed that every miner in the Yukon had heard the good news and was rushing to the diggings – everyone, that is, except Robert Henderson who, unaware of the discovery over the hill, continued to prospect on Gold Bottom Creek for another three weeks. By then the best locations on Bonanza Creek had been staked. Henderson did stake a claim on nearby Hunker Creek, which might well have been profitable, but he did not work it, preferring instead to search for another Bonanza. Perhaps, like some miners, he had a psychological will to lose. He left the Yukon with only a thousand dollars in gold, and that was stolen from him before he reached the South. Because he was popular in the North, and because he had in truth pointed the way to the riches even if he had not discovered them, the federal government eventually gave him a pension of $200 a month. He continued to prospect in northwest Canada almost until the day he died, in 1933, but never struck it rich.[6]

That was the first phase of the Klondike gold rush. By Labour Day, virtually all the men in the region had converged on Bonanza Creek, the entire creek had been staked, and many of the claims were already producing a rich harvest. Several of these had been staked by cheechakos, for some of the veterans pooh-poohed the discovery, believing that Carmack's find was a flash in the pan and that large amounts of gold would never come out of Bonanza. They were wrong, of course, but there was an even bigger surprise in store. On 31 August 1896 five men decided to try the "pup" flowing into Bonanza Creek from the south. They went half a mile up this nameless tributary and did some panning. To their surprise, there was gold in the stream. They staked claims and named the creek Eldorado. Each of the original claims eventually produced more than a million dollars, and most of the fifty or so claims that were soon staked there reputedly produced at least half a million each before they were worked out – $30 million or so from a creek no more than five miles long. The same amount of gold would be worth about CDN $776 million, or US $560 million, in 2004 dollars.[7]

The maddening thing about the claims on the Klondike creeks was the great amount of work needed to tell whether they contained a lot of gold or hardly any. The gold must have once been in a mother lode, probably on a mountain. Water and glaciation had eroded the mountain over the centuries, dislodging the gold, grinding it finely, and washing it downhill via the small creeks, where it settled into the sandy creek bottoms. Although most of it was in small grains, there were occasional nuggets, some quite large – one found on Bonanza Creek weighed more than 64 oz (1.8 kg), worth about CDN $35,000 at 2004 prices. Over the centuries these creeks changed course and built up layers of sediment, so although some gold was at the surface like that Carmack and his partners found, most of it was five to twenty feet below the surface, at bedrock. And because of the shifting of the creeks, the miners could never be sure where the original creek had been; it might be right underfoot, or it might be somewhere else. In some cases it was halfway up the banks of the hills that lined the creeks. The only way to find out was to dig down, through the sand and muck, through the permafrost, then haul the dirt to the surface and wash it out in a pan or sluice box. If there was no pay dirt in the first few feet, the temptation to sell out and try elsewhere was strong.

Thus, the wealth of the Klondike was a matter of chance; some of the great strikes were made by veterans, and others by cheechakos. And the strikes were big. There was not as much gold in the Klondike as there had been in California, or as in South Africa, but what gold there was was concentrated in a small area. Some of the claims had incredibly rich pay dirt. Before 1896, ground yielding ten cents a pan was considered well worth working. Whereas on Fifteen Above Eldorado, three Scotsmen got four hundred dollars' worth in two pans of pay dirt – more than a year's wages for a working man washed out of the sand and gravel in a couple of minutes. Later, some men claimed to have got as much as a thousand dollars from a single pan.

A famous story that conveys the surreal flavour of the period is the tale of Dick Lowe's "fraction." By the autumn of 1896, there were hundreds of claims up and down Bonanza, Eldorado, and neighbouring creeks. Some of the richest had been carelessly or inaccurately measured, and since 500 feet was all a miner could claim, it was vitally important to know the exact boundaries of each one. Fortunately, William Ogilvie was on the scene to perform honest and impartial surveys, and Charles Constantine and his twenty policemen were there to preserve order. When Ogilvie surveyed Two Above Bonanza, he found the claim was wider than the law permitted, and a "fraction" – a pie-shaped piece of ground, in this case 86 feet (26 m) wide at the base – was eligible for claim. Ogilvie, as a civil servant, was barred by law from staking a claim, so Dick Lowe, one of the chainmen on the survey crew, claimed it.

Lowe was an archetype of the Yukon miner. An American by birth, he had found gold in the Black Hills of South Dakota and started a transportation business, only to lose it all in the Indian War. He had been a muleskinner in the American Northwest before coming to Alaska and then to the Yukon. His fraction did not look promising, and he first tried to sell it for $900 and then to lease it, but no one would invest in a claim that small. He finally decided to work it himself. His first shaft hit nothing. In the second, he got $46,000 in eight hours. Eventually the fraction yielded more than half a million dollars, the richest claim per square foot ever staked in the Yukon.

According to Pierre Berton, "Lowe's ground was so rich that a wire had to be strung along the border of his claim to prevent trespassers. Whenever a nugget was found along the boundary line, its ownership was determined by a plumb bob which slid along this invaluable wire ... It was said that as much gold was stolen from Lowe's property as he himself recovered from it, for in some places glittering pieces were visible from a distance of twenty feet."[8] True to the image of the miner, Lowe became an alcoholic, married a dance-hall girl, threw his money away, and died broke in San Francisco in 1907.

Some, though not many, of the miners who got in on the ground floor of the rush made fortunes and kept them. Clarence Berry, an American who worked with his wife Ethel on Five Above Eldorado, became a millionaire. Perhaps because he had a wife, he avoided the temptations of the saloons, held on to his money, and died in San Francisco in 1930 worth several million dollars. Alex McDonald, the "King of the Klondike," on the other hand, made a fortune through investing in other men's mining properties and lost that fortune the same way, dying broke in the Yukon, still dreaming of new opportunities.

In the fall and winter of 1896–97, while men worked and grubbed in the muck of the Klondike tributaries, a new town emerged. Dawson City, named after George M. Dawson of the Geological Survey of Canada, was located on flat swampy land at the confluence of the Klondike and Yukon rivers, about 9 miles (14 km) from the site of the discovery on Bonanza Creek. Behind the town rose a steep hill, the Dome. Although Dawson lies more than 125 miles (200 km) south of the Arctic Circle, the midnight sun can be seen from the top of the Dome at the summer solstice, and a picnic there under its glow is a ritual of early summer. The town was ideally located to be the centre of the mining community, since it lay an easy day's journey from the major creeks as well as being on the Yukon River, which was navigable from Dawson upstream to the Whitehorse Rapids, and downstream all the way to its mouth on the Bering Sea. Its physical location was less ideal, for the land was flat and prone to flooding.

During the first months after the discovery, the news spread downstream through Alaska and upstream and south as far as the Alaska panhandle. Hundreds of men began to converge on the new town of Dawson City, where Joe Ladue, a Yukon veteran since 1882, had in 1896 bought land from earlier prospectors at $10 an acre, as well as some cabins from aboriginal people living on the site, and he was soon selling town lots at $1,000 each. Ladue built the two essentials of a gold-mining town: a sawmill and a saloon. By the spring of 1897 there were perhaps fifteen hundred people in Dawson. Some of them had come up the Yukon River from mining camps in Alaska, and others had come over the Chilkoot Pass from Juneau and Skagway. These were the men and women who "mined the miners," as the contemporary phrase put it – the saloon keepers, dry goods merchants, hotel keepers, laundresses, and all the various townspeople who supplied and made money from the mining activities.

After the ice broke up on the Yukon River in May 1897, more people arrived in the new town, and by midsummer the population numbered about thirty-five hundred. At the same time, those who had found gold in the initial rush and were anxious to take their wealth south boarded the steamers for St Michael in the Yukon River delta. There they embarked on the Alaska Commercial Company's *Excelsior* for San Francisco or took the North American Transportation Company's *Portland,* bound for Seattle.

These two small ships were the golden armada that brought the news to the attention of the world. On 14 July 1897 the *Excelsior* steamed into San Francisco harbour with more than $500,000 in gold, and the news went out over the wires. Three days later, when the *Portland* docked at Seattle with sixty-eight miners carrying more than a million dollars in gold, a crowd of over five thousand was waiting at the dock. There was, literally, a ton and a half of gold on the *Portland.* A million dollars' worth weighed well over that when gold sold for twenty dollars an ounce, and since there were no banks in the Yukon, the metal had to be hauled south by travellers. And there they were, coming down the gangplanks in Seattle and San Francisco, dragging rope-tied, battered suitcases which contained thousands – tens of thousands – of dollars' worth of gold.

The news created a sensation. The steamship companies were swamped by inquiries. It seemed as though half the population of North America, together with most of that of Europe, was planning to go to the Klondike, though few people had much idea where it was. Within a few months, thousands of people were headed north. Thousands more were laying schemes to profit from the rush in other ways. It occurred to owners of ships along the Pacific coast that passage could be sold on any old tub as long as it was Yukon-bound. The dry goods merchants in Vancouver, Victoria, Portland, Seattle, and other cities realized that all the would-be miners would have to buy supplies somewhere, and there arose a tremendous civic rivalry for the right to the title of main jumping-off point for the Yukon.

Why did they go? For wealth, for adventure, for a change, for a second chance, for a last chance – there were almost as many reasons as there were gold seekers. Nearly a century later it is difficult to think as these people did, for they lived at the end of the Victorian era, when there were still limitless opportunities in the wilder parts of the "colonies" for a man with the right spirit. It was an age when a phrase like "limits of growth" would have been incomprehensible. Men such as Harry Pepper, twenty-one years old in 1897, a ticket clerk at the railway station in Winthrop Highlands, Massachusetts, dreamed of something more exciting than selling train tickets to Boston. One morning he shut his ticket window and took off for the Yukon. There were thousands like him.

In the fight for the Yukon trade, Seattle had a head start, since it had been supplying the Yukon and Alaska trade since 1891. Now, with the news of the discovery, the Seattle Chamber of Commerce went into high gear, setting up a committee led by Erastus Brainerd to trumpet the city's advantages to the world. Thousands of dollars were collected from local businessmen and spent on advertisements in periodicals and newspapers throughout the United States. Would-be miners arriving in town were urged to write home extolling the virtues of Seattle. In October 1897 the Seattle newspaper printed a special eight-page Klondike edition, which was sent to every postmaster and public library in the country as well as to thousands of businessmen and politicians.⁹ Vancouver and Victoria tried the same tactics, but the vociferous boosterism of Seattle overwhelmed its rivals.

There were a number of possible routes to the goldfields. The easiest was by steamer to St Michael near the mouth of the Yukon River, then up the Yukon by a smaller steamer to Dawson. This entailed no effort at all on the part of the traveller, but it was expensive, and space on the Yukon River steamers was almost impossible to come by. The shortest route was up the Pacific coast by steamer to the little settlements of Skagway and Dyea at the head of the Lynn Canal, then over the White or Chilkoot passes to Lakes Lindeman and Bennett (the headwaters of the Yukon River), and then down the river to Dawson. This route was later called the Trail of '98; it was the poor man's route and the one most people used.

But these two routes had a drawback in the eyes of patriotic Canadians: they both required passage through the United States. This was more than a theoretical problem, since miners' goods brought into the United States were subject to customs duties, which meant that Canadian miners would be better off buying their supplies in American towns than in Canadian ones. Consequently, Canadian patriots and merchants both looked for an all-Canadian route to the Klondike. There were several of these, but only two important ones. The first involved a journey inland through British Columbia. Travellers left Vancouver and made for Ashcroft. Then, heading north through the Cariboo mining district, they hit the old trail that had been blazed in the 1860s for the telegraph line to Russia. The line had never been built, but its path, though abandoned for more than thirty years, could still be distinguished. Eventually the trail reached Teslin Lake on the B.C.-Yukon border, from where passage to Dawson was easy.

This trail, however, was a horror, and of the fifteen hundred or so people who started out on it, very few got to Dawson. Those who did take it arrived much too late to find gold. It was one thing for Native people to move on such a trail; they travelled light, lived off the land, and were in no particular hurry. But the goldseekers were unsure of where they were going, were loaded down with all sorts of junk that the merchants had sold them as indispensable ("cholera belts" to ward off disease were a popular item), and they did not have the time to live off the land. The trail turned to mud, their horses died, and so did some of the men – at least one by suicide.

Even more unlikely were the routes to the Klondike originating in Edmonton. In 1897 Edmonton was a town of little significance on the edge of prairie settlement, but it had two advantages: energetic civic boosters and the fact that it was the end of steel on a branch line of the Canadian Pacific Railway. Edmonton's business community immediately promoted it as the jumping-off point for an all-Canadian route to the Yukon.

There were three versions of this route. One went via Fort St John and the Liard and Pelly rivers to the Yukon River. The second went via Fort Nelson to the Pelly; the North-West Mounted Police sent a party over this one, and it took them fourteen months to get to Dawson. The third, and perhaps the most bizarre, went from Edmonton to the Athabasca River, to Lake Athabasca, and Great Slave Lake, then down the Mackenzie River to Fort McPherson (far to the north of Dawson), then via the Rat, Bell, and Porcupine rivers into Alaska, and then back up the Yukon River into Canada to Dawson. A variant of this route crossed the northern Yukon via the Wind River Valley from Fort McPherson to Dawson. It is hard to believe that anyone who looked at this route on a map of North America would have attempted it. The Hudson's Bay Company had used it successfully for years – but its employees were not amateurs. The wonder is that of the sixteen hundred people who tried these routes, about half actually reached Dawson. Every summer, Edmonton commemorates its rather inglorious part in the gold rush by holding a festival called Klondike Days (to the fury of Yukoners, who would prefer to use the name themselves).[10]

Nor were the Americans immune from this kind of foolishness. About a hundred people tried to reach the goldfields via the Malaspina Glacier at the head of Yakutat Bay in Alaska. Nearly half of them died. At the hamlet of Valdez (now a thriving port) three thousand men landed in an attempt to cross the Valdez Glacier and reach the Yukon via the Kluteena River. The result of this absurd, almost criminal, idea was that during the winter of 1898–99 men at Valdez actually died of scurvy, a disease not generally associated with North American society. Episodes such as these were part of what came to be called the Klondike madness.

But the most famous of the routes, and the ones that became fixed in the public mind, were the two that went over the two passes – particularly the Chilkoot Pass – the so-called Trail of '98. It is a short trail. A remarkable fact of geography is that the end of the trail at Lake Lindeman, from which it is possible to go by boat to Dawson (and right past it more than a thousand miles to the Bering Strait) is only about 30 miles (50 km) from salt water at Skagway. All through the summer and autumn of 1897, boats loaded to the gunwales with would-be miners and their supplies, and those who hoped to live off their labours, steamed north from the West Coast ports, up the Inside Passage off the coast of British Columbia, and into the Lynn Canal, a long, narrow fiord that pointed like a finger at the goldfields. At the head of this inlet lay two towns, Skagway and Dyea. Skagway was the bigger of the two, a roaring frontier town, which by late 1898 had a transient population of 10,000. Today it has about 750 people and survives off the tourist trade, while Dyea is not even a ghost town.

But in 1897 both towns were alive and boisterous. Skagway was like a town out of western American fiction. Although it had a sheriff and a U.S. marshal, it was in fact ruled by a thug in the classic American cowtown mold – a man named Jefferson "Soapy" Smith. Smith was a small-time crook who organized a gang that which held Skagway and Dyea in an iron grip. His agents preyed on the greenhorns, offering them advice and then robbing them, steering them into gambling halls where they were fleeced, buying them drugged drinks, or simply knocking them out and picking their pockets.

Sam Steele, who commanded the North-West Mounted Police in the Yukon at the height of the rush, passed through Skagway in the early months of 1898. "Robbery and murder were daily occurrences," he recalled. "Shots were exchanged on the streets in broad daylight ... At night the crash of bands, shouts of 'Murder!' cries for help, mingled with the cracked voices of the singers in the variety halls; and the wily 'box rushers' [variety actresses] cheated the tenderfeet ... In the White Pass above the town the shell game expert plied his trade, and occasionally some poor fellow was found lying lifeless on his sled where he had sat down to rest, the powder marks on his back and his pockets inside òut."[11] In July 1898, Soapy Smith was killed by vigilante Frank Reid in a Skagway street shootout that left both men dead. Smith's fame lingers on. In that strange way in which western towns transform their villains, he is no longer a vicious thug but a "character" from Skagway's colourful past. The two graves lie near each other in the Skagway cemetery, but although Reid "died for the honor of Skagway," it is Smith's grave that has had to be fenced off to discourage souvenir hunters from cutting away pieces of it.

Having survived Skagway, the traveller who wanted to take the shortest route to the goldfields would trek around the spit of land that separated that town and the smaller (though equally corrupt) community of Dyea to find the beginning of the Chilkoot trail. The first few miles of the trail were deceptively easy – a pleasant walk through spruce woods bordered in summer with wildflowers, marred only by the men, horses, and mules which clogged the path. Soon, however, the trail began to steepen, and small glaciers could be seen hanging from the mountains that crowded in on it. The path became swampy, a mixture of dirt, mud, and snow, depending on the season, and travellers had to make their way past great round boulders, dead horses and mules, and, increasingly, piles of goods and supplies cast off by men he had second thoughts about carrying them over the pass.[12]

When the stampeders disembarked in 1897 in Skagway or here in Dyea, they found their supplies piled in a huge jumble on the shore. Having found their goods, their next task was to find some way of getting them over the coastal mountains and into the Yukon (authors' collection).

Slowly the trail became steeper; then, at the timber line, there was a widening, where a community named Sheep Camp had grown up to provide travellers with crude meals and lodging. This was a tent community, which at its height had a floating population of more than a thousand. One of the main occupations of the denizens of Sheep Camp was packing goods for miners at high rates (some men made fifty dollars a day carrying supplies – twenty times the industrial wage in the south). It was heavy going, but the local Native people, for instance, had made a good living as packers for several years before the rush and were conditioned to the work.

The other occupation at Sheep Camp was crime, for this was the last chance before the Canadian border for the crooks to fleece the travellers. In some ways Sheep Camp was worse than Skagway, for there was an urgency about the place. A short distance ahead was the Canadian border, past which the crooks could not operate. Steele described the place: "Neither law nor order prevailed, honest persons had no protection from the gang of rascals who plied their nefarious trade. Might was right; murder, robbery and petty theft were common occurrences. The shell game was there likewise, the operators could be met with on every turn of the trail, pushing the business to the utmost limit so as not to lose the golden opportunity which could not be found on the other side of the pass, where life and property were safe."[13]

There were dangers of other kinds too. In early April 1898 an avalanche crashed down on the trail above Sheep Camp, killing more than sixty people. Some of the victims were taken to Dyea, where Soapy Smith's men robbed the corpses. Today the wooden markers of their graves stand in a fenced enclosure, with grass neatly trimmed. Outside the fence is second-growth forest, the tall spruces, ferns, and grass hiding the few collapsed buildings that are the rotting remains of Dyea. Other than the graves, there is little to indicate the location of this once-turbulent town.

A few miles beyond Sheep Camp was a rock formation known as Stone House, and then came the final climb to the summit. Here – ironically, in American territory – one of the epics of Canadian history took place, commemorated in photographs almost as famous as the one taken of the CPR's last spike being driven in thirteen years earlier. The final climb to the summit of the Chilkoot Pass was only a few hundred yards long, but it rose at nearly a forty-degree angle. The only way to get over the pass was on foot, carrying everything, and in the winter of 1897–98, when the trail was at its busiest, steps for that purpose were cut in the snow. An enterprising businessman had built an aerial tramway, rather like a primitive ski lift, to carry goods over the pass, but it was too expensive for most people. Thus, day after day, for months, men and some women trudged up the path, step by step, in an unending line. Those who left the path for a rest might wait for hours to get back on, for the line was unbroken.

If it had been a question of a single climb, with perhaps a packsack containing a bedroll and some food, it would not have been such a torment. (In fact, for a single trip, it is an easier climb in winter than in summer, when the absence of snow uncovers huge boulders that block the trail.) But the Mounted Police who guarded the summit of the pass would not let anyone into the country without enough money or supplies to last six months, and for most people that meant taking as much as a ton of goods over the pass. A man could manage a hundred pounds, which meant that the average miner would have to make the trip perhaps twenty times. The ordeal could take weeks, unless the travellers were rich enough to afford to hire the professional packers, many of them First Nations men, who charged what the traffic would bear – as much as a dollar a pound – to take goods over the pass. And they were not dressed in modern synthetic clothes, which weigh little but keep one warm. They were wrapped in heavy wool serge or canvas duck, which became wet with snow and sweat, chafing their skin and weighing them down. Yet up the summit steps they went, gasping, sobbing for breath, the last steps on their hands and knees. They were still only about 19 miles (30 km) from Dyea and they had climbed 3,500 feet (1,000 m), most of it in the last few miles.

One of the most famous scenes in Canadian history, this photograph of people climbing the Chilkoot Pass in the winter of 1897–98 gives an idea of the terrible effort involved (RCMP photo).

Some members of what the Victorians called the "frailer sex" went over the Chilkoot Pass, though they were generally not burdened with heavy packs. Like the men, they were all types: miners' wives, prostitutes, and women out for change or adventure. A member of this last category was Martha Black, one of the most vivid personalities in Yukon history. Born Martha Munger in 1866, she was from a wealthy Chicago family and was married at nineteen to a young railway executive. In 1897, bored with middle-class life, the two decided to seek adventure in the Yukon. When her husband changed his mind and decided to go to Hawaii, she left him and went north with her brother. (She never said why she preferred Dawson City to Honolulu. This part of her autobiography is somewhat disingenuous.)

Martha, pregnant at the time, walked the Chilkoot trail in July 1898, and forty years later she wrote: "In my memory it will ever remain a hideous nightmare. The trail led through a scrub pine forest where we tripped over bare roots of trees that curled over and around rocks and boulders like great devilfishes. Rocks! Rocks! Rocks! Tearing boots to pieces. Hands bleeding with scratches. I can bear it no longer. In my agony, I beg the men to leave me – to let me lie in my tracks."[14] But she was a tough woman. She survived the journey, reared the child of her broken marriage alone, went into the lumber business, married a Yukon lawyer, George Black, who was eventually appointed commissioner of the Yukon Territory, and followed him to England during the First World War. And in 1935, when she was almost seventy, she became the second woman in Canadian history to be elected to the House of Commons. She died in 1957 at the age of ninety-one, virtually the personification of the self-reliant northern woman. Like so many others who went over the pass, her feelings about the experience were mixed. Would she do it again? she asked herself. "Not for all the gold in the Klondyke ... And yet, knowing now what it meant, would I miss it? ... No, never! ... Not even for all the gold in the world!"[15]

Once she and the thousands of other travellers reached the top of the Chilkoot Pass, they were in Canada – not in the Yukon, but in a small corner of British Columbia which separated the territory from Alaska. Just where the Canada-American boundary was in this part of North America was a matter of dispute in 1897, and the issue was not resolved until the Alaska boundary controversy was settled in 1903.[16] But when the rush began, Ottawa had ordered the Mounted Police to establish posts at the summit of the Chilkoot and White passes, and there the boundary remained – and remains to this day.

At the summit of the Chilkoot Pass, the miners cached their goods and returned for another load, sliding down the hill on the seats of their pants like children. Once all their goods were over the top, they checked in with the police (who also acted as customs officers), submitted to the mandatory search for forbidden liquor, paid what duty was necessary, and trekked their supplies to the shore of Lake Lindeman, about 9 miles (15 km) from the summit, where they hoped to build boats and float downriver to Dawson.

The other trail, which ran from Skagway over the White Pass to Lake Bennett was not so steep and was 656 feet (200 m) lower, so horses could be taken across it – but it was longer, stretching about 45 miles (72 km). It was also muddier, and in wet weather, which occurred often, it became congested. By the fall of 1897 it was impassible, and traffic all but ceased. The horror of the White Pass trail was the fate of the horses, mules, and oxen who were driven along it. Nearly everyone who wrote reminiscences about it included a gruesome description of the section called Dead Horse Gulch. Here is how Jack London, who went over the trail in the fall of 1897, described the scene:

The horses died like mosquitoes in the first frost and from Skagway to Bennett they rotted in heaps. They died at the rocks, they were poisoned at the summit, and they starved at the lakes; they fell off the trail, what there was of it, and they went through it; in the river they drowned under their loads or were smashed to pieces against the boulders; they snapped their legs in the crevices and broke their backs falling backwards with their packs; in the sloughs they sank from sight or

At the top of the Chilkoot Pass, looking back across the border into Alaska, early 1898. Miners' outfits are piled everywhere. By order of the police, each person had to bring a ton of goods into Canada (NA, C 14474).

smothered in the slime; and they were disembowelled in the bogs where the corduroy logs turned end up in the mud; men shot them, worked them to death and when they were gone, went back to the beach and bought more.[17]

Of the many thousands of stampeders who headed for the goldfields in the summer of 1897, only a handful actually made it to Dawson before the Yukon River froze in late October. Most of those who went over the White and Chilkoot passes spent the winter on the shores of Lakes Lindeman and Bennett. For the thousands of people living under canvas at Bennett – the main community on the lakes – the winter was not a time for relaxation, for the only way to Dawson, 560 miles (900 km) down the Yukon River, was by boat, and the boats had to be built on site. Thus, the collection of greenhorns who had left their clerking jobs, classrooms, workshops, and offices – these men who had been turned into beasts of burden on the passes – now had to become boat builders.

Photographs of Bennett taken in the winter of 1897–98 show a community that looked as though it was having a gigantic garage sale. Thousands of tents, not only small ones but large marquees that served as saloons, hotels, and businesses, were surrounded by all the gear that had been carried

At the top of the Chilkoot Pass the NWMP tent marked the international boundary, and the sunburned police checked each man and woman entering Canada. The cables overhead belong to an aerial tramway built to carry goods over the pass. Few could afford to use it (NA, 16151).

Boat building at Lake Bennett, 1897–98, shot by E.A. Hegg (1867–1948), the Swedish American photographer who took many of the best photographs of the gold rush. Since the boats are all the same size and shape and look well built, this was probably a commercial operation (NA, C 4688).

over the pass: sleds, stoves, canned food, furniture, and mining supplies of every description. Alongside were piles of rough-sawn boards. Thousands of boats were being built, and the surrounding hills were rapidly stripped of trees for lumber. Nails and caulking had been hauled over the passes. The planks were produced in sawpits – platforms on which one man stood pulling up on a six-foot saw while his partner stood underneath, covered in sawdust, cutting the wood on the downstroke. It was bitterly hard work, and the suspicion that a man was shirking his part of the job led to the breakup of more than one partnership. One pair whose friendship had snapped under the strain divided all their goods, including the completed boat, down the middle. Then, on 29 May 1898, the ice on the lakes went out, and more than seven thousand boats began the race for Dawson. Some did not get far, sinking in the short river that linked Lakes Lindeman and Bennett.[18]

Every aspect of the Klondike gold rush invites superlatives, and the trip downriver to Dawson was no exception. Contemporaries used words like "armada" and "argonauts" to describe the fleet and the crews that drifted, poled, and sailed with jury-rigged masts down the river. It was not all clear

The NWMP insisted that all boats heading for the Klondike stop at Tagish and register before continuing downstream. This was done for safety reasons – the police inspected the boats – but it was also useful in keeping track of potential and actual criminals (YA).

sailing, for the turbulent Miles Canyon lay in their path, and Whitehorse Rapids was almost immediately after that. The canyon, though still an impressive sight, has now been tamed by the Whitehorse hydroelectric dam, which has partly filled it, but it was a fearsome obstacle in the spring of 1898, with its sheer cliffs narrowing the river to less than a third of its normal width. The rush of water through the canyon wrecked more than a hundred boats and drowned five men before the North-West Mounted Police (NWMP) realized that a catastrophe was in the making and arrived to avert it. The police ordered that boats be inspected and registered, that no boat judged unsafe be permitted to carry men through the canyon, and that women and children must walk around it. An entrepreneur named Macaulay built a tramway, with wooden logs as rails, to haul boats around the obstacle, and he made a fortune that spring. Once past the canyon and the Whitehorse Rapids, and then downriver past the less dangerous Five Finger and Rink rapids, it was virtually clear sailing the rest of the way to Dawson.

The picture of a police corporal at Miles Canyon laying down regulations for thousands of miners raises another icon of the gold rush era. The miners

This well-known photograph shows boats on a calm day being rowed across Marsh Lake, heading downstream towards Dawson City in the spring of 1898. There are dozens of boats in the picture – appearing as specks in the distance (NA, C 22486).

Four men in a scow (which they probably built themselves) shooting the rapids in Miles Canyon on the Yukon River on their way to Dawson City (NA, C 15022)

are a famous symbol of the Klondike gold rush, but equally so is the NWMP constable – braving danger, holding the passes, facing down bad characters, helping the unfortunate, and demonstrating to the world that the Yukon was an outpost of British-Canadian law and justice. The writ of the Yankee desperado would not run there.

At the beginning of 1896 there were twenty police in the Yukon. Now their reputation, already rebounding in southern Canada from the controversy over their role in the 1885 Northwest Rebellion, was about to be tremendously enhanced. After the discovery, the strength of the force in the Yukon was increased: to 40 in May 1897 and to 196 by February 1898. Eventually it reached over 300. Commanding the police in the Yukon was Sam Steele, a veteran of the 1866 Fenian raids in Ontario and the Red River Expedition of 1870, the man who had brought the law to Native people on the prairies and to striking Canadian Pacific Railway workers. Steele was one of the most impressive figures of the gold rush, the quintessential example of the Anglo-Canadian imperial spirit of the late nineteenth century, and a man determined to prevent disorder in the territory.[19]

The NWMP adopted a flexible policy in establishing its detachments in the Yukon. Whenever a discovery was made, a new community sprang up almost overnight, and the police were among its first citizens. If it looked as though the settlement might be permanent (which in gold rush terms meant a year or so), the police built a log cabin as a detachment; if not, they put up a tent. Most of the smaller detachments were manned by only one or two men. By the end of the rush there were thirty-three of these detachments in the Yukon and adjacent parts of British Columbia.[20]

Because they were for several months the only representatives of government in the Yukon, the police were compelled to provide a tremendous range of services beyond simply enforcing the law. They collected customs duties at the border until Ottawa sent up civilians to take over; for several months they carried the mail in and out of the territory and ran the local post offices. They were the original recorders of mining claims and land titles, and they acted as coroners, Indian agents, health officers, tax collectors, jailers, magistrates, guards for the Dawson banks, and later as returning officers at elections. There was little going on in the Yukon that they did not know about. Sam Steele, whose headquarters were in Dawson City at the height of the rush, described his working day: "My working hours were at least nineteen. I returned to rest about 2 A.M. or later, rose at six, was out of doors at seven, walked five miles up the Klondyke on the ice and back over the mountain, visited every institution under me each day, sat on boards and committees until midnight, attended to the routine of the Yukon command without an adjutant, saw every prisoner daily, and was in the town station at midnight to see how things were going."[21]

The NWMP had a definite idea of what a gold rush society should be, and it bore no resemblance to the kind of community that had developed in the California gold rush and other American rushes. The police were appalled by the traditions of the small frontier democracies that had developed in the American mining communities, where lack of public order had led to the rise to power of villains like Soapy Smith, and the ensuing disorder and vigilante justice. They and their superiors in Ottawa were determined that nothing of the sort would happen in the Yukon.

They were particularly alarmed by the fact that the majority of people coming to the goldfields were Americans. As representatives of the eastern Canadian establishment view of what the ideal society should be, they were deeply suspicious of Americans, especially the lower-class types who seemed to be crowding into the Yukon. As one officer of the force put it, "A considerable number of the people coming in from the Sound cities appear to be the sweepings of the slums and the result of a general jail delivery."[22] The criminal nature of Skagway was exactly what the police and the government wanted to avoid in the Yukon.

In order to make sure that the Yukon remained orderly, the police did not hesitate to invent law to fit the unusual circumstances they encountered. When Steele laid down regulations for navigating Miles Canyon, he prefaced them by a speech to the miners, which began: "There are many of your countrymen who have said that the Mounted Police make up the laws as they go along, and I am going to do so now, for your own good."[23] There are several instances of law invented ad hoc by the police in the Yukon. For instance, their policy of barring people from entering the country without adequate provisions was illegal. So was the common police practice of warning bad characters to get out of the country while the going was good.

In these actions the police were fully backed by the Laurier government in Ottawa. To reinforce the police, the government detached a force of two hundred men from the Canadian army – a quarter of the entire army – named it the Yukon Field Force, and sent it north in the summer of 1898.[24] The existence of this body of men is one of the lesser-known aspects of the gold rush, but it played an important part. The field force was designed not only to assist the NWMP in such duties as guarding the banks and escorting the shipments of gold out of the country (another of the many duties shouldered by the police), but also to demonstrate to the world, especially the United States, that Canada was determined to enforce its sovereignty in the Yukon. It was no coincidence that the Yukon Field Force was sent north at a time when Canada and the United States were quarrelling over both the location of the international boundary and the question of customs duties collected on the routes to the goldfields. The United States had four companies of the regular army stationed in Alaska, and the Canadian government felt compelled to make some demonstration of military force.[25]

There was good reason for a display of firmness, for there were a few moments of international tension in the Yukon during this period. A group of Americans organized themselves as the Order of the Midnight Sun, and it was rumoured that they and their supporters in Skagway were planning to liberate the Yukon from British tyranny. But it was all barroom bravado, and nothing came of it. On another occasion there was alarm in Dawson when someone hauled down the Union Jack at the summit of the White Pass, but the culprit turned out to be a drunken railway navvy in need of a blanket. Most of the scares were of this sort.

The Yukon Field Force was commanded by Lieutenant-Colonel T.D.B. Evans of the Royal Canadian Dragoons and consisted of officers and men of the Royal Canadian Artillery and the Royal Regiment of Canadian Infantry. Because they were military men in uniform, they could not travel through American territory without permission, which it was considered politic not to seek. They thus used an all-Canadian route. Travelling from eastern Canada to Vancouver, they went by steamer up the west coast to Glenora on the Stikine River and then marched north on the old telegraph trail to the headwaters of the Yukon River. With them they carried two Maxim machine guns with 12,500 rounds each, 300 rounds for each man's rifle, and nearly 200,000 pounds of food. All this gear and two hundred men were landed at the muddy hamlet of Glenora in May 1898.

Although the field force went over the same telegraph trail that had defeated so many civilian gold seekers, it had little real difficulty in achieving its goal, and it reached Teslin Lake in early July. The reason for this was that the force had what others lacked: good organization and money. The government was able to hire more than three hundred pack animals to haul the supplies, and the members of the force, rather than adopting the "every man for himself" philosophy that characterized the civilian effort, were under strict discipline. Of course, it was a hard trip, particularly for the four members of the Victorian Order of Nurses who were attached to the expedition at the urging of Lady Aberdeen, the governor general's wife. Nurse Georgia Powell was one of them:

Through deep forest we went, where the trail was narrow and the branches of trees threatened our eyes or tore our [anti-mosquito] veils disastrously, through tracts of burnt and blackened country, in some cases the ashes still hot ... through forests of wind-fallen, upturned trees, whose gnarled roots and tangled branches made insecure and often painful footing; over sharp and jagged rocks where slipping would be dangerous ... a strain that only the strongest and most sinewy woman could bear.[26]

The force built its headquarters at Fort Selkirk, and fifty men were sent to help the police in Dawson. Half the force returned south in the fall of 1899, and in the spring of 1900 the rest went home. Most of them were soon in South Africa as part of the Canadian contingent serving in the Boer War.

The experience of the Yukon Field Force's trip to the Yukon points out another fact about the Trail of '98: its rigours depended very much on the wealth, experience, and common sense of the individual. Some of the people who went to the Yukon had lots of money, and for them the journey was a pleasant adventure. Such a person was Nevill A.D. Armstrong, age twenty, son of an English baronet, who in 1898 was sent to the Klondike as assistant manager of the Yukon Goldfields Mining Company, an English concern. He took the roundabout route by steamer from San Francisco to St Michael and up the Yukon River. He had the price of a steamer ticket – the steamship companies, knowing a good thing when they saw it, were charging $1,000 for the fare to St Michael by the fall of 1897 – and for him it was all colour and adventure. Tales of hardship and privation meant nothing to him. "The enthusiasm of youth is not easily quashed," he wrote. "Besides I was luckily not in the position of thousands of these men who had flocked here without proper provision and nothing to fall back upon ... I was the accredited representative of a substantial firm to buy what holdings I thought promising." Armstrong must have been an unusually reliable young man – he had already worked for three years on farms in the American Southwest – and in fact he was able to buy Yukon properties that brought his backers substantial profits. It was he who found the famous giant nugget on Bonanza Creek.[27]

When the flotilla of boats reached Dawson in the late spring of 1898, the great gold discovery was nearly two years in the past. There was still gold to be discovered, but the irony of the Trail of '98 is that most of the people who participated in it did not get rich, for the best locations had long since been staked. Dawson City was still a young town that spring, only twenty months old, but it had already seen two hard winters.

In the first of these, the winter of 1896–97, about a thousand people lived in the new city. They were almost all veterans of the North, since this was the winter before the news got out. During the winter there was feverish activity both in Dawson and on the creeks nearby. In town the sawmills ran non-stop, and saloons, hotels, and dance halls were quickly built by those who had come in from Circle City and Fortymile to profit from the rush. Small houses were beginning to line the streets stretching back from the river.[28] The town was built almost entirely of lumber, most of it green, and fires were an ever-present menace. Three great blazes – in the autumns of 1897 and 1898 and in April 1899 – swept Dawson. The last one, which was the worst, destroyed 117 buildings and more than a million dollars' worth of property.

At the height of its glory, in the summer of 1898, Dawson was full of the frenetic bustle typical of boom towns. Front Street, the main thoroughfare of business and entertainment, was crowded with people, gossiping, discussing business, or simply walking around the town: many men and women, having successfully reached the Klondike, had no idea what to do once they discovered that not only were the streets of Dawson not paved with gold (though some enterprising men sifted gold dust from beneath the floors and foundations of the saloons) but that the gold-bearing creeks were fully staked. Some left almost as soon as they reached Dawson, while others took labouring jobs to earn enough money to get home. Dawson's population, like that of most boom towns, was extremely fluid. People left the territory on the same kind of sudden whim that had brought them there in the first place.

On the creeks, men built fires on the frozen ground, then dug up the thawed muck and piled it in preparation for the spring work of sluicing. There was a tremendous element of suspense in this, for unless the muck was studded with nuggets, it was difficult to tell how rich the ground was until it could be sluiced. This meant that a huge pile would be built up over six months of winter; in the spring it might yield a fortune or almost nothing. On the other hand, some of the diggings were so rich that every shovelful thawed over a stove yielded gold. It was mostly a matter of luck.

Perhaps the greatest surprise of the gold rush came in the fall of 1897, after all the good locations on the creeks had been staked. It occurred to a few cheechakos, relative newcomers to the territory, that perhaps not all the gold had settled at the bottoms of the gulches – that perhaps higher up the sides of the creek beds, where the ground level had been thousands of years before, they might find old gold-bearing beds. It was an inspired guess, though the veterans scoffed at it, and when Oliver Millett of Lunenburg, Nova Scotia, tested the theory by prospecting on a hill far above George Carmack's claim on Bonanza Creek, he staked a claim that produced half a million dollars' worth of gold. The place was called Cheechako Hill. Soon every hill in the region was covered with claims, making the terrain even more like a moonscape as trees were cut down for fuel and sluice boxes and as the dirt and muck was heaped up everywhere.

In town and on the creeks there was a great deal of gold, but there was little to spend it on. Dawson was woefully undersupplied, because by the time the discovery had been made in August 1896 it had been too late to place orders with wholesale merchants in the South. There was plenty of liquor in the town, for that was a commodity that always found a path to a mining community, but there was a shortage of clothing, food, and consumer goods of practically every kind. The result was inflation, as any economist could have predicted. Salt cost twenty-five dollars a pound. Eggs were a dollar each (in the south they cost less than a penny). Men gambled for huge sums in gold because there was nothing else to do.

The next winter, 1897–98, saw more of the same. This was still before any appreciable number of people from the outside had reached Dawson, and again there was a shortage of everything. Charles Constantine, commanding the NWMP in Dawson, made an effort in the fall of 1897 to convince people not to stay in the town over the winter, as supplies of food were so low that he feared scurvy or actual starvation. Though no one did actually starve that year, there was certainly some malnutrition among the miners, and even the police had to go on short rations for a time.

The exaggerated rumours of starvation that reached the outside world were so harrowing that the United States Congress authorized the expenditure of $200,000 to have a herd of 539 reindeer shipped from Norway to New York and then by train to Seattle and by ship to Haines, Alaska, from where Lapp and Norwegian herders drove the unlucky beasts over Dalton's Trail. The trip from Haines to Dawson lasted from May 1898 to January 1899, and when the 114 surviving animals reaching their destination it was they, not the miners, who were starving. The episode was one more monument to the ignorance and hysteria that marked the world's reaction to the rush.

This period spawned some of the great legends of the gold rush era. Legends seem to need nicknames, like that of Bill Gates, who was named Swiftwater when he boasted once too often about his career as a boatman in Idaho. Gates had been one of life's losers until a strike on Eldorado Creek made him fabulously wealthy. He was short and homely, with a straggling moustache, and had been reduced to washing dishes in Circle City before his luck changed. Now he dressed like a lord and spent like a drunken sailor – he was reputed to have bathed in wine on more than one occasion.

Swiftwater Bill, according to Pierre Berton, had a crush on Gussie Lamore, one of the prostitutes from the mining towns downriver who flocked to Dawson when news of the rush got out. Gussie was fond of eggs, a luxury item in Dawson, and one day, probably in the winter of 1896–97, Swiftwater Bill saw her in a restaurant on the arm of a gambler, eating fried eggs. He retaliated for the snub by paying two coffee tins full of gold for all the eggs in Dawson and then, depending on the account, frying them one by one and feeding them to stray dogs, or presenting them to Gussie as a present, or feeding them to other dance-hall girls in revenge. Of course, Swiftwater Bill died poor, but not until he had survived the rush by nearly forty turbulent years that saw him involved in bigamy, fraud, and mining swindles in South America.

During the twelve months that followed the spring of 1898, the gold frenzy reached its height, and the population of the Yukon peaked at about forty thousand – no one is sure of the exact numbers because people came and went continually, and an exact census was not taken until 1901. On 13 June 1898 the Yukon was made a territory,[29] partly in response to the demand of the citizens, who wanted some measure of local self-government, and partly to forestall the desire of the Government of the North-West Territories in Regina to make money by selling liquor licences in Dawson. The commissioner of the Yukon was appointed by the federal government in Ottawa, and the members of the territorial council were appointed by the commissioner. The first man to hold the office was James Morrow Walsh, one of the great figures of the early pioneering days on the prairies. He was not a success as commissioner, quarrelling with the police and others, and soon resigned, to be replaced by William Ogilvie, who knew the country, was popular among the miners, and had good political connections (he was the uncle by marriage of Clifford Sifton, minister of the interior).[30]

The members of the first territorial council were all government administrators, including Sam Steele of the NWMP Council meetings were at first not even open to the public. Ottawa had no intention of permitting any kind of local self-government in a turbulent community that had a strong American element. Only later were local citizens appointed to the council, and only after the rush had ended were elections for the council permitted.

Thus, Dawson was not a democratic town in the American frontier tradition. On the other hand, it was an amazingly peaceful community, in the sense that there were few crimes of violence. The Yukon was not a good country for murderers, since the police were, as one commentator put it, "rapid, simple and severe" in their methods. And there was virtually nowhere to hide. Very few men had the native skills necessary to live off the land, and there was at least one policeman in every community to watch for bad characters. There were only a few practical ways to leave the Yukon, all of them closely guarded by the police. The physical geography of the Yukon thus made it much easier to control than other places. There were several high-profile murder cases, but they were all rapidly solved, with the killers arrested, charged, convicted and executed in quick succession, to the general satisfaction of Yukoners.[31]

Methods of justice in the Yukon may have been rough-and-ready, but they were effective. Sam Steele was presiding as a police magistrate one day when a blustering American came up before him on a charge. When Steele found him guilty and fined him fifty dollars, the man said, "Fifty dollars – is that all? I've got that in my vest pocket." Steele added, "And sixty days on the woodpile. Have you got that in your vest pocket?"[32] The woodpile was behind the police barracks. The government offices consumed a thousand cords of wood each winter, and this was sawn and split by prisoners working ten-hour days on the huge woodpile which, Steele noted with satisfaction, was "the terror of evil-doers."

In 1898 Dawson became the largest city in Canada west of Winnipeg. This, the last great year of the rush, was the year in which all the excitement and razzle-dazzle that made Dawson City famous reached a peak. Along with the miner panning gold and the upright Mountie, the image appearing

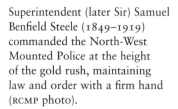
Superintendent (later Sir) Samuel Benfield Steele (1849–1919) commanded the North-West Mounted Police at the height of the gold rush, maintaining law and order with a firm hand (RCMP photo).

in most people's minds at the words "gold rush" is the dance hall. In some ways, these dance halls stood at the centre of Dawson life, at least for the miners, for they were a combination of saloon, gambling hall, and theatre.[33]

The first theatre was the Opera House, built in 1897, a building with a saloon and gambling tables in the front and a theatre in the rear, with a stage, benches on the floor, and boxes at the side – all the theatres in Dawson followed this pattern. It was lit by candles, and the stage curtain was made of blue denim.[34] The Opera House was followed by the Monte Carlo, the Novelty, the Pavilion, and others, but the largest and most famous was the Palace Grand, which was opened in 1899. Built by Arizona Charlie Meadows – a hustler from the United States who had made his fortune with a souvenir newspaper extolling the virtues of wealthy Yukoners – the Palace Grand held a reported 2,200 people, and like its rivals its theatrical fare was a combination of the absurd and what passed for "high-class" entertainment. On the opening night at the Palace Grand, an actress dressed as the Fairy Queen alighted gracefully from her carriage and sang "All Coons Look Alike to Me."

The theatres became social centres for miners who could afford to patronize them, and those that did not burn down proved highly profitable. The clientele was almost exclusively male. A man could drink in the saloon at the front of the house and then watch the show at the back. If he was flush with gold and wanted to show off, he could rent a box and treat the dancers

This was, as the original caption says, "One of the Girls," a prostitute drawn to Dawson City in 1898 to "mine the miners." She is smoking a cigarette, something no respectable woman would be seen doing in that era (NA J 6215).

and actresses who worked in the establishment to champagne at fifty dollars a bottle (the women made a 10 per cent commission on each bottle). If he was really rich, he might treat the whole house.

Most of the actresses and performers who played Dawson were second-rate at best, since it was not worthwhile for a real star to make the effort to go so far for a week's engagement. The Dawson newspapers frequently complained that the actresses could not act, nor could the singers sing. However, those who did have some talent, or those whose personality appealed to the crowd in some way, could have a tremendous success in the town. Cad Wilson, a redhead who played the Orpheum and the Tivoli, had something about her that made the miners want to lavish money on her. She had the biggest belt of nuggets in the Yukon and was reported to have persuaded a man known as the Sawdust King to spend $1,700 on champagne in one evening. She eventually left town with $26,000 in earnings. Maggie Newman, billed as the "Princess of the Klondike," reduced the homesick miners to tears with her sentimental songs, sung in a childish voice. Weeping into their moustaches, they threw coins and nuggets at her, and she left the Yukon with a fortune.

Dawson City was a rough place during the rush, both socially and physically. Here a team of horses hauling lumber has become stuck in the main street. The year was 1898, and judging by the flag and bunting in the background, it may well have been the Fourth of July (NA C 666).

When the actresses were not actually on stage, they were expected to hustle the miners for drinks, and this led to more than one evening's memorable entertainment. On one occasion, an actress named Nellie Lewis, cast as Madame Prudence in *Camille*, had been drinking with some miners in a box while waiting for her cue. The actress playing Marguerite called her several times from the stage but got no reply. Eventually, Nellie's head, considerably dishevelled, appeared between the curtains of the box, yelling, "Madame Prudence ain't a-comin' tonight. Don't you think she's a-comin' to-night." Although dragged from the box, she was as good as her word, and the play had to finish without her. The crowd loved it.

But immorality in the theatres was not tolerated – not for Dawson the strip-tease exhibitions of Circle City. When Freda Maloof, a "seductive Greek damsel," did a belly dance at the Novelty Theatre, she was fined twenty-five dollars for indecency, despite her plea that she was performing a "Mohammedan religious dance" that was educational rather than pornographic.

The authorities did tolerate gambling and prostitution in Dawson – so long as they were orderly. After an initial period of confusion, in which there was uncertainty about who had the right to regulate the sale of liquor in the Yukon, the police and Commissioner Ogilvie took firm control of the situation. Saloons were ordered to close from midnight Saturday until midnight Sunday, and women were forbidden to drink in them. The prostitutes were herded into a specified section of town (much to the rage of the citizens who were there already) and were later forced to cross the footbridge over the Klondike River to Klondike City, or "Lousetown" as it was popularly called.[35]

Prostitution was, of course, illegal in every jurisdiction in Canada in 1898. It was tolerated in Dawson for the same reason that it was tolerated in most cities on the Canadian prairies in the early days: the authorities concluded that it was too prevalent and too popular, and probably too necessary to public order, for it to be to suppressed it in a community in which the population was made up of a high proportion of single young men. For a time the prostitutes were arrested and fined, but since this made it seem that they were being licensed, the police adopted the policy of ignoring them unless they made a public nuisance of themselves, in which case they were told to leave the country. Eventually, both prostitution and gambling were outlawed in the territory, but this did not occur until 1901, when the rush was over and Dawson had become a more settled community.[36]

It is as common today as it was in the 1890s to romanticize the gaudier aspects of gold rush history. The prostitutes of Lousetown did not as a rule have hearts of gold, nor did they all end up marrying rich miners. When, as a young woman, Pierre Berton's mother Laura and her friend crept out one day to spy on the prostitutes from the hill above Lousetown, Laura was charmed by what seemed to be their gay manner, their chatter, and their

Dawson City, photographed looking south, at midnight on 21 June 1899. The large space in the middle is the government reserve, and the bridge to Lousetown can be seen near the top centre (NA C 20813).

colourful clothes. But this was a middle-class fantasy, which bore slight resemblance to the reality. Some of the prostitutes led miserable lives, abused by pimps or succumbing to alcohol. At least one committed suicide. But in the main, these were women of sturdy stock – they had to be to have survived the trek over the Chilkoot Pass. And if photographs of women such as Snake-hips Lulu are accurate, a touch of *embonpoint* was no impediment to a successful career as a prostitute.

Of course, not all the women in the Yukon during the gold rush were actresses, prostitutes, or dance-hall girls, but it was these colourful ones that the contemporary journalists and later legend spinners focused on. It is not always easy to separate fact from fiction. This is particularly true when the lives and behaviour of these women did deviate so spectacularly from the lives and behaviour of "decent" women in southern Canada. Some of these lady legends did eventually achieve "respectability." Lulu Mae Eads, for instance, worked the Floradora and the other hotels in company with Diamond-Tooth Gertie, Babe Wallace, the Oregon Mare, and others, but she married the hotel's owner and stayed in Dawson after the rush to become a mainstay of the community.

GODESSES OF LIBERTY ENLIGHTING DAWSON, Y.T.

This photograph was labelled "Godesses of Liberty Enlighting Dawson, Y.T." Although dance-hall girls have gone down in legend as being typical of the Yukon's female residents, other women came north, often with their husbands, to follow more conventional occupations, sometimes as mothers and housewives. Note the liquor bottle on the tray in the foreground (NA C 18642).

The fantasies about life in the Yukon nurtured in the rest of the world were fed by the poetry of Robert Service, who made a fortune telling readers what they expected to hear about the gold rush. The fact that he did not arrive in Dawson until several years after the rush made it easier for him to shade the truth, for by that time even the residents of the Yukon were gilding some of the harsher realities of gold rush life. His first poem to achieve success, "The Shooting of Dan McGrew," was written in 1906 while he was working in a bank in Whitehorse, far from the site of the events he described. Like so much of his poetry, it depicts a gold rush that is part truth and part fantasy. The first stanza is accurate enough:

A bunch of the boys were whooping it up in the Malamute saloon,
The kid that handles the music-box was hitting a jag-time tune;
Back of the bar, in a solo game, sat Dangerous Dan McGrew
And watching his luck was his light-o-love, the lady that's known as Lou.

Where Service goes wrong is when he gets to the violence:

Then I ducked my head, and the lights went out, and two guns blazed in
   the dark;
And a woman screamed, and the lights went up, and two men lay stiff
   and stark;
Pitched on his head, and pumped full of lead, was Dangerous Dan McGrew,
While the man from the creeks lay clutched to the breast of the lady that's
   known as Lou.

Miners found themselves lying on the floors of Dawson saloons often
enough, but not because they were full of lead. L.E. Karp, in an article about
Service in *North* magazine, remarks that his poetry is a "fresh, imaginative,
and vivid portrayal of a unique phase of North American history, the fabu-
lous gold rush."[37] Whether it is fresh or not is for the literary critics to decide, though it seems that Service borrowed heavily for form and inspiration
from Kipling. Vivid his verse is and also highly imaginative. In fact, since it
sold so widely, it was a major influence in shaping the English-speaking
world's perception of the gold rush. (It is worth noting that Karp, in his article, thought of the rush as a "North American" rather than Canadian phe-
nomenon.) But Robert Service's Dawson City, with shots ringing out and
bullet-riddled miners lying on the floors of saloons simply did not exist. In
fact, it was illegal to carry a handgun in Dawson.

Nonetheless, the territory was by no means free of crime. At that time,
more charges were laid per capita in the Yukon than in any other part of
Canada. This was particularly true for such offences as theft, fraud, larceny,
and assault – the kinds of crime one would expect in a community where
there was much loose money lying around in the form of gold. The rate for
larceny was five times that of Ontario, and for fraud sixteen times. For assault and battery it was eight times Ontario's, though only marginally higher than that of British Columbia and the North-West Territories (which then
included present-day Alberta and Saskatchewan).

Interestingly, however, once arrested, an accused person's chances of
being convicted were lower in the Yukon than anywhere else in Canada. Although the crime rate was high, the conviction rate was low. The conviction
rate for assault and battery in the Yukon was one-sixth that of Ontario, for
fraud about half, and for larceny two-thirds. This surprising fact was a result of the police methods used in the territory. One technique the NWMP
found effective during the gold rush was to bring charges against petty criminals, bad characters, and those who offended in other ways, and to tell them
that if they left the territory forthwith the charges would be dropped.[38] This
practice was referred to as "getting a blue ticket." Of course, it was illegal;
it amounted to a kind of deportation, and neither the police nor anyone else
had the right to deport citizens or aliens without due process. Nonetheless,
the order to leave seems to have been widely obeyed, since the alternative
was likely to be a conviction and many weeks on the woodpile.

An example of the process in action was given by Sam Steele. The offender, presumably the type of Yankee the police disapproved of, had not even broken the law; but he had spoken disrespectfully of Queen Victoria: "Some of the people objected to Royalty in general, did not like monarchs, and would speak slightingly of ours. One of those was an actor in the theatres in Dawson, and when his conduct was reported by the sergeant he was given an opportunity to say he would sin no more or take his ticket for the outside. This had the desired effect."[39] In this case, the man was given a chance to repent, but the incident illustrates how the social order was preserved in the Yukon at the expense of what today would be considered ordinary civil rights. As the American anthropologist Thomas Stone has pointed out, the police did more than merely enforce the law in the territory; they also performed the function of "symbolizing class dominance"; that is, they made sure that the Yukon was not only peaceful but that it conformed as much as possible to the eastern Canadian middle-class social norms of that era.[40]

Before the rush, the federal government had virtually ignored the Yukon, but once the scale of the Klondike discovery became apparent, it sought a means of extracting revenue out of the miners' good luck. This money was not intended for the development of the territory or to invest in its future, but to enrich Ottawa's coffers. Clifford Sifton expressed the official policy when he observed: "The Yukon is not the same as any other gold mining country in the world, and the difference consists in the fact that it is good for nothing except mining, which in all probability will be temporary."[41] In accordance with this attitude, he several times raised the royalty schedule on gold extracted from the creeks; but each time, his efforts to increase Ottawa's share of the riches ran into violent opposition from the miners and the Yukon business community – who shared Sifton's view of the region's future and wanted to maximize returns before the gold ran out – and he was forced to withdraw the regulations.

On a more positive note, Sifton did plan to integrate the Yukon into the nation through an all-Canadian rail link between the northern interior of British Columbia and the Yukon Valley. This scheme, hatched in response to pressure from the Canadian business community, was aimed at diverting the Yukon trade from Seattle to Vancouver and Victoria. The proposed route was by steamship from the two B.C. cities to the Stikine River (where Canada had right of passage through Alaskan territory under the Treaty of Washington), up the river into British Columbia, and then north by rail to the Yukon. Sifton had personally investigated the feasibility of the route on a trip to the region in the autumn of 1897, in which his party went over the Chilkoot Pass to Lake Lindeman, came back over the White Pass, and visited Taku Inlet and the Stikine River, both possible routes for a railway.

Sifton entered into negotiations with the entrepreneurs William Mackenzie and Donald Mann, but the plans fell through under the weight of

American obstructionism and Canadian political wrangling. The death of this railway scheme and the subsequent construction of the White Pass and Yukon Railway cemented the transportation link between Skagway and the Yukon and dealt a mortal blow to Sifton's goal of capturing the Klondike trade for Canadian business – the cornerstone of his Yukon policy.

It is clear from Sifton's actions that the federal government viewed the region as a potential source of short-term profits for Canadian business. The Yukon was an annoyance rather than a source of pride to Sifton and the government. Charges of political corruption levelled at the Yukon civil service (some of them well founded) and battles over railways, royalties, and mining concessions dissipated what interest Sifton had in the region. Eventually, he handed the economic destiny of the territory over to large corporations, which were more efficient than individual miners and complained less.

As often happened in North America when a gold rush or other such event took place, the aboriginal people of the area were considered peripheral, and some were overwhelmed or pushed aside by the rush of white settlement. Although common enough in the history of North America, this was particularly ironic in the Yukon, given the fact that aboriginal people, were the co-discoverers of the great treasure on Bonanza Creek. Nor did the Canadian government concern itself much with the fate of the Yukon First Nations before, during, or for many years after the gold rush. The Native people of the territory were not even encouraged to sign a treaty or to establish themselves on reserves.[42]

The reason why the Government of Canada did not sign a treaty with the Yukon First Nations, of whom there was a declining population of about two thousand in 1898 (government population figures for the northern aboriginal people were notoriously inexact), was that Ottawa did not want to have them choose land for a reserve on which gold might later be found. Nor did it want them to move into the communities. The government felt that the Native people were "best left as Indians," – living as nomadic hunter-gatherers as far away from the settlements as possible.[43] Since Ottawa believed that the gold rush was a transitory event and the Yukon would never have a a large white population, there was no need to be concerned about the welfare of the indigenous people, who, rather than making demands on the government, could simply carry on as usual.

The majority of Yukon First Nations did exactly that. A few, weakened by disease or trapped by alcohol, gravitated to the settlements, where they lived a precarious existence on the fringe of white society. A few turned to begging, but even those Native women who had prostituted themselves to the miners before the rush were put out of work by the many white prostitutes who swarmed north after 1897. Thus, the majority of aboriginal people continued in their traditional way of life. What they gained from the gold rush was the opportunity to sell food to the miners; moose meat and other game could always be sold at the mining camps. In some cases they found seasonal wage employment as woodcutters for the steamboats on the Yukon River, or occasionally as day labourers on the creeks (though there was reluctance to hire them in many cases). But such jobs were an overlay to their way of life – an additional means of earning money for food and supplies for a few weeks or months before going back on the land.[44]

Certainly, the First Nations population of the Yukon was reduced to some extent by introduced diseases – the Tron'Dëk Hwëch'in people, for instance, who lived in the area of the Klondike, were all but wiped out by illness – yet the gold rush did not have as catastrophic an effect as might be expected. The miners did not really take up much space in the territory; Dawson City and the other communities occupied only a minuscule fraction of its land area, and the rest was left relatively undisturbed. A combination of the whites' racial prejudice and the aboriginal people's desire to retain their way of life meant that many of the Yukon Natives took from the gold rush only what they wanted and avoided being completely overwhelmed by it. Nearly half a century was to pass before the welfare state tied them firmly to white society.

Although the gold rush was a spectacular manifestation of human preoccupation with material wealth, there were some people in the mining communities who served God instead of Mammon. A number of missionaries of various denominations were active in Dawson by 1898. The most notable was Father William Judge, a Jesuit missionary to the Native people at Nulato, downriver in Alaska, who was ordered by his superior to Fortymile in 1894 and who followed the rush to Dawson in 1897. He built a church and a hospital, staffed with nuns and lay nurses (some of them male), and devoted himself to the care of the sick and injured, to the detriment of his own health. When he died in January 1899, worn out by his labours but known throughout the territory as the "saint of the Yukon," he was not yet forty-six.[45]

Bishop William Carpenter Bompas, the other great religious figure of the period, pursued a different goal during the rush. His main concern continued to be the indigenous people, who by 1898 were not only ignored by the government but were largely neglected by the traders who had once eagerly sought their business. Bompas moved his mission from Fortymile to Dawson, justifying his action not on the grounds that the miners needed him but that the local Native people did. He was not popular with the authorities, especially the police hierarchy, who accused him of being more interested in the welfare of the First Nations than of the general population. As one government official noted: "My complaint with regard to the missionaries is that instead of teaching the Indians self-reliance and independence they aid most strongly in making them mendicants. I am daily in receipt of letters from Indians, written by a missionary, asking for all sorts of favours."[46] In 1901 Bompas moved again, to Caribou Crossing (Carcross), where he died in 1906, still lamenting the events that had made his aboriginal charges only bit players in the great drama being played out in the Yukon.

The population of the Yukon reached its peak in 1898–99, but by the end of that year the notorious Chilkoot Pass was all but deserted, for a modern and far easier method of reaching the goldfields had become available. Early in 1898 a group of British financiers, expanding on an earlier idea, had decided to build a railway from Skagway over the White Pass to the head of navigation on the Yukon River, and in April of that year the White Pass and Yukon Railway Company was organized. Construction began immediately. With the thousands of travellers and tens of thousands of tons of goods destined for the north, it appeared to be a project that was bound to be profitable. There were all sorts of logistical difficulties. As many as two thousand men were needed to labour on the project, and since most men in the area were intent on finding gold, the company had to employ those down on their luck, or men from Skagway who had been robbed by Soapy Smith and needed work to get another grubstake.

The engineering difficulties were even more immense. The line rose from sea level to 2,880 feet (879 m) in just under 21 miles (34 km), winding through canyons and hanging on the sides of sheer cliffs. The decision to build a narrow-gauge line of 3 feet (0.91 m) instead of the North American standard of 4 feet 8½ inches (1.434 m) made the task easier. A tunnel 83 yards (76 m) long was blasted out of the granite, and a steel cantilever bridge was built 216 feet (66 m) above Dead Horse Gulch. For a time it was the highest railroad bridge in the world.

In contrast to earlier North American railway projects, the men who built the Yukon and White Pass do not seem to have been exploited and mistreated, probably because labour was hard to come by in the region – and there was always the alternative of getting a labouring job on the creeks. On one occasion the navvies all downed tools and left work at the news of a new gold strike at Atlin. There were few serious accidents on the projects, and the men were paid three dollars for a ten-hour day and given free lodging, though they had to pay for their meals. The project was a resounding success. The first train ran to Carcross on Lake Bennett in July 1899, and the line was finished to Whitehorse, 110 miles (177 km) from Skagway, a year later.[47]

The White Pass and Yukon Railway laid the foundation for a significant change in the territory, since it was the basis for the growth of the new town of Whitehorse. Whitehorse was ideally suited as a transportation centre. Located downstream from the treacherous Miles Canyon and Whitehorse Rapids, it was the head of safe navigation on the Yukon River. From the railway station, which sat on the west bank of the river, dominating the town, it was only a few steps to one of the steamers – many of them also owned by the railroad company – which took freight and passengers to the goldfields. From the very beginning, Whitehorse contained the seeds of future growth. But it remained only a transfer point until the defence exigencies of the Second World War made it the territory's focal point.[48]

In the summer of 1899 the Klondike rush ended when a gold was discovered on the beaches of Nome, Alaska. Because very few of the people who had come to the Yukon after 1897 had found enough gold to make their trip worthwhile, there was a large floating population in Dawson and elsewhere in the territory anxious to participate in another rush. When the strike at Nome was announced, many of these people left for Alaska. Others left for the south. But this did not mean that Dawson turned into a ghost town; simply that there was no gold for newcomers.

Those who had good properties continued to work them. The year of greatest gold production in the Yukon, in fact, was 1900, when over $22 millions' worth was taken out of the creeks (in 1897 the figure was $2.5 million; in 1898, $10 million). After 1900, production began to decrease, but very slowly; by the end of 1911, $140 million in gold had been taken out of the ground. The population of the Yukon declined from about forty thousand at the height of the rush in late 1898 to just over four thousand in 1921,

A crew of miners operating a large sluice box on Bonanza Creek in May 1903. Although this was rather late for that kind of mining, it gives an idea of the work involved (NA, PA 16515).

This photograph of mining operations on Bonanza Creek in 1899 shows the amount of wood that was needed for the heads of shafts and for the sluice boxes and other structures. It also shows some of the effect of mining on the landscape (NA, PA 16944).

of whom nearly half were aboriginal. Gold was still being taken out of the creeks more than sixty years after the rush, and with the sharp increase in world gold prices in the 1970s there was another flurry of activity.

The most dramatic change in gold mining at the end of the rush was not the loss of population but the change in mining methods. There was an almost incredible concentration of gold on some of the claims, where, it was said, hundreds of dollars' worth – literally, two pounds of gold or more – could be taken from the ground in one shovelful. This could not last. Soon the concentration of gold in the ground began to decline, so it became uneconomical to work the claims in the old, wasteful, labour-intensive way. For a time, more efficient methods helped to reduce the cost of labour. Thawing frozen ground by means of fires was supplanted by steam points, which were driven into the permafrost. Then hydraulic mining was introduced; water was pumped under high pressure through hoses, which were directed at the banks and hillsides, washing away large amounts of dirt and gravel in a short time.

The final phase of the transformation of mining was the introduction of the dredges. These giant machines were so efficient that they could make a profit processing as little as a few cents' worth of gold in a cubic yard. They were enormous floating machines. Launched on the creeks, which were dammed up to float them, they chewed their way up the creeks, reworking the claims (which had wasted a considerable proportion of their gold in the comparatively inefficient sluicing process), leaving the serpentine trails of tailings – like castings of some monster worm – which today are still a striking feature of the landscape in the vicinity of Dawson City.

In order to make the dredging process feasible, the original claims had to be consolidated. Shortly after the gold rush, large mining corporations became interested in acquiring gold properties. Clifford Sifton was originally opposed to the idea of consolidation, writing that there was "no possibility of any mining companies getting a group of claims. A policy of that kind would simply blanket the whole country and stop development." As early as January 1898, however, he changed his mind and presented new regulations that permitted corporate control of large stretches of gold-bearing ground.[49] Twenty-year dredging leases extending up to five miles each along the creeks were now authorized. Some claims were bought from their owners, who were no longer making a profit or who wished to sell out, and many were acquired from the territorial government after having been abandoned. Large corporations, or "concessions" as they were called – the Treadgold, the Guggenheim – came to dominate the economy of the Yukon, and day labour began to replace grubstaking on the creeks. Of course, prospecting continued, as it does to this day, in hundreds of creeks all over the territory, but near Dawson, where most of the gold was located, corporate capitalism had replaced the individualism of the mining frontier. It was when this happened that the rush could truly be said to be over.

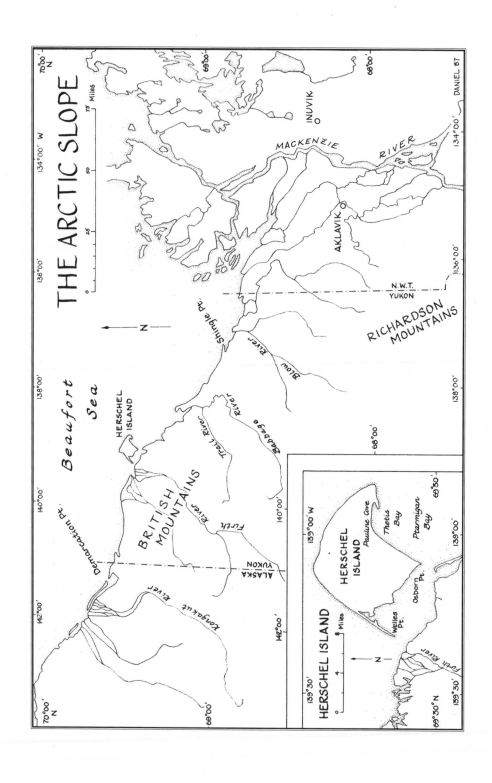

THE ARCTIC SLOPE

Beaufort Sea

MACKENZIE   RIVER

INUVIK ○

AKLAVIK ○

RICHARDSON
MOUNTAINS

N.W.T.
YUKON

HERSCHEL
ISLAND

BRITISH
MOUNTAINS

ALASKA
YUKON

Demarcation Pt.

Kongakut River

Firth River

Babbage River

Trout River

Blow River

Shingle Pt.

N

Miles
0   25   50   75

70°00'
N

69°00'

68°00'

134°00' W

136°00'

138°00'

140°00'

142°00'

136°00'

138°00'

140°00'

142°00'

70°00'
N

69°00'

DANIEL 87

HERSCHEL ISLAND

HERSCHEL
ISLAND

Pauline Cove

Thetis
Bay

Ptarmigan
Bay

Osborn Pt.

Welles
Pt.

Firth River

N

Miles
0   4   8

159°30'

159°00' W

159°00'

68°00'

69°50'

69°00'

69°50' N

FIVE

Herschel Island
The Unknown Yukon

The first part of the present-day Yukon to be reached by Europeans was a region far away from the modern communities of Dawson and Whitehorse. It was in fact a part of the territory that most southerners have never heard of. In the Beaufort Sea, a couple of miles off the northern coast of the Yukon and 30 miles (50 km) east of the Yukon-Alaska boundary, lies Herschel Island, a small rectangular piece of land. Most of the island is flat, but at one point it rises to an elevation of 656 feet (200 m). It is timberless, almost featureless, but it has one advantage that made it attractive to Europeans – it possesses the best harbour along that part of the Arctic coast.

Before the Europeans arrived, a number of Inuit lived on the island, and others crossed over periodically from the mainland to hunt caribou and to fish in the waters surrounding it. Then and later, the local waters teemed with fish and with whales, and it was easy to keep warm by burning the driftwood that floated down the Mackenzie in large quantities and fetched up on the island's low, flat beaches. In the year 1800 there were perhaps as many as 2,500 Inuit living on the island and the adjoining stretch of coastline between the Alaska boundary at the 141st meridian and the Mackenzie River delta, a hundred miles to the east of the island.[1]

The coastal Inuit knew of the existence of the *kabloona*, the white man, for Russians had been trading with the Native people of Alaska since the middle of the eighteenth century, and news of these traders – and some trade goods – had circulated as far as the Beaufort Sea region by way of First Nations middlemen. But none of these outsiders had actually visited the Inuit before the second quarter of the nineteenth century.

Herschel Island appeared on the map of the known world as a result of the twists of European power politics of that era. After the British victory in the Napoleonic Wars was capped by the triumph at Waterloo in 1815, Great Britain was for a while the most powerful country in the world. At the same time, as a result of a general downscaling of the British armed forces, there were hundreds of unemployed and underemployed British naval officers available to establish Britain's glory in peacetime exploits. Fully 80 per cent of naval officers had neither ships to command nor duties to perform. In the early nineteenth century the Canadian Arctic played the same role as outer space did in the mid-twentieth: it was a field of adventure, rivalry, and scientific discovery for the great powers of the world. By this time there was no longer a commercial rationale for finding the Northwest Passage; in the words of John Barrow, second secretary to the Admiralty, the search was "one of the most liberal and disinterested that was ever undertaken … having for its primary object that of the advancement of science, for its own sake, without any selfish or interested views."[2] In the field of scientific exploration, as in industry, Britain was determined to be paramount. Thus, in 1825, John Franklin, a forty-three-year-old veteran of the British navy, was sent to map North America's Arctic coastline. It was his third northern expedition. In 1818 he had been second-in-command on a voyage to Spitsbergen, and in 1819–21 he had led an expedition to the mouth of the Coppermine River, which had resulted in the death of ten of his men from exposure and starvation, mostly because of bad planning.

On the 1825–27 expedition Franklin was better prepared. He descended the Mackenzie River in two boats, following the path pioneered by Alexander Mackenzie thirty-three years earlier. Passing through the delta, he sent one of his boats east to map the coast to the Coppermine River and took the other boat west along the Arctic coast, the first European to do so. Shortly after reaching the open sea, he met a large group of Inuit camped on the shore. He had previously determined to open "communication with the Esquimaux by landing amongst them, accompanied only by Augustus, his interpreter." The Inuit, however, realizing that Franklin's boat contained objects of great value to them, pressed forward in a manner he found menacing. "At no time did they appear to have hostile intentions, but the Inuit pressed close around the stranded sailors, carrying off supplies, trade items, even a pistol, anything that the beleaguered seamen could not preserve … As the looting became more intense a violent conclusion seemed likely, until suddenly the boats were released by a rising tide and the expedition scurried away down the coast."[3]

The name Pillage Point commemorates the incident. Franklin later claimed that another group of Inuit told him that the first group had intended to murder his party, something that is difficult to judge, given the cultural gap between the two races. Certainly, there were what one student has called "fundamental misunderstandings" present in these early contacts between the Yukon Inuit and Europeans. James Richardson, in charge of another part of the expedition, reported that the Inuit followed the boats in amazement; in their culture only women rowed, yet here were people with beards bending at the oars.

On 17 July 1826 Franklin sighted a low island just off the coast and named it after the well-known British chemist and astronomer Sir John Herschel, son of the even more famous Sir William Herschel, who had discovered the planet Uranus and was astronomer royal to King George III. Perhaps to his surprise, Franklin found that the island and the Arctic coast nearby did not constitute a kind of uninhabited northern desert. There were many Inuit on the island, and more along the coast. At one point a fleet of Inuit boats set out from the coast to meet him, and Franklin's men counted seventy-three kayaks and five umiaks before they lost count.[4]

Franklin found the Inuit of the region to be a friendly people, in contrast to those at the mouth of the Mackenzie. Although these people appeared to have never seen a European before, they were carrying steel-tipped arrows, and Franklin learned through an interpreter that these had come from Inuit living farther west, who had got them from Russian traders. He gave them presents and continued his mapping of the region. He did not quite succeed in his mission, which was to rendezvous with a British ship west of Point Barrow. Plagued by ice and bad weather, he turned back in mid-August 1826, 155 miles (250 km) short of his goal. He returned to his base at Great Bear Lake and the next year went home to England.

A decade later, two more Europeans came along the northern coast of the Yukon, this time as part of an expedition commissioned by the Hudson's Bay Company to survey the stretch of coast that Franklin had left blank. The company was a surprising participant in "scientific" exploration, for its earlier exploratory thrusts had all had a singular commercial purpose. There was a connection, however. Its monopoly in Rupert's Land was under review, and the company wanted to press for an early renewal of its licence, so HBC Governor George Simpson sponsored a major Arctic expedition as a sure-fire technique of winning public support. In command was Peter Warren Dease, an HBC employee who had spent many years in the Athabasca and Mackenzie districts. His companion was Thomas Simpson, cousin of the governor, George who had worked for some years as a clerk for the company. In the summer of 1837 the two men came down the Mackenzie with fourteen men and two boats, turned west, and headed for Point Barrow. Like Franklin, they had problems with ice, wind, and fog, but they persevered and reached their destination. The whole of the Arctic coast west of the Mackenzie had now been explored.

Also like Franklin, Dease and Simpson found that the Inuit of the Western Arctic were friendly but inclined to pilfer. In the account of the expedition that Simpson published, he had few good words to say about the Inuit. Even their friendliness he called "deceitful good-humour," and he warned that when they got guns, white men would not be safe in the Arctic.[5] Simpson was not only a racist (he disliked Indians and Metis as much as the Inuit), but he seems to have been mentally unstable – subject to periods of depression – and he hungered for glory. On a trip back east to press his case for a new expedition, he was shot to death south of the Red River Settlement in circumstances that have never been fully explained.[6]

For the next fifty years the Inuit of the Herschel Island region remained relatively undisturbed. In 1840 the Hudson's Bay Company established Fort McPherson at the edge of the Mackenzie Delta, providing a closer alternative to Russian traders for the supply of European trade goods. But the main theatre of European activity in the North in this era was in the Central and Eastern Arctic, where the search for the lost expedition led by Sir John Franklin in the 1840s absorbed the energies of the British and the attention of the entire world. In 1867 Alaska was purchased by the United States, and in 1870 and 1880 Canada acquired formal title to the North-West Territories and the Arctic Islands, respectively, making the Inuit officially Canadians – but this meant no more to them than it did to the Canadian government, which neither knew nor cared about the region. In the 1880s, however, a series of events occurred that changed forever the lives of the people of Herschel Island.

Although the Inuit of the Herschel Island region had little material wealth as white people reckoned it, their country had a resource that aroused the acquisitive instincts of nineteenth-century southerners in much the same way as gas and oil do today. A century ago the lure also was oil – whale oil – as well as other products of the bowhead whales that teemed in the Beaufort Sea.[7]

Whaling was a centuries-old industry. In the United States, the New England ports had been centres for the whaling fleet since the beginning of the republic. By the mid-nineteenth century the industry had spread to the Pacific coast, and hundreds of whaling ships were operating out of San Francisco and other ports. There was a booming market for the products of the hunt. Whale oil was used for lubrication and lighting, especially before the development of the distillation process for petroleum. But an even bigger prize was baleen – the tough, flexible cartilagelike substance that hangs from the top of the whale's mouth, filtering out large fish and enabling the animal to swallow large quantities of the shrimp-sized krill that is the mainstay of its diet. From the baleen were made fishing rods, buggy whips, and particularly stays for the corsets that were a necessity for women who wished to follow the dictates of Victorian fashion. In order to achieve, as nearly as possible, the desired eighteen-inch waist (some managed it, to the detriment of their health), something flexible yet strong was needed, and baleen was perfect.

There was a lot of money in whaling, at least for the captains and the owners of the ships. Around 1900, whale oil sold for $15 a barrel and baleen $6 a pound. A bowhead whale could yield a hundred barrels of oil and two thousand pounds of baleen, making the whale worth up to $15,000 – this in an age when the average worker counted himself fortunate to make $400 a year. A lucky ship could catch $400,000 worth of whales on one voyage. Whales were caught by shooting a kind of small grenade at them that exploded deep inside the animal (the days of hand-held harpoons were decades in the past). A special darting gun was developed for the Arctic whaling industry which permitted the whalemen to harpoon and shoot the whales in one action. Previously, wounded whales had often escaped into the ice pack, dragging the gear with them. The animals were taken as fast as they could be hauled aboard and stripped of their baleen and blubber.

Naturally, scores of entrepreneurs entered the trade, and by the 1880s they had thinned out the whales of the northern Pacific region considerably. By that time the whaling ships were passing through the Bering Strait and hunting off the north shore of Alaska, though they hesitated to go east of Point Barrow (the northernmost point in Alaska) for fear of being trapped in the ice over winter. But eventually some of the whaling captains decided to risk the trip to see whether the rumours they had heard from the Inuit about the fabulously rich whaling grounds east of the point were true.

Thus, in the summer of 1888, the manager of the Pacific Steam Whaling Company's station at Point Barrow sent one of his harpooners, Joe Tuckfield, with a small Inuit crew hired for the journey, five hundred miles east in an open whaleboat to scout the region and report whether it was worth the whaling fleet's trouble to risk conditions east of Point Barrow. Tuckfield spent the winter of 1888–89 with the Inuit near the Mackenzie Delta. He returned the next summer with the sensational news that bowhead whales were "as thick as bees" in the region – bees that were worth $10,000 to $15,000 each. Furthermore, there was a first-rate harbour at Herschel Island. The news stimulated tremendous interest. The government agent at Point Barrow wrote to a friend in the south that Tuckfield had "returned with accounts that made almost everybody crazy, of the great amounts of whales down there ... The beaches are lined with driftwood so there is no danger of freezing and there is plenty of game."[8] It is worthy of note that there was a U.S. government agent at Point Barrow, while there was no permanent representative of the Canadian government at Herschel Island or within nine hundred miles of it.

As soon as the news broke, the *Thetis,* an American revenue cutter on duty in the region, steamed to Herschel Island to determine whether the story was true and whether the island might be in American waters. Commander C.H. Stockton, captain of the *Thetis,* found to his disappointment that it was part of Canada. Nevertheless, he named the natural harbour Pauline Cove.

It is significant that the Americans were very much on the spot as the new opportunities opened up. The fact that Herschel Island was part of Canada mattered not at all to the whalers or to the Canadian government. It was the *Thetis* that took the soundings and the observations on land that made possible the publication in 1890 of the first chart of the island, wherein it was dutifully noted that Herschel Island was part of the Dominion of Canada.

In the summer of 1890, two American ships arrived at Herschel Island. The island was so far from the ships' home port, San Francisco, that it was impossible to go north, hunt, and return home in one short season. Thus, from the beginning it was planned to have the whaling ships remain in the Arctic for at least one winter. That is why Pauline Cove, at the southeast corner of Herschel Island, became the centre of whaling operations: the ships had to find a safe anchorage for the winter. In the open sea they could be crushed by ice. This had happened on more than one occasion to vessels that had lingered late in the season in open waters. Thirty-two ships had been crushed by ice off the Alaska coast in 1871, and five years later twelve more had met the same fate.[9]

The first ships to exploit the whales in Canadian waters were the schooners *Mary D. Hume* and *Grampus*. Because they were the smallest ships in the Pacific Steam Whaling Company's fleet – the *Mary D. Hume* was only 98 feet (30 m) long – it was considered that they would be best suited for operations in the shallow waters of the Beaufort Sea near the Mackenzie Delta. The two vessels arrived at the island on 20 August 1890, unloaded their supplies, and built a warehouse on the sandspit at Pauline Cove. The ships were frozen in by 15 September, and the crews began to prepare for the long winter ahead. More than a hundred cords of driftwood were collected and stacked near the warehouse. Emergency supplies and the ships' boats were put on shore for use in case fire broke out on the ships. The ships' decks were roofed over with lumber and canvas, then insulated with blocks of sod, cut from the tundra. Later in the season, blocks of snow were banked up against the ships, and ice from a nearby pond was cut and put on racks to provide fresh water. Periodically, the ice was cut from around the rudders and propellers of the two ships to prevent damage.

In addition to the food which the ships brought with them, supplies of fresh meat were obtained through trade with the sixty or so Inuit who camped near the ships, and sometimes with First Nations from the Old Crow region, who crossed the mountains south of the coast to trade. The meat – caribou, goose, and ptarmigan – was stored in cellars blasted out of the permafrost and roofed with sod. It gave variety to the men's diet and also helped prevent scurvy.

Although the crews were well housed and well fed, they had problems with the climate, particularly with frostbite, for they were unprepared for living in conditions where the temperature dropped to -40°C. Hartson H. Bodfish, first mate on the *Mary D. Hume,* became skilled at performing sur-

Pauline Cove, Herschel Island, is the best natural harbour between Point Barrow, Alaska, and the Mackenzie River delta. As a result, it became the logical wintering point for the whaling fleet (RCMP photo).

gical operations, especially the amputation of frozen toes. His first operation was on one of his own, which had been crushed by a falling piece of rigging:

I sent the steward for the captain to do the job, but he was busy at the time and asked me to wait. I thought rather fast. My foot was numb from the accident. I knew that the longer I waited, the more painful the amputation would be, so, with the steward and cabin boy looking on and groaning, I whetted up my knife and cut it off myself. The way it was injured made it necessary for me to unjoint the bone from the foot, too, but I did it, and there was considerable satisfaction in having performed my first surgical operation.[10]

The crew also suffered from boredom, and in midwinter six of them deserted and headed for the Hudson's Bay Company post at Rampart House. The ships' officers went after them to recover the goods they had stolen and found them about seven hours' travel from the ship, badly frozen and glad to be caught.

The whalemen soon found that Tuckfield had told the truth – the Beaufort Sea was a whaler's paradise. In July 1891, as soon as the ships were freed from the ice, they headed eastward, and the *Mary D. Hume* found a treasure in whales near Cape Bathurst. In less than two months her crew took twenty-seven whales, and during the same time the *Grampus* took more than twenty-one.

The *Grampus* stayed one winter at Herschel Island, and the *Mary D. Hume* stayed two. In the winter of 1891–92 the first death occurred among the crew when John Meyers, a sixty-year-old black seaman from Baltimore, died of "inflammatory rheumatism." His body was covered with snow and logs until the ground thawed enough to permit a proper burial.[11] His was the first of many bodies which over the years filled a small cemetery on the island with plain wooden markers. By the middle of the second winter the crew of the *Mary D. Hume* were starved for news from the outside world, so William Mogg, the ship's third mate, walked the 300 miles (500 km) to the Hudson's Bay Post at Rampart House for news. But the Hudson's Bay men and the local Anglican missionaries knew little more than he did and were able to tell him only that Queen Victoria was alive and Lord Salisbury was still prime minister. When Mogg got back to his ship after an equally long walk, Hartson Bodfish wrote that this was "wonderful news for a bunch of New England Yankees who had received no mail for over twenty-six months!" And Mogg was reported as saying as he left Rampart House that "he needed [the missionaries'] prayers to protect him from damnation from profanity on the return trip."[12]

Both of the pioneering ships made a fortune. The *Mary D. Hume* returned to San Francisco in 1892 with $400,000 worth of baleen and whale oil aboard – one of the most profitable whaling voyages in American history. It is difficult to appreciate the size of this sum in today's sadly depreciated currency, but it was about a thousand times the average annual wage of a factory worker. When the *Mary D. Hume* docked at San Francisco in September 1892, her crew looked as if they had been marooned, as in a sense they had: "The sailors looked like a lot of wild men when they came ashore; they had long hair, longer beards and clothing that was patched and tattered beyond recognition of the original hue and texture of the garments. There were only three pairs of shoes in the party, the remainder of the crew being shod with deerskin and rubbers."[13] *Mary D. Hume* was a tough as well as lucky ship. Rebuilt in 1954, she was still afloat in the late 1970s, working as a tug in Puget Sound, her hull nearly a hundred years old (though she is now a mouldering wreck).[14]

News of the wealth to be found in the Beaufort Sea drew other ships north, and during the winter of 1894–95, fifteen ships wintered at Pauline Cove. The community became a virtual boom town, with about five hundred whalemen living there, as well as a number of Inuit families. In 1896 it was reported that twelve hundred people were at the island, living either on the ships or in buildings erected on shore.[15] Herschel Island became an economic magnet that drew Native people from a wide area. Vast quantities of food were required – a naturalist has estimated that each ship at the island consumed more than ten thousand pounds of caribou meat a year – and meat had to be brought in from as much as two hundred miles away. The bulk of the meat was provided by the Nunatarmas, the Inuit of the northern Alaskan interior, who came east to exchange meat for trade goods at the island.

The whaling ships had a reputation for being filthy and stinking, since the process of rendering whale blubber into oil, which took place on deck in large iron kettles, produced clouds of greasy black smoke. Other sailors claimed that the whalers could be smelled twenty miles to leeward. But the ships had a certain amount of style, and between hunts were carefully cleaned:

The captain's quarters on the *North Star* were certainly handsomely appointed, "the wood being of curly and birdseye maple, the door panels of French laurel, pilasters of mahogany, coving of rosewood, and other parts inlaid with black walnut and gilt, and the ceiling is painted white. The furniture is in harmony with the general fittings, and on the floor is a tapestry carpet of subdued hues." Even the pantry "was finished in black walnut." The crew's quarters were, admittedly, considerably more modest.[16]

For a dozen years – from 1891 to 1903 – the whaling crews operated as if Herschel Island was a no man's land, which in a sense it was. Until 1894, when the first member of the North-West Mounted Police arrived in the Yukon, there was no official representative of the Canadian government within a thousand miles of the island, and even after the discovery of gold in the Yukon in 1896 brought the police to the territory in force, they were still a long distance away and had no effect on the whalers. Ottawa simply balked at the expenditure that would be involved in sending government officials north, and in any case saw no need for action, believing that the rumours that began to filter south about what was happening to the Inuit were exaggerated.

The barter economy at Herschel Island involved more than trading for food. The crews needed their clothes mended, and Inuit women were paid in trade goods for this service. Away from home for a year or two, the men were also lonely and felt the need of sexual comfort. Some captains solved this problem by arranging to have Inuit women live with them in dwellings on land. Beginning in 1894, other captains brought their wives with them. Presumably, the latter pretended not to notice their husbands' friends' companions. The arrangement usually involved some sort of barter with a woman's husband or male relative, and the Inuit did not object to this. In fact, the women involved reportedly felt honoured and were envied by their friends.

For the members of the crew, it was a different story. In the first place they had little money. Many of them were deadbeats of one sort or another who had signed on with the ships in a kind of desperation. Some were "not sailors at all," reported a police officer: "[They] have never been to sea before signing on, some are men who have come to sea to get away from the drinking habit, and a few... have done time for some offence in the United States ... Altogether they are rather a rough lot."[17] These men were forbidden to have regular Inuit companions and could not have afforded the luxury in any case. The arrangement under which they had signed on for the trip was known as the "lay" system. The lay was a percentage of the take: captains got $1/2$ to $1/15$, cooks and engineers $1/25$, and ordinary seamen as little as $1/35$. What was really inequitable was that the value of the lay was calculated differently according to a man's rank. The officers' lays were based on a price for whalebone of $5.00 per pound; those of the mates, of $2.50 per pound; and those of the remainder of the crew, of $1.50 per pound. The crew were often charged exorbitant prices for their supplies, and since these could easily amount to the whole of their share of the profits, they often arrived home as poor as they had left, or even in debt.[18]

The combination of sexual frustration and the knowledge that they were not going to strike it rich, together with the harsh climate and hard work and the fact that many of the crew were bad characters from the West Coast waterfronts, led to periodic outbursts of violence. This was especially true after 1896, when word filtered north that gold had been struck near Dawson City. On more than one occasion whalers' crews deserted and tried to hike overland to the diggings – a journey of more than 400 miles (640 km) that few of them could have made alive. Some had to be dragged back to the ships by force; others froze to death on the way to Dawson. On 21 January 1896 seventeen men deserted the ships, and twelve more did so on 12 March. A party of ships' officers and Inuit were sent after them, because "as long as any number of deserters remained at large, it was a temptation to other men to desert and join them." The episode ended with a confrontation straight out of a Hollywood western:

In March ... a pursuit party was again dispatched and again "held up" by the deserters, who this time took two sleds and dog teams as well as supplies from their pursuers. A few days later a pursuit party of officers again reached the deserters, but were driven back twice in attempts to shoot it out with the ... Ten days after the initial desertion, natives reported being robbed by the deserting crewmen, and a third party was sent out ... A pitched battle again took place when the party reached the deserters' camp; this time the officers returned with six of the deserters, one of them shot to death in the gun battle and another badly wounded. The survivors were put in irons and chained to the decks for a month.[19]

A recent study that has analysed the isolated society that existed at Herschel Island during this period concluded that much of the violence and discontent among the crews was rooted in the fact that the officers and men were separated by a profound social gap.[20] Part of the problem lay with the method used for recruiting the ships' crews. Men were often more or less shanghaied from among the waterfront drifters of San Francisco, Honolulu, and other Pacific ports, and were considered by most captains to be scum not worth much consideration. They could be a violent lot, and the whaling captains had to be handy with their fists – as was the *Mary D. Hume*'s Hartson Bodfish, who later became captain of the *Beluga*:

In 1896 the second mate of the *Beluga* "had trouble" with a crewman and hit him. The crewman responded by seizing a handspike and attacking while others in the crew urged him to go ahead and kill the officer. The mate escaped, and reported the incident to the captain ... who immediately went after the crewman in question, "laying him out without any delay," but the affray escalated when one of the crewman's supporters jumped in and stabbed Bodfish. Bodfish, undeterred by his wound, grabbed a squeegee and continued the fight, decking his attackers and some others before the fight ended. Bodfish had his attacker put in irons and "triced up" in the rigging for twenty minutes, by which time "he had experienced genuine contrition and promised to behave himself."[21]

Members of the crew wreaked even greater havoc among themselves. In 1894 there was a "knifing affair" on the *Newport*, and in 1895 one man stabbed another in an argument over laying out a baseball diamond. In 1896 the second mate of the *Jeanette* got drunk and shot a sailor through the leg. In the same year Captain Bodfish noted that he had "kicked the cook this morning for threatening the Steward with a cleaver." In 1903 a crew member on Bodfish's vessel was so tormented by his mates that he took a knife to one of them, delivering "eight cuts on his body, one near the collar bone and another in the upper arm being very serious" and another "along his lower ribs that was ten inches long." In 1905 a member of the *Karluk*'s crew named Nugent stabbed another man in a quarrel over loading ice from a pond. He was put in irons, and after he had been so confined for two months, the crew petitioned the captain to keep him in irons indefinitely, since he had threatened the lives of several of them.[22]

Not everything at Herschel Island was darkness and violence, especially after some of the senior officers began bringing their wives and children north with them. Herschel Island saw amateur theatrical productions and minstrel shows, performed either on stages built on the ships' decks or in a large frame storehouse that contained a billiard and games room. This building, constructed by the ships' crews in 1893, was still standing over eighty years later, the oldest frame building in the Yukon. There was also a baseball league in summer with four teams: the Herschels, Northern Lights, Arctics, and Pickups. The officers' wives organized elaborate dinner parties (members of the crew were not invited to these), and ornate hand-written invitations to New Year's Eve and other parties still exist in private collections.[23] Each week there was at least one social gathering – dinner, dance, birthday party, whist party – and most weeks there were several. The Fourth of July saw a universal celebration, not least because it was the approximate date on which the ships could be freed from the sea ice.

But despite diversions, the picture of life for the crews of the whalers was one of overwhelming misery and hardship. They were not invited to the fancy dress balls held by the officers. Instead, they had to resort to "cards, whiskey and visits to an Eskimo house when nature demanded the company of women."[24] And the loneliness and discontent among the crews had a bad effect on the Inuit. The men tried to get around the ban on cohabitation with Inuit women by teaching the people how to make homebrew out of molasses, raisins, and potatoes, with a view to seducing the women. In this they were frequently successful, and the drunken parties that resulted led to the rumours of "orgies" that trickled south even as far as Ottawa.

But as usual, the worst effect of the whalers on the Inuit was the diseases they introduced. Because very few whites had visited the Western Arctic before 1888, the Inuit had not built up immunity to common European illnesses. When the whalemen infected them, not only with venereal diseases but also with measles and influenza, the Inuit had no resistance and died in shocking numbers. By the mid-1890s, the local population had shrunk to such an extent that the whalers had to import Inuit from Alaska to work for them. Diamond Jenness, the great anthropologist of northern Canada, estimated that by 1930 only a dozen of the original 2,000 to 2,500 Inuit population of the Western Arctic remained, the rest having succumbed to imported diseases.[25]

The trading activity at Herschel Island attracted First Nations as well as Inuit. Because trading was a secondary activity to whaling, which bore the overhead costs of the voyages, the whalers could trade goods with the Native people at a cost considerably below that of the Hudson's Bay Company at Fort McPherson and Rampart House to the south. As one captain wrote, "Arctic whalers were trading ships as well as whalers, and it was quite on the cards that a good profit might be made in trade even if very few whales were taken. There had always been some trading, but I think the trading developed to a new high level at about this time, owing to the increased knowledge among the whalers and likewise among the natives."[26] Because these men were not "traditional" traders, they did not limit themselves to the traditional trade goods: muzzleloaders, tobacco, tea, and blankets. Instead they offered repeating rifles, alcohol, and canned goods, which attracted aboriginal traders from a wide area.

There was also a "respectable" element on the island, for missionaries reached it as early as 1893, not long after the whalers. In 1891 Bishop W.C. Bompas, whose vast northern diocese included the northern Yukon, wrote to the Church Missionary Society, warning that Americans had penetrated the region and were "inclined to offer them [the Natives] liquor." He asked for men and money to establish a mission on the island, and the society acceded to his request.

The man sent to open the new mission was Isaac O. Stringer, who arrived in 1893, having spent the previous winter at Fort McPherson, getting used to the country and learning something of its customs and languages. Stringer later become famous as the "bishop who ate his boots" when his food ran out during a long sled trip across the Richardson Mountains in 1909. In 1893 he was at the beginning of his career, twenty-seven years old and straight out of Wycliffe College in Toronto, full of enthusiasm for his task.[27]

Stringer had been recruited for northern work by Bishop William Reeve of the Diocese of Mackenzie River, and from 1893 to 1897 he divided his time between Herschel Island, the mission post at Peel River, and other Inuit settlements in the region, such as the summer camp at Kittigazuit. After four years of periodic visits to Herschel Island, Stringer returned in the summer of 1897 to establish a permanent mission. Accompanying him was his wife Sadie, whom he had married in 1895, and her uncle, W.D. Young, who was to assist him in running the new mission.

To Stringer's surprise, on his first arrival at the island in 1893 the whaling captains welcomed him, made him comfortable, and even provided quarters for him. "I was doubtful as to how I would be received," he wrote, "and I thought I would be very satisfied if they would let me stop with the Indians [who had accompanied him] in their quarters. But I was invited at once into the Captain's cabin and received a hearty welcome."[28] He found himself in a rather awkward and ambivalent position. On the one hand, he was anxious to cultivate good relations with the whaling captains, and he welcomed the opportunity to socialize with men of his own class, or closer to it than the crewmen were. On the other hand he was personally and officially opposed to the trade in liquor with the Inuit. He wrote of this dilemma:

I could not have been much better used under the circumstances if I had been the President of the United States. But I can't help feel that a little indiscretion on my part or some undue circumstances might cause just as hearty an opposition. Why should they be friendly to a lonely missionary, who, if he says all he thinks, would condemn some of their darling sins? ... I know that many of them would do a great deal for me or anyone else in my place under the circumstances in this country. But this winter I got a better insight into their life and manner of living – and seven ships instead of four does not make matters any better.[29]

Despite his opposition to the spread of liquor and promiscuity among the Inuit, Stringer was wise enough to be discreet in his criticism of the whalemen. He did preach at least one sermon on the evils of drink, but the ships' officers did not take offence, probably because the sermon had little practical effect. The captains were glad to have an educated man to talk to in the long winter days, and they agreed with the missionary that drunkenness and disorder were bad things. When these continued despite Stringer's reasoning, he threatened to complain to Ottawa, and the captains signed an agreement to put an end to the liquor traffic – an agreement that was honoured very loosely.

The Stringers' primary purpose was to bring Christianity to the Inuit, and to this end the missionary began to preach weekly sermons, which were interpreted by an Inuit named David Copperfield. The couple also provided more practical services. They ran a school, which was attended by Inuit and whalemen, and Mrs Stringer gave lessons in shorthand to several crew members who longed for a steady job once they got back to San Francisco. She also bore two children in that lonely spot.

When the couple left the island in 1901 to return south, they were replaced by the Reverend C.E. Whittaker and his wife Emma. Whittaker had a rougher time than Stringer. Moreover, he suffered personal tragedy on the island: one of his children died there. (The explorer Roald Amundsen, visiting Herschel Island in 1906, recorded the sad sight of the Whittakers leaving the island forever, dragging their daughter's body with them on a sled.)[30] Whittaker's difficulties in his post seem to have been the result of his personality, which was acerbic and inflexible. Unlike Stringer, he was not popular with the whaling fleet, and in turn complained of them on many occasions to the government. The police officer in charge of the Herschel detachment wrote of him in 1903: "This man is so much disliked by the whalers that some of them tried to make the natives believe that Mr. Whittaker was the cause of Leviauke [a local Inuk] being arrested."[31]

Oddly enough, the Inuit seemed not to have objected to the state of affairs at Herschel Island. They were all there of their own free will, and they seem to have thought it a wonderful place, where there were parties and games all the time and where fascinating and useful goods could be acquired. Such, at any rate, is the impression given in the memoirs of a man who spent several years of his youth at Herschel Island. Nuligak was a Mackenzie Delta Inuk. Born in 1895, he lived there throughout the later part of the whaling period, and as an old man he dictated his memoirs, which have been translated into English. They clearly reflect the delight which the Inuit found in the food and gadgets the whalers brought:

When summer came Uncle Kralogark took us west to Herschel Island ... Crowds of Eskimos came there. That fall I saw some very large ships. The sailors we met always had something in their mouths; something they chewed. It so intrigued me that I kept staring at their jaws. One certain day that "thing" was given to me. I chewed – it was delicious. It was chewing gum. From that day I was able to recognize some of these white men's things.[32]

Although the Inuit do not seem to have minded the state of affairs at Herschel Island, the missionaries did, and complaints from Stringer and Whittaker found their way to Bishop Bompas at Fortymile. He in turn complained to the North-West Mounted Police when they first arrived in the Yukon in 1894, and the police forwarded the stories to Ottawa. In 1895 Inspector Charles Constantine reported from the Yukon the evil rumours that had reached him via a ship's engineer who had deserted and made his way south to the NWMP post at Fortymile: "The carryings-on of the officers and crews of the whalers there was such that no one would believe ... Large quantities of whiskey are taken up in the ships ... As long as the liquor lasts, the natives neither fish nor hunt, and die of starvation in consequence ... The captains and mates of these vessels purchase for their own use girls from nine years and upwards."[33] This was probably a bit overstated – Inuit died, but seldom from starvation – but the tone was accurate enough. Bishop Bompas echoed these complaints and for a number of years nagged the government to take some action before the violence and debauchery at the island led to the "utter ruin" of the Inuit. Earlier, in 1894, Stringer had described a similar scene:

As I write some geese are passing and they [the Inuit] were banging away with their rifles. It is a wonder some are not killed with all the rifles and rum. Almost every man has a rifle. Now Kokhiks wife comes in and takes the drum telling me its all right not to be afraid and now she drums away and sings as if mad ... Outside many are dancing and staggering and swaggering around after the manner of drunkards in general ... At times they were very wild in their demonstrations one or two began crying for children they had lost.[34]

In fact, it is difficult to give an accurate assessment of the nature of Herschel Island society in the 1890s, since perceptions of it varied so widely from one observer to another. Was it an "outpost of civilization," as the explorer Stefansson described it? Or was it, as the Nome press called it, "the Sodom of the Arctic"? It seems to have depended on the moral standards of the reporter. The Rev. Whittaker, a stickler for morality, said that "the scenes of riotous drunkenness and lust which this island has witnessed have probably never been surpassed,"[35] – which seems a bit strong. Perhaps Whittaker, during his English education, had never read Edward Gibbon's descriptions of the Roman Empire, which make Herschel Island seem tame by comparison.

Certainly, the authorities thought that the missionaries' tales of immorality were exaggerated. The comptroller of the Mounted Police complained that it was difficult "to convince the goody-goody people that in the development and settlement of a new country allowances must be made for the excesses of human nature."[36] Many of the tales of debauchery and "bacchanalian orgies which beggared description" that were breathlessly retailed in southern Canada were exaggerations. According to one excited author, "Down the gangplanks surged a motley horde of mixed humanity till the sand[s]pit was overrun with a drunken mob of dark-visaged kanakas, bearded Russians, ebony-faced Negroes, and the off-scouring of the Barbary Coast. Rum flowed like water. Fighting, drinking, and debauchery became the order of the day."[37] But as one expert noted, if this picture had literally been true, few whaling masters would have wintered at Herschel, and certainly none would have brought their wives along.

The Canadian government was initially reluctant to move to assert its authority in the Western Arctic, especially as it discounted the missionaries' tales of horror. After 1894 Ottawa had asserted its authority in the central Yukon, but the northern part of the territory continued to be ignored. What finally moved the government to action in the northern Yukon was the question of sovereignty. The presence of American whalers operating in the Beaufort Sea contravened a number of Canadian laws, including a ban on trading alcohol with the Native people and selling them repeating rifles. No royalty was paid on whales taken, which by the First World War amounted to over $13 million in total value, nor was duty paid on goods traded with the Inuit, which came to another $1.5 million.[38]

Worse still, because there was no official Canadian presence in the region and no Canadian laws enforced, the possibility existed that Canada's claim to sovereignty there might be placed in doubt. As an official in the Department of the Interior commented, "It is feared that if American citizens are permitted to land and pursue the industries of whaling, fishing and trading with the Indians without complying with the revenue laws of Canada and without any assertion of sovereignty on the part of Canada, unfounded and troublesome claims may hereafter be set up."[39]

The law came to Herschel Island in 1903. By then the government had, in the NWMP, a police force with wide experience in Yukon service. It was also the year of the settlement of the Alaska boundary dispute – an agreement that disappointed and infuriated Canada and made Ottawa determined not to let more of the North go to foreigners by default. The fact that American whaling ships were operating in Hudson Bay in the same way as in the west lent urgency to the government's desire to assert its northern sovereignty.

Two NWMP detachments were set up in the Western Arctic in the summer of 1903: the main one at Fort McPherson, with a satellite at Herschel Island. The detachment at the island consisted of Sergeant Francis J. Fitzgerald and Constable F.D. Sutherland. Fitzgerald, born in Halifax in 1869, was a veteran of fourteen years' service in the NWMP, and had served in the Yukon during the gold rush. He exemplified the qualities that were expected of a Mounted Police officer: he was fit, resourceful, fair, firm, and unmarried (which freed him for lengthy periods of northern service).

Sergeant Francis J. Fitzgerald established the North-West Mounted Police detachment at Herschel Island in 1903. He died in the ill-fated "lost patrol" of 1910–11 (RCMP photo).

When Fitzgerald and Sutherland arrived at Herschel Island after a long trip in an open boat, they were practically destitute, for the government had sent the expedition north woefully undersupplied, expecting the police to improvise according to conditions. The two men had little food, no fuel, and nowhere to live, and they had to borrow a sod house and coal from the whalers. They were expected to enforce compliance with Canadian laws among a foreign population that naturally might be expected to be hostile to their mission. Their only assets were the force of their personalities and the tenuous authority of the Canadian government, a very long way away.

But the police at Herschel Island had other, less obvious factors favouring their mission. In the first place, they and the whaling captains were not necessarily antagonists. The captains also feared the disorder that could be caused by unruly crew members and were glad to have officials on the scene to help keep them under control. After Fitzgerald had subdued a drunken sailor or two, hauling them back to ship to be placed in irons, the captains realized that the police were as much allies as enemies.

More important still was the fact that the police had no drastic effect on the operations of the whaling ships. By 1903 the whaling industry was in decline, the whales in the Beaufort Sea were beginning to thin out, and some ships were wintering at Baillie Island, 250 miles (400 km) to the east of Herschel Island. The most practical demonstration of Canadian sovereignty in the region was the collection of duties on whales caught and goods traded with the Inuit, but if captains wished to avoid payment, they simply did not call at Herschel Island. The police had no ship of their own and could not patrol the coast to bring the law to ships that avoided their post. Nor could they insist on a thorough search of all the ships that came their way, particularly when they were under obligation to the whalers for fuel and housing.[40]

The result was that Sergeant Fitzgerald was reduced to doing a certain amount of bluffing. He asked the captains for a list of the goods brought in for trade and required them to pay duty according to these lists. They complied and produced the lists, accurate or not, and Fitzgerald collected a small sum based on them. In international law, it was the demonstration of Canada's authority that counted as proof of Canadian sovereignty in the region; the actual sum collected was immaterial. As far as the liquor traffic was concerned, Fitzgerald reported that he had checked the flow – but to what extent it is difficult to judge. Certainly, those who wanted liquor could still get it, but the presence of the police compelled a certain amount of discretion.

There was in fact a fair degree of harmony among the residents of Herschel Island in its days of glory, with the possible exception of the Rev. Whittaker, who seemed to have a talent for alienating people – a considerable liability in a remote northern post. In 1907 he ran afoul of the police when he interfered in their internal affairs. The episode casts light on an aspect of life in the Arctic that for obvious reasons received little publicity – sexual relations between whites and Inuit. Again, it concerned Francis Fitzgerald. Like many white men stationed in the North for years at a time, Fitzgerald had taken an Inuit woman as a common-law wife. She was called Unalina. Eventually he decided to marry Unalina and applied to his superiors for permission to do so, as all Mounted Policemen in that era were required to do. Whittaker, who as a clergyman was keen on formal marriages, also wrote to the police urging them to grant permission. But at that time and for many years thereafter, it was unthinkable that a police officer should marry a Native woman. Fitzgerald's immediate superior rebuffed Whittaker in no uncertain terms, writing that "he would prefer reporting to Ottawa that Fitzgerald had blown his brains out rather than that he had married a native woman."[41]

This story had a sad ending. Unalina and Francis Fitzgerald had a daughter, Annie, who was crippled in an accident while a child. In 1926, long after Fitzgerald's death, Annie surfaced at the Hay River Residential School, where the principal tried to get the Royal Canadian Mounted Police to assume responsibility for her. She was in a "pitiable" condition – a hunchback – but the commissioner of the RCMP, while expressing concern (and surprise), refused to provide funding for her. Eventually the government provided an annual grant of $145 for three years for her to continue at school so that she could be trained for housework, but she died soon after, at the age of eighteen.

By the time the First World War broke out in 1914, the whaling industry in the Western Arctic was dead, and so was Francis Fitzgerald. Whaling was killed by the invention of synthetic substitutes for baleen; Fitzgerald was killed by overconfidence and bad luck. As leader of the four-man 1910–11 winter mail patrol between Fort McPherson and Dawson City, Fitzgerald, then an inspector, had tried to set a speed record, and had the misfortune to get lost in the Richardson Mountains during a particularly severe winter. He kept trying to find his way to Dawson until it was too late to return to Fort McPherson, and in February 1911 he and his companions died, three of starvation and exposure, and one of suicide.

Members of the Dempster patrol preparing to leave Dawson City in search of the "lost patrol," around Christmas 1910 (YA)

On the occasion of this tragedy, Whittaker made another gaffe. When the bodies of the four men from the "lost patrol" were brought to Fort McPherson, Whittaker somehow got hold of Fitzgerald's diary and, based on its contents, wrote a sharply critical letter about the patrol, accusing Fitzgerald of setting out ill prepared, ill guided, and with poor dogs. The Mounted Police were extremely sensitive about their public image, which was damaged by this episode, and the fact that Whittaker's comments were partly true did not help matters. They reacted with huffy denials of his allegations.[42]

Despite the decline of the whaling industry, Herschel Island continued to be a trading and administrative centre for the Western Arctic. Inuit who could no longer earn trade goods by working for the whalers turned to hunting fur, particularly muskrat and fox. By 1915 the fur trade had grown to the extent that it partially replaced whaling as a source of income for the Inuit. The trade was intensely competitive, with the Hudson's Bay Company, some San Francisco firms, and both Canadian and American independents competing with one another. In 1915 the HBC opened a post on the island. Three other posts operated on the Yukon's north coast in this period. The HBC ran a post at Demarcation Point between 1921 and 1924, and another at Shingle Point from 1920 to 1928. H. Liebes and Company also operated at Shingle Point between 1917 and 1921. By 1923 the HBC had established posts eastward along the Arctic coast from Herschel Island as far as King William Island.[43] But the company never made much money from the trade in that part of the North, even when fur prices were high. The Herschel Island post was kept open primarily to deter competition from other

Buildings used by the whalers at Herschel Island, seen at the end of the whaling era, c. 1910 (RCMP photo)

traders and as a regional transportation depot to assist in the shipment of supplies from ports such as Vancouver to company posts to the east of the Mackenzie Delta.

In the 1920s silver fox pelts sold for $50 each, and some Inuit made enough money to buy large motor schooners and other material goods; one trapper made nearly $15,000 in a year – a fortune in those days. White trappers also came north, lured by the high fur prices. The Inuit hunter Nuligak remembered this era as a happy, prosperous time: "From Christmas to New Year's the dancing drums never stopped ... On Christmas Day we were all invited by the minister to dinner. On New Year's it was the HBC's turn to entertain us with all kinds of good things to eat. The RCMP also gave us a day, in between these two. We had all kinds of games, and we returned home only when we felt like it."[44]

A number of explorers visited the region in this period and used its harbours as a base or a stopping place. Roald Amundsen navigated the Northwest Passage between 1903 and 1906. In 1905, near the end of his journey, his ship, *Gjoa* was beset in ice for the winter at King's Point. The crew built two small houses of driftwood and erected a small observatory (which later became a crypt for one of Amundsen's men who died during the winter). The explorer visited Herschel Island several times that year and in late October decided to travel overland to Fort Yukon to spread the news of his successful voyage. Amundsen was disappointed to discover that there was no telegraph station at the trading post, so he pushed on to Eagle City, where he dispatched word of his Arctic adventures. He then returned to King's Point for the winter. In July 1906, the last season of his famous expedition, he cast off from his northern Yukon harbour and headed west. The tumultuous welcome he received at Nome was a foretaste of the enthusiastic reception awaiting him throughout the world.[45]

Yet another explorer-adventurer, Vilhjalmur Stefansson, similarly focused public attention on the Canadian Arctic. Stefansson made several highly publicized expeditions to the Western Arctic, stopping often at Herschel Island for supplies. He recognized few boundaries between promotion and science; some of his discoveries, such as the alleged "blond Eskimos" of Victoria Island, brought hoots of derision from traditional scientists but earned the explorer much public acclaim. He had, however, become a figure of considerable note, and when he approached the Canadian government for financial support for a major Arctic expedition, the government could not turn him down.

This Canadian Arctic Expedition (1913–18), Canada's most ambitious northern undertaking, was under the direction of Stefansson and R.M. Anderson. The venture floundered from the beginning. The *Karluk*, carrying Stefansson's Northern Division, was caught in floe ice in September 1913 and after drifting westward for three months, sank off Wrangel Island with the loss of eight lives. Stefansson had left the ship long before the sinking, so anxious was he to push on with the explorations.[46]

The work continued in an atmosphere of recrimination and anger. Stefansson, always the loner, put his own needs ahead of those of his colleagues. He routinely angered the Mounted Police and the missionaries with his carping criticism, his publicity-seeking activities, and his unrelenting self-promotion. Stefansson fell seriously ill at Herschel Island. After more than a month in the police barracks, he was sent south for medical care. A special police patrol carried him as far as Rampart House, and from there he secured Native guides to take him down the Porcupine River to Fort Yukon.

Stefansson left a legacy of bitterness, but he focused North American attention on the Canadian Arctic. He was, in the words of his best biographer, "less of a scientist, in the strict sense, and more of a publicist and promoter."[47] The police officers disliked the pretentious explorer and feared that his naive notions of the "friendly Arctic" would attract unprepared adventurers to the North. As Sergeant Fitzgerald noted, "Such men as Stefansson claim they can live on the country: they can by some one else supplying the food. All those people are a drain on our supplies ... [It] is impossible to refuse a white man if he is short of food."[48]

When Stefansson publicly deprecated the efforts of Arctic missionaries, they responded with bitter denunciations of their own. And his fellow scientists protested his lack of attention to research. One later wrote: "Mr. Stefansson has persistently misquoted, libelled or ignored the work of every scientist member of the late Canadian Arctic expedition, so that instead of feeling an honest pride in having been engaged in more or less valuable work in the North, most of us feel inclined to apologize for having been Arctic explorers rather than be connected in any way with Mr. Stefansson or his schemes. He had made a laughing-stock and a byword of the name of explorer."[49] Another crew member was even more direct: "I learn here [Herschel Island] that V.S. completely succeeded in 'getting the goat' of everybody here and at Fort McPherson. It is strange, but no one seems to have a good word for him; seldom have I seen a man for whom there were fewer good words than is the case with V.S. along the coast. It may be due to the climate or the men here, but some or rather most of it must be due to V.S. himself."[50]

The work of Stefansson and the other explorers did have an impact. Members of the Canadian Arctic Expedition surveyed the Arctic coastline of the Yukon and explored several of the rivers flowing into the ocean. They also conducted extensive surveys of the natural history of the region. Perhaps their greatest contribution, highlighted by Stefansson's promotional efforts, was to keep Herschel Island and the Arctic slope in the public eye in the years after the demise of the whaling industry.

Herschel Island did not die with the end of the whaling industry in the Western Arctic. It remained the centre of government activities and the supply depot for fur traders working the area. Here the schooner *Arctic* is seen at the island in 1923 (authors' collection).

The explorers could use Herschel Island as a base because the Mounted Police maintained their detachment there throughout this period. When the whaling stopped, there was not a great deal for the police to do except survive, which in that environment seemed to take up most of their time. The entries in the Herschel Island detachment diary for the autumn of 1906 give the flavour of police life there:

Sept. 29th – Saturday. 24 [°F] above, strong wind. Scrubbed out quarters.
Sept. 30th – Sunday. 24 above. Very strong gale.
Oct. 1st – Monday. 25 above, fine. Hauling wood to storehouse.
Oct. 2nd – Tuesday. 27 above, strong wind. Hauling wood to storehouse.
Oct. 3rd – Wednesday. 24 above, strong wind. Hauling wood to storehouse.
Oct. 4th – Thursday. 22 above, foggy. Cleaning up storehouse.
Oct. 5th – Friday. 25 above, fine and calm. Repairing dog harness.
Oct. 6th – Saturday. 21 above, fine and calm. Cleaning stove pipe and
scrubbing out quarters.[51]

When in 1928 the RCMP (as the force was called after 1920) finally acquired the *St Roch,* a seaworthy patrol vessel of its own, the ship, commanded by Henry Larsen, called regularly at the island and sometimes wintered there.[52]

Still, by 1920, probably not one Canadian in ten thousand had ever heard of Herschel Island. What brought it to public attention in southern Canada was a sensational criminal case tried on the island in the summer of 1923. Alikomiak and Tatimagana, two men from the Coppermine region, were charged with the murder of a Hudson's Bay Company trader. Alikomiak, while under arrest at the Tree River detachment, east of Herschel on the Arctic coast, shot and killed Corporal W.A. Doak of the RCMP. A judicial party went north from Edmonton to hear the case, and the two Inuit were convicted and sentenced to death. The case aroused great public interest, and a lively debate took place in the press over whether the sentences should be commuted. But this was not the first time that Inuit had killed whites in the Western Arctic, and the government was determined to make an example of the two men. Thus, on 1 February 1924, the two were hanged in an abandoned whaling shed – the first Inuit executed for murder under Canadian law.[53]

What killed Herschel Island as a community was the Great Depression of the 1930s. The 1929 stock market crash put a stop to luxury consumption, sending prices for furs plummeting. Inuit hunters such as Nuligak who had been called plutocrats in the 1920s were now practically reduced to starvation. Because of its isolation, Herschel Island had always been expensive to supply, and pressed by the harsh economic realities of the depression, government and private industries alike tried to economize on their northern operations as much as possible. In 1937 the Hudson's Bay Company trader on the island noted that there was "No Fur this year. Mostly cash sales."[54] The company moved its post to Tuktoyaktuk, and the RCMP moved its Western Arctic headquarters to Aklavik and eventually closed the detachment on the island. A government official commented: "The new routing of the Western Arctic freight by way of Mackenzie River has meant the desertion of Herschel Island as there is no longer any shipping by Point Barrow. The Hudson's Bay Company and the R.C.M.P. have left there. Captain Pedersen, who had brought in supplies around by Alaska for the past 42 years has this year shipped everything by the H.B.C. boats down the Mackenzie."[55]

With the government and the traders gone, there seemed little reason for the Inuit to stay. Occasional Inuit trappers from the Mackenzie Delta came into the region for a season of hunting, but when the Inuit left the area, there was no permanent trapping base left to sustain trade. By the Second World War the island was deserted.

The shift towards the Mackenzie Delta was a gradual one. The Anglican missionaries had been trying for years to establish schools among the Inuit, but a shortage of teachers and money had reduced their effort to occasional classes taught by clergy and their wives. In 1922 a mission was established at Shingle Point, on the coast midway between Herschel Island and the Mackenzie Delta, in response to the growing local Inuit population at this favoured fishing and trading site. When the Roman Catholics opened a residential school at Aklavik in 1924, the Anglicans felt compelled to respond in kind. They feared that otherwise they would lose the attention of the Inuit of the Western Arctic, who were opposed to the church's policy of removing the children from the district and shipping them south to Hay River for years at a time.

Such an undertaking promised to be expensive, however, and the church could not proceed without federal government assistance. The Anglicans' Arctic Mission, established to coordinate work in the Far North, decided to proceed with a temporary school in order to gauge the Inuit response. The missionaries settled on Shingle Point as the site and in 1929 welcomed the first children into their humble establishment. The Inuit responded enthusiastically to the new school, so much so that many children had to be turned away. As was the pattern with northern residential schools, the teachers sought, more successfully here than elsewhere, to integrate a Canadian curriculum taught in English, along with a Christian education and training in traditional skills:

The boys are taught to hunt the caribou, the birds, white whales, etc., as well as to make nets, catch the fish, dry them, etc. The girls are taught cooking, how best to utilize everything that comes to them, and in many other ways to become suitable citizens in Eskimo settlements in days to come. The fact that we have two Eskimo hunters at the school who take the boys hunting and fishing, etc., and two Eskimo women who teach the girls to sew boots, clothes, etc., is sufficient proof of the seriousness of our intention regarding these matters.[56]

The Arctic Mission was convinced that the Shingle Point school had demonstrated its usefulness, but it was not wedded to that site. Problems with sea ice and food interfered with the work of the school, and when the Anglican Church looked for a permanent location, it turned away from the Arctic coast. The Department of Indian Affairs built a new facility for the church at Aklavik, a Mackenzie Delta community that was emerging as the administrative centre of the Western Arctic. Shingle Point was closed, and in August 1936 the staff and students, almost fifty in total, moved to their new quarters.

It is difficult to assess the effectiveness of the missionary activities in the Herschel Island region. Many whites had little use for the missionaries, either personally, as in the case of Whittaker, or on philosophical grounds. Stefansson despised them, believing that they taught the Inuit useless lessons and customs and interfered with their ability to survive in their environment. K.G. Chipman of the Canadian Arctic Expedition accused the missionaries of Herschel Island of saving souls for profit: "Most of the natives have what is known as a 'fox skin' name, Pete, Harry, Elias, Carry, Tommy, etc. These names they are proud of and consider them as a mark of distinction. It seems that Bishop Stringer and Mr. Whittaker christened the natives, big and little, and gave to them names. For this service they received a fox skin for each person. That is a good business."[57] The missionaries defended themselves vigorously, Stringer writing in 1927: "Gradually they [the Inuit] were brought to a knowledge of God in spite of all the severest kinds of temptations through the whalers and other white people along the Arctic coast. Now the majority of the Eskimos along five hundred miles of the Arctic coast from the Alaska boundary have been baptized, and most of the adults confirmed."[58] Of course both men could have been right; it depends on one's personal view of the value of Christianity to Native people.

The police returned to Herschel Island in 1948, using it for a number of years as a dog-breeding station, but the day of patrolling by dogsled was drawing to a close, and the detachment shut down in 1964. From time to time the island was visited by hunting parties; in 1962–63 eight Inuit trapping licences were issued for the area, and the following year, four.[59] Inuit families occasionally used the old buildings (in the 1980s there was one family living there), but for the most part the place was left to a slow process of decay. The wooden headboards marking the graves of the whalemen who died there in the 1890s were blown flat in the 1970s, but the names on them can still be read. At least one is a child's grave – that of George Edson, son of a whaling captain, who died at Herschel Island in February 1898, ten days before his first birthday.

The Government of the Yukon had always ignored this northernmost part of its jurisdiction. Since communications between Herschel Island and the Mackenzie River were far easier than between the island and Dawson, it seemed only sensible to let it become de facto a part of the Northwest Territories. Indeed, for a time there was some confusion about which territory it was in. There was even a proposal in 1928 to transfer it to the Northwest Territories on the grounds that it could be better served by access to the Mackenzie River than via Dawson. One government official wrote: "I think if the present boundary is changed to cut off all that area within the watershed of the Beaufort Sea, together with the islands in the Beaufort Sea, north of the Yukon, and to add this area to the Mackenzie District, it would not greatly concern the people of the Yukon."[60] He was right about Yukoners' indifference; but because of apathy and the gradual disappearance of the Herschel Island community, nothing was done about the matter.

With the energy crisis of the 1970s, however, the island assumed new importance. Discoveries of gas and oil deposits in the Beaufort Sea and talk of constructing a modern port at Pauline Cove impelled the Yukon government to take action to demonstrate its authority over the island. In June 1972, Commissioner James Smith of the Yukon Territory flew with some reporters and members of the territorial council to raise the flag of the Yukon for the first time above Herschel Island.

Once the busiest community in the Western Arctic, Herschel Island is now all but abandoned, though oil and gas exploration in the region in the 1970s led to renewed interest in the island and its natural harbour (Yukon Government photo).

Oil exploration off the north coast of the Yukon began in 1973, and over the next fifteen years the stupendous sum of $6.5 billion was spent by oil companies exploring and drilling for gas and oil in the Beaufort Sea. Some very substantial finds have been made, notably in the Amauligak field 45 miles (72 km) northwest of Tuktoyaktuk, where in 1986 Gulf Canada announced a find of 700 to 800 million barrels.[61]

Herschel Island and the Yukon's Arctic slope, all but ignored from the 1930s to 1940s, have become the focus of considerable debate in the last decade. The Berger Commission recommended that the northern Yukon, home of the massive Porcupine River caribou herd, be set aside as a wilderness park. At the same time, the Committee for Original Peoples' Entitlement (COPE), representing the Inuit of the Western Arctic, laid claim to aboriginal land rights in the region, as did the Council of Yukon Indians, representing the claims of the people of Old Crow. The competing demands, further clouded by corporate plans for port developments at Herschel Island or Shingle Point, made the region a focus for the conflicting Native, business, and government interpretations of the future of the Arctic.[62] In July 1978 the federal government announced that the northern Yukon, including Herschel

Island, was closed to development, pending the establishment of a national park. Again, there was little consultation on the decision, although it did ensure that Native needs and rights in the area would not quickly be ignored in favour of short-term commercial interests. But controversy surrounding the area continued.

In the mid-1980s the United States government announced that it was granting oil exploration permits for the Alaskan lands contiguous to the northern Yukon, even though that area was on the migratory path of the Porcupine caribou herd.[63] When the issuing of permits was extended to the off-shore, the Reagan administration challenged Canada's long-standing but unofficial boundary in the Western Arctic – the northward extension of the 141st meridian to the 200-mile limit. Perhaps the most significant change, however, was in the new Yukon attitude to the north slope. In 1987 the Yukon government announced the establishment of Herschel Island Territorial Park, the first such park in the Yukon, a fitting symbol of the renewed interest in this long-ignored region.

SIX

After the Gold Rush
1900–1918

The Klondike gold rush was too rich and too frantic to last long. There was not enough gold in the world, let alone in the Yukon, to satisfy the hunger for wealth of the tens of thousands who rushed north to find it. At first there was gold to spare and even to waste. Ripped out of the earth, washed by crude and inefficient methods, gold worth untold thousands of dollars was lost to the Yukon's streams and rivers. The gold never ran out completely, of course, and it was mined with reasonable profits for the next six decades – it is still mined when the world price goes high enough to justify the expense – but within a year or two the rich diggings were played out. There was still work in and near Dawson, but the era when a couple of men with picks and shovels could make a fortune was over, and the age of the machines had begun.

The Yukon did not die after the rush, but as early as the end of 1898 its population began to shrink, as men began to look elsewhere for the big strike. In that year the discovery of gold at Atlin, British Columbia, just across the border from the southern Yukon, drew some miners away. During the Atlin rush two astute businessmen saw a different opportunity. Isaac Taylor and his partner Bill Drury, saw that many of the prospectors, having carried a ton or more of supplies over the coastal mountain passes, were quitting the area shortly after their arrival. Taylor and Drury bought up these supplies for a fraction of their worth and used them as the basis of a successful retail operation. They then moved into the fur trade, opening their first post at Little Salmon. From this beginning was to grow the Yukon's largest retailing operation, with posts scattered throughout the territory.[1]

But Atlin was a sideshow. The first great blow to the Klondike came from Alaska, where in the winter of 1898 gold was discovered in paying quantities on the beaches of Nome. In Dawson, a city overflowing with unemployed stampeders, many of whom had come far to discover little, the news rekindled an old excitement. Although the police warned the miners about the dangers of winter travel, hundreds set off down the frozen Yukon River, hoping to beat other prospectors to the new find and to avoid coming in second once more. When the ice broke in the spring, the human trickle out of Dawson turned into a flood. The first steamers to leave town were jammed with prospectors, and the river was once more filled with makeshift rafts, though this time they were leaving Dawson, not arriving. Thousands abandoned Dawson. The gold rush, which had never stayed in one place for long, had moved on once more.[2]

Dawsonites did not despair, however. In 1898–99 the Klondike fields were still producing well, and stampeders from the south continued to arrive, though fewer every month. Meanwhile, some of the Nome adventurers came back to Dawson City, discouraged by the slim pickings of the new strike and the violence and disorder that attended it. In the spring of 1900, Dawson City and the Klondike enjoyed a modest recovery. Although the boom times were gone, many Yukoners believed that a stable, lasting community would now emerge from the turmoil of the gold rush. Commissioner William Ogilvie predicted that Dawson would stabilize at around ten thousand people and that the rich Klondike deposits would sustain a prosperous community for at least twenty years.[3]

The next blow caused more damage. In the summer of 1902 an Italian immigrant, Felix Pedro, struck gold near a makeshift trading post that had been opened the previous year near Alaska's Tanana River. Additional strikes on Cleary, Fairbanks, and Ester creeks confirmed the richness of the Tanana gold field. The rush would centred on the new community of Fairbanks, which soon challenged Dawson City as the cornerstone of the Yukon basin's gold frontier.[4] The Klondike once more emptied in response to the new discovery, but this time most of the miners did not return. Tanana had much more to offer than Nome, and the miners and workers who rushed downstream in 1903 found opportunities long since gone in Dawson. As Fairbanks grew, and Dawson's slide picked up speed, a number of businessmen joined the exodus. On the frontier, national boundaries had little meaning; the people went where the gold and the opportunities were. The lemming-like impulse that drew people to the gold rush also worked in reverse; when enough people began to believe that Dawson was doomed, the prophecy became self-fulfilling. It was Fairbanks's turn for glory now, and Dawson would have to wait and see if this blow would be fatal.[5]

By the summer of 1904 the writing was on the wall: Dawson was no longer the brightest hope for the Northwest. Many of the original Dawsonites had left for the new field. Experienced miners in the Klondike fields could see that the high-grade deposits had already been worked over and that new mining techniques would be required to sustain gold production. Faced with the harsh realities and high costs of modernization, many simply sold out to the companies consolidating claims in the Klondike and headed for Fairbanks, where it was said that individual prospectors still had a chance.

There were social as well as economic changes in Dawson. The rowdy, boisterous community of the first years of the gold rush was becoming "civilized." Dawson was beginning to look respectable, as the reform efforts of the middle-class residents, particularly the Women's Vigilance Committee, challenged the gambling halls, brothels, and dance halls that had once made the city seem so sinful. However, the new morality in Dawson owed as much to depopulation as to moral crusades, for by 1901 the town's population had fallen to half of its gold rush peak. There was less sin partly because there were far fewer sinners.

It was ironic that as the economy of Dawson began to collapse, it gained an outward appearance of permanence and stability. Responding to Commissioner Ogilvie's optimistic forecasts about the Yukon, the federal government had authorized the construction of an elaborate administration building, a new courthouse, a new post office, and an imposing residence for the commissioner, which became the social focus of Dawson. As the population declined, the new civil service buildings proclaimed that Dawson was the administrative, legal, and commercial centre for the upper Yukon River basin. This period, in the words of Hal Guest, author of a history of Dawson City, was "Dawson's golden age," an age of elegance that masked a valiant but losing battle to maintain the status and prosperity of the Klondike gold rush.[6]

The numbers told a sad tale. No census had been taken of the Yukon at its height in 1898, since the next regular census was not due until 1901. The best estimate of the territory's maximum population was perhaps as much as 40,000. It fell to slightly over 27,000 people in 1901, of whom more than 9,000 lived in Dawson City, while most of the rest were on the Klondike creeks. Ten years later, the Yukon had only 8,500 people, more than a third of whom lived in Dawson. The city's collapse continued, and in 1921 it could claim fewer than a thousand residents. Dawson City would never regain the energy and excitement of the gold rush days, nor would it again have the status and authority it enjoyed in the first years of the twentieth century. The city was clearly on the skids, but it did not go down without a fight.

One way in which Dawsonites reacted to the decay of their community was by attempting to prove that it was indeed a going concern – that it was just as vital and "civilized" as any town in southern Canada. In particular, there was a strong desire on the part of middle-class citizens to make Dawson a "moral" place. If Ontario's capital in this era was known as "Toronto the Good," then Dawsonites aspired to make their town "Dawson the

Better." Southern Canadians and some federal officials had always thought of Dawson as a sinful place, so there was both public and private support for the campaign to clean it up, to make it the kind of place where decent folk could live without being confronted daily in the streets by gamblers and harlots. Since there were still hundreds of single young men in Dawson in the first decade of the century, the campaign for moral purity was bound to produce a certain amount of civic tension.

The restructuring of Klondike society began in 1901. In short order the government put restrictions on gambling, the sale of alcohol, and prostitution. These actions did not, however, satisfy the reformers. The Reverend J. Pringle, the Presbyterian minister in Dawson, continued to use his seat on the territorial council to wage further battles against immorality.[7] The Mounted Police supported these battles, even though their own men often succumbed to the temptations of the flesh. Sam Steele was particularly anxious to control the "fast women and 'tin horn gamblers' galore" who made a profitable living off the miners' weaknesses.[8] But Steele and other police were concerned more with order than morality, and concentrated mostly on harassing the gamblers. Steele did not try to close the saloons as long as they were orderly; and after he left the Yukon, Commissioner James Ross proceeded slowly with new measures, always being careful to consult the business community.

At times, efforts to regulate the saloons ran afoul of administrative manoeuvring. Ross's successor, Frederick T. Congdon, a passionately partisan Liberal, used liquor licences to reward his supporters, undercutting the effort of several years to regulate drinking. When Congdon left office in 1904, the police moved quickly to eliminate the practice of paying women a percentage for drinks they solicited, and imposed further regulations on gambling. With the next commissioner, Alexander Henderson, the forces of morality found a new and powerful backer. Like many of the church people and social leaders, Henderson saw no justification for the remnants of the frontier lifestyle in Dawson City, and he ordered an immediate clamp-down on the saloons, hotels, and brothels. But as he soon discovered, there was a substantial demand for the services of these establishments, and there were many people, particularly men from the creeks, who scoffed at the moralizing of the Dawson elite. Their protests, plus the fact that the taxes paid by these establishments were crucial to the municipality, forced a hasty retreat. Morality in the Yukon had to be tempered by a little common sense and an eye on municipal revenues.[9]

The battle against prostitutes was similarly clouded. Several of the women who had crossed the passes in 1898 to mine the miners had married wealthy men. No longer "langorous lilies of soulless love," they now moved in comparatively respectable circles. Nor could those who were still in their original business be ignored, for Dawson was a small place, and these women were only too evident when they appeared in public. Early in 1901, Major Z.T. Wood of the NWMP announced that prostitutes were banned from Dawson City. Many left the Yukon for Nome or Tanana, while others went south, but some simply moved across the Yukon River to West Dawson, or across the Klondike River to "Lousetown" – Klondike City. This cut into their business considerably, for Lousetown was connected to Dawson by an open bridge, and the parade to the brothels required an exposure which many men – at least, those who worried about their reputation – did not care to undergo. The moral crusade continued, for prostitutes still came into town to shop, and their very presence offended some good citizens. Some even dared to continue their business in Dawson, flouting public authority but doing a land-office business. Civic officials and the police harassed them constantly.

The government, led by Commissioner Henderson, broadened the attack to include the dance halls, on the principle that cleaning them up would eradicate most of Dawson's immorality. This effort was ultimately successful, leading Mayor Wood to claim that Dawson City was "as free from immorality as any Eastern City, and much more so than any mining camp that has hitherto been known."[10] The saloons remained, as did the prostitutes, but by 1905 the reformers' protests had largely been satisfied. Brothels were forced to operate discreetly, as in southern cities, and the saloons had to obey a lengthy series of regulations. The police kept a close eye on all operations and moved quickly to stamp out any expansion of vice. The battles themselves represented Dawson's struggle for social respectability and the community's intense sensitivity to comments in the national press and in the House of Commons about immorality on the northern frontier. Dawsonites wanted to prove that civilization could flourish in the Northwest and that social stability had followed the heady and chaotic days of the gold rush.

The increasingly middle-class nature of Dawson society in the new century showed itself in other ways too. The civil servants, businessmen, police officers, and professionals who made up the middle class – and particularly their wives – struggled to erase the frontier nature of the community. Access to this group was strictly controlled; only those of suitable social and economic background were admitted. The arbiters of correct behaviour were the women, who made strenuous efforts to reproduce the social life of southern Canadian communities. Each woman had a "day," for which she produced elaborate invitations and hosted an "at home." Callers, dressed in their best, were feted with a fancy tea and refined conversation. Laura Berton, whose day fell on the second Tuesday of the month, described the process:

On one's day, one was at home to the entire town during the hours of the late afternoon and early evening. One spent many days before *the* day salting the almonds, preparing the olives, churning the sherbet in the freezer, preparing trays of home-made candies. One made sure the proper people were honoured by being allowed to "pour" or "pass," and the coefficient of success was calculated in direct ratio to the number of people who turned up. Thus it was possible to compute mathematically the social standing of the entire upper crust of Dawson City.[11]

The ritual was comical and rather sad in its artificiality – the irony was that Laura Berton, as an elementary school teacher, would not have been included in such a circle in Toronto or Vancouver, but in Dawson the definition of what constituted the "upper crust" had to be loosened considerably. In winter the social set went snowshoeing and sleighing or out on dogsled trips, or attended one of the town's many evening dinners and dances. Fancy-dress balls, which sent men and women scurrying to buy, make, or send outside for elaborate costumes, were held throughout the year – on St Andrew's Day, New Year's, Washington's Birthday, Easter, Discovery Day, and so on.[12] This, clearly, was a class-conscious society, fighting to eliminate the stigma of the town's frontier heritage and trying to be as modern and fashionable as their counterparts to the south. In this, Dawsonites were only doing as people have always done in similar situations, struggling to put a good face on their isolation and their distance from the centres of society, and anxious to make as few concessions as possible to their situation. Dawson was, at least in its pretensions, a society that could well have been plucked from southern Ontario and recreated on the banks of the Yukon River.

A society that aspires to elite status must of course have people to exclude, and the ones left out of Dawson's upper crust tended to be the colourful characters of the gold rush days who had given the community its unique character in the first place. According to Laura Berton, three of the richest and most influential businessmen in the Yukon – pioneer Big Alex McDonald, mine developer A.N.C. Treadgold, and the one-time sailor, boxer, and promoter extraordinaire Joe Boyle – were not welcome in the homes of select society. The former dance-hall girls, no matter who they had married, were beyond the pale, as were the miners, labourers, and transients who continued to make up a large percentage of Yukon society.[13]

The Yukon social pyramid was small after 1900, but it had sharply defined lines, in contrast to the rough egalitarianism of the years preceding the strike. At the top stood the commissioner and judges, the officers of the North-West Mounted Police, top civil servants, clergy (particularly the Anglican bishop), lawyers, bankers, leading businessmen, and single women from respectable professions – nursing and teaching – who though not of the financial elite, were welcome at the top as women who would balance the sex ratio somewhat. Below the upper crust and occasionally welcomed into its ranks, was the "downtown crowd," less prosperous merchants and small businessmen. Lower on the social ladder were the labourers, mine workers, and the constables of the North-West Mounted Police (who did not, in this period, come from the best of social backgrounds and were, moreover, miserably paid). At the bottom of the social heap were the white men with Native wives, mixed bloods, dance-hall girls, and prostitutes. Below them all were the First Nations people, most of whom stayed on the tiny Moosehide reserve downstream from Dawson City.[14]

There was another line that sharply divided Dawson society: politics. Patronage was, of course, a deeply entrenched Canadian tradition at this time, and when Laura Berton arrived in Dawson City the community was highly politicized: "Dawson at this time was a predominantly Liberal town. The Liberals held all the Government jobs and as a result most of the prominent socialites were Liberals."[15] While territorial Conservatives complained about the blatant favouritism, solidly Liberal newspapers carried the government's advertising, party supporters received preferential treatment on the awarding of the controversial mining concessions, and loyal Liberals received the lion's share of construction and supply contracts.

The federal election of 1911, which returned a majority Conservative government for the first time in fifteen years, demonstrated the strength of political influence in town. Dawson Tories went wild with delight, for the patronage plums were now theirs for the picking. Liberals, who held their government jobs primarily as a result of their political allegiance, skulked out of the territory, some not even waiting for official notice of their firing. Many Conservatives who had long since left the territory rushed back to take their places, notably George Black, long one of the city's dominant Tories, who claimed the prize of commissioner of the Yukon Territory. Political loyalties overlay all other divisions of the community, which owed so much of its existence to government patronage.[16]

Not everyone in Dawson conformed to the divisions of class, politics, and race. Bishop Stringer and his wife Sadie, who had moved the headquarters of the Yukon diocese to Dawson City in 1906, paid less attention to the social conventions than most others did. Sadie, in particular, welcomed Native people to her home, referring to them as "the roses around my door," and she often had the wives of First Nations missionaries staying there. The wife of Julius Kendi, a Native minister from Mayo, visited several times and was included in Mrs Stringer's social gatherings. Although the other ladies were clearly upset with this breach of social convention – as she well knew – she continued the practice.[17] But few followed her lead, for most members of the social elite found the social code a comfort, a barrier separating them from the harsher realities of life in the North.

It was within this social world that Robert Service, the "bard of the Klondike," operated. He wrote his first gold rush poems while working as a bank clerk in Whitehorse, before he had even visited the Klondike region, and he published his first volume, *Songs of a Sourdough*, shortly before he was transferred to the Dawson City bank. Service became a familiar if

Robert Service, bank clerk, poet, and "bard of the Klondike," was living in this modest cabin in Dawson City when this picture was taken in 1909 (YA).

shadowy figure on the social landscape, a loner who avoided social occasions and seldom sought companionship. At first he was a poet without honour in his own country – most Yukoners had never heard of him. When Governor General Earl Grey asked to meet him during his visit to Dawson, Service had to be rounded up and produced, since no one had thought of inviting him to the official reception. Eventually, he became the most famous Yukoner, and to his obvious discomfort his attendance at social functions became almost mandatory.

When the royalty cheques started rolling in, Service quit his job with the bank, but he remained in the North for a few years. He became even more reclusive and thought little of his own work. In a conversation with Laura Berton, he commented of his poetry, "That's the stuff the public wants. That's what they pay for. And I mean to give it to them."[18] Sensibly, he continued to profit by doing so. Eventually, he left the Yukon for southern France, where he continued to write, turning away from the Klondike to deal with other themes, but his inability to reproduce the commercial magic of his gold rush poetry darkened his later years.

By the time Service reached Dawson City, the appearance of the goldfields had changed tremendously. Just as Dawson society struggled to overcome isolation and gain some measure of stability, so the Klondike fields were undergoing major transformations. The days of the individual prospector and the mining methods that had produced the gold rush were finished as an important economic force, though a few loners still continued to work the more distant creeks. Now the symbol of the goldfields was not the pan but the dredge – the enormous, mechanical beast that slowly chewed its way like a dinosaur along the riverbeds. Dredges processed tons of gold-bearing gravel each day and could make a profit on a trace of gold in each cubic yard – pay dirt that could not support a miner working with simpler techniques. The first dredge arrived in the Yukon in 1900 and was moved to Bonanza Creek after a short but unsuccessful trial on the Yukon River. The second test was a success and demonstrated that the Klondike had life after the prospectors. High-tech mining was obviously the way of the future.[19]

The mining regulations of the early Klondike were, of course, not suited to the new technology, which required a consolidation of the old claims. The regulations had to be changed, with the backing of the federal government. Ignoring the recommendations originating in the North, which called for the preservation of the existing system, Clifford Sifton, minister of the interior, had decided that the future of the Klondike field lay in the introduction of these modern mining techniques, he had chosen James H. Ross as commissioner to undertake the difficult task of steering the new mineral regulations into operation.[20]

The basis of the system introduced by Sifton was the "concession" – a grant from the government permitting the concessionaire to buy up existing and lapsed claims, control water rights, and otherwise manage large areas of the goldfields. Although concessions had been granted as early as 1898, the system did not pick up steam until after Sifton introduced the new regulations in 1900, permitting the consolidation of claims and regulating the potential conflict between the needs of placer mining and those of the much larger concessions. By 1904 some forty-four concessions had been granted, some of them comprising 5 miles (8 km) or more of creek bed. The concessions were controversial from the beginning, not least because of charges of political favouritism in granting them – it was almost mandatory for an applicant for a concession to be a contributor to the Liberal Party.[21]

The most famous of the concessionaires was A.N.C. Treadgold, a former British public school master who had come to the Yukon in 1898 as correspondent for the *Mining Journal* and the *Manchester Guardian*. A short, energetic man, who in old age looked rather like a wizened gnome, Treadgold had an audacious vision of the new Klondike. He began to buy up claims, purchased an interest in other concessions, sought backing in England for his schemes, and came to Sifton with a plan for a massive reorganization of the Klondike creeks into one giant concession. To make it work, Treadgold asked the government for a virtual monopoly over water resources – the essential element in placer mining – plus large amounts of land, tax exemptions, and other privileges. Sifton was enthusiastic: "It is the chance of a lifetime to have the country put upon an enduring basis and development started upon a scale hitherto unknown in mining in Canada. Too much hypercriticism will wreck the whole plan."[22]

Despite some resistance in the Liberal cabinet, Treadgold was given a concession in 1901, though some of the more extreme elements of the original plan were modified. The concession gave Treadgold and his partners exclusive rights to a large part of the Klondike goldfields, including water and timber rights, for a period of thirty years.

The news was greeted with horror in the North, and Yukoners rallied against the scheme, which threatened to destroy the Klondike as they knew it. Public meetings, editorial protests, and dozens of letters to the government spelled out the general hostility. The Dawson board of trade complained of the "monopoly of [the] Treadgold Octopus" and demanded that the entire concession scheme be scrapped.[23] Although the protests were vehement and widespread throughout the territory, Sifton persisted. But in 1903, in his absence, the government agreed to the establishment of a royal commission, under Justice B.M. Britton, to be dispatched to the Yukon that summer to investigate the Treadgold affair. The commission's report was inconclusive, but the federal government, bowing to the storm, cancelled the concession in 1904.

Sifton blamed this debacle on Treadgold's "stubborn narrowness & complete incapacity for business of a large scale."[24] Sifton himself remained convinced that large-scale mining was the only possible future for the Klondike fields, an opinion echoed in the Britton Report. However, he was losing interest in the Yukon, which he now held responsible for its own economic distress. Gold production had been falling precipitously, from over a million fine ounces in 1900, worth $24 million, to slightly over 420,000 ounces in 1905.

In fact, consolidation was already underway, as miners banded together to operate their claims more efficiently. But the gold discoveries at Nome and Tanana had drained much of the entrepreneurial vitality from the region. Change was coming, but not on the scale the government wanted. Sifton believed that the violent reaction to the Treadgold proposal had probably deterred potential investors. Moreover, he had other struggles to tend to, including the political battle that would soon lead to his resignation from the Liberal Party.

The immediate future of the Yukon looked gloomy. James Ross, who had now become the Yukon's first member of parliament, was still well respected in the North but had fizzled in Ottawa, seldom attending the Commons and proving unable to defend Yukon interests adequately. As the *Dawson News* editorialized, Ross was "as impotent as a katydid in a simoon."[25] With the cancellation of the Treadgold concession and the report of the Britton Commission, the Yukon was left without a plan for its economy. The old methods were failing to sustain the territory, the new proposals had been rejected, and the future was unclear.

Treadgold's dream of consolidation had not yet died, nor had the concessions been completely eliminated. Obviously something had to be done to update or replace the old placer-mining system, and efforts to modernize the operations continued. The Klondike Mines Railway was under construction from Dawson to the creeks – it passed over one of Treadgold's Bonanza Creek claims – and was completed to the creeks in 1906. Construction of the line led to an incident which showed that there was still something unique about life in the Yukon:

Treadgold did not like the fact that the railway crossed one of his claims ... so he proceeded to the claim ... and removed a rail from the track ... Jerome Chute, railway contractor, politely picked up Mr. Treadgold and lifted him off the track and deposited him some feet from the track. Treadgold in the meantime made an effort to free himself, but not until the more skookum Mr. Chute deposited him beside the track as aforesaid. The railway crew relaid the track, while Contractor Chute held Mr. Treadgold. Treadgold afterwards returned to the middle of the track and refused to get off to let the engine pass onto his claims. Dave Curry, foreman, took Mr. Treadgold in charge, and knelt upon the chest of Mr. Treadgold until the engine passed. The story of the incident ... was the subject of considerable talk.[26]

But the railway never showed a profit, and it closed in 1914.

In 1905 Treadgold continued to lay financial plans, flitting about the Yukon, then leaving in the fall to seek out financial backers. The following year, a construction team arrived with orders from Treadgold to build a water ditch 70 miles (112 km) long, stretching by means of ditch, flume, pipe, and inverted siphon from Twelve Mile River to Bonanza Creek. Thus did Treadgold hope to get around the contentious matter of water supplies – the issue that had stalled his earlier grandiose scheme to corner the Klondike fields.

Treadgold continued to buy up properties, picking up small claims and some of the remaining concessions, that increasing his already impressive list of holdings in the Klondike. Word leaked out that he had the financial backing of the wealthy Guggenheim family, and when two of the Guggenheims visited the Klondike in 1906 it seemed as though the dreams about a revitalized gold-mining operation were about to come true. Work continued on the water ditches, additional dredges were built, and a power plant to supply

This flume, 6 ft wide and 3 ft deep (roughly 2 x 1 m), was part of the Yukon Gold Company's "Yukon ditch," which carried water for more than 70 miles (115 km). The water was used for the company's hydraulic operations in 1908 (YA).

Even as the last wave of Klondike prospectors were scouring the creeks for gold, more sophisticated developers were introducing new technology to northern mining. These hydraulic operations at Hunker Creek, c. 1900, were among the first in the Yukon (authors' collection).

the electric dredges was begun. In October 1906, the registering of a large block of claims surrounding Bonanza, Eldorado, and Hunker creeks under the Yukon Consolidated Goldfields Company and Northwest Hydraulic Mining Company provided final confirmation of the scale of the Guggenheim interest. The consolidation process was well underway.

By 1907 the results of the new investments were apparent. A sawmill at Twelve Mile Creek, water ditches, the Twelve Mile power plant, and the new dredges – each weighing close to eight hundred tons – were all in service. New steam-thawing techniques were used to loosen the permanently frozen gravel. Through the summer, work also started on the construction of four new dredges from parts brought in during the previous year. Operations were streamlined under the newly formed Yukon Gold Company, which was still controlled by the Guggs, as the family was known in the Yukon. Treadgold sat on the company's board of directors but was not as active in the Yukon operations as he had been. So dominant was the new enterprise that many of the remaining operators worked over their richest ground and then sold their holdings to Yukon Gold.

These developments brought the Yukon squarely into the mainstream of the world economy, a process that raised new problems. In the old days, the Yukon mines succeeded or failed on the initiative of individual miners and the richness of the ground. Now the mines were at the mercy of distant stock exchanges and the vagaries of international capitalism. In 1908 a stock market collapse in the United States raised questions about the Yukon Gold Company's strength. Some questionable promotion of its stock by a financier named Thomas Lawson resulted in bad publicity for the company and some difficulty in continuing with the work in the Yukon. There was a public outcry when the company tried to bring in low-paid contract labour from Vancouver. Eventually, however, Yukon Gold put its operations in order and began mining. When the Twelve Mile Ditch opened in 1909, there was a major expansion of hydraulic and dredging operations. The company continued to buy up gold properties, and although gold production remained far below the level of a decade earlier, the company continued to show a profit.

But Yukon Gold and the Guggenheims had little commitment to the Yukon. Profits from the operation were, after the first years, transferred to southern investors through dividend payments. There was little reinvestment and no real attempt to diversify. As Yukon returns dipped during the First World War, with labour in short supply and costs high, the company began to shift its operations to new goldfields in such places as Alaska, Idaho, and Malaya. One by one, the dredges were shut down and dismantled. By the middle of the war, the Guggenheims had lost interest in the Yukon and abandoned any hope of long-term profits. According to one estimate, the company took more than $31 million in gold from its Klondike

Hydraulic mining extracted a considerable toll from the environment. In addition to diverting water supplies, it involved the systematic stripping of dirt and gravel from gold-bearing hills, such as this one at Lovett Gulch, in 1911 (YA).

properties during this period, delivering more than $9.8 million in dividends to its shareholders. In that day, few asked what Yukon Gold delivered to the Yukon in return.

Despite its size and dominance, Yukon Gold was not alone in the goldfields. Joe Boyle, best known as a tough and aggressive mining promoter, was a formidable competitor. Boyle had been involved with the Klondike since 1897, when he bought into a large concession near Hunker and Bonanza creeks. He and his partner Frank Slavin were boxers, who with some others had applied for a large concession and later discussed selling it to Treadgold. Some preliminary work was done on the project, but the concession was soon embroiled in the leasing controversy that ended with the establishment of the Britton Commission.[27]

Boyle could do little more than cut wood on the property, trying in vain to raise enough money to start full-scale mining. Facing considerable opposition within the Yukon, he headed outside in an attempt to raise money. In 1904 he found supporters in the Detroit Yukon Mining Company, a small concession that was already active in the Klondike fields and was building a railway to help with mining operations. Boyle negotiated a deal with the group, which led to the formation of the Canadian Klondyke Mining Com-

The final stage in extracting gold from the creeks was dredging. The piles of tailings deposited by dredges such as this one are still a feature of the lower Klondike River valley (authors' collection).

pany. The new company began work in 1905, establishing a power plant on Bear Creek and constructing a new dredge. The other principals, particularly the famously wealthy Rothschild family, took an active interest in the property, visiting the Yukon several times to oversee mining operations.

In 1907 Boyle found himself embroiled in a legal controversy with his fellow investors. The Detroit group had agreed to sell to the Guggenheim interests, a move that Boyle protested vehemently. The court case was initially decided in Boyle's favour, but the struggle continued. In 1909 Boyle and his former partners finally settled the matter in a deal that permitted him to buy out the outstanding shares in the company, leaving him in full control of Canadian Klondyke, with the financial resources necessary to keep his mining operation in the field. Always anxious to outstrip Yukon Gold and Treadgold, and ever the optimist, Boyle announced in 1910 that he was building the world's largest dredge – Canadian no. 2 – a behemoth costing over $300,000 and capable of handling more than 350,000 cubic feet (10,000 m³) of gravel each day. Boyle, his finances secure, now represented a formidable challenge to Treadgold's plans for control of the Klondike.

Although Treadgold had helped create the Guggenheim empire in the Klondike, he disliked working for others. He eventually decided to sell out his holdings in Yukon Gold and go it alone. Work on his properties began in earnest in 1909–10, marked by the construction of a substantial power plant on the Klondike River. Treadgold split his time between supervising the construction and mining crews in the Yukon and floating deals in the financial centres of North America and England. His new company, Granville Mining Company (which included a future American president, Herbert Hoover, among its partners), now moved to dominate the Klondike.

Key to the scheme was an amalgamation with Joe Boyle. A complex stock deal, which allowed both Treadgold and Boyle to control their operations while permitting joint ventures on projects of mutual importance, was struck in 1912. Boyle appears to have got the better of the deal, and he gained considerable control over the goldfields as a result. The two men did not work well together, for Treadgold's regal demeanour was at odds with Boyle's more confrontive and abrasive style. Both sought to be "King of the Klondike." Neither was comfortable sharing the spotlight. They tried to unravel their complex affairs, trading stock, forming new companies, adopting new technology, and expanding mining operations in new directions. Treadgold's gamble did not pay off. His supporters tired of his endless promises and began to pull out of the Granville Mining Company. By the middle of the First World War he had lost control of the gold-mining empire he had built. By 1920 he was bankrupt, and his dream of controlling the Klondike seemed dead.

Treadgold's loss was Boyle's gain. Under his direction, Canadian Klondyke continued to expand operations, its balance sheet showing a healthy profit. The paper machinations also continued, as Boyle created a new entity, Boyle Concessions, to combine his various holdings. Assets were shifted back and forth between his various corporate shells. Boyle was now truly the "King of the Klondike." His trains ran regularly between Dawson City and the creeks, new dredges were put into use, gold production expanded, and in 1913 he purchased the Northern Light, Power and Coal Company, which supplied electricity to Dawson City. Boyle was a "hands-on" administrator, routinely involved with the field operations of his Klondike holdings. But it was not all clear sailing, for Boyle found himself embroiled in numerous court cases, several involving Yukon Gold. The companies' properties were so close that Boyle's dredging operations threatened even the physical stability of the Guggenheim facilities.

The two companies were dramatically different. Boyle was a Yukon booster, revelling in his stature as the local magnate. He was active in community affairs, including a bizarre scheme to take a Yukon team to compete for the 1905 Stanley Cup that ended in ignominious failure. The Guggenheims, in contrast, were outsiders, exploiting the territory's resources, doing most of their purchasing and hiring in the south, only marginally committed to the stability and future of the Yukon. Boyle made many investments in the territory, some of which (his ownership of the Dawson utilities, for instance) brought him much grief and controversy.

Boyle's operation ran into difficulty during the First World War. Like Yukon Gold, Canadian Klondyke had trouble finding enough workers and faced continually rising prices. The company also ran into financial problems and at times had trouble meeting the payroll. Boyle's credit dried up, and his legal troubles – an ever more complex web of corporate and personal entanglements – continued. When in 1916 he left for Europe and his strange, dramatic future, he put his son, Joe Boyle Jr, a training mining engineer, in charge of his company. But Joe Jr could not pull the company out of its financial and legal morass, and in January 1918 Canadian Klondyke passed into receivership. The short-term reign of the "King" was over; the pretender to the throne was in the wings and would return shortly.

While Boyle's struggle for the Klondike had captured the territory's attention, other miners had turned their eyes to other parts of the Yukon. The transition from Dawson to other regions was difficult and painful, hampered by fears that the Yukon's wealth was played out. As economist Kenneth Rea has noted, "by 1914 the public conception of the Yukon as a land of quick wealth had been transformed into a growing conviction that the territory was not worth the expense associated with maintaining it."[28] Nonetheless, the ever-optimistic prospectors were determined to put life back into the Yukon economy. It would not be easy, and the returns would be slow in coming.

Before the gold rush, miners had found promising traces of gold on Livingstone Creek, and there had been a modest rush to the district. Joseph Peters, in partnership with George Black, had developed a good deposit of placer gold. A small community sprang up with the usual dancehall, saloon, stores, roadhouse, and Mounted Police detachment. But the creek was hard to reach – 44 miles (70 km) by a twisting winter trail from Lake Laberge – and the gold was limited. Nonetheless, the original claims produced an estimated $1 million by 1920.[29]

Early in the century, gold had been discovered on creeks emptying onto the west side of Kluane Lake. Prospectors and speculators once more raced to the strike, set amidst the towering mountains and ice-cold lakes of the southwest. The stampede, like so many others, lasted a year or two. A couple of the prospectors, Eugene and Louis Jacquot, stayed on, their imagination captured by the dramatic beauty of the Kluane district. The Jacquots established a trading and shipping company and were among the first to recognize the opportunities for big-game hunting in the territory. But their hopes of reproducing the success of Joe Ladue, the fast-moving businessman who had capitalized on the Klondike rush, were dashed by the inconsequential gold discoveries. However, the brothers were captivated by the beauty of the region, and both married local First Nations women and settled in the Kluane district.[30]

The search for a new Bonanza reached to all corners of the territory. Small gleanings of gold had been taken before 1900 from the Firth River, which flows north into the Arctic Ocean, but little development had ensued. Excitement soared when Ben Smith and Jujiro Wada, a Japanese adventurer and prospector, made a promising strike in March 1908. Ten groups of prospectors headed into the isolated zone the next summer, scouring the Firth and Old Crow regions for further evidence of major deposits. They failed, though a few hopeful adventurers continued their explorations. By 1913, most of the prospectors had abandoned the field – yet another illusory "Eldorado" that kept alive dreams of a second Klondike."[31] Only slowly did Yukoners begin to consider the possibility that their future might not lie in gold. The rapid improvement of transportation, stimulated by the opening of the White Pass and Yukon Railway and the expansion of steamship service, made it reasonable to think of exporting other ores of greater bulk but lower value.

Miners had been active along the Stewart River for decades. There had been sporadic strikes, and prospectors had pushed up the river, hoping that the many creeks and rivers held another great gold deposit. The arrival in 1901 of some two hundred miners led to the development of a small community at Mayo and the construction of a road to the lower Stewart River. New gold discoveries followed in subsequent years, enough to maintain enthusiasm, but not sufficient to set off a full-scale rush. Mayo developed into a minor regional centre, the terminus of steamboat travel along the Stewart River, and connected to Dawson by winter "stage" (a giant sled that served as a stagecoach).

In July 1903 Jacob Davidson had uncovered a rich deposit of silver and lead near Galena Creek, a small pup some 19 miles (30 km) from Mayo. The claim was permitted to lapse, but Davidson's partner, H.W. McWhorter, regained control of the property and arranged for a trial shipment of ore to the Consolidated Mining and Smelting Company's smelter in Trail, British Columbia. Shipping costs were steep, but the high-grade ore paid for them and provided a healthy return besides. The Silver King claim was sold to Thomas Aitken and Henry Munroe, who also tested the waters, sending a shipment of a thousand tons of ore to a San Francisco smelter. Shipping costs continued to plague the enterprise. It cost more than sixty dollars a ton to transport and process the ore, one-third of the expense being on the short journey from the mine to Mayo. Shipments continued but only of the highest-grade ore, for the owners simply could not support a larger operation. Yet the richness of the original strike was sufficient to encourage other prospectors to continue the search for additional silver and lead deposits. They did find their new Bonanza, though not until after the First World War.[32]

Copper was also added to the Yukon's short list of marketable resources. During the gold rush, prospectors had discovered a massive copper deposit surrounding Whitehorse. Although the deposit was large and rich, low prices for the metal and the high cost of transporting ore to the railhead by road kept excitement in check. In 1900 two prospectors named McIntyre and Granger developed their Copper King deposit and made a trial shipment. But copper prices were extremely volatile, and the Whitehorse mines were subject to the fluctuations of the international market. In 1906 prices skyrocketed, leading to preliminary construction of a railway spur line towards the mines. When prices fell by half the following year, work stopped, not to pick up again for another three years.

After 1912 copper prices stabilized, and under pressure from Ottawa the White Pass and Yukon Railway reduced its rates. With the onset of the First World War, demand picked up and the copper mines became profitable. Atlas Mining dominated the field, operating such rich properties as Pueblo, Arctic Chief, War Eagle, and Grafter. Production rose from 286,000 pounds (130,000 kg) in 1910 to over 1,800,000 pounds (816,500 kg) in 1913, and peaked in 1916, when more than 2,800,000 pounds (1,270,000 kg) of copper ore left the territory. The mines, operating on the temporary wartime profitability, did not last long. They were doomed by a combination of water seepage (which made pumping costly) high transportation costs, and unreliable markets. Operations ceased in 1920, to be revived temporarily late in the decade. Only in the 1960s did copper mining again form a major part of the territorial economy.[33]

Here and there throughout the territory there were other hopeful signs. For a couple of years a silver mine operated at Conrad, on Tagish Lake; and the Engineer Mine, a major gold operation on the lake, was based on a discovery by Captain Alexander, an English Boer War veteran who had been active in the region since 1903.

Despite the widespread perception that mining was the Yukon's sole economic activity, the fur trade remained very much alive in this period. High prices, improved transportation, and the opportunity to combine prospecting with trading led to a rapid expansion in the number of independent traders active in the field. Many had little attachment to the area, and they exploited the trade for a quick profit. But in contrast with the general northern experience, a number of reputable, reliable, and trustworthy traders also opened shop in this period. Taylor and Drury quickly expanded throughout the territory, and Eugene and Louis Jacquot put down roots at Burwash Landing. In the Far North, Dan Cadzow moved into the void left by the departure of the Hudson's Bay Company. Like many of the Yukon traders, Cadzow planned to stay for a long time and treated the First Nations people with respect and honesty. Thomas Riggs, who visited Rampart House in 1911, said of Cadzow's operation: "The place is run as closely to old Hudson's Bay practice as possible. Practically all material was traditional Hudson's Bay,

Rampart House enjoyed renewed life in the early twentieth century as a revitalized fur trade brought traders back into the Porcupine River valley. Dan Cadzow, the most prominent of the traders, established a profitable trade there (YA).

such as the old-time axe shapes, the Assomption sashes, blankets, etc. I think Dan liked to think of himself as a Hudson's Bay factor."[34]

While the Yukon escaped some of the abuses that plagued the northern fur trade, there were still many problems. Prospectors, desperate to get a grubstake for future exploration, joined the hunt for furs, often paying little attention to the long-term future of the resource. As Frederick Congdon wrote in 1910, "One difference between hunting by trappers and by Indians is that, while the Indian always leaves a stock of all fur bearing animals in a district to continue the species, the white man does not. He goes into a 'creek' and absolutely extinguishes all the individuals in it and therefore makes it impossible that it should be restocked from any animals left in the district."[35]

The territorial government did little to regulate the fur trade, which was considered to be of minor importance to the Yukon economy. Because there were no export taxes, the government did not keep track of the thousands of pelts leaving the Yukon each year, most of which found their way to American markets. Not until 1919 did the Yukon government begin to extract some revenue from the resource and start to take note of the substantial contribution the fur trade made to the regional economy.

While officials paid little attention to Yukon furs, international dealers had long noted the quality of the region's production. This was particularly true of fox skins, among the most valuable pelts in the early twentieth century. The demand for Yukon foxes was such that trappers and traders did a substantial business in live-trapping the animals for shipment to southern fox farms. In time, Yukon entrepreneurs saw the wisdom of establishing their own fur farms. The territorial council began to regulate the trade in 1914, requiring licences to operate fur farms and limiting the live-trapping operations. Within two years, seventeen fox farms, most small in size, were in operation. Fox farming seemed to offer greater stability than the hunt for wild animals, but it too was vulnerable to the fluctuations of international markets. Fox farming fell off dramatically in the next decade, and many operators went out of business while others shifted to the trickier task of raising mink.[36]

That the Yukon economy kept afloat at all reflected the continued improvement of territorial transportation. Construction projects undertaken during the Klondike gold rush reached fruition only after the Klondike fields had gone into decline. As the economy declined, regional transportation actually improved, a reflection of the White Pass and Yukon Railway's commitment to the area and the technological advances in navigation.

The completion of the White Pass and Yukon Railway to Whitehorse in 1900 was the major turning point. The railway did not replace river travel. Since Whitehorse was more than 300 mile (500 km) from Dawson, the sternwheelers remained very much in use. But with access from Skagway to Whitehorse now assured, the pattern of bringing supplies and people in by way of the Bering Strait and the lower Yukon River was quickly altered. The upper Yukon, and hence the Skagway, Carcross, Whitehorse, and Dawson City corridor, dominated the regional transportation system during the first half of the twentieth century.[37]

As the dominant force in Yukon transportation, and anxious for the advantages of controlling the entire transportation system, the White Pass and Yukon Railway (WPYR) began to diversify into river operations. A subsidiary company, the British Yukon Navigation Company (BYNC), was created, and shipyards were built in Whitehorse and Dawson. The BYNC began to build sternwheelers and to buy out its competitors. Others could not compete with the co-ordinated rail and river system, and by 1904 the BYNC had all but eliminated the competition on the upper Yukon.

On the lower Yukon, a similar consolidation of American carriers ensued, a reaction to the rapidly contracting economy in the area. By 1910 it was clear that the Yukon basin could not support two separate transportation systems – either the upper or the lower river networks would have to go. After a battle made brief by the fact that neither side was financially strong, the American-owned Northern Navigation Company surrendered. A new White Pass subsidiary, the American Yukon Navigation Company, was formed in 1914 to operate the lower Yukon boats in cooperation with the upper river service. The upper Yukon had wrested control of the Yukon River from Alaska, thus ensuring the continued viability of the railway and the Whitehorse-based steamers.

The resolution of the transportation battle ensured the continuation of the unique international community in the Yukon and Alaska. Many of those who had rushed to the new goldfields in Nome and Tanana or to later strikes in Ruby and Iditarod had previously lived in Dawson City. Klondike experience became a link between the people of the Yukon basin as they followed the careers of pioneers who had moved elsewhere in the North. The revised transportation system required that almost anyone entering or leaving the Northwest had to pass through Skagway, Whitehorse, or Dawson. National boundaries meant little to people so tied together by history, common surroundings, and now a single transportation route linking them to the outside.[38]

The economic condition of the region was such that transport companies did little to extend the riverboat network. Traders in isolated areas either operated their own boats, as Taylor and Drury did, or contracted with small operators to carry supplies up the Porcupine, Pelly, or other rivers. Where possible, government steamers, particularly those operated by the Mounted Police, were made available to the public. The government even provided modest subsidies for companies such as Side Streams Navigation, founded in 1909, which were willing to operate along the Stewart, a shallow, rock-filled river that required special shallow-draft sternwheelers.

The British Yukon Navigation Company's triumph over its rival gave it tremendous influence over the territory. Its freight rates determined the survival of businesses in the Yukon, as the Whitehorse copper miners and the Mayo developers discovered to their chagrin. The same was true of Whitehorse, the Yukon's first real company town. Businesses had watched the construction of the railway carefully. When the railhead neared Whitehorse, the Yukon retailers Whitney and Pedlar and their rivals Taylor and Drury rushed into town. It was soon evident that the landholdings, freight yards, and boat docks of the railway would dominate the community. By 1910, most of the people in town worked for the WPYR or its subsidiary, the BYNC Those who did not were wise enough to realize that the fate of their community rested on the success of the rail and river system.[39]

Despite its power, the WPYR was not omnipotent. High freight rates, seen by the company as essential for corporate survival but by most customers as exploitation, led to a series of confrontations. Businesses strug-

FE.WHITE   WHITEHORSE YUKON   Nov 1901

Whitehorse, seen here in 1901, was the link between the railroad and steamboat
traffic on the Yukon River. The town grew little before 1940, partly because
of the seasonal nature of river traffic and partly because of the control exerted
by the British Yukon Navigation Company, which owned most of the land
in the town (NA, PA 17211).

gling to survive in a rapidly declining economy pleaded with the WPYR to
keep rates low. At times, freight rates to the Yukon exceeded the wholesale
value of the goods carried. The company was clearly putting its investors'
needs first: "The directors of the White Pass and Yukon Route recognized
that the days of the 'fast buck' in the Yukon were over and they followed
a conscious policy of 'getting all that they could, while the getting was
good.' The shareholders extracted every last possible profit from the operation, oblivious to the needs of the Yukon and to the detriment of the physical facilities of the railway."[40] It was a familiar corporate tale, one too
often repeated in Yukon history. Yukoners struggling to make a home in the
North and to establish some measure of stability viewed the transportation
companies' prices as exorbitant and a tremendous affront. They protested

often and loudly to Ottawa, and in 1911 the WPYR agreed to a voluntary re-duction in the tariffs.[41]

Elsewhere in the territory the progress of transportation was more cloud-ed. The Klondike Mines Railway was never a success, despite government subsidies. The Overland Trail, linking Dawson to Whitehorse during the winter months, suffered a similar fate. It had its genesis when the Canadian Development Company secured a contract to deliver the mail – one of the few secure sources of revenue around – and used this as a basis for its over-land operations. The WPYR, continuing its efforts to control all aspects of Yukon transportation, bought out the Canadian Development Company in 1901, and the following year the government awarded it a contract to build a winter trail between Whitehorse and Dawson. The Overland Trail, some 330 miles (530 km) long, was open by November 1902, permitting regular movement between Whitehorse and Dawson City for all but a few weeks each year. The journey took about five days, with meals and overnight stays at some of the many roadhouses built along the route – a rough, jarring ex-pedition that tested the endurance of travellers.

Beyond this, little was done to improve transportation in the Yukon. The gradual introduction of automobiles – the first car arrived on the Overland Trail in 1912 – encouraged improvements to the main trails and the con-struction of short roads near the communities. But the small population and the paucity of automobiles convinced the government not to spend the money necessary to build a proper road system. The Dawson area received most of the road-building grants, as befitted its needs and political clout. Continued activity across the river from Dawson City led to the construc-tion of a cable ferry across the Yukon River, thereby providing for regular and inexpensive transit throughout the area.

While roads, a railway, and riverboats moved people and supplies more expeditiously around the territory than had previously been possible, the Yukon was still very much an outpost of Canadian civilization in the years before the First World War. Communication with southern Canada, partic-ularly with the federal government in Ottawa, was painfully slow at first, leaving Yukoners with an uneasy feeling of isolation and adding to their well-founded sense of being ignored by other North Americans. In 1899 the Department of Public Works opened a telegraph link from Dawson to Skag-way. By sending telegrams on the coastal steamers to Vancouver, messages could reach Ottawa in four to five days. The Department of Public Works then began construction of an all-Canadian telegraph line, linking the Yukon with the British Columbia telegraph grid. The new system became operative in 1901, cutting the delivery time in half and making Yukoners more a part of the North American mainstream.[42]

The federal government was not interested in investing in the economic future of the Yukon, but neither was it prepared to let the Yukon manage its own economic destiny. The country's hold on its northland was too weak and too recent to permit the largely American frontier community to determine its own future. Fortunately for Ottawa, there was a ready means of reconciling parsimony and the responsibilities of token sovereignty – the Mounted Police.

Renamed the Royal North-West Mounted Police (RNWMP) in 1904, the force found itself with even more duties than it had shouldered during the hectic years of the Klondike gold rush. When the government began laying off civil servants early in the twentieth century and decided in 1904 to disincorporate the city of Dawson, additional duties fell to the police. New posts were established in the southern Yukon, at Teslin and Dalton Post, in an attempt to regulate the flow of liquor from British Columbia and Alaska to the aboriginal people in the Yukon. These posts were largely ineffective, since the aboriginal people could cross the border into Alaska to drink, but the government felt that the gesture had to be made. When new communities opened up – Mayo, Livingstone Creek, Conrad, and Burwash – the police were there almost as soon as the prospectors. The force also moved into the fur-trade districts, providing some measure of control and support for the largely indigenous population along the Pelly and Porcupine rivers.[43]

The RNWMP did not ignore the enormous area and the hundreds of Yukoners who were not served directly by the permanent settlements. Before the day of extended radio service and the airplane, routine police patrols carried the mail, made scheduled visits to trappers or settlers in the backcountry, registered mining claims in new districts, carried supplies, and checked on local game conditions. These patrols were usually undertaken on foot in the dead of winter. At other times river navigation provided faster and more reliable. There were also many special patrols – to search for criminals, investigate complaints of overhunting, search for lost prospectors or hunters, carry sick people to hospital, or conduct surveys of previously unexplored territory. Although many Mounties were stationed in the territory for only a short time, some stayed for many years and made a sustained effort to integrate themselves and the law they represented into their communities.

The churches contributed significantly to the post-rush Yukon. Most retained at least some presence after 1900. The Anglican Church predominated, largely because of its strong presence in the Yukon before the gold rush. But like the other denominations, it had difficulties. Bishop Bompas, whose sponsor, the Church Missionary Society, supported only Native missions and was not particularly interested in spiritual work among the mining population, had trouble attracting enough clergy and paying those who came. However, the church did send a few men. Isaac Stringer (who had left Herschel Island on leave in 1903) was followed by the Reverend Hiram A. Cody, later a well-known novelist and the biographer of Bompas, who arrived in 1904. Some southern clergy came north because they had been infected by an ecclesiastical variant of gold rush fever. E.P. Purdy, rector of St Matthew's Cathedral in Brandon, Manitoba, succumbed to the disease, left his charge, and came north to Dawson to work with the miners. Like that of many of the stampeders, Purdy's interest in the territory quickly waned, and he left after two years.

Attempts to secure more clergy ran afoul of a national church that was more interested in international missions than northern work. Bompas, in his usual undiplomatic style, condemned the lack of support: "We in the west have [allowed] ourselves to be completely mastered by the east. They use us as they like, give us what small modicum of help they like and assume control of our work and expenditures & restrict us from our efforts to raise funds. The MSCC [Missionary Society of the Canadian Church] is I think a failure. Our connection with it should be dissolved and the west be independent. The future belongs to the west & it may soon control the east."[44] Never comfortable with whites, Bompas retreated to the security of a First Nations pastorate in Carcross, where he remained until he relinquished control of the Yukon church to Bishop Stringer in 1905, on Stringer's return from his leave.

Stringer quickly moved to raise the church's profile. Having moved the diocese's headquarters to Dawson City, he organized a territory-wide synod for 1907, which resulted in a strongly worded series of resolutions calling for protection of Native harvesting rights, better housing for Native people, and government grants for day and residential schools. Stringer was well suited to his task. While he had enough of the social graces to be accepted by Dawson society, he was also able to relate to the aboriginal people and workingmen who belonged to his church. A careful and practical administrator rather than a mystic, Stringer was a welcome change from Bompas.[45]

Other denominations were also active in the years following the gold rush, especially around Dawson. The Presbyterians had the fiery reformer John Pringle. Roman Catholic work fell under the control of the Reverend Bunoz of the Oblates, who oversaw a series of mission stations around the territory. Meanwhile, the Sisters of St Anne operated a school and hospital in the gold rush capital. While the Yukon was not a conventionally religious society, the number and variety of churches in Dawson and the existence of clergy in Whitehorse, Mayo, and Conrad added a civilizing touch to the area.[46]

While most denominations worked with the miners, the Anglican Church tried to balance service to the white population with a large Native mission field. Even though Stringer had moved to Dawson, largely to re-establish a few bridges to the white community, the church remained active in the backcountry. In 1911, for example, the church supported stations at Moosehide, Fortymile, Selkirk, Whitehorse, Teslin, Champagne, Carcross, and Rampart House. As mentioned above, filling the missions was not easy. Whereas Bompas had found most of his recruits in Britain, Stringer enjoyed greater success with recent graduates from Canadian theological colleges. A few of the missionaries served lengthy terms, but most stayed only a few years, working up the ecclesiastical ladder from Native mission to a non-Native congregation to a placement outside. Cecil Swanson, whose career followed such a path, thought little of the process: "I felt that I should have been left there [Little Salmon] for at least seven years. It takes time to develop a trusting relationship with the Indians, and a lifetime to learn and use the language ... Short-term missionaries are useless."[47]

Stringer solved the manpower shortage, at least in part, by hiring Native clergy. Bompas, though fond of aboriginals as people, had had little confidence in them as clerics, but the new bishop was more sanguine. A number of First Nations lay readers were ordained and assigned to Native congregations in the northern half of the territory. Native clergy required greater supervision than their academically trained white counterparts, but their Christian determination, willingness to stay in the North, and much lower salaries justified their employment. Although the Anglican Church was slow to recognize it, the widespread use of aboriginal lay readers and clergy played a major role in the long-term allegiance of the First Nations of the Yukon to that denomination.[48]

The church was determined to prepare the aboriginal people for a modern, industrial future. The cornerstone to this plan was a modest day-school program and an aggressive campaign to secure government funding for a residential school. Day-school classes were run by missionaries, white church members, and, in a few cases, aboriginal lay readers. Parents seldom kept their children in classes for long; the dictates of harvesting almost always won out over the protests of the teachers. The quality of the staff varied widely. Bishop Stringer defended the hiring of Jacob Kendi, a Native man, at Rampart House in 1916 in a rather back-handed fashion: "He is perhaps not as well qualified to teach as most of our teachers, but he was the best man available. Again, at this place the Indians have to go off for weeks and months to hunt and fish, so that school can be held only when they come to the Post for a few weeks." Under such conditions little could be expected. T.G. Bragg, superintendent of education for the Yukon, bemoaned the effort: "The ordinary day schools are practically useless, and the energy and money expended in maintaining them are comparatively barren of results." Not surprisingly, the Anglican clergy thought that a residential school would show better results.[49]

Residential schools had been in place in southern Canada for several decades, but the results had been disappointing. By 1905, both the Anglican Church and the federal government were questioning their usefulness. When approached on the topic by the Yukon clergy, Frank Oliver, minister of the interior, commented,

My belief is that the attempt to elevate the Indian by separating the child from his parents and educating him as a white man has turned out to be a deplorable failure ... The mutual love between parent and child is the strongest influence for the betterment of the world, and when that influence is absolutely cut apart or is deliberately intended to be cut apart as in the education of Indian children in industrial schools the means taken defeats itself ... To teach an Indian child that his parents are degraded beyond measure and that whatever they did or thought was wrong could only result in the child becoming, as the ex-pupils of the industrial schools have become, admittedly and unquestionably a very much less desirable element of society than their parents who never saw the schools.[50]

But such opinions were unfashionable in that era, and political considerations soon forced Oliver to ignore his own advice.

Bishop Bompas had moved his small church-funded boarding school – an orphanage, really – when he shifted the centre of church operations from Fortymile to Carcross in 1904. He and his successor were anxious to expand the school and repeatedly petitioned the government for the necessary funding. Bompas did not live to see his dream fulfilled. He died in June 1906, his passing much mourned by his Native friends, though by few whites. In 1908 Ottawa agreed to send two educational inspectors to assess the schooling needs of the Yukon First Nations. They reported favourably on the Anglicans' efforts and encouraged the government to fund the school. The new facility, built at a cost of more than $10,000, opened in Carcross in 1911, the jewel of the Anglican plans for the moral and cultural improvement of the Yukon First Nations. It would take a decade or more for the first children to work their way through the school. For the time being, Stringer and his clergy turned to the difficult task of convincing aboriginal parents to part with their children and send them to the new residential school.[51]

While the government responded favourably to this program for aboriginal people, it was far less generous in its treatment of the territory as a whole. Led by an active and vocal Dawson City press, Yukoners voiced their displeasure over planned mining regulations, new royalties, government services, and alleged corruption within government ranks. They had much to complain about, from the lack of elected representation at the local and federal level, to misguided or ill-timed federal attempts to regulate the placer-mining sector. The tremendous furor over the concession system had only added to regional resentment.

Improvements came slowly. Back in 1896 and 1897, as the gold rush gathered momentum, the government had to take some action. Consequently, money started to trickle north for roads, bridges, wharves, more civil servants to handle the deluge of government business, an expanded police force to supervise the swarming mob of prospectors, and an improved mail service – a constant concern of isolated northerners. That the progress was so slow reflected both Ottawa's determination not to offer provincial status to this isolated, transient society and a fear that the largely American population might, if given the political power, move in directions contrary to Canadian interests in the North.

A general description of federal legislation in the Yukon would tell little about the actual nature of the evolution of government structures. The handling of administrative matters – the point of contact between citizens and government – reveals the extent of Ottawa's apathy more clearly. Under federal legislation, the appointed commissioner had – and was expected to exercise – sweeping power over local administration. Through his four senior associates – the gold commissioner, the crown timber and land agent, the legal adviser, and the comptroller – he had effective control of the territory. Significantly, the legislative separation of federal and territorial jurisdictions was more apparent than real. J.T. Lithgow, for example, was both comptroller and territorial treasurer, and was paid by both the federal government and the territorial government. Before 1908, the top civil servants usually filled the appointed positions on the territorial council.[52]

Even after the council became an elected body, councillors had only limited control over expenditures, which remained the bailiwick of the commissioner and his staff. Nor did they have the authority to hire the civil servants, a prerogative that belonged to the commissioner. Attempts to increase the council's power failed. The awarding of the electoral principle proved an empty victory, for real power did not accompany the right to select political representatives. This was in part a result of the decline of the Yukon. As people departed, leaving political and administrative structures intact, a smaller and smaller elite found itself wearing more and more hats, increasingly unable to separate their functions as territorial councillors from their other duties and positions.

The collapse of municipal government in Dawson City illustrates the failure of political development in the Yukon. After much debate and consideration, Dawson was incorporated as a city in December 1901. Another debate ensued over the nature of civic government. The business community preferred an appointed council, while others wanted an elected mayor and council. The latter option prevailed, a municipal election was held, and early in 1902 the council began its work. But as the population declined, many political leaders departed for the outside, leaving holes in the political fabric while simultaneously eating into the tax base. As the hastily built and poorly planned city aged, the expenses of maintaining its services mounted. Faced with rising costs, a number of citizens began in 1904 to circulate petitions calling for the disincorporation of the city. By September of that year the city council was dissolved and Dawson City lost its charter. From 1904 on, the

In the early years of the twentieth century, there were signs that the Yukon was maturing politically. A completely elected territorial council (seen here) was established, but this proved to be only a temporary victory. In 1918 the federal government abolished the council (YA).

complex and expensive issues of municipal administration were dealt with by the territorial government. Taxpayers had saved themselves some money but in doing so had edged the city one step closer to its grave.[53]

The dismantling of the government and administration continued throughout the federal and territorial administration. The territorial court had been established in 1897, with the arrival of Judge Thomas H. McGuire. McGuire was replaced by Judge Calixte A. Dugas the next year, and Dugas was joined two years later by Judge James A. Craig. The two men – Craig rigid and formal, Dugas more light-hearted and not as hard-working – had much to do. They were joined in 1901 by Charles D. Macaulay as police magistrate, an appointment that made possible the hearing of appeals within the territory.

There were endless difficulties with the administration of justice in the Yukon. The law required that jurors be British subjects, a major problem given the high percentage of Americans in the population. The movement of people out of the territory caused numerous delays in cases and resulted in the dismissal of many charges. Also, within a decade of the establishment of the court system, it was obvious that the three judges did not have enough work to do. Dugas and Craig, like many Yukoners, routinely took extended vacations outside the territory. In 1912 both were pensioned off, with the provision, never enforced, that they had to return to the Yukon if the court required their services. Judge Macaulay was left to act as justice of the peace, police magistrate, and territorial judge. Any challenge to his decisions had to be taken to the Court of Appeal of British Columbia. As was the case elsewhere in the administrative structure, the Yukon received the full services of government but then faced the steady bleeding away of political rights and government offices. The wholly elected council remained, but that too would go in time.[54]

The miners' meetings of the early years, which had been suppressed by the Mounted Police, resurfaced as the principal forum for registering displeasure with government policies when in February 1900 a gathering of British subjects loudly proclaimed their opposition to the lack of elected institutions. Out of this meeting came the Citizens' Committee and a formal petition. Other meetings followed, and the protest gained force when the census reported that there were more than four thousand British subjects in the territory. The first battle was won – two territorial councillors were to be elected in 1900.[55] When Governor General Lord Minto visited the territory that same summer, the Citizens' Committee presented a petition calling for a fully elected council, representation in the House of Commons, and changes to liquor and mining regulations. The same committee steered two Conservative candidates to victory in the territorial election, thereby issuing a stinging rebuke to the Liberal Party and increasing the problems of the minister of the interior, Clifford Sifton.

In the aftermath of the election loss, and still smarting from wide-ranging antagonism to the federal administration in the Yukon, Sifton reluctantly conceded that the original commissioner, William Ogilvie, was ineffectual, and with little notice he arranged for Ogilvie's removal (he was officially permitted to resign) and for him to be replaced by James Ross. Ross was a perfect choice and managed to calm matters considerably. A former polititian and administrator from the North-West Territories and well versed in the politics of the periphery, he sided with the Yukoners and carried their protests into the inner sanctums of power in Ottawa. By 1902, Ross had secured three additional elected seats on the territorial council and, his greatest coup, the right of citizens to elect a representative to the federal parliament.

As mentioned above, it was Ross himself who took up this seat – though that had not been his intention. While he was away negotiating a better deal for the Yukon and singing the praises of a territory making major strides towards self-government, the catastrophic Treadgold concession scandal hit. Sifton found himself under unrelenting attack in the House of Commons, hounded by an opposition that loved to see the arrogant minister on the defensive. In the midst of the scandal, the by-election for the new House of Commons seat loomed. Fearful of having an opposition member from the Yukon in the seat, Sifton was desperate for a Liberal win. He urged Ross to resign as commissioner and accept the Liberal nomination. In the face of personal disaster, Ross did so. His wife and daughter had recently died in a boating accident, and on his way back to the Yukon he suffered a stroke. Yet he still agreed to stand for office, offering only his widely admired name to a campaign that he left entirely to his supporters.

Ross was aided, ironically, by the Citizens' Committee's choice of candidate. They selected Joe Clarke, a combative, intemperate politician, who often flirted with libel and slander. The contest saw both the vituperative Clarke and the more dignified Ross campaigning strongly against the Treadgold concession. Ross won by a narrow margin. Sifton could breathe more easily, but only temporarily, for another Yukon politician soon began to cause him grief. Seeking Ross's replacement as commissioner, he accepted the Yukoners' advice and appointed F.T. Congdon, an active Yukon protest leader.

Congdon, a newspaperman-turned-lawyer who had worked hard on behalf of the Yukon Liberal Association, had strong political and administrative credentials. He also had intense ambition and the sense of direction of a loose cannon on a slippery deck. As commissioner, he used his office and the strings of patronage to build an impressive political machine, one tied more to him than to the Liberal Party. The actions of "King Congdon" quickly aroused public discontent, but he had widely co-opted many potential opponents into his group of cronies. The battle started within the Liberal Party – between the "Tabs" (Congdonites) and the "Steam Beers," led by a Liberal brewer – and provided an opening for the Conservative Party in the territory. While Congdon tried to oil his machine, the territory's Tories went about building their opposition force.

Congdon's partisanship quickly divided the Yukon. The next federal election, slated for December 1904, provided a test of his strength. Congdon secured the Tab nomination and resigned his position as commissioner. His opponents rallied around Dr Alfred Thompson, a well-respected Yukon figure. The campaign was corrupt even by the standards of the time. Patronage positions were offered, threats issued, bribes given, newspaper columns controlled, voters added illegally to the lists of electors, and election officials given strict orders to aid Congdon's campaign. Even with the manipulation, Congdon lost by a sizable margin. Thompson would take the opposition Tory message to Liberal Ottawa. Supporters of the former commissioner lobbied in an attempt to get him his job back, but the government had had enough scandals from the Yukon, and the British Columbia politician William W.B. McInnes was appointed commissioner.

By 1905 the political landscape had been completely transformed. Sifton was gone, at odds with his own party over the question of separate schools on the prairies. Ross had resigned, soon to be rewarded with elevation to early oblivion in the Senate. Congdon, too, was gone, his patronage machine in tatters. Their replacements, Thompson and McInnes, proved well suited to the task of pressing for political reform. And Frank Oliver, Sifton's replacement, was sympathetic to the North and supported their efforts. After years of acrimony, the discovery that federal and territorial politicians and administrators could work together towards a common end was reassuring to the few Yukoners who remained in the North.

There were still problems. Congdon resurfaced in territorial politics as legal adviser and began to toss darts at his replacement and his political foes. Commissioner McInnes, facing criticism from within the Liberal Party about the conduct of his administration, resigned to return to the less tumultuous world of British Columbia politics. Eventually Congdon, too, had had enough. He resigned his position and left for Ottawa, where he hoped his organizational and political skills would be more appreciated. But the struggles that Congdon had initiated would live on in bitterly contested territorial elections and a general distrust of elected and appointed officials. Such was the legacy of the man who wanted to be the political "King of the Klondike." The federal government was again inundated with suggestions for a new commissioner, but this time advice from the Yukon was overruled and Alexander Henderson, the former B.C. Attorney general, was recruited for the post.

The Yukon was by now reeling from economic collapse and the steady decline of Dawson and the creeks. Ironically, in 1908 the federal government finally acceded to the long-standing request that the territorial council be made wholly elected. But the new council had little real power, and people invested little emotional energy in the legislative process, except for the distribution of patronage. In the winter of 1908, following Alfred Thompson's resignation, a federal by-election was called for January 1909. Yukon cold did little to quell the political steam, for the combatants included none other than the boisterous Joe Clarke, staunch Tory George Black, breakaway Liberal Robert Lowe, and, most remarkably, the once-disgraced Frederick T. Congdon, seeking a last hurrah. Political rhetoric flew wildly, most of it focusing on the personal, professional, or moral failings of the candidates. Congdon won the January 1909 vote by a healthy margin and returned to Ottawa in triumph. The 1908 by-election campaign was the last real political battle in the Yukon for many years. As the territory continued to decline, the federal government reduced its expenditures there and regional revenues shrivelled.

Through a quirk of the electoral system, the territory was in a unique political position. Federal elections in the Yukon took place well after the elections in the provinces – a full month afterwards in 1911. Although Congdon's excesses had forced a break in the tradition, Yukoners as a rule wisely
voted for the governing power. When the results of the 1911 election revealed a Conservative victory, Tory hopes in the territory were immediately
revived. As Laura Berton described it, the party faithful were quick to see the
opening: "What celebrating there was that night among the Dawson Conservatives. Within an hour of victory the Tories had every possible party
worker (and some impossible ones) slated for the coveted jobs so long held
by the enemy ... The next stage (or so it seemed to me) was jammed with
Conservatives pouring back into the country. John Black, George Black and
all the others who had left with me more than year before on the last boat,
ostensibly for ever, were now preparing to return in triumph."[56]

The plums, what few remained, now went to the Conservatives. George
Black got the first prize, the job of commissioner. The Tories wanted to add
the Yukon seat to the government benches in Ottawa. Those veterans of the
1904 election, Thompson and Congdon, went head to head in yet another
bitterly fought personal campaign. The Conservatives won handily, aided in
no small measure by the Yukoners' realization that the support of the government was crucial to the territorial economy.

The two men faced each other for the last time early in 1918. That year
the Yukon voted after the Unionist victory of the previous year. Both Thompson and Congdon tried to present themselves as nonpartisan Unionist candidates, the latter on the slimmest and most creative of pretences. The majority of Yukoners voted for Congdon, but the weird confrontation was not
yet over:

Alfred Thompson was declared their Member of Parliament by a vote on division in the Canadian House of Commons. That odd turn of events occurred as
a result of the rather difficult problem of distributing the votes of Yukon soldiers
for and against Borden's government between two men who both claimed to be
Unionist candidates. After an initial period of confusion, the Commons, by a majority decision, chose to assign Thompson the Unionist ballots and Congdon the
Liberal ones, thereby turning the doctor's defeat of 110 into a victory of 10.[57]

It was a suitably bizarre ending to the Yukon career of Congdon, the man
who had done so much to sour the political atmosphere in the territory, diverting a potentially powerful, regionally based protest movement into a
mud-slinging political environment in which the only constant losers were
the long-term interests of Yukoners and the political stability of the territory. The Yukon was, in the final analysis, ill served by its politicians. But perhaps they were only reflecting the society from which they had emerged. Like

most miners, workers, businessmen, and corporate investors in the Yukon, the politicians placed personal gain ahead of regional needs. They could not, in fact, see the underlying problems in their society, seeking instead to respond to the short-term demands of their supporters and to use public office to reward those who put them there. In power, the Conservatives were no different from the Liberals. The Yukon was one of the country's most unusual patronage posts, used by both parties to pay off partisans. In the face of this unrelenting self-interest, there were few standing up for the Yukon. The territory could only suffer as a result.

In the midst of this period of gloom, partisanship, and retrenchment, the First World War provided an interval of unity and a feeling of shared purpose. Despite the territory's feeling of isolation and neglect, or perhaps in part because of it, Yukoners responded to the war with an enthusiasm that matched or exceeded that of all other parts of Canada. The Yukon's per capita rate of enlistment was the highest in the country, as was the rate of purchase of war savings bonds. Although the Yukon newspapers carried a good deal of international news, the outbreak of war in August 1914 was unexpected, falling "like a bombshell" on the residents.[58] The response was instantaneous and enthusiastic. Martha Black, the commissioner's wife, described the effect of the news on a theatre party:

As though answering an overwhelming urge, they stood in unison and commenced to sing "God Save the King." The effect was electrical. With one move, the audience was on its feet, and never in the world, I dare say, was our national anthem sung with greater fervour or more depth of feeling than in that moving picture house in that little town on the rim of the Arctic. Although eight thousand miles of mountain, land and sea separated us from London, the heart of the Empire, yet England's King was our King, and England's Empire was our Empire.[59]

During the war, Yukon women played their usual strong role in shaping the community's response to external events. They took an active part in supporting the war effort, not confining themselves to rolling bandages, knitting socks, or supplying tobacco and other "comforts" to the troops, but actively moulding opinion in the territory. The women's organization most to the fore was the Imperial Order Daughters of the Empire (IODE), which founded several chapters in the territory to promote the war effort and loyalty to Britain. Through the IODE, women served as tireless propagandists for the Allied cause. The minutes of the monthly meetings of the IODE record the presentation of books to the schools as prizes for student essays on patriotic themes, the disbursement of large sums for Belgian relief, presents for the troops at Christmas, and the like. The December 1915 meeting of the White-horse chapter of the order opened with the reading of a patriotic verse:

So that tyranny will fall
Canada will give her all;
With her dearest she will part
For the cause that stirs her heart.
Take this message to the Huns,
Canada's behind the guns.

The chapter then received one hundred copies of a pamphlet entitled "Why Don't You Wear a Uniform?" to be sold and distributed locally. The Whitehorse chapter was asked by Commissioner Black if it would like to contribute money to buy a machine gun for the Yukon machine gun detachment. Government employees had already bought one at the cost of a thousand dollars. The ladies of the IODE gladly complied, and raised another thousand for a second gun.[60]

One unfortunate result of the Yukon's patriotism was an increase in the drift of population out of the territory. A number of Yukoners were members of militia units in southern Canada, and they quickly left to join their regiments. Between a hundred and two hundred men volunteered for service in the first days of the war, and by the end of 1914 several hundred more had gone outside to enlist.[61] Since the population of the Yukon in 1914 was only about seven thousand, the departure of so many healthy men in their

At the end of the First World War a squadron of American military aircraft, commanded by the famous General Billy Mitchell, visited Dawson City en route to Alaska. The whole town turned out to see them. Three Mounted Police officers are in front of the right wing of the middle plane (Glenbow Archives, NA 513-52).

twenties and thirties obviously had a depressing effect on the territory's economy. Indeed, all through the war the operators of mining concerns in the Yukon complained of labour shortages, and some had to curtail their operations.

Most Yukoners enlisted quietly, for there was little hoopla associated with recruiting in the territory, no "inspiring sounds of marching bands nor the thrilling sight of magnificent battalions marching past," as Martha Black put it.[62] An exception to this rule was Joe Boyle's Yukon Detachment of the 2nd Regiment, Canadian Mounted Rifles. He was probably the richest resident in the territory in 1914, and as soon as hostilities broke out he organized a machine gun company of fifty-four men at a personal cost of $50,000.[63] The regiment was accepted into the Canadian Expeditionary Force by Colonel Sam Hughes, minister of militia and defence, and left Dawson by steamer on 10 October to a tremendous ovation: "Under the blaze of lights and with the band playing and the populace shouting, the boys of the Boyle-Yukon detachment got away for war."[64] Boyle became famous in the later stages of the war as the "saviour of Roumania" from the Bolsheviks and as the supposed lover of the glamorous Queen Marie. After his European exploits he did not return to the Yukon to repair his ruined empire. Instead, he turned his energies to promoting oil deals in eastern Europe. He died in England in 1923.

The patriotic enthusiasm for a distinctively Yukon contribution to the war effort continued when Commissioner George Black organized another Yukon contingent. Black, in his forties when the war broke out, resigned his post, enlisted in the army, and was given permission in August 1916 to organize a company of infantry, which later became the 17th Machine Gun Company. That the rush to the colours was not quite as spontaneous in 1916 as it had been in 1914 is suggested by the recruiting letter Black wrote and circulated in the territory:·

Hundreds of Yukoners volunteered for overseas service during the First World War, including these members of the 17th Yukon Machine Gun Company. Most of the young men who served in the forces never returned to the Yukon (YA).

You cannot fail to realize that it is the duty of every able-bodied man in Canada, who is not supporting helpless dependents, to offer his services to fight for the Empire in this great crisis. That Yukon has done well, that many of her Men have gone, that Yukon women are doing their duty, does not relieve you. It is a matter of individual manhood. Each must decide for himself whether or not he will play the part of a man. We have remained at home in safety while others have been fighting our battles for over two years, although no more obligated to do so than you or I have been. They have, for us, in many cases, made the supreme sacrifice. They are calling to you and to me for help. Are we going to fail them, or will you come with us?[65]

In 1916 Black led his men to England, and the formidable Martha bullied politicians until she was permitted to go with him, the only woman on the troopship with several thousand men. The fact that she had just turned fifty made this devotion to the cause (and to her husband) all the more remarkable. Of course, Martha always liked adventure.

While the men were, in the words of the popular war song, "somewhere in France," patriotic activity continued at home. Support for the war effort in the Yukon did not seem to dim even as the dreadful casualty statistics mounted. Although the members of the IODE prayed at every meeting that the war might end, they fulminated against the Hun right up to Armistice Day. Virtually every social, political, cultural, and athletic event held in the Yukon throughout the war became a fundraising event, and the Yukoners' efforts continued at a high level until the very end. It was a matter of intense pride to Yukoners that their per capita contribution far exceeded those for Canada as a whole. The Canadian Patriotic Fund, one of the more important of the numerous war relief organizations, reported in June 1916 that the Yukon, with a population of eight thousand, had contributed $62,000, or nearly $8 per capita. The average for Canada was about a dollar.[66]

Some forms of patriotic self-denial, however, the Yukoners shunned. The First World War saw the triumph of prohibition in much of the rest of Canada, as patriotic Canadians, anxious to share if only vicariously the suffering of the troops, voted to deny themselves the pleasures of the cup. Not so the Yukon. Although the territory was intensely patriotic, the use of alcohol was too thoroughly ingrained in the fabric of its society to be uprooted even in the cause of thrashing the Kaiser. A plebiscite held in August 1916 on the question of territorial prohibition saw the anti-prohibitionist "wets" win by three votes out of the more than seventeen hundred cast.[67]

The territory's contribution of manpower and wealth to the war effort only accelerated the Yukon's decline. Each year more and more people packed their bags and left Dawson and Whitehorse for the last time. Even those who retained some measure of commitment to the Yukon had fallen into a pattern of spending as much as half the year outside. For those in the

North, the annual leave-takings of fall had become a mournful symbol of the Yukon's decay:

The last boat's departure was a considerable rite in Dawson City, for it effectively marked the beginning of winter. It was invariably a sad and sentimental occasion. The dock was jammed with people, for the entire town turned out for the ceremony of leave-taking. The last boat was always packed with the wealthy going out for the winter, the fortunate going out forever, and the sick going out to die. The atmosphere was electric with brave untruths. Every last soul on the boat pretended to be returning the following spring, but in point of fact few ever did so. The last boat had a curious and depressing finality about it. For some reason those people who were quitting the country for good always waited for the last boat, and the last moment, before they did so. Thus it became more than just another boat leaving town; it became a symbol of the town's decay. There was always a forced joviality among those on the dock who called "see you next spring" to those on the deck, but when the final whistle sounded everybody on dock and deck began quite openly to weep. Then the boat pulled out into the river and turned its prow towards the south, leaving a little crowd of people standing on an empty wharf, looking cold and miserable and quite forlorn.[68]

In the fall of 1918, this ritual of leave-taking turned into an unthinkable tragedy which, in a sense, tore the heart out of the Yukon. That year the last boat from Dawson was crowded with the usual mix of seasonal transients – Yukoners, Alaskans, and others – leaving the North forever. Lulu Mae Eads, the former dance-hall queen, was leaving, as was the O'Brien family of Dawson and many other citizens of the territory, including the well-known Captain Alexander of Atlin's Engineer Mine, who joined the party at Whitehorse. They were all heading south, up the Yukon River by steamer and then across the White Pass on the railway to the docks at Skagway. There they waited, celebrating their liberation from the northern winter, for steamship passage south.

At the end of October, close to three hundred of them found passage aboard the ss *Princess Sophia*. Commanded by Captain Locke on its regular run down the Lynn Canal from Skagway to Vancouver, its cabins jammed to overflowing with a cross-section of northern society, the ship ran onto Vanderbilt Reef in a blinding snowstorm. It sat on the reef for a day and a half, while the captain and would-be rescuers in ships hovering nearby debated the wisdom of attempting to take the passengers off across a low reef swept by a heavy swell. Then, on the night of 25 October, the wind increased and blew the ship off the reef, splitting her plates. The *Princess Sophia* sank quickly; there were no survivors. All 354 of the passengers and crew died of drowning, suffocation by bunker oil, or exposure. Close to 10 per cent of the territory's white population had perished in less than half an hour.[69]

ncess Sophia" ten hours after striking Vanderbilt Reef.   Winter To Sone

The *Princess Sophia,* grounded high on Vanderbilt Reef in the Lynn Canal, north of Juneau, Alaska, photographed from a fishing boat at about 11 AM on 24 October 1918. At dusk the next day the ship sank, killing all 354 passengers and crew (Alaska State Archives, PCA 87-1704).

With the Yukon weakened by the ravages of a far distant war and the decimation of the *Princess Sophia* disaster, regional politicians had little fight left for the series of body blows delivered in 1918 by Minister of the Interior Arthur Meighen. With little warning, Meighen announced the abolition of the position of commissioner, the dismantling of the elected territorial council, a slashing of the federal budget for the territory by almost half, and the closure of several government offices. Protests were registered, and for a time it seemed that the energy and commitment of the early reform drive had re-emerged, but the federal government and the House of Commons paid virtually no attention to cries of distress from the frontier, and the proposals passed with little debate. The evisceration of Yukon government and politics met with indifference in the rest of the country. Later representations to Meighen and the government succeeded in reversing some of the measures, and re-establishing the territorial council, but at a weakened level.[70]

In twenty years the Yukon had gone from fame to obscurity. Having gained, after a concerted fight, some significant political reforms, Yukoners suffered the ignominy of having the federal government declare to the country that the territory no longer deserved the financial and political resources it had come to count on. There could be no greater symbol of how far the Yukon had fallen from the heady days of the Klondike gold rush than the sight of territorial representatives scurrying off to Ottawa to beg for political rights only slightly greater than those of a large city and to plead with authorities to keep a few government buildings open in Dawson City. The gold rush was surely over. Could the future hold more bad news? The few Yukoners who remained could be excused for wondering if worse was to come.

SEVEN

The Lean Years
1918–1939

At the end of the First World War the Yukon was in a sorry state. An economic recession, war losses, and finally the *Princess Sophia* disaster had pushed the territory into the doldrums. Ignored by the federal government, with a transient population, it seemed to many Yukoners almost as if the gold rush had never happened. In 1921 there were only 4,157 people in the Yukon Territory, less than half the population of ten years earlier. Dawson had shrunk to one-third of its size in 1911, a twentieth of that of 1898. Even Whitehorse, whose population usually grew in the summer months with the increase in transportation activity, held only 331 people in 1921, down from 727 in the previous census. Close to fifteen hundred of the Yukoners were aboriginal people – the major constant in the region – who continued to live off the land and could be found in the isolated seasonal camps of the fur trade districts. Most whites, except for some missionaries, a small number of fur traders, and some of the Mounted Police officers, lived in the towns.

Before the war it had seemed that the Yukon was headed toward social stability. There was an increasing ratio of families to single men in the territory, and the ratio between males and females had become more nearly even. But the war had reversed that promising trend. In 1921 there were about twice as many males as females. The gold rush pattern of a territory dominated by young single males on the move had been re-established. But the prospectors themselves, who had given the territory so much of its character had left. Gone, too, were many of the businessmen and promoters who had swarmed north during the gold rush. Most Yukon communities seemed continually to be saying goodbye to someone, either at the steamboat dock or, increasingly, at the funeral parlour.

The demographic slide was, of course, the result of the implosion of the Yukon economy. Gold production declined steadily in the aftermath of the war, falling as low as 26,000 fine ounces of gold in 1926, a shocking collapse from a high of over 1 million ounces in 1900. The fabulously rich Klondike goldfields had, it seemed, finally been picked clean. At war's end, there was little to replace the decaying gold-mining sector. Promising gold returns, during the war years, from the Mayo-Keno area (the post-rush hope for the Yukon) aided by temporarily high prices had turned sharply downward in the early 1920s, with production declining from 360,000 ounces in 1916 to only 19,000 ounces four years later.[1]

Other minerals were hit equally hard. The copper mines, primarily in the Whitehorse copper belt, demonstrated the continued vulnerability of Yukon mining to world market forces. High wartime prices had fuelled a major expansion, enabling producers to overcome the otherwise prohibitive production and transportation costs. The end of military purchasing forced prices down to prewar levels and tore the heart out of the Yukon copper sector. Yukon mines had shipped more than 2,800,000 pounds (1,270,000 kg) of copper in 1916, the peak year of production. Shipments fell to only 165,000 pounds (74,800 kg) in 1919 and stopped altogether in 1921. Trial shipments were sent outside in 1928 and again in 1930, but low prices and high transportation costs made the exercise unprofitable.

From time to time there was a glimmer of hope, but each one seemed eventually to flicker and die. The Silver King mine near Galena Creek had seemed to be one such glimmer. Trial shipments of silver ore had been sent to smelters in Trail, B.C., and San Francisco, but transportation costs were so high that only the highest-grade deposits could be developed profitably, and within two years the mine closed. The closure of the Silver King property in particular made the glory of the Klondike years seem a rapidly fading dream.[2]

Interest had, however, been spurred in the district, and prospectors continued to scour the hills for other minerals. On 10 July 1919, Louis Beauvette staked a silver claim, which he named Roulette, atop Keno Hill. News of the strike reached A.K. Schellinger, a mining engineer with the Yukon Gold Company, who interested his superiors in the new prospects for silver and lead. The company quickly invested in the property, and a small rush to Keno Hill followed. Over six hundred claims were filed in the next year, and by the summer of 1920 some one hundred men were at work on the property.

But the Keno Hill mines, although rich, were hard to reach, since the swift and shallow waters of the Stewart River made navigation difficult. The Yukon River steamers could not ascend this tributary; even the shallow-draught vessels used on the river could go no farther than Mayo. Carrying the tons of ore from the mines, located some 30 miles (50 km) away, was almost prohibitively expensive. Through much of the 1920s, it cost more to move the silver and lead from Keno to Mayo than to ship the supplies from Mayo to markets in the South. Only the fact that the deposits on Keno Hill were extraordinarily rich made working them worthwhile. The company held back from expensive investments in the property, preferring to develop only silver-rich veins, which permitted the ore to be shipped directly to market. The Yukon Gold Company exploited its properties until 1924, at which time it leased its claims to the Treadwell Yukon Company.

The Keno Hill properties were given a future by the work of Livingston Wernecke, a geologist working for Alaska Treadwell. A shy, intense man, who ran his mining camps with a firm hand and a strong sense for minerals, Wernecke started work on a property close to the Yukon Gold Company's mine. Unlike Yukon Gold, the newly formed Treadwell Yukon Company was prepared to make long-term commitments to the Keno Hill property. Well informed as a result of Wernecke's thorough work and careful observations, Treadwell looked for ways of making its mine more cost-efficient. Transportation, of course, remained the major barrier. In the winter of 1922–23, Treadwell brought in a caterpillar tractor train to move supplies and ore, which radically changed the economics of mining on Keno Hill. Then, in 1924, Treadwell constructed a concentrating mill, further reducing transportation costs and permitting the development of the less valuable milling-grade ores.

The Yukon Gold Company and the Treadwell Yukon Company controlled the Keno field. Both now poured large amounts of money into the venture, gambling that as yet uncovered deposits would pay off their investment. Smaller operators, unable to raise enough investment capital, had no option but to sell to the two dominant firms. The purchase of the assets of the United Keno Hill Company in 1924 allowed Treadwell to rationalize its mining operations. This corporate concentration forced many small developers out of business or required them to rely on Treadwell transportation and milling facilities. Treadwell Yukon Company had made major strides in adapting mining and transportation technology to the conditions of the Mayo-Keno region and had enabled the silver-lead mines to take over the lead in the territorial economy. The project was not large – Treadwell directly employed only one hundred men in 1924 – but by the middle of the 1920s the Keno mines were clearly carrying the Yukon economy.

With the Treadwell Yukon Company in the forefront, lead production reached almost 8,900,000 pounds (4,000,000 kg) by 1930; silver output also reached a new peak that year, topping 3.7 million ounces, 14 per cent of all Canadian production. Most importantly, the Keno deposits were rich enough and the Treadwell operations sufficiently stable and well-financed to survive fluctuations in world prices. Exploratory efforts, now aided by the use of airplanes, continued as Treadwell attempted to expand its reserve base. Even the best planning, however, could not offset the chaos that befell

Silver-lead ore, mined here in the Elsa-Keno area, was stockpiled along the riverfront at Mayo awaiting shipment to the southern refineries (YA).

the Treadwell operations in the early 1930s. The onset of the Great Depression, declining world prices, and the final exhaustion of the principal Keno Hill deposits threatened the demise of the industry. In the fall of 1932, the concentrating mill on Keno Hill was closed. Having carried the Yukon for a decade, the Keno mines seemed about to collapse, and after several unprofitable attempts to develop new properties, Treadwell closed its Yukon operations in 1934.

The expansion of mining activity had changed Keno from a transient tent village to a seemingly permanent settlement. A townsite had been set aside in 1922, and cabins, a liquor store, and a stable were built. The apparent stability and richness of the Keno Hill strikes had encouraged a small number of miners to bring their wives and families into the town. Now they found themselves faced with upheaval.

But then, to the delight and surprise of corporate investors and labourers alike, work on Galena Hill uncovered several new rich veins; and major U.S. government purchases of silver ore following the passage of the Silver Purchase Act of 1935 pushed the price back up. A concentrating mill was built on site, and in the midst of general economic chaos, Treadwell Yukon Company announced that the firm was about to expand. The development of new mines, such as Calumet, offset the closure of worked-over properties such as Silver King. In 1937 Yukon mines produced almost 4 million ounces of silver, a record for the territory, and more than 6,000,000 pounds (2,720,000 kg) of lead, with most of the ore coming from Treadwell properties.

The Keno operation demonstrated the radically different approaches to northern mining. The Yukon Gold Company had high-graded its properties, taking the best ore out as quickly as possible, investing minimal amounts in local infrastructure, and abandoning the mines at the first hints of unprofitability, a common pattern in the Yukon. Treadwell Yukon, which invested heavily in roads, equipment, mills, and other facilities, took a longer-term view. Its activities sustained the local and territorial economy, encouraging the growth of Mayo and the development of a new community at Keno. Both the Yukon Gold and Treadwell Yukon made money on their investments; according to one estimate, the companies earned a profit of approximately 20 per cent on the $23 million worth of silver and lead taken from the area between 1919 and 1942. However, even Treadwell fell into the pattern of removing corporate profits from the territory. Although Wernecke attempted to expand company exploration activities, he had to defer to company officials, who wanted the Keno profits for operations outside the Yukon.

From the beginning, miners and companies had petitioned the territorial and federal governments for assistance with roads and river transportation. But the territory did not have much money at its disposal, and the federal government provided only modest aid. Even in the provision of roads, for example, private enterprise in the form of Treadwell Yukon was compelled to contribute close to one-third of the cost of road construction in the Mayo to Keno area. The territorial council assisted with bridges and subsidized the Side Streams Navigation Company (a subsidiary of the White Pass and Yukon Route Corporation). It also provided an airfield, and it moved the territorial assay office to Keno City for the convenience of the miners. Political representation came more slowly. The Mayo district lacked a voice in the territorial council until 1926, when it was permitted to elect one of the four members.[3]

The Keno Hill mining development lacked the drama and excitement of the Klondike gold rush. Certainly, Louis Beauvette is not as well remembered as George Carmack, Skookum Jim, and Dawson Charlie. Nor was Treadwell investing in concentrating mills and access roads as colourful as the stampeders straining up the Chilkoot Pass. Silver and lead, for all their value, lacked the mystique of gold – there was no Robert Service at Keno to immortalize "the men who moil for lead." In the 1920s and 1930s, however, Yukoners were grateful for the Keno Hill mines, for they played a major role in sustaining the territory. Only the silver and lead operations of Yukon Gold and especially Treadwell Yukon prevented a total economic collapse in the lean years after the First World War. The importance of the silver-lead mines also emphasized the continued deterioration of the Klondike goldfields. Territorial gold production had started to decline during the First World War but during the 1920s it dropped precipitously. In 1900 the Yukon had produced almost 80 per cent of Canada's gold; by 1926, it produced only 1.5 per cent. Canadians could almost be forgiven for believing that the Klondike had disappeared.[4]

Gold mining did continue, of course, but not in a way that Klondike stampeders would have recognized. By the end of the war the once-prominent dredging companies were facing bankruptcy. Granville Mining, North West Corporation, and Canadian Klondyke were all in receivership, and the situation at the other companies was little better. Three companies – Yukon Gold, New North-West Corporation, and Burrall and Baird Company – accounted for three-quarters of the territorial production. About eighty small operators, some still using the techniques of the gold rush era, could be found in the goldfields, but their returns continued to decline. The once rich gravels of the Klondike Valley had been all but picked clean. New techniques and machinery that could of handle vast quantities of material quickly and efficiently were required to produce a profit. The development of new ground-thawing techniques, for example, enabled dredges to move more quickly through the gravels. But in spite of such advances, the companies were not in a strong financial position.[5]

During this period the federal government continued to support the concentration of ownership and production in the Klondike goldfields. Despite loud protests from the small operators, the government again amended mining regulations to permit even larger concessions in the Klondike fields. In 1923 a number of investors created the Yukon Consolidated Gold Corporation (YCGC) out of the existing firms, including the three largest: Burrall and Baird, New North West, and Canadian Klondyke. The transition reflected the stagnation in gold production. It was a sign of the times that in 1929, the year of the great consolidation, placer gold operations produced less than 30 per cent of the Yukon's total mineral production. Gold was no longer king in the Yukon.

But there were still vivid characters in the goldfields, notably the ever-controversial A.N.C. Treadgold. Although his financial affairs were tangled, Treadgold now controlled the YCGC. He and his rival Joe Boyle had once been the Klondike's great gold entrepreneurs, and now he made a triumphant return – a symbol of the Yukon's past optimism, and perhaps of Dawson's last hope for a prosperous future. Lewis Green described Treadgold's re-entry into Yukon life: "He was bubbling over with enthusiasm for his new dreams, and the local people, having watched the struggle of the operating companies under receivership, were certain that better days lay ahead. At Bear Creek, he recognized all the old-timers who had worked with him in the past and greeted each one by name as if only a few days had lapsed since he left the Klondike of 1912."[6]

Behind Treadgold's confident exterior, however, lay only half-formed plans for the troubled Klondike mining operations. Treadgold showed little interest in the dredges, thus leaving the most profitable side of his operation starved for cash, while he spent great sums on experimentation, bringing in electric shovels in 1925 to excavate the gravels. His financial position, based on intricate financial dealings in England, remained shaky. He was away from the Yukon for long stretches and had to depend on managers such as Andrew Baird and W.J. Rendell to handle the day-to-day operations of the YCGC. His constant stream of instructions from London was too much for the strong-willed Baird, who was eventually fired.

Treadgold paid little attention to shareholders, ignoring the advice of his employees and dealing ruthlessly with anyone who questioned or challenged his authority. Lack of planning brought on numerous crises. In the spring of 1929, uncertainty about the solvency of his operations caused a number of suppliers to withhold their goods and convinced many of the employees to campaign to unseat Treadgold. The protest group, labelled "The Conspiracy" by Treadgold supporters, attempted a shareholders' revolt, which was met by the determined opposition of their target. By 1930 they had wrested control of the day-to-day operations from Treadgold, but the speculator kept his grip on the financial strings. They also petitioned the secretary of state to investigate the YCGC's internal affairs, and the Ottawa accountant G.T. Clarkson was appointed to conduct the inquiry. Clarkson's report, issued in the midst of the shareholders' struggle, offered a damning critique of Treadgold's administration and provided fuel for a court challenge to his control of the company.

The judgment of the court, issued in the spring of 1932, contained a strong denunciation of Treadgold's affairs, focusing particularly on his secretiveness. The judge ordered a cancellation of Treadgold's shares in the YCGC. While Treadgold sulked – his friends thought him near-suicidal – his opponents moved to take over the company. Andrew Baird managed the Klondike operations, while Tom Patton took over Treadgold's role as president. But Treadgold was not finished. While company affairs in the Yukon staggered on, underfinanced and without long-term direction, Treadgold received a new hearing in Toronto in 1933. He lost again, the judge once more agreeing that he had acted improperly in promoting the company. Treadgold had devoted much of his adult life to the Klondike mines, and now these decisions had stripped him of all shares and involvement with his creation, the YCGC. He continued his appeals to the Canadian courts and later tried his luck in front of British judges. These failed as well, but Treadgold persevered, obsessed with regaining control of his Yukon company. In the end, separated from his wife and bankrupt, he borrowed money from anyone who would lend it to him, promising them a share of the YCGC when he finally won his case. He died in 1951, very much a Yukon promoter of the old style, still pursuing the dream of regaining his crown as King of the Klondike.

The Treadgold controversy had drawn much attention away from the practical problems of mining in the Yukon. As Treadgold himself had demonstrated, only large, well-capitalized companies could continue in this increasingly marginal industry and region. To exploit the resource efficiently and quickly, a multifaceted organization was essential, one that included expensive and complex dredges and hydraulic facilities, power plants, work camps, and miles of roads.

Ironically, the onset of the worldwide economic calamity in 1929 led to the return of some prosperity to the Yukon goldfields. The price of gold, locked at around $20 an ounce for decades, was officially raised to $35 in 1933, making many operations in the Yukon suddenly profitable. Much of the credit for reversing the tattered fortunes of the YCGC belonged to its manager, W.H.S. McFarland, who straightened out the mess left by Treadgold's quixotic administration. Dredging and stripping operations were reorganized and expanded, and the company returned to profitability. By the middle of the 1930s, gold production had reversed its downward trend. In 1939 Yukon producers delivered to the market more than 88,000 ounces of gold – worth over $3 million, the highest level in twenty years – and prospectors returned to the field in large numbers, particularly in the Carmacks district.

The improved economic picture did not come without problems. The YCGC faced many complaints, especially from its employees. The workers demanded better wages and complained bitterly about their working and housing conditions, particularly as long as Andrew Baird remained in charge. He was, nonetheless, a better employer than Treadgold had been. As the wife of one employee told him in 1931, "I admit that you are a tightwad and a skinflint but as long as you are in charge the employees know that their wages will be paid promptly."[7] Workers' complaints were, of course, limited by the high levels of unemployment outside and the comparative stability of work in the Yukon. With McFarland in charge, and with company shareholders looking with enthusiasm towards the future of the industry, working conditions improved and the industry gained a measure of stability it had not known for years. The revitalization of the Klondike fields came as a pleasant surprise, for most people had written the industry off as an aging relic of the gold rush. Collapse had been close at hand, but survival now seemed assured, at least for the short term.

In the midst of the economic uncertainty of the postwar period, the Yukon fur trade remained stable. The international demand for furs had picked up appreciably in the last years of the war, and it escalated even more quickly in the 1920s. The territorial government had previously paid little attention to this seemingly minor component of the regional economy, but surging prices and demand, expanded competition, and the prospect of widespread overhunting forced the government to consider measures to regulate the industry.[8]

Initially, the Native people had much of the Yukon trade to themselves, though prospectors and miners occasionally brought furs to market. Once the stability and profitability of the Yukon trade had been well established, however, white trappers were attracted in increasing numbers. Fur prices remained high through most of the 1920s and 1930s. As Louis Levy, a San Francisco fur merchant wrote in 1927,

Lynx, Red Fox, Cross Fox and Mink are in very strong demand and in fact all furs from the Yukon are bringing around 25% more than last year at this time ... I handle all Shorty Chambers' furs, and have Johnny Johns the native buying furs around Carcross country. Am handling Thayer's furs from Carmacks. These traders are up against Taylor and Drury's who are hard competitors, and we can pay more than they do, as I get better prices and can pay more ... Business has been very good for the past four months and all indications point to a good season.[9]

Pauline Cove, Herschel Island, in 1922. Outside the Dawson-Whitehorse corridor, the fur trade remained important between the two world wars. The Inuit of the Arctic coast made enough money from fox and other furs to buy these schooners, moored at Pauline Cove (NA, PA 172822).

The territorial government left traders and trappers alone to establish their own rules of exchange, counting on the RCMP to control any abuse of the game resources. The trapping of individual species, particularly beaver and marten, was suspended on several occasions when overhunting threatened the long-term stability of the resource, but these regulations were imposed cautiously in order to prevent hardship on the largely aboriginal hunting population. The Yukon remained out of step with southern conservation concerns, its comparative lack of regulations contrasting with the more heavily controlled conditions elsewhere in Canada. A major redrafting of the Yukon Game Ordinance in 1938 brought Yukon practices closer to national norms, but throughout most of the territory, trappers continued to do much as they pleased.

The fur industry contributed thousands of dollars to the territorial economy, making up nearly 10 per cent of its revenue. Returns on the trade fluctuated from a low of $78,000 in 1920–21 to a high of over $600,000 in 1927–28, an exceptionally good year in which furs almost matched the value of gold produced. The industry required limited capital investment, except by the largest fur-trading companies, and provided a regular source of income for several hundred First Nations and white trappers throughout the territory. For these reasons, it quickly expanded through the Yukon. In 1921 there were twenty-seven licensed fur traders in the territory working out of eighteen locations; nine years later, there were forty-six posts in operation, owned by thirty different operators.

The fur trade was an industry unlike the other main sectors of the economy. The trappers were independent workers, not wage labourers, and were not tied by contract to a particular trading company. While most of the trappers were First Nations people; almost none of the traders were. Dominating the trade was the locally owned Taylor and Drury Company, run by Isaac Taylor and William Drury. They operated their own supply steamer, freeing them from dependence on the White Pass and Yukon Route ships, a necessity given the eleven widely scattered posts operated by the company in 1930.

The trading system, like the mining economy before the gold rush, operated largely on credit. Reliable and skilful traders had no difficulty securing a winter's outfit from one of the many traders operating in the territory on the understanding that, the loan, or "jawbone," would be repaid with the returns from the winter's harvest. First Nations trappers, of course, knew the intricacies of the fur trade well by this time and readily exploited competitive situations when these worked to their advantage. Those in isolated areas, such as Ross River, often had to travel long distances if they wished to benefit from competitive bidding; but in periods of intense competition, small independent traders carried their wares throughout the territory. The traders, of course, sought to tie the aboriginal trappers to their posts. Taylor and Drury accomplished this by paying the trappers for their furs with company tokens, which were usable only at the firm's outposts. But the Yukon escaped the corporate concentration that had overtaken much of the northern fur trade. In the neighbouring Northwest Territories, the competitive traders drawn to the region during the 1920s sold out one by one to the powerful and well-financed Hudson's Bay Company, which controlled much of the industry to the east by the 1930s. Although the HBC did return to the Yukon, re-establishing its long-abandoned post at Fort Selkirk in 1937, it did not expand much from that base.[10]

In general, native people benefited from the prosperous fur trade of the 1920s and 1930s. Because of their ability to live off the land, they were able to wait out temporary declines in fur production and short-term fluctuations in fur prices. White trappers, in contrast, arrived when prices were high and usually left when returns fell off. There were occasional problems between aboriginal and white trappers over the latter's use of poison, as well as complaints against each other for overhunting. A number of white men who entered the trade (for instance, Dan Cadzow at Rampart House, Poole Field at Ross River, and Eugene Jacquot at Burwash) married Native women and stayed in the Yukon with their families.[11]

The vitality of the fur trade rested on the persistence of indigenous harvesting. As long as the First Nations continued to live off the land and away from the mining communities, the fur trade flourished. Through the 1920s and 1930s, when the mining economy struggled for stability and offered few openings for any Yukoners, the Native people continued to stay away from it, preferring the harvesting lifestyle to the dubious benefits of mining. Sustained by Native participation and steady international demand for northern furs, the Yukon trade remained a vital element of the regional economy.

While the First Nations played a crucial role in the stability of the Yukon's oldest commercial activity, they also participated in the territory's newest industry – big-game hunting. Native people and many of the whites still depended on wild animals for sustenance. That rich Americans were prepared to pay hundreds of dollars to hunt for big-game trophies on the last frontier seemed rather odd to people who still regularly hunted for food, but it brought in money – provided that no one laughed openly at the Yankee hunters.[12]

Big-game hunters had come north before the First World War, but their numbers increased steadily in the 1920s. The Yukon had a good reputation for the quality and size of its animals. The White River area, the southern lakes, and the Mayo region in particular attracted considerable attention from hunters, and about thirty of them came to the territory each year through the 1920s, though the number dropped off sharply during the depression. Many of the Yukon's most prominent long-term residents – the Jacquot brothers, Shorty Austin, Charlie Baxter, and First Nations guides

Paddy Smith and Jimmy Kane, among others – participated in the new industry. Most of the guides operated on a part-time basis only, for there was not enough business to sustain them all full-time. Only a few, the Jacquots, Baxter, and the most famous, Johnny Johns, achieved much stability in their operations.

Native people, who did much of the actual guiding and thus ensured the successful reputation of the Yukon industry, had limits placed on their participation in it. Under a 1922 regulation, they were barred from serving as chief guides. This regulation was later eased, giving the commissioner wide discretionary powers to determine whether the would-be guides were capable of handling the financial and administrative tasks associated with the job. Johnny Johns, a First Nations man from Carcross, got around the regulations by becoming enfranchised. Others, such as Billy Hall and George Johnson of Teslin, had their applications turned down and were forced to hire on with white guides if they wished to work in the industry. Pressure for such racist regulations clearly came from the white guides' desire to eliminate competition. Upon learning that Johnny Johns had received a licence, one government agent complained, "It really means the taking away of the livelihood of guiding from the white men if any more Indians are granted the privilege of acting as Chief Guides."[13]

Big-game hunting earned the Yukon much favourable publicity, for the hunters wrote widely and enthusiastically about their frontier experiences. But although the territorial government exacted its toll through large non-resident licence fees, and although the hunters spent freely during their short stay in the Yukon, their numbers were so small that the overall economic impact on the region was comparatively slight.

There was, however, another side to the tourism industry in the Yukon. The mystique of the Klondike gold rush had grown rather than diminished over time. During the rush, dozens of travelogues, diaries, and novels had been written about it. Newspaper articles by the hundred had helped fuel widespread interest in all aspects of the Klondike, and in the 1910s and 1920s the publication of Robert Service's poetry and Jack London's short stories strengthened a growing North American fascination with the Northwest. Migration to the last frontier was a possibility for the young and adventurous, and the passion to see the Yukon was still there.

The costs and difficulties of access to the Northwest seemed an unavoidable barrier to regular tourist traffic. Yet each summer a number of people made their arrangements and ventured north to see the land they had read so much about. But Yukon business leaders did little to encourage or exploit this southern fascination with their territory. While there were many hotels still standing, remnants of the gold rush days, most stood abandoned and decaying. In the busy summer months, when business travel on the trains and steamboats peaked, room for casual travellers was often scarce. A few saw the potential, however, and following the example of the big-game guides, they began to organize for annual migrations of tourists.

The territory had much to offer tourists: the dramatic mountains and lakes of the southern Yukon, the historic Yukon River journey aboard the fascinating and well-appointed riverboats, and of course the many attractions of the Dawson area. The White Pass and Yukon Route company did its utmost to develop the business, for it was desperate to find passengers and cargo for its underutilized train and stern-wheeler service. Coastal steamship firms, including the Alaska Steamship Company, the Pacific Steamship Company, and the Canadian Pacific Steamship Company, were persuaded to arrange two-day stopovers at Skagway, giving the travellers time to ride the train to Carcross, with longer trips possible.

Special excursions were organized out of Carcross, taking travellers on a beautiful journey along Tagish Lake and through "Canada's Alps." The highlight of the trip was Ben-My-Chree, a gardener's oasis on the edge of the frontier at the south end of Tagish Lake, established by a retired English couple, Mr and Mrs Otto Partridge. The trip continued from there to Brooks Inlet, where tourists travelled a tiny railroad that joined Tagish and Atlin lakes. Another boat carried them across the lake to the old gold-mining town of Atlin. Altogether, it was a wonderful journey, marked by signs of the famous Klondike rush and some of Canada's most striking scenery. Those who made the journey spoke enthusiastically of the expedition, but they were not able to convince southerners in sufficient numbers to make the southern Yukon a major tourist destination.[14]

In the interwar years, access to the Yukon continued to be a major problem. In an era when most major investments were put on hold pending a major economic revival, emphasis was placed on maintaining existing transportation facilities and lowering the still excessive costs of moving about the territory. The Yukon's modest road system became increasingly important after the war, serving as an off-season adjunct to the river steamers. This was particularly true in the Mayo district, where unnavigable rivers forced developers to construct roads to the mines. Yukoners, however, ran into strong resistance from the federal government on this score, for road construction in the North was costly and the returns to the nation were slight. Thus, repeated territorial requests for assistance failed to sway a federal government that still doubted there would be permanent development in the territory. Through most of the 1920s, the Yukon government could do little more than maintain existing roads and assist with the construction of trails to promising mining areas.

Even the Yukon's main land route, the winter Overland Trail from Whitehorse to Dawson City, had fallen into serious disrepair, with declining traffic. As Laura Berton noted: "Many of the roadhouses which in the old days had been spotted every twenty-two miles along the winter road were closed. Passengers now had to provide their own lunches and these were eaten in the open after being thawed out by a bon-fire on the side of the trail. In the old days we had made the journey in less than a week. Now the stage only made a post a day and, if the trail was bad, the trip often took longer than a fortnight."[15]

The White Pass and Yukon Route company (WPYR) cancelled its overland service in 1921, no longer needing the route to maintain control of the lucrative summer mail contract. Various small operators tried to keep the trail going, but with little financial success. Dawsonites lost out further when the trail was diverted towards Mayo, which now generated the bulk of the winter traffic. George Black protested to the federal government: "What my constituents are more interested in are roads, for in so vast a country transport is a vast problem." But the government was not listening.

River transport was more stable, but even here the corporate concentration and declining service that characterized the entire Yukon economy was evident. The collapse of Side Streams Navigation a year before the end of the war had removed the only major competitor to the British Yukon Navigation Company upstream of Dawson, and the latter moved into the void left on the Mayo route. With the exception of Taylor and Drury's pup steamer *Thistle* (later replaced by the *Yukon Rose*), which supplied the firm's widely scattered posts, the British Yukon Navigation Company had the Yukon rivers almost to itself.

For the first few years of the 1920s, Dawson City maintained its central role in river transport. Ore from Mayo was shipped via Dawson, where it was loaded aboard American Yukon Navigation Company steamers (owned by a WPYR subsidiary) and sent downstream to the Bering Strait. Improvements on upstream navigation, particularly the development of a new, shallow-draft barge, permitted the WPYR to reverse this pattern, moving the ore to Whitehorse, where it was loaded onto the train for Skagway. When the Alaska Railroad reached Fairbanks in 1922, the American Yukon Navigation Company was pulled off the lower Yukon, cutting the commercial link which for fifty years had tied together the two territories of the Yukon River valley. Although few noticed the change immediately, the shift represented the first major barrier between Alaska and the Yukon, an early brick in what would later become a solid wall.

A transportation development that attracted more attention at the time was the struggle to improve river navigation along the treacherous and shallow Stewart River. The construction of the ss *Keno* in 1922, specially designed for low-water service, helped, but the addition of lining cables and the removal of rocks in the waterway were also required to ease transit on the river. Attempts to open navigation upstream from Mayo proved to be less successful, leaving transportation in the area to the roads and the winter tractor-trains.

Winter may have stopped the riverboats, but Yukoners found ways to get around. This automobile, with chains on its tires, is pulling sleds loaded with freight and passengers across Lake Laberge in 1922 (YA).

Among the many problems of subarctic transportation was the short season. The late breakup of the ice along the Yukon River and the shallow water of Lake Laberge routinely delayed the opening of navigation and cut into the shipping company's ability to move supplies in and out of the Yukon. Several attempts were made to extend the season. In 1925 the WPYR constructed a dam across the Yukon River between Miles Canyon and Marsh Lake. By holding water back during the winter, the company could create a flood in the spring to force the ice out of Lake Laberge and extend the season by as much as three weeks.

Environmentalists of a later day would have shuddered at the WPYR 's second method of improving water transportation. Late each winter, company trucks discharged gallons of oil, diesel fuel, and carbon black on the lake ice. If the weather cooperated, the enhanced heating action could eat through several feet of ice and permit ships to get through the lake to the open river below. In conjunction with the government, the company also undertook minor dredging operations in an attempt to improve river navigation, but grants were so small that little work of substance could be undertaken.[16]

That the ships continued to run on a regular schedule provided further evidence of the impact of the Mayo-Keno mines. The shipment of supplies into the mines and the removal of ore and concentrate kept the WPYR steamers on the river during the Yukon's lean years. But the cost of rebuilding the *Klondike* and *Casca*, both of which ran aground in 1936, bit deeply into company profits and stalled additional efforts to improve river navigation. The steamers, like much else in the Yukon, were holding on and waiting for better times. The combination of tourist traffic and mine-related cargo kept the company afloat, but barely. For all its monopoly control of Yukon River

The *Maid of Orleans*, a schooner owned by the trader Charlie Klengenberg, locked in the ice at Herschel Island, c. 1924 (NA, PA 172867)

transport, the WPYR had trouble paying its bills in the troubled 1920s and 1930s. Cargoes had fallen off dramatically from the prewar period: in 1928 the WPYR carried about half the tonnage it had in 1914. Company officials sometimes spent their own money to keep ships on the river, and commercial customers were often required to pay in advance in order to keep operations moving. There were no great corporate profits drawn from the WPYR operations; no dividends were paid between 1912 and the 1950s. This, perhaps, explains the absence of sustained criticism from Yukoners, because in these doldrum years the company's ships and other operations were among the Yukon's few economic constants.

While the familiar river steamers served as the foundation for the Yukon economy, the development of air transport in this period held out the prospect of a more promising future. Surplus airplanes and demobilized pilots looking for work were peculiarly well suited for the transport needs of the North. The first planes, part of the First Alaska Air Expedition, reached Whitehorse in August 1920, moving on to Dawson City and then to Nome. The Yukon Airways and Exploration Company, owned by a small group of Whitehorse and Mayo businessmen, started operation in 1926. Although within three years the firm fell victim to weak management, insufficient capital, and a series of crashes, it made many think about the potential for air transport in the Yukon.[17] Treadwell Yukon also got into the business, purchasing two planes to fly prospectors around Mayo and to deliver mail from Whitehorse to Dawson when the Overland Trail was closed.

The early Yukon pilots were a courageous lot. There were few landing strips – wheeled planes usually landed on sandbars – through the region's many lakes and rivers provided relatively safe landing for planes equipped with pontoons or skis, depending on the season. Pilots had treacherous winter conditions to deal with, and there were few roads or other landmarks to indicate routes. Crashes were frequent and often fatal. Although the need for air travel was obvious, it is not surprising that the industry had to struggle to succeed in the Yukon.

Northern air service came into its own in the 1930s. Within the space of a few years, Canadian Airways, Northern Airways, and United Air Transport began operations in the territory. Not to be outdone, the WPYR established its own airline, British Yukon Aviation, in 1934. Regularly scheduled service was now available to Whitehorse, Mayo, and Dawson City. The highly skilled pilots and engineers who manned the northern planes paid particular attention to the special needs of subarctic navigation and devised ways of dealing with the vagaries of the northern climate. The federal and territorial governments joined with private companies to build, expand, and maintain a rapidly growing network of Yukon airfields.

The introduction of air travel brought sweeping changes to the North. Airmail service began in 1927 when Andy Cruikshank, aboard the *Queen of the Yukon* (owned by Yukon Airways), flew a planeload of mail from Whitehorse to Dawson and Mayo. It was not an official flight – people mailing letters had to affix a special Yukon Airways stamp issued for the service. The pilot's wife actually delivered the mail, in a unique fashion. The plane did not land at Dawson. Instead, Mrs Cruikshank simply threw the mail bag out of the window as they flew over Dawson, after which the plane continued on to Mayo. Soon mail delivery by plane became more routine, bringing previously isolated communities back into the mainstream of regular communication.

As with any technological advance, the change from surface to airmail service gradually but inevitably brought old traditions and techniques to an end. Percy DeWolfe, widely hailed as the "Iron Man of the Yukon," had been an 1898 stampeder, but unlike many, he had stayed after the rush. After years of freighting, fishing, hunting, woodcutting, and other ventures, DeWolfe landed a contract to deliver the mail between Dawson City and Eagle, Alaska. His initial contract had called for a lump-sum payment of $125 per round trip, 200 miles (330 km) by dogsled in the winter. The journey, challenging at the best of times, was particularly dangerous in the weeks before breakup and after freeze-up. His exploits were legendary in the North, his stamina, reliability, and good humour the stuff of which northern folk heroes were made. By the mid-1930s, however, his work had lost its lustre, having been replaced by the more daring and even more dangerous flights of the early Yukon pilots. DeWolfe remained a fixture on the Yukon landscape with his Dawson-to-Eagle run until 1950, but long before that date the Percy DeWolfes of the Yukon had largely been replaced by the faster but no more reliable airmail service.[18]

The availability of air transport brought other benefits. Supplies could be flown into remote mining camps, allowing industrial operations to continue where in the past they had had to close for weeks while supplies came overland. Fur trappers no longer had to transport their supplies hundreds of tortuous miles upstream to their traplines; now, bush planes could drop them near their outposts and retrieve them again at the end of the season. Seriously ill patients, once doomed for want of a doctor, could be delivered to hospital by plane. Yukon pilots regularly risked death themselves on their many flights of mercy.

The addition of air service, along with improvements in internal transportation, brought Yukoners closer to the mainstream of North American society. They could now keep in touch with changing developments on the outside and could maintain closer contact with friends, family, and associates within the territory. But this represented one of only a few improvements in Yukon society. The souring of the gold-mining sector, though offset in part by the new silver-lead mines, sapped much of the vitality from a community already weakened by war and the wreck of the *Princess Sophia* on Vanderbilt Reef.

The signs of decline were particularly evident in Dawson City. Once the gem of the Klondike and famed throughout the world, Dawson now had the appearance of an overgrown graveyard. Dozens of dilapidated and crumbling buildings lined the streets. As Laura Berton wrote, "Those people who were left in the town had by this time taken on some of the qualities of Dawson's aging buildings."[19] There was room for several thousand residents, but by 1921 only 975 remained in town; ten years later, the number had fallen to 819 (though Dawson rebounded somewhat during the depression years, and by 1941 the local population had grown to 1,043 people). As Laura Berton sadly noted, funerals were the major social event in the Dawson of the 1920s. Symbols of decline could be seen everywhere. The U.S. government removed its consulate in 1918, the *Dawson Daily News* stopped daily publication in 1920, more businesses closed each year, old-timers moved "outside" (or into hospital), and commercial life slowed to a crawl. The town seemed to be in its death throes.

The revitalization of the goldfields after Treadgold's disastrous consolidation attempt provided a much-needed respite and, to a degree, put Dawson back on its feet. But it was now little more than a standard company town, though corporate control was offset somewhat by the presence of the territorial government. But it could no longer even claim economic pre-eminence, since the centre of mining had moved to the Mayo district. Still, Dawson City was avoiding the long-expected total collapse.

Old traditions died hard, and Dawsonites clung to the rituals of the past. The familiar social whirl – fancy bridge parties, engraved calling cards, and elaborate dances – remained in evidence, although for lack of people the strict class barriers of the past had to be relaxed slightly. RCMP constables, formerly considered too plebeian for the town's top social events, were now welcome in the winter round of soirees. "Scarlet fever," an affliction of the heart affecting many of the town's single women, still struck with some regularity in town, though the prize was now a constable rather than an inspector.[20] And there were lingering signs of the old pretensions. Literary clubs, well-attended church services, the dances and receptions, and a stratified society that kept government officials and business leaders distinct from the mine workers and other wage labourers offered faint reflections of the "sophistication" and "culture" that community leaders so anxiously sought. Outsiders, however, were far from impressed with the shrivelled and form-ridden community on the banks of the Yukon River.

Dawson was no longer the frontier town of old. Although a few old-timers were still around, as witnessed by their continued attendance at the Yukon Order of Pioneers meetings, the glitter of their earlier dreams for Dawson had worn dull by years of hard news. Most of the townsfolk were short-timers from outside, who stayed a year, perhaps two, before trying their luck in more promising places to the south. For those struggling to make a go of life in the North, the constant movement of people in and out of the territory was a bitter sign of its greatest failing – the lack of commitment by the very people who were making a living from its once-famous resources.

Whitehorse, on the other hand, had changed little since the gold rush years. It remained under the thumb of the White Pass and Yukon Route company, which controlled the local economy and owned much of the land around the townsite. The city lived by the seasons of the river, flourishing in the spring when workers arrived to lower the dry-docked steamers into the river, and falling into somnolence each fall as the same workers departed for winter jobs and better weather in the south. The town had few ambitions, and even the episodic development of the local copper belt did little to fuel dreams of its future.[21]

Although Whitehorse was the transportation hub of the territory, and hence vital to the Yukon's economic health, it felt ignored. Federal officials paid little attention to the town, which was perhaps to be expected, but the territorial government similarly dismissed the town's repeated claims for financial assistance. Dawsonites looked down their noses at the seasonal town, which they saw as little more than a train station, docks, and a few hotels. Whitehorse was, as a result, a quiet town, well controlled by the police, where everyone seemed to be passing through. Evidence of WPYR domination was everywhere to be found. Company officials and local businessmen lived in a small enclave to the southwest of the Main Street business district. The skilled workers, most of them employed on the WPYR's trains, in its boatyards, or on its steamers, lived in more modest homes in the adjacent districts. Transient workers, who made up the bulk of the town's summer workforce, put up makeshift dwellings near the railway yards. There were a few First Nations people in the community, despite attempts to keep them out, but they lived to the north, on the small residential reserve set aside for them. They too were transient, moving back to the traplines and hunting grounds as seasons dictated.

The entire community lived on the rhythms of the WPYR steamers, though the trains operated all year, providing the one reliable contact with the outside world. The arrival of the trains, although routine, was an important ritual: "Train day was an event in Whitehorse. It meant mail, fresh milk and green vegetables, strangers in town ... It was considered no more than a patriotic duty for every true Whitehorse booster to swell the crowd at the station or dockside. As one socialite explained ... 'I think it's our duty to show the tourists that we're not all Indians and Eskimos and that we know how to dress decently.'"[22] For all its modest appearance, Whitehorse was the Yukon's third community, the transportation entrepot that stood behind Mayo's mines and Dawson City's gold mines and administrative offices. That this small, seasonal, company town would hold such an important place in the territorial scheme of things reflected the slow pace of Yukon development and the collapse of the glorious dreams of the Klondike era.

There were a few Yukoners – for instance, Isaac Drury and William Taylor – who dedicated themselves to the commercial future of the North and reinvested in the Yukon. But most people – from the unskilled workmen to the investors in the Treadwell Yukon Company – viewed the North in a different light. For them, the Yukon was a place to make money in and then escape from. The companies took their profits out of the territory and reinvested them in other ventures, with the result that the Yukon lost the benefit of any spinoff spending. Most workers were little different, migrating like the geese with the change of seasons, taking much of their pay packets with them to their families and homes in southern Canada. The Yukon paid the price of instability, marginal business opportunities, and the absence of enough committed residents to sustain pressure on the federal and territorial governments to change the status quo. It seemed that the Yukon was destined to be forever a land of yesterdays and tomorrows, whose best days lay far in the past or well in the future.

The Yukon First Nations viewed the region differently. For them, this was home, as it had been for their ancestors. They were not particularly noticeable in the 1930s. They could be seen in towns, but under controlled circumstances; their cabins and camps lined the Yukon's rivers, and they often worked as woodcutters and packers for the river steamers. But they were not to be found in the mines or in the service industries, nor did they have a political presence.[23]

In the backcountry, away from tourists and government officials, aboriginal people and whites mixed freely and easily. Fur traders such as Dan Cadzow, Shorty Chambers, Pool Field, Eugene Jacquot, and Del Vangorder were their friends, business partners, and often their relatives by marriage. Other men, attracted by the high fur prices of the 1920s, came only temporarily and did not seek to make their relationships with Native women permanent. The missionary doctor Grafton Burke, writing of the white men of the Porcupine River area, commented that "traders in these isolated places vie with each other as to who can 'swell the population.'"[24] Those who did take Native wives often found themselves shunned by white society in the Yukon. Laura Berton gives a poignant example:

She was a pretty little thing, bright and neat, and I think could have made him a good wife, but the parents were so shocked they would neither see nor speak with him. This attitude drove him from the town and back into the bush, where his life was spent among the Indians, hunting and cutting wood for a living. Now here he was, standing by the river with his dark, wiry children clustered about him, the fish wheel in the background turning slowly with the current, the salmon smoking under the trees. In all intents and purposes he was a native.[25]

Away from the towns, the numerical dominance of the aboriginal population ensured that aboriginals and whites would get along well. The process was aided by the presence of the RCMP, which maintained a number of posts in outlying areas and controlled relations between the two groups. There were only a few flare-ups, very seldom violent, a testament to the accommodation reached between the races away from the mining camps and river ports. It was clear, however, that the Native traders and trappers were not free to shift their families to the mostly white towns, where a different reception awaited them.

Whitehorse, Dawson, and Mayo, were white enclaves. Native people were permitted inside the communities only under very specific conditions. They came as temporary labourers, to fill a void caused by a lack of white workers, to buy goods in the stores, and, on occasion, to participate in parades and festivals. They came also to visit the missionaries or to seek help from the doctors, the hospital, the Indian agent, or the Mounted Police. Although welcome for such short visits, provided they stayed sober, they were not encouraged to stay.

The communities, working through the police and the federal government, had various ways of controlling aboriginal settlement. Special residential reserves were established for the First Nations. The Mayo reserve, a particularly symbolic example, was located two miles downstream from the main settlement and on the opposite side of the river. Thus, the First Nations could live close to the towns, as many did on a temporary basis each year, but not so close as to annoy local citizens. Faced with protests from whites, the government established a curfew restricting First Nations' access to Dawson and, in 1933, invoked a permit system for any Native person wishing to move into Dawson City. Although such measures were privately acknowledged to be illegal, they served their purpose.

There were many such examples. The Mayo hospital, financially supported by the Treadwell Yukon Company, refused to admit aboriginal people into the general wards; they were treated in a tent attached to the outside of the building. The races did not often mingle in Whitehorse, Dawson, and Mayo. Police officers and men such as Yukon Indian Agent John Hawksley, a former missionary, implemented such measures as were necessary to placate white protests and to control Native incursions into the white enclaves. This discrimination was justified on the grounds that First Nations people had to be protected from the baneful influence of white society until they were ready for full assimilation. However specious this argument, it was widely accepted by whites involved with aboriginal affairs.[26]

While the government and police concentrated on keeping Native people out of town (and, in fact, they were more interested in hunting and trapping anyway), the task of preparing them for assimilation fell to the churches. The Anglican Church, in particular, had deep roots in the territory and served both aboriginal and white congregations. The other denominations had fallen on hard times after the gold rush, and many clergy had left the territory.

The Anglican Church had always had difficulty attracting suitable candidates for northern service. The problem was magnified by the poverty of the Yukon diocese and the national church's limited support for Canadian missions. Bishop Stringer's many efforts to recruit missionaries for northern work were rejected by people who felt that God had called them to serve in the pleasanter surroundings of a middle-class urban parish in southern Canada. Unable to attract suitable full-time candidates, Stringer turned in the 1920s to student preachers at the Anglican Theological College in Vancouver. The government provided small salaries and expenses for teachers at Native day schools. By offering to have his missionaries run a day school while the Native people were in camp, Stringer was able to get the government to subsidize Anglican missionary efforts in the Yukon. The summer students were an earnest, energetic bunch, who took to their work with the enthusiasm of youth and Christian commitment. But they knew little about the realities of northern missionary work, could seldom speak the Native languages, and did not stay long enough to make an appreciable impact.[27]

Much the same could be said for the full-time missionaries that Stringer recruited. By the 1920s, almost all of the new members were Canadians, a change from the largely British missionary corps of the previous century. They were an upwardly mobile group, many of whom used their Yukon service as a stepping stone to a more fashionable parish elsewhere in Canada. Even those of long service were moved about so frequently that their work was hampered. The redoubtable A.C. McCullum, a quiet, modest man, worked at five different stations during his seventeen years in the Yukon. Cecil Swanson, who had served for four years among the Carmacks and Little Salmon people, was moved to Whitehorse, and from there he moved south. Like a number of other missionaries, he was convinced that the missionaries' mobility was undercutting their impact on the Native people.

To discover that many Anglican clergy used the Yukon as a stepping stone to a middle-class career in southern Canada should be no surprise. Why should the missionaries be any different from other whites in their approach to the Yukon? There were a number, of course, who saw the missionary enterprise differently and dedicated their lives to their Native congregations, in the manner of Roman Catholic priests. But such people were clearly the exception among the Protestant clergy in the Yukon.

There were alternatives to bringing white missionaries north, one of them being the recruitment of aboriginal clergy. Although the training of aboriginal catechists had long been an Anglican objective, Bishop Bompas had had little faith in their ability to spread the gospel. Bishop Stringer, more flexible and open and without the manpower to staff his widely scattered missions, took a different tack. During his tenure, which ended in 1932, Stringer recruited seven First Nations priests – Julius Kendi, K. Kunizzi, Richard Martin, John Martin, Amos Njootli, J. Pelisse, and John Tizya – and others as lay readers. Adapting the church to the presence of Native spiritual leaders was not always easy; they often expected more freedom, status, and salary than the church was prepared to give. Some whites within the church were troubled by the Natives' lack of formal education, and their concerns were heightened when several of the Native priests ran afoul of the church administration over financial and personal matters.

The church had other troubles. When John Machray, the financial officer of the Ecclesiastical Province of Rupert's Land and the University of Manitoba, absconded in 1932 with several hundred thousand dollars of trust funds, the northern missions faced a serious crisis. A.H. Sovereign, the current bishop of the Yukon, was transferred to the Diocese of Athabasca, and Bishop Geddes of Mackenzie River was given charge of the Yukon in addition to his other duties. In 1939 the Diocese of the Yukon was transferred to the Ecclesiastical Province of British Columbia, severing the connection with Red River and Winnipeg that had originated in the 1860s with the work of W.W. Kirkby and Robert McDonald.[28] Despite these struggles with finances and personnel, the Anglican Church pushed on with its missionary program for the Yukon First Nations. The cornerstones of this effort were the church's

The Anglican residential school at Carcross educated several generations of Protestant aboriginal children before it was destroyed by fire in 1939. The Roman Catholic children went to a school in northern British Columbia (Anglican Church Archives).

two residential schools, the Carcross (Choutla) school for Indians and St Paul's Hostel, which housed mixed-blood children, who were not eligible for entry into the Indian school.

The Carcross school, financed by the federal government, had opened in new quarters in 1911. The schooling program ran into numerous difficulties, not the least of which was the reluctance of most parents to part with their children for long periods of time. The devastation wrought by disease took its toll on the students, many of whom came to school already suffering from tuberculosis, and the tragic incidence of children dying while at Carcross eroded public confidence in the school. Through the years, the Anglicans constantly struggled with the First Nations' concern about the school and had great difficulty keeping it filled. The school's academic program was limited to basic writing and arithmetic, and promoted loyalty to Christianity and the British Empire. Particular emphasis was placed on practical skills. Native boys were taught carpentry, hunting, gardening, and, for a time, how to run a printing press. The girls were trained in domestic service and were expected to assist with the kitchen and cleaning work in the school. The teachers hoped that their students would leave school as missionaries in their own right, carrying to their communities a reverence for God, middle-class morality, southern standards of hygiene, and the Protestant work ethic. If properly prepared, the argument went, these young people would become the guiding lights for their villages, leading the Native population towards Christianity and the mainstream of Canadian culture.[29]

As the first graduates emerged from the school in the 1920s and 1930s, the missionaries' hopes were in most cases dashed. The shift from the rigidly controlled surroundings of the school dormitory to the more open lifestyle of the hunting camp required a sweeping transformation for which most students, after years in the school, were not prepared. In 1926 an Anglican from the Porcupine River area pleaded with Bishop Stringer not to send a girl back home:

If C— M—'s girl comes back, she is going into the filthiest hovel in the country ... A dirt floor, two tiny windows which cannot be seen for the flies, stinking meat and fish being all over the cabin, the stench unspeakable, six people already there, and now a seventh, and under the willows on the dirt floor, all the filth of a long winter throwing off a deadly effluvia, in a stifling heat ... Bishop, I plead with you not for humanity's sake, but for the sake of the Dear Lord who redeemed us, not to send a decent girl back to untold misery and evil, where she cannot help but curse the very day she was born.[30]

While whites seldom saw much value in indigenous lifeways – hence the almost hysterical tone in letters such as this – there was some reason for this concern. Children raised in the residential school under strict church discipline and in an environment totally unlike that of the Native village, would undoubtedly have difficulty readjusting to the old way of life. Moreover, the mission school specifically and systematically taught the children that village customs and traditions had no place in twentieth-century Canada.

There were a few "successes," as the church called young adults such as James Wood, Jacob Njootli, Johnny Johns, and Maggie Daniels, who became models of what the Anglican teachers hoped to produce. But for every success there were many who did not make the required adaptation and who found themselves struggling between the expectations raised by their education and the realities of life in the Yukon. A summer missionary at Carmacks in 1934 offered a succinct and accurate assessment of the issue. Graduates, he noted, "are potential outcasts of their own people and are not quite up to the standards of the white intellect. In other words, they are 'betwixt and between' – a condition of pitiful helplessness."[31]

From the beginning, the mission school was a complex and disruptive force in the lives of the Yukon First Nations, though no one familiar with the school doubted the zeal and commitment of the educators. The missionaries truly cared about the Native people, fervently believing that they were doomed unless they made an accommodation with the new literate and industrial order. However, their methods – their way of showing their love – left an indelible scar that ran through Native society in the territory, a scar that deepened and festered to become one of the most contentious points in aboriginal-white relations in the Yukon.

The Anglican Church followed a different policy with its school for mixed-blood children, St Paul's Hostel, which opened in Dawson City in 1920 and moved to the old Good Samaritan Hospital in 1923. The federal government made a special concession for this institution, providing financial support even though it was not legally required to do so. The school, supported initially by the Anglican Forward Movement, was under the control of Miss E.J. Naftel, formerly of Carcross. She was replaced in 1923 by C.F. Johnson, an old-time pioneer who, while on his way to the Klondike, had been convinced to join the missionary corps in the Mackenzie River district.[32] The hostel provided housing and close supervision for about thirty mixed-blood children, who attended regular classes in the Dawson public school. Out of school hours, they received additional instruction in practical skills.

Here there was no attempt to change the lives of the mixed bloods completely. To the church and the government, the fact that these children had at least half non-aboriginal parentage meant that they were closer to the norms of white society. As Bishop Geddes later commented, the hostel wanted only to allow each child "to fit himself to take his place in the community as a white man."[33] Most of the children had fairly regular contact with their parents, many of whom supported the school financially. St Paul's Hostel was far less intrusive, and hence less disruptive, than the Carcross residential school. Still, it stirred up its fair share of controversy. Some white parents protested the inclusion of mixed-blood children in the regular school system. The *Mayo-Keno Bulletin* in its September 1925 editorial bluntly stated the views of at least part of the community:

Why should the people's money be used to house, feed and clothe the somewhat prolific progeny of able bodied men who have mated with native women? ... Does the Federal Government realize that the result of its misplaced generosity is to encourage a certain class known as "squaw-men" to shift their parental responsibilities on the shoulders of an unwilling public?[34]

In an era of general financial restraint, the government seldom initiated programs specifically for the Yukon First Nations. Although John Hawksley, the Yukon's Indian agent, did look after the specific and local needs of the Natives, he did not travel around the Yukon a great deal and seldom sought out work for his office. He saw his job as one of mediating between First Nations and whites, and responded swiftly to any particular Native request, but he was not a strong or vocal advocate of aboriginal rights in the Yukon. Even this modest protection was lost, however, when Hawksley retired in 1933. No replacement was appointed. Instead, the government assigned responsibility for Indian affairs to the RCMP, which in turn made the job a part-time responsibility for one of its officers, on a rotation basis. For their part, the First Nations people placed few demands on the government. Those suffering from illness and able to get to a doctor or hospital received free medical attention, and relief was available for Natives facing privation, with the provision that able-bodied men and women were expected to work for their supplies. Only a few Natives, mostly widows and the elderly, availed themselves of such charity.[35]

Despite government expectations to the contrary, First Nations people did not provide much work for the police. In the 1920s the Old Crow people repeatedly ignored government regulations against gambling and drinking. They were confident that they would not be arrested, for the nearest court was hundreds of miles away in Dawson City. The government moved with glacial slowness in response to frequent police requests for the power to deal with the problem. Eventually, in 1928, the local missionary A.C. Mc-Cullum was appointed justice of the peace, but the commission looking into the affair arrived after he had moved away. Although the police continued to have problems imposing their will on the aboriginal people, few serious crimes in this period involved the latter. For instance, a 1921 rumour that the people of White River were planning a raid on a neighbouring band proved, on police investigation, to be groundless.

For both the First Nations people and the government, the issues of greatest concern were connected with land and harvesting rights. When Natives faced competition for resources in Old Crow in 1929 and at Little Atlin in 1932, the government stepped in and offered protection. Both First Nations and Indian agents supported more sweeping measures to assist Native interests and to prevent the overhunting that accompanied the revitalization of the fur trade in the 1920s, but these were not often implemented. When in 1932 Joe Squam requested ownership of his family's traditional lands around Wolf Lake, his application was rejected. Several years later, Harper Reed, Indian agent from the Stikine River Agency, proposed that a Native-only hunting reserve be established in the southern Yukon. But Mounted Police reports failed to substantiate Reed's claims that the land was being seriously overhunted. Charles Camsell, deputy minister for the Department of Mines, offered a more general reason for turning down the proposal: "If we are not going to reserve our northern regions exclusively for the use of the natives but are looking to encourage the opening of these regions to the people of Canada generally, then I think we must limit the extent of these preserves to meet the pressing needs of the natives but no more."[36]

While the federal government had clearly decided that the Yukon was not to be retained as a Native preserve, it had no clear idea of how the territory might develop. In the wake of the collapse of the Klondike goldfields, the government had all but given up on the Yukon, content to spend minimal sums maintaining a formal administrative presence. Because it retained control of natural resources, Ottawa had the power to set the pace for regional development. By contrast, the territorial council, which was the focal point for demands for government assistance, lacked the money and authority to assist or encourage expanded economic activity. The Yukon was not alone in this. Before 1930, the prairie provinces also lacked control of natural resources, and they devoted little attention to their northern lands until they had the rivers, lakes, minerals, land, and timber under their jurisdiction.

The federal government had a rationale for not investing more in the North. To expand too rapidly, it argued, would upset the balance of Native life, forcing hundreds of aboriginal people to depend on government support to survive. And a country as large as Canada had many demands on its meagre resources. Through the 1920s, much energy and capital was expended on readjusting to the postwar world, completing the settlement of the southern plains, and building the country's still limited industrial capacity. In the next decade, while governments across the country struggled with the Great Depression, even less attention was directed to the Canadian North. In the past, government-supported ventures, particularly railways and canals, had fuelled the country's economic expansion. The collapse of the national railway system during the First World War had taken the bloom off the Canadian tradition of mixed government and private investment.[37]

For these reasons, northern development was left to the marketplace and the investment patterns of southern corporations. The Treadwell Yukon Company, A.N.C. Treadgold's Yukon Consolidated Gold Corporation, and the White Pass and Yukon Route Corporation made the decisions that shaped the future of the Yukon. These decisions naturally rested on a concern for profits. By removing itself from the development game, the federal government lost the right and ability to regulate the economic development of the Yukon Territory. Since most of the corporations, with the notable exception of the White Pass and Yukon Route, acted with little concern for the long-term interests of the territory, the boom-and-bust pattern of the past was almost certain to continue.

Throughout these years the Yukon did, somewhat surprisingly, retain its single member of parliament. For much of that time, the member was George Black, ably aided by his formidable wife Martha. George was an old-time Conservative and an unabashed partisan, and his wife was, if anything, even more so. She dominated Dawson and Yukon society, assuming the British and Canadian mannerisms appropriate to her position as wife of a leading lawyer and, from 1912 to 1916, as wife of the territorial commissioner. George Black's wartime service, his solid Tory contacts, and his following throughout the Yukon brought him victory in the 1921 federal election. He was re-elected in 1925, 1926, and 1930, and during the government of R.B. Bennett he was made speaker of the House of Commons. In 1935, when he was stricken with a serious illness, Martha ran in his stead, appealing to Yukoners to elect her to office as a reward for her years of service to the territory.

The unabashed appeal to sentiment succeeded (but just barely), and Martha squeaked into office, the second woman ever elected to the House of Commons. George regained the seat in the next election and remained in office until 1949.[38]

George Black was a Tory of some note, but he was not a regional booster and did little to generate support for Yukon government. Although he made the obligatory backroom moves, he was unable to staunch the continued shrinkage of federal funding for the Yukon Territory. Perhaps no one could have stirred up much national interest in the Yukon's problems between the wars, but at a time when the territory required a vigorous and unabashed defender, it sent south a man with good political connections and personal ambition but not a great deal of fire.

Black's last years in office were somewhat troubled. He became a bit of a character, notorious for taking pot-shots at rabbits on Parliament Hill, and he had serious trouble with Prime Minister Mackenzie King, who refused him the usual prize of appointment the Privy Council, an honour finally accorded to him by Prime Minister Louis St Laurent. He died in 1965 at the age of ninety-two. Martha had predeceased him in 1957 aged ninety-one, still the grande dame of Yukon society.

Having decided to stay out of territorial development, the federal government continued to dismantle the territorial administration. The process had begun in the wake of the gold rush, but it intensified under Arthur Meighen when he was minister of the interior in Robert Borden's government. In 1918 Ottawa gave itself the power to disband the elected ten-member territorial council, planning to replace it with an appointed council of two. The territorial subsidy was slashed in half, forcing many civil servants out of their jobs and out of the territory. Yukoners protested, hoping to ward off yet another bodyblow to a society on the verge of total collapse. The government relented and decided to maintain an elected three-member council, with representatives from Dawson, the Klondike (shifted in 1926 to Mayo), and Whitehorse. While this was a far cry from the larger representative council of earlier years, the preservation of at least some local democracy was greeted enthusiastically in the region.

But the council had little effective power. The appointed commissioner controlled it and could veto its legislative and budgetary decisions. As the official representative of the federal government in the Yukon, the commissioner also controlled federal expenditures. He was like a British governor dominating unsophisticated colonials. The council and its small civil service found themselves constantly deferring to federal administrators. The major federal departments, especially the post office, the RCMP, and the Department of Public Works, controlled most of the money and thus much of the Yukon.

The territorial government itself had little money. Its revenue came from federal grants and a variety of sources, particularly the tax on liquor, but also

Left: George Black (1873–1965) served as commissioner of the Yukon from 1912 to 1916 and was the territory's member of parliament 1921–35 and 1940–49. He was speaker of the House of Commons 1930–35 (NA, PA 123538).

Right: Martha Munger Black (1866–1957) came north during the gold rush, raised a son alone, started a successful business, married George in 1904, and was the second woman elected to the Canadian parliament (1935–40). She and her husband were the Yukon's "first family" in the 1930s and 1940s (NA, C 23354).

hunting licences, fur export taxes, municipal levies, and registration fees. These sources provided some $200,000 in 1927, but the money was never enough to maintain the schools, libraries, health programs, roads, and bridges. Even more costly, as the Pioneers of '98 aged and became infirm, were the hospitals and welfare programs; Dawson's aging population was particularly expensive and, in economic terms, nonproductive. The regular addition of old-timers to the welfare rolls or their entry into hospital represented yet another drain on an already strained budget and was further confirmation of the continuing collapse of the Yukon economy and society.

Eventually the Yukon government turned into a single person. As funding dried up, civil servants laid off, and government work curtailed, George Jeckell emerged as the dominant administrative force in the Yukon. A solid if unadventurous man who adhered closely to his superiors' instructions, Jeckell – like the mounted police in the 1890s – had an unusual variety of titles. He had been named comptroller in 1913 (changed to "controller" in

1936), and later became public works agent, income tax inspector, mayor of Dawson (ex officio), registrar of land titles, and senior territorial executive officer, the latter following the abolition of the office of gold commissioner in 1932. It was, as Jim Lotz observed, "a withering away of the state in a way which Marx never envisaged. One man wore many hats, and the Commissioner was a virtual dictator, ruling the territory on behalf of the federal government."39

The Yukon's political impotence was emphasized by the re-emergence in the late 1930s of the proposal that British Columbia should annex it. The instigator was T. Duff Pattullo, who became premier of British Columbia in 1933. Pattullo had been a civil servant and businessman in the Klondike at the turn of the century and was enthusiastic about the prospect of northern development. After a term in office, with his province suffering through the depression, Pattullo linked the annexation of the Yukon to his plans for the construction of a highway to Alaska. The road, to be built as a public work, would open up the North, stimulate tourist traffic, and help offset the economic distress of the 1930s.

The federal government, anxious to be rid of a financial burden, had by April 1937 tentatively agreed to the transfer. Nobody asked what Yukoners thought; Ottawa had no constitutional duty to do so. Responding to organized complaints from the territory, Pattullo remarked, "It does not seem reasonable that the destiny of a territory as large as the Yukon should be finally determined by the few residents living there." The proposed annexation, announced with such fanfare and seemingly inevitable, failed over the question of continuing a territorial grant to St Mary's Catholic School, which at the time had only fifteen students. Prime Minister Mackenzie King, remembering what a political hot potato the funding of separate schools had been on the prairies, skipped deftly away from the issue, and the project fell through. The Yukon had been saved, not because Ottawa cared about it but through sectarian prejudice and political cowardice. The lack of concern in southern Canada for the integrity of the Yukon Territory was a cruel blow for those fighting to maintain a semblance of stability there.40

By the end of the 1930s, the Yukon had resignedly adjusted to its new condition, one very similar to its situation before the Klondike gold rush. The population was small, Ottawa's interest negligible, and economic returns modest, but for a few, hopes lived on. With the Klondike goldfields back in operation and the Mayo-Keno mines carrying the territory, its future looked promising, if not bright. There were, however, two Yukons by the end of the 1930s. In the mining corridor – Skagway to Whitehorse to Mayo to Dawson – the imperatives of the industrial age dominated. Here whites dominated the communities, and Native people were generally not welcome. Buttressed by government offices, seasonal transportation activities, and a small tourist trade, this sector of Yukon society clung to the legacy of the gold rush, living off the faded dreams of the Klondike and the belief that persistence would be rewarded in yet another boom. But many saw the Yukon only as a place to make money, and whether they were labourers, skilled workers, entrepreneurs, or industrialists, they invested their time and money and took their returns with them to southern Canada. It was not much of a basis on which to build stability.

The more stable part of Yukon society lay away from the mining corridor, along the streams and in the hills that made up so much of the territory's land mass. There was little here to excite the politicians or to fuel dreams of empire. But it was here that the First Nations people lived, almost alone in their commitment to the Yukon. There were a few whites in the "always afternoon years"[41] who shared the Native people's dedication to the people and land of the Yukon and who sought a better future for the North. But it was the First Nations who had the deepest and most enduring connection to the Yukon, past and present. They were not like their ancestors of a century before – technology, schools, missions, disease, and economic change had altered much of their pattern of life – but they remained uniquely adapted to the contemporary realities of life in the North. They were there for the long haul and were determined to be around when the goldfields ran bare and the silver and lead veins had been picked clean.

The irony is that to most observers the First Nations no longer seemed to be part of the Yukon. Visitors saw the decaying remnants of the Klondike rush and the modern machinery of the mining frontier. They saw white settlements and the signs of technological progress. In these surroundings, the aboriginal people seemed anachronistic, their hunting and trapping ways already outdated by the advance of western civilization. But the Yukon remained theirs in many ways. No treaties had been signed with them, and they the native people moved freely about the land, ignoring the seasonal migrations of other Yukon workers. In the winter months, when whites had left the territory or else stayed close to their communities, the Yukon seemed to have reverted back to the days of the fur trade.

The 1920s and 1930s were perhaps the Yukon's "winter years." For Yukon boosters, these were hard, bad times: the population had fallen, business was down, and productivity had dipped dangerously low. There was some hope that the next decade would bring a return to prosperity and a revitalization of the Yukon. This did happen, but not in a way that anyone could have guessed and not in a fashion that pleased the long-term residents of the Yukon. For in the next decade the Yukon Territory was be caught in a flood tide that was not of its own making, swept up in the forces of world power politics and another great war.

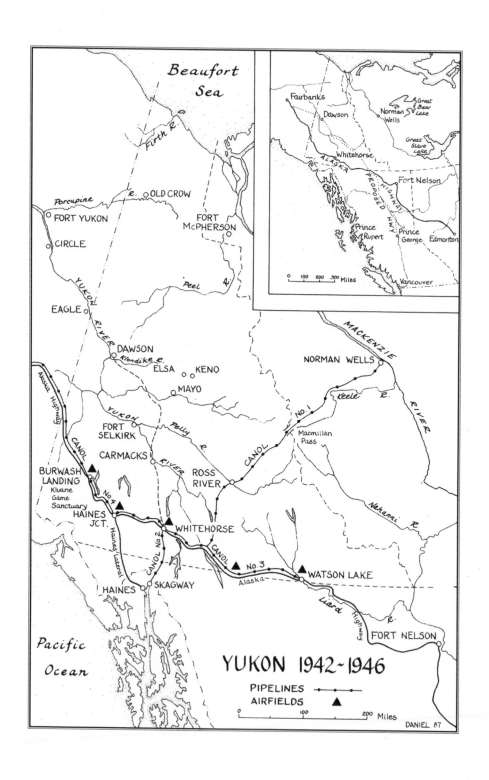

Beaufort Sea

Firth R.

Porcupine e. OLD CROW

FORT YUKON

CIRCLE

EAGLE

DAWSON
Klondike e.
ELSA   KENO
MAYO

FORT McPHERSON

Peel Ri.

Yukon River

FORT SELKIRK

CARMACKS

Yukon

Pelly R.

ROSS RIVER

BURWASH LANDING
Kluane Game Sanctuary
HAINES JCT.

Alaska Highway

CANOL

No. 4

No. 2

Haines Lateral

CANOL No. 2

WHITEHORSE

CANOL

HAINES   SKAGWAY

No. 3

Alaska Highway

WATSON LAKE

NORMAN WELLS

MACKENZIE

Keele R.

No. 1

Macmillan Pass

CANOL

Nahanni R.

RIVER

Liard R.

FORT NELSON

Pacific Ocean

YUKON 1942~1946

PIPELINES •——•——•
AIRFIELDS ▲

0   100   200 Miles

DANIEL 87

Inset map:

Fairbanks

Dawson

Norman Wells

Great Bear Lake

Whitehorse

Great Slave Lake

ALASKA HIGHWAY

PROPOSED HWY.

Fort Nelson

Prince Rupert

Prince George   Edmonton

Vancouver

0   100   200   300 Miles

EIGHT

War and Upheaval
1939–1946

By 1939 the Yukon seemed to have disappeared from the national consciousness. Tourist interest in the territory had dwindled to almost nothing during the Great Depression, as had the region's general economic vitality. The Yukon had returned almost to its pre-gold-rush roots, sustained only by the fur trade and a relatively stable dredge-mining sector based in the Klondike. But by 1943 this pattern had been overturned as tens of thousands of people once more flooded into the Yukon, upsetting the economic and social structure and setting the territory on a new course.

Yukoners in 1939 were not expecting a boom. Like other Canadians, they acknowledged the outbreak of war in Europe with resignation. The young men, many of whom had been without jobs for years, went off to recruitment centres and training camps. Klondike mining operations faced serious dislocations, especially the Yukon Consolidated Gold Corporation (YCGC), the Yukon's largest employer, which hired as many as seven hundred men a year to keep its dredges and subsidiary operations functioning. The wartime manpower shortage made it difficult to keep operating. While the YCGC's frustrations mounted – the gold was there but profits could be made only if the men could be found – there was little the company could do, but it kept going as best it could. In 1940 ten dredges were in operation, 625 men hired, and more than $2.6 million worth of gold recovered.

Bigger troubles lay ahead. Through the 1920s and 1930s, the YCGC had capitalized on the workers' need for employment by keeping wages relatively low and deferring improvements in the workplace. Lewis Green offers a dismal picture of the life of Klondike gold miners during those years:

The working conditions were often difficult. Despite protective clothing, the men on the stripping and thawing crews would be wet much of the day in temperatures that were often close to zero Fahrenheit towards the end of the season. Most shifts were ten hours long, seven days a week, all paid at the going hourly rate without overtime. All employees were required to produce. Any unable to meet the company's expectations, whether for physical or other reasons, were replaced immediately. The camps were spread out along the creeks, up to fifty miles from Dawson. Even though new buildings had been added, the camps were often crowded and lacked many amenities, such as adequate washing facilities. There were many complaints over the food.[1]

Before the Second World War, workers in the North had little option but to accept these terms, if only for one season before they could leave for the outside. Now, with a great demand for skilled industrial workers throughout the country, Klondike miners were in a sellers' market. In July 1941, at the height of the mining season, the YCGC workers demanded a cost-of-living bonus of a dollar a day. When the company refused to negotiate, the men dropped their tools and marched to Dawson City. The arrival of close to five hundred men worried the townsfolk. What were their intentions? Would the local economy collapse? The protest leaders kept the men in close check and prevented any violence, and they waited for the company to act. The company offered to meet the workers halfway, but the men held out for more. Finally, after nine days on the streets of Dawson, discussions between the labour leaders, company officials, and a federal negotiator flown in specially to deal with the crisis resolved the impasse. The workers received a substantial wage boost – sixty-two cents per shift – and also gained recognition of their "employees' council," a major concession from the anti-union YCGC.

Although improved wage rates and some small improvements in living conditions stabilized the workforce temporarily, opportunities on the outside were too attractive for many Klondike miners. From a prewar level of more than 700 men each season, the YCGC could put only 400 men in the field in 1942, only 172 two years later, and 186 the following year. The company had no choice but to close down dredges; in 1944 only three of the massive machines remained in operation. Eventually, the company took the unprecedented step of hiring Native workers. The experiment was not a success – though the men were "dependable employees" – because the Natives continued to follow the seasonal cycles of the harvesting economy and were not prepared to alter their patterns to suit the gold-mining industry's requirements.[2]

The workforce returned at the end of the war, but in the interim YCGC's production fell precipitously. From a high of $2.8 million in 1942, returns fell to slightly over $610,000 in 1944, even though the price of gold rose from $36.00 to $38.50 an ounce in the early 1940s. The dislocation of gold-mining operations knocked out one of the cornerstones of the territorial economy – and it was not the only foundation to be eroded.

The Treadwell Yukon Company had carried the Yukon through much of the 1920s. The company had explored extensively through the mountains in the Mayo-Keno-Elsa area, seeking out new silver-lead deposits in an attempt to keep operations alive. Throughout the 1930s, the firm maintained a high level of production and profits while rapidly depleting the known resources. Returns fell off dramatically in the late 1930s. The Silver King property went out of production in 1939, followed by the Elsa mine and processing mill. When the U.S. government stopped the purchase of foreign silver during the Second World War, Treadwell Yukon lost its principal market. The combination of closed markets, lower prices, and the near exhaustion of the major ore bodies was too much for the company. In its 1941 annual report, Treadwell Yukon announced that it would be unable to continue operating, and in May 1942 the Treadwell Yukon Company was formally dissolved. The company had few regrets. It had reinvested in the Yukon only those sums necessary to increase the productivity and profitability of its operations; the profits had been exported and invested outside the Yukon. According to one conservative estimate, Treadwell Yukon profits had reached $4.6 million, or 20 per cent of the total value of the mineral production from the area. Now the mines that had carried the Yukon were closed.[3]

In other circumstances, the closure of the Treadwell properties would have devastated the Yukon Territory. The territorial government had invested heavily in public services and transportation facilities for the Mayo region. This expenditure, and the people working for the government, were now redundant. The White Pass and Yukon Route company relied heavily on the silver and lead mines; close to 40 per cent of the company's earnings came from this single region, permitting it to maintain its full Yukon operations. In normal times, the ripple effects would have ruined the territorial economy, but these were far from normal times, and the closure of the Treadwell Yukon properties seemed scarcely important in the hyperinflated wartime economy of the Yukon.

During the First World War, Yukoners had struggled to show their interest and involvement in the international confrontation. They faced no such challenge in the Second World War, for the war came to them. Between 1942 and 1946, thousands of American soldiers and civilians poured into the territory, preparing the way for the defence of the far northwest. In a fashion reminiscent of the Klondike gold rush, the Yukon was transformed while once more attracting attention across North America. The Yukon had been rediscovered and would never be the same again.

The story begins back in the days before the war. For years, the politicians of Alaska and the Yukon had been lobbying unsuccessfully for a highway link to the south. They had, at different times, received support from fellow promoters in British Columbia, the Pacific northwestern states, and Alberta, and from other provinces and states that hoped to capitalize on the future development of the Northwest. The fate of these proposals reveals much about the nature of northern isolation and southern interest in the Yukon and Alaska.[4]

The most highly publicized venture originated with T. Duff Pattullo, premier of British Columbia in the 1930s. As mentioned above, he had been in the Klondike during the gold rush – he was a Liberal patronage appointee assigned to assist the commissioner of the Yukon – and he had been captivated by the prospects for the North and recognized the need for an all-Canadian overland link to the Klondike. Pattullo's predecessor as premier, Simon Fraser Tolmie, also had dreamed of a highway to the North, and had even convinced the United States to sponsor a joint commission to investigate the prospects for such a road. At the time, partisan concerns had forced Pattullo to oppose the venture, but when he became elected premier in 1933 he quickly revived his own dreams for the North.

Pattullo took office in the midst of a severe depression and found the provincial treasury bare. Nonetheless, he believed that government spending on major public works such as bridges, hospitals, and highways could lead the provincial economy out of the economic collapse. His problem was that he had no money for such ventures. When the United States Congress voted $2 million in 1935 for a highway to Alaska, the idea that had simmered in Pattullo's mind for many years came to the fore.

The Alaska Highway took on special life in 1937. Pattullo turned for support to the Liberal prime minister, William Lyon Mackenzie King, but King, as usual, was cautious about anything that smacked of innovation or expenditure. U.S. President Franklin D. Roosevelt, on the other hand, supported the plan and encouraged Pattullo to continue his efforts. The federal government resented the British Columbia premier's intervention in what was clearly a matter for the diplomatic service. King was particularly incensed, confiding to his diary that Pattullo, "like a fool, has been telling the Americans what to do to get under way with public works in Canada." Nevertheless, the British Columbia initiative had forced the federal government's hand. More formal planning would have to follow, though Ottawa remained unconvinced of the value of such massive expenditures in the isolated and voter-less frontier.

In 1938 the U.S. government established the Alaska Highway Commission to investigate the various proposals for a road to Alaska. At the Americans' urging, Pattullo then pressed Ottawa to establish a similar commission in Canada. Although King did so, he appointed as chairman of the Canadian Highway Commission a man named Charles Stewart, who happened to be very seriously ill and thus was unable to devote himself fully to the commission's work. The two commissions made extensive studies and visited the North, and in 1940 they wrote their reports. The American study supported the construction of a coastal route, running behind the Alaskan panhandle and providing for future access to coastal areas. The Canadian commissioners offered an uninspired and inconclusive summary of the two main routes proposed, favouring the interior route – north from Prince George to Dawson City – rather than the line preferred by the Americans. Ottawa was obviously counting on the commission to stall deliberation of a serious and, to the people of the Northwest, important issue, and much to Pattullo's chagrin, it worked. Pattullo resigned as premier in 1941 and was not around when new circumstances forced a hasty re-examination of the 1930s work of the highway promoters.

At the same time that British Columbia's Duff Pattullo and Warren Magnusson of Washington State were promoting a highway north through British Columbia, politicians on the Canadian and American prairies were also talking of a highway to Alaska. A well-organized group, the United States–Canada–Alaska Prairie Highway Association, drew financial and political support from North Dakota, Saskatchewan, and Alberta (especially Edmonton, which saw itself as the natural gateway to the Northwest). The organization was slower off the mark than Pattullo in British Columbia, but by the early 1940s it had established a political pressure campaign, hoping to convince American and Canadian decision makers to opt for a prairie route to Alaska. F.S. Wright, a tireless promoter of northern development, provided much of the inspiration and data for the campaign.[5]

While the talk of a highway wa sgoing on, work was underway on the improvement of airplane facilities in the Northwest. The most enthusiastic promoters spoke of a "Great Circle Route" connecting the Canadian Northwest, Alaska, Siberia, and China. For British and Canadian authorities anxious to tap into the Far East, the proposal was especially attractive. As early as 1935, Dan McLean, an employee of the Department of Transport, had flown an aerial reconnaissance throughout the Northwest with the famous northern bush pilot Punch Dickens, and just before the outbreak of war in Europe, the federal government authorized preliminary survey work on the planned airway to the Orient. Airfields were laid out at Grande Prairie, Alberta, at Fort St John and Fort Nelson in British Columbia, and at Watson Lake and Whitehorse in the Yukon. Later work led to the establishment of similar emergency airstrips between the major fields. The route was usable for daylight flying in 1941 and radio stations were opened along the flight path by the end of the year.[6]

As the war progressed, the function of these fields, initially intended for commercial traffic, was transformed. The Northwest Staging Route became particularly important with the entry of Russia into the war in 1941. The Lend-Lease program, authorized by Congress in March 1941, was extended to the Soviet Union three months after it entered the war. Now, Allied war machinery was shipped by air through the Northwest and across Siberia to the front lines of the battle with the forces of Nazi Germany. The Red Star became a routine sight in the skies of the Northwest, as a steady stream of planes headed to Fairbanks, where Russian pilots took them over. But even this was only a preliminary to the main show.

On 7 December 1941, Japanese fighter planes and bombers attacked Pearl Harbor in Hawaii. The daring raid caught the United States unprepared. Where would the next attack come? Residents of the Pacific Coast, their discriminatory attitude towards Orientals now tinged with a genuine fear of Japanese militarism, prepared for an attack. Although a realistic appraisal of the military significance of the region suggested that the danger was less than it appeared, North America's northern flank was unprotected. Something had to be done quickly, if only to soothe public opinion.

It is difficult today to recreate the fear and unease of those troubled days of late 1941 and early 1942. The forces of freedom around the world were in retreat. France had fallen to the Germans and Britain was facing the ferocious attacks from the Luftwaffe. The American fleet in the Pacific had been badly damaged; Hong Kong, Manila, and Singapore had been captured by the Japanese, and the British navy had lost much of its Pacific fleet. As the months went by, matters only worsened. Allied forces were in retreat across North Africa as General Rommel pressed towards the Nile, and German armies had the Soviet forces on the run on the Eastern Front. For Canadians, confirmation of the severity of the wartime situation came in August 1942 with the fatally flawed attack on Dieppe, in which many Canadian soldiers were killed and wounded. One could well understand how, in those desperate days, North Americans might wonder if their continent, too, was about to face the full power and destruction of an enemy invasion.

Alaska and the Canadian Northwest seemed particularly vulnerable. The Aleutian Islands chain reached to within 800 miles (1,300 km) of Japan, and in 1942 the Japanese began to move up the islands, capturing Kiska, Attu, and attacking Dutch Harbor. While the military challenge was met by a combined Canadian and American force in several bloody battles in what has been labelled "the forgotten war," the broader question of North American defence had yet to be addressed. Within days of Pearl Harbor, in fact, discussions had started on how best to protect the region from Japanese attack. Even as the military response was being mounted, work was underway on solving the long-term defence requirements of the Northwest.

Before the war, Canadian and American planners had dismissed the need for a highway to Alaska, claiming that the advantages of such a costly venture were "negligible," but with the attack on Pearl Harbor, political pressure for the highway increased dramatically. President Roosevelt and others who had supported the project before the war – notably, the territorial delegate Anthony Dimond of Alaska – welcomed the reopening of the discussion. The politicians asked their advisers in the War Plans Division to examine the strategic value of the highway. Professional soldiers studied the prewar surveys and weighed the project against the country's many pressing needs. Their advice went against the prevailing political wisdom. Not only was a highway not needed for military purposes, but expenditures on a project of this type would take away from more urgent military requirements. The rationale was simple. The U.S. Navy argued that it could continue to supply Alaska with all strategic goods. Moreover, the major military sites in Alaska were located along the coast and would not be accessible via the highway in any case. As M.V. Bezeau concluded in his study of the strategic planning process, the road was "a magnificent achievement carried out as a military project in time of war. But it was not needed for defence. The highway was actually planned and built for other reasons."[7] On 12 February 1942, the U.S. government ignored the professional advice and decided to proceed with the highway.

There was another potential stumbling block. Although the highway ended in Alaska, it had to cross vast reaches of Canadian territory. It followed, therefore, that Canadian permission had to be secured before construction started. Canadian authorities disagreed with the American decision to build the highway, echoing the concerns of the U.S. military about the lack of strategic value. But they would not – and perhaps could not – block it. Since the Americans were going to pay the entire cost, Canada could scarcely stand in the way. As Hugh Keenleyside, assistant undersecretary of state for external affairs, noted, "The United States is now so insistent ... that the Canadian Government cannot possibly allow itself to be put into the position of barring ... land access to Alaska." Further, he pointed out, "this argument should be recognized, in our own minds at least, as being based on political and not strategic grounds. The political argument, given the attitude of Washington, is inescapable; the strategic argument, in my opinion, is a most dubious egg."[5] On 5 March 1942 the Canadian government approved the Americans' request. Construction could begin on the Highway to Alaska.

As yet, no one knew which route the highway would take. A public hearing was called before the Committee of Public Roads in Washington in early February to deal with submissions on possibilities. Halvor Halvorson, president of the United States–Canada–Alaska Prairie Highway Association, spoke for proponents of the prairie route. Halvorson faced considerable opposition to his presentation, particularly from the many supporters of the inland highway through British Columbia. To his delight, however, the U.S. government decided to proceed as he had recommended; a prairie route would be built under treaty with Canada, and not as a project undertaken by Congress and therefore subject to political pressure. As he later wrote, somewhat sanctimoniously, "We won the fight on the merits. What political pressure was used, was entirely from the opposition, who carried their story and opposition to not only the Army, and the Secretary of State, but directly to the President of the United States himself."[9]

Seldom has a project of this magnitude been undertaken with such haste and so little planning. The earlier work of the Canadian and American highway commissions was consulted and then rejected, so the whole project had to begin as if the idea were entirely new. The task of managing this unwieldy project fell to the solid, thick-jawed Colonel William Hoge, a veteran of the U.S. Army Corps of Engineers. Hoge had impressive First World War battle credentials, advanced study in engineering at Massachusetts Institute of Technology, and had considerable experience with frontier road construction. He faced an enormous challenge. But he had little to work with, except an order to push through the pioneer road in the first year (1942) and a requirement that his highway must link the existing airfields of the Northwest Staging Route. Beyond that, Hoge had no idea of where the highway would go. However, he could call on the assistance of Canadian surveyors already in the area. Knox McCusker, the dominion land surveyor, offered to guide the trailblazing crews into the field before spring breakup called a halt to winter operations. Hoge relied heavily on McCusker and his crews, who played a major role in laying down the initial path north from Fort St John.[10]

Hoge divided the highway into two sections: north of Watson Lake and south of it. Fort St John was named the southern headquarters, while the main administrative centre was located in Whitehorse – the centre with the best combination of river, rail, and air facilities north of Edmonton. Hoge separated the two commands, retaining control of the northern sector and placing Colonel James "Patsy" O'Connor in charge of the Fort St John headquarters. In addition to the crews working north and south from Whitehorse, north from Fort St John, and south from Big Delta in Alaska, Hoge, again with McCusker's assistance, rushed a work crew into the Fort Nelson area before the spring thaw of 1942. This manoeuvre allowed construction to begin north of the Peace River through the spring and early summer.

Work on the pioneer road proceeded at a breakneck pace, for almost 1,500 miles (2,400 km) had to be finished before winter. Carefully managed workcrews pushed into the forest:

Two men ... blazed the initial rough trail. After them came the stadia party. Its members ran the preliminary line and cut a pack trail of sorts for the use of advance transport. The surveyors were quickly followed by a single bulldozer cutting a swath through tree growth along the centre line so that the next bulldozers, in squads of six, could concentrate on cleaning up the resulting debris. This clearing operation made way for rough as well as finished grading work all along the line of construction. After the Cats had levelled the roadway for grading, subsequent parties located the final route, building corduroy roads wherever required. The general scene was one of intense activity. Pack trains threaded their

Colonel William Hoge was in command of the first phase of the Alaska Highway construction, surveying most of the route from the air (United States National Archives [USNA], 13974).

way through tangles of tractors, graders and men. Radio equipment enabled workers to keep in close, constant touch with each other's work all along the line. At this stage of the project, men worked extremely long shifts. Motors were seldom turned off. Trucks moved night and day.[11]

Work was off to a great start. But the actual route had still not been finalized!

Hoge worked on the road survey with engineers from the Public Roads Administration, an American civilian agency that would be responsible for turning the army's hastily built pioneer road into a usable, year-round highway. While the area north of Whitehorse was well known – there was a

Colonel Hoge and Colonel E.G. Paules of the 18th Engineer Regiment inspecting
the highway route around Kluane Lake in the southwest Yukon in the spring
of 1942 (authors' collection)

wagon trail of sorts from Whitehorse to Kluane Lake – selecting the route
from Fort St John to Whitehorse was another matter. Native guides were extremely useful for local work, helping army crews find their way through
river valleys and around the mountains which the Natives knew so well.
They could not, however, help with the siting of the entire road. That task
fell largely to Bill Hoge.

Knowing only that he had to connect up the airfields, Hoge set out to select a route. After exhausting all the available information, he turned to Les
Cook, one of the region's best bush pilots, and day after day Cook and Hoge
flew over the land between Fort Nelson and Whitehorse. Cook was instru-
mental in locating a suitable pass between the Mackenzie River and Yukon

The first intimation that some First Nations people in the southern Yukon had that a highway was being built was a bulldozer crashing through the trees near their community (USNA, 139746).

In the early stages of highway construction, the U.S. Army Corps of Engineers brought supplies in by pack train (USNA, 144826).

River watersheds. By early June, reconnaissance parties had travelled the route laid out by Cook and Hoge.[12] Construction crews could now proceed with reasonable confidence that they knew where they were going. Few Canadians had been consulted on the general path of the highway, a cause for concern in some quarters: "While there is unanimous approval of the decision to build the highway and almost equally unanimous satisfaction that the advice of qualified military experts is being relied upon, especially in the controversial matter of the choice of route, nevertheless there have been a few isolated expressions of discontent on the choice made."[13]

Hoge's problems were not over once the route was selected. He did not get along well with Brigadier General Clarence Sturdevant, who had overall responsibility for the highway. Nor did his operation mesh well with the Public Roads Administration's activities in the area. (The latter's initial plan had called for the improved highway to follow the route set out by army crews). Hoge faced many difficulties managing the large number of workers under his direction. The men often were sent into the field without the proper equipment and supplies. As one regimental historian recounted, work north of Whitehorse started slowly; the soldiers worked "in coolie fashion, bending pick points in frozen ground and mucking around in rivers of mud, going nowhere." The heavy equipment eventually arrived, allowing the men to proceed in an orderly fashion. But ice, snow, spring rains, hot summers, and mosquitoes complicated the work and added to the workers' frustrations.

From an engineering perspective, permafrost and muskeg presented the greater challenges. Where possible, the highway was routed around the muskeg; otherwise, corduroy roads (logs laid side by side at a right angle to the roadway) were built over the surface. Dealing with permafrost was more difficult. In many places, surface soil and vegetation were scraped off, exposing an apparently hard surface underneath. Within hours, as the hitherto insulated soil thawed, the hard pack turned into a quagmire. Only slowly did the engineers discover the need to build up a "blanket," or extra level of insulation, over the permafrost.

In the middle of 1942, Bill Hoge was abruptly fired. His superior officer, Brigadier General Sturdevant, had visited the highway in July 1942 and liked what he had seen but suggested that Hoge try to coordinate his work more closely with the Public Roads Administration. News that the highway was well ahead of schedule, coupled with mounting criticism of the route selected, convinced Lieutenant General Brehon Somervell, commanding general for services and supply, that he too should visit the area. Somervell, "whose reputation for pomp, show, and grand designs was unrivaled in the United States Army,"[14] was not impressed by the apparent chaos throughout the Northwest. With little warning – and little justification beyond a dislike for

Hoge – he relieved the highway commander of his duties. Colonel "Patsy" O'Connor was given charge of a revamped administrative structure, which was called the Northwest Service Command and was based in Whitehorse. Hoge's career picked up with little interruption. He played a major role in the Allied landing in Europe, continued up the ranks, and ended his career as commander-in-chief of the United States Army in Europe.

Under Hoge and then O'Connor, the U.S. Army Corps of Engineers completed its assigned task on schedule. The more than ten thousand men assigned to the project (including several regiments of African American engineers) pushed the pioneer road through expeditiously. The highway was officially opened to much fanfare on 20 November 1942, at Soldier's Summit near Kluane Lake. It was a striking engineering accomplishment, even though it was far from the finished highway that government officials had promised. Some 1,500 miles (2,400 km) of rough pioneer road had been pushed through the Northwest in a single year. Despite all the celebration, and a sense throughout North America that the project was all but finished, a major part of it still lay ahead.

A White Pass and Yukon Route train leaving Skagway in 1942 loaded with trucks and equipment to be used on Alaska Highway construction. The company's rolling stock was worn out by the end of the war (USNA, 150175).

Before the bridges were built, the engineers sometimes used cable ferries, using the power of the current to push a raft attached to a cable strung from shore to shore (USNA, 143380).

There were many accidents and some fatalities along the highway during the construction period. Trucks that broke down or ran off the road were abandoned and cannibalized for spare parts (U.S. Army Corps of Engineers Archives).

Black troops of the U.S. Army Corps of Engineers building a timber bridge over a small river somewhere along the Alaska Highway in the summer of 1942 (USNA, 139940)

The Public Roads Administration (PRA) had been involved with the project from the beginning. Their task, using staff engineers and civilian contractors, was to improve the military road to the appropriate civilian standard, to replace temporary bridges, and otherwise to make the Alcan Highway (as it was called) usable on a year-round basis. Since this was wartime, supplies were hard to come by, but fortunately the PRA had many warehouses filled with material left over from depression-era construction projects. In the haste of the moment, the contents of these warehouses were loaded, almost intact, onto railway cars and shipped north to Dawson Creek, in northern British Columbia. Much of the stuff was unnecessary – only a certain number of typewriters and filing cabinets could be used – and was discarded upon arrival in the Northwest. PRA crews took most of 1942 to get started, although their engineering divisions were extremely active, laying the plans for an extensive push in 1943 to complete the highway.[15]

Already in 1942 the PRA had begun to line up the contractors. Most were American: Dowell Construction, Okes Construction, Lytle and Green Construction, and W. Green Co. But there was one major Canadian participant, R. Melville Smith Co. These companies managed major sections of the highway and hired subcontractors (forty-seven in 1942 and eighty-one the following year) to handle specific tasks. Together, these companies supervised

VIEW ALONG THE NEW ALCAN HIGHWAY THROUGH CANADA'S WILDERNESS
BUILT BY A WELCOME ARMY OF U. S. SOLDIERS
BY PERMISSION OF WARTIME INFORMATION BOARD

There were several "suicide hills" along the Alaska Highway. This one shows why the road had to be rerouted after the initial construction period. This photo was made into a postcard whose caption read "View along the New Alcan Highway through Canada's Wilderness Built by a Welcome Army of U.S. Soldiers" (authors' collection).

the work of 7,500 workers in 1942 and more than 14,000 in 1943. Work was done on a cost-plus basis – the contractors were paid all expenses plus a percentage of the profit – an arrangement that eliminated the need for time-consuming tendering delays.

The division of labour between the Corps of Engineers and the PRA caused some difficulties. The PRA found its men and equipment being diverted to assist with the high-priority task of completing the Alcan Highway in the first year. According to one estimate, PRA crews, alone or together with the army, built more than three-quarters of the pioneer road. In 1943 the PRA turned to the task of improving it but quickly discovered that huge sections of the original road were unusable and would have to be abandoned. Engineers of the PRA began to survey a route for the new road that often deviated by miles from the army one. In many places, the pioneer road would serve as little more than an access route to the new highway, eliminating much of the value of the initial project.

The U.S. government was understandably angered by this costly and seemingly unnecessary duplication. In 1943 it admitted that the Alcan Highway was not needed for military and supply purposes, beyond providing a land link for the airfields. The project was downgraded considerably, and the U.S. government even approached Canadian authorities and asked them to take over control of the route. Boastful newspaper and radio accounts still talked of the "high-quality, well-finished road" to Alaska, but Canadian authorities, well-informed by C.K. LeCapelain, its liaison officer in the area, knew better. The U.S. government had reneged on its promise to complete a proper civilian road, though Canada could hardly object, since the Americans were dedicated to a major war effort and had built the road without Canadian involvement. However, the federal government could, and did, ignore American requests in 1944 that Canada assume responsibility for the highway, since the initial agreement required that the United States would maintain the highway until six months after the war.[16]

In regions of permafrost, bulldozing the trees and tearing off the top layer of dirt led to thawing and spectacularly bad driving conditions (USNA, 146243).

Washouts in the spring of 1943 did extensive damage to the highway (USNA).

Many of the original bridges were destroyed by flooding in the spring of 1943 and had to be rebuilt or replaced. Note the new bridge in the background (authors' collection).

The Alcan (renamed Alaska) Highway was but one arm of the American "invasion" of the Canadian Northwest. In one of the most ill-conceived construction projects of the war, one producing many boondoggles, the U.S. government authorized the development of the Norman Wells oilfield in the Mackenzie River valley, the building of a pipeline overland to Whitehorse, and the erection of a modern refinery in Whitehorse. The pipeline cut across one of the most isolated portions of the Yukon Territory, providing access to the Macmillan Pass area, crossing the Pelly River at the village of Ross River, and joining the Alaska Highway north of Teslin Lake. Known as the Canol Project, the undertaking promised the highway and associated airfields a ready supply of inexpensive fuel, which would be delivered throughout the North by pipelines running from Whitehorse south to Watson Lake and north to Fairbanks. Another branch connected Whitehorse to the coast at Skagway.

The undertaking was beset with problems from the beginning, not the least being the building of a pipeline through hundreds of miles of undeveloped territory. Shoddy construction of the line, a lack of understanding of northern conditions, and a shocking lack of attention to fiscal concerns inflated the project's costs wildly. The project was completed but "was allowed to wither, subject to some fancy diplomatic footwork which upset the Americans, and remained a junkyard monument to military stupidity."[17]

The transformation of the Northwest was clearly underway, and there was more to come. The backlog of supplies at Skagway and along the White Pass and Yukon Route convinced the Americans that an additional access road was required. As work continued on the main highway, workers pushed south from what is now Haines Junction towards the coast. Other crews started from the fishing town of Haines, Alaska, and worked north. The construction of the Haines Road allowed for the movement of supplies from the coast into the interior, without relying on the overtaxed Skagway-Whitehorse railway. There were other projects as well. Airfields were upgraded, hangars built, and access roads constructed. Additional emergency airstrips were constructed. A telephone system was built along the highway, providing greater contact with the outside than Yukoners had ever known.

The impact of all this on the Yukon Territory went far beyond the provision of a new road, airfields, a pipeline, and a telephone line. The Yukon had had fewer than 5,000 people in 1941, 30 per cent of whom were Natives. The white population lived in a few communities – Whitehorse, Dawson, Mayo – with only a few missionaries, police officers, and fur traders in the outlying areas. Almost overnight, 10,000 American military and an equally large number of civilian workers (some Canadian but mostly American) flooded into the Northwest. By the end of 1942, the Whitehorse area alone had a population four times that of the prewar Yukon. The American invasion affected all aspects of Yukon life, created the greatest boom since the Klondike gold rush, and set the territory on a markedly different course.

It was not a course that Yukoners directed or even influenced. They had, certainly, often petitioned for the construction of a highway and, regardless of the circumstances, they were pleased that they were about to get their connection to the outside. But more than a few expressed severe disappointment with the selected southern route, which entirely missed the heavily mineralized Mayo area and ran far south of Dawson City. Only the residents of Whitehorse could be pleased with this highway, which ignored the social and economic realities of the territory.

The disruptions hit all levels of Yukon society. In 1942 the U.S. Army leased the White Pass and Yukon Route, and only two months later a Canadian official reported that Yukoners were furious:

The U.S. Army has taken over the White Pass Railway on a lease. Before the lease was given, Ottawa was consulted and approved of the transfer. It was distinctly understood that shipments for the Canadian Government Departments and for the needs of the civilian population of the Yukon, were to be handled with reasonable dispatch. The operation of the railway under the U.S. Army has been very unsatisfactory and the service rendered to the people of the Yukon has been just about as bad as could be. The military handling the operation of the railway simply takes the attitude that the army comes first and Canadian Government, airport supplies and freight for the civilian population can take what is left, which, at the present time is NOTHING.[18]

The Americans ran the railway hard, pushing it twenty-four hours a day during the summer and keeping trains going all winter long. They did not, unfortunately, pay much attention to roadbed and running-stock maintenance, leaving the railway in bad shape when the lease ended. The army gave highway-related shipments top priority on the railway, making it difficult for commercial and domestic consumers to plan for their own needs. Repeated protests by George Jeckell, the highest ranking territorial official, on behalf of the Yukon government were ignored, and it was only when construction demand slowed after 1943 that civilian needs were given a reasonable priority. This was wartime, after all, and Yukoners knew they had little right to complain about such comparatively trifling inconveniences. The federal government helped out somewhat by not applying national rationing to the territory, though shortages of key commodities ensured long line-ups in front of the stores – especially the liquor store – when supplies arrived.

The construction projects also created opportunities. Workers from around the territory were drawn to the high-paying jobs along the highway or pipeline complex, making it extremely difficult for local employers to find suitable employees. C.J. Rogers, president of the White Pass and Yukon Railway, complained to George Black, "Our Labour and Wage situation is all snarled up here on account of the arrival of American contractors who are

George Jeckell came to the Yukon early in the twentieth century, was appointed comptroller in 1913 and served as the Yukon's senior executive officer from 1932 to 1947. He was a "virtual dictator, ruling the territory on behalf of the federal government" (NA, PA 164029).

competing for local labour and paying a wage scale away in excess of that prevailing for any similar kind of work such as on the airfield here. They initially agreed not to disturb the local scale."[19]

Not surprisingly, Yukoners preferred the high-paying American jobs to low-paying Canadian work. Eventually Humphrey Mitchell, Canada's minister of labour, stepped in and ruled that only Americans were eligible for work with American companies. Horace Moore, publisher of the *Whitehorse Star*, protested this policy as manifestly unfair: "It might reasonably be construed as placing a penalty on one's nationality ... As long as Canadian labour is available here there is no real necessity or reason for the U.S. contractors being compelled to import U.S. citizens, none of whom will contribute a single cent toward Canadian taxation and whose earnings, for the most part, will be transmitted to the United States."[20] Moreover, as the initial agreements took effect, Yukoners found that they did not have equal access to all the jobs.

Because the Americans were supervising and paying for the construction of the defence projects, the Canadian government agreed to their request that American wage rates and wartime regulations would apply to American nationals working in the Northwest. Canadians came under the jurisdiction of the Western Regional Labour Board, which decided whether labour could be spared for specific tasks and set wage rates for all Canadian workers. Canadian contractors and subcontractors hired Canadian personnel, while Americans sought their employees in the United States. Given that most of the contractors were American, this meant that the majority of the work was undertaken by U.S. citizens. While a general shortage of workers throughout the Northwest limited Canadian protests, there were occasions when Yukoners found themselves barred from high-paying jobs in favour of workers brought in from the United States.[21]

The regulations were not rigidly enforced, especially in the isolated camps along the highway and the Canol pipeline, far removed from the watchful eyes of highway administrators. Canadians raised no objections when an employer agreed to pay the prevailing American scale – a better option perhaps than having a bitter employee. Most workers imported from the outside approached highway work in a "get rich quick" frame of mind, an attitude that discouraged a strict imposition of the rules. Rigidity on this question, officials realized, "would probably have created some friction particularly when most Canadians were looking for some of this 'easy American money.'"[22]

The wage differentials were substantial enough to create considerable hostility. Bechtel, Price, Callahan, one of the largest contractors on the northern defence projects, paid its American labourers on the Canol project US $1.00 per hour; a Canadian employee doing the same job received CDN 50¢ (and the Canadian dollar was fixed at US90¢ throughout the war). The pattern was the same for other job classifications: American truck drivers received $1.40; Canadian 85¢. An electrician from the United States was paid $1.50 an hour; his Canadian counterpart, working in his own country, received $1.00 Other companies followed the same basic scale. Although the difference was narrowed through the war years, high American salaries remained a major grievance for Canadian workers in the Yukon.

The grievances over wage rates spilled over into intense controversies concerning the application of American laws in Canada's North. Negotiations between Ottawa and Washington resulted in the establishment of concurrent jurisdiction in the Northwest. While Canadian laws remained in force, American soldiers and workers came under the authority of U.S. military and civilian regulations. Initially, these regulations applied only within the confines of American work camps, a situation few Canadians found unsettling. But as time passed and as it became increasingly evident that the Canadian government was reluctant to press its own authority in the region, the Americans expanded their authority beyond their own establishments.

Although the American presence was generally benign, there were enough unsettling situations to cause concern among Yukoners. In a number of criminal cases, for instance, American military police arrested the offenders and spirited them back to the United States before the Royal Canadian Mounted Police even had a chance to question them. In a controversial case, a doctor escorting two young ladies home from a dance at the airport was accosted and beaten by two American soldiers. By the time the police had been alerted, the men were in a truck heading for the Alaskan border. Numerous protests were registered, including a strongly worded letter by Yukon member of parliament George Black, but to no avail. In such instances, the Americans preferred to try their soldiers and civilians under American military law rather than letting the Canadian legal process run its course.

Incidents such as this generated considerable anger, particularly among Canadians who wondered if justice was truly being served. On one occasion, two two soldiers found guilty of having sex with underage girls were fined $24 and $20 each by an American military court, whereas a conviction for the same offence in front of a Canadian judge would probably have carried a jail sentence. However, the situation could, and did, work in reverse. There were occasions when American military law provided for much faster and harsher punishment than would have been possible through the Canadian courts. For instance, when two soldiers entered the girl's dormitory of the Carcross residential school, severe penalties were handed out – much more severe than they would have been given under Canadian law (in this case, almost certainly because the culprits were African American). In what became known as "sofa laws" (as in the phrase "to hide under the sofa"), Canadian authorities often delivered the accused to American officials and left the dispensation of the case in their hands. However, the judicial systems were only intermittently in conflict. As with other aspects of highway work and administration, cooperation was the norm. If there was a problem on the legal front, it had to do with enforcement, where charges of American high-handedness were more commonplace.

Although the Royal Canadian Mounted Police moved its Yukon headquarters to Whitehorse in 1943–44, the thirty-man detachment could not patrol the entire southern Yukon. The U.S. Army Military Police, therefore, had an important enforcement role. Its men took to the task with enthusiasm, often overstepping legal and national barriers. For example, they arrested the assistant fire chief of the Whitehorse Volunteer Fire Brigade for investigating a fire that followed a plane crash on the streets of his town.

The activities of the American military police were evident throughout the territory. Security investigations were carried out on a number of Yukon citizens, sometimes over the protests of Canadian authorities. The military sites, around Whitehorse were off-limits to Canadian personnel, a situation that sparked several confrontations between the police and local residents. The military police controlled access to the Alaska Highway, barring even local traffic, though the residents had been promised relatively free use of the road after initial construction. They American police also enforced highway regulations, once more stepping beyond their authority, and were accused on several occasions of handling civilians in a rude and abrasive fashion. While the complaints resounded with the moral indignation of people who felt that they had been treated unfairly, they contained the additional frustration of being mistreated by foreign nationals. "Whose country *is* this?" they could ask with some justification.

For the soldiers and workers, northern work quickly lost its lustre. The excitement of the journey north was offset by the isolation and frontier conditions of the land they now worked in. They found themselves working ten-to sixteen-hour shifts, made possible by the long summer days. Not many complained about the workload, in part because they had little reason for being there except to make money, but also because there was little else to do. Construction camps were rudimentary affairs. Most of the soldiers spent the winter in dome-style tents. As time passed, the ubiquitous Quonset huts[23] sprang up in the construction and maintenance camps along the highway. Eventually, wooden barracks were erected at the more important centres; Whitehorse was filled with the long, low "temporary" buildings that housed the workers and offices of the Northwest Service Command.

As the workers soon discovered, the northern climate had its vicious side. Most were not familiar with the dangers of a subarctic winter. Several men died when they ignored the oft-repeated warning to stay with their vehicles if they broke down along the road; they froze to death while trying to walk to the nearest highway camp. The cold weather made machinery hard to operate; it limited outside activities and generally made life miserable for the men. They also complained about the summer, when the long days not only made it possible for their bosses to extend the workday, but gave the mosquitoes plenty of time to feast on them. The food offered little relief from what rapidly became a dreary existence. Difficulties with supply forced the army and construction cooks (never known for creativity) to feed the workers a distressingly monotonous menu of Yukon Shrimp (Vienna sausages), hash, and chili.

Army and civilian managers recognized the dangers of unhappy work crews and sought to provide some recreation for them. The U.S. government asked for and received permission for its men to hunt along the highway, subject to a one-dollar licence fee – a privilege that Alaska did not extend to the soldiers. The fee was the same as that for resident Yukoners and was substantially less than the standard non-resident fee of $75 for British subjects and $100 for foreign nationals.[24] While locals, especially Native people, complained about overhunting and wastage of game, the government accepted such losses as necessary evils. As Bill Hoge noted, "if permission was not granted the men would hunt anyway."[25]

American military personnel in Whitehorse lived in a large tent city throughout the winter of 1942–43 (YA).

And hunt the Yankees did. The slaughter was too much for one employee of the E.W. Elliott Company: "There are guns in every camp killing everything from the smallest to the largest ... The soldiers kill anything. What is your people [RCMP] going to do? Stand by and see your game destroyed? It hurts a lot of us to see these trusting animals killed."[26] The area surrounding construction and maintenance camps faced the greatest pressure, for few of the visitors risked the journey into the backcountry. Although the long-term damage was comparatively slight, the impact on local game resources was noticeable. The fur supervisor of the Indian Affairs Branch observed that "the decimation of the big game resources in the area was the direct result of too intensive big game hunting by whites generally and particularly by U.S. Army personnel."[27]

Allowing Americans to hunt also revealed a fundamental truth about federal policy towards Yukon First Nations' harvesting. R.A. Gibson, a federal official, noted that "there has always been a fundamental difference in wild life management in the Yukon and Northwest Territories. In the Yukon hunting for sport has been encouraged. In the Northwest Territories the wild life is reserved for those who depend on it for a living, chiefly our increasing population of Indians and Eskimos."[28] While the Natives did not appreciate or agree with the distinction, the federal decision permitted the Americans at least one outlet for their energies.

There were, of course, other outlets. Card playing competed with complaining about the weather and food as a major pastime. The "beer bust" was an important part of an otherwise dreary social life, and workers near the handful of major centres joined the long line-ups at the liquor stores. The U.S. Army established a radio network along the highway which reached most construction camps and provided the best of modern music and timely newscasts to the widely scattered crews. The army also delivered first-run movies, fresh out of Hollywood, preceded by patriotic newsreels outlining the progress of the war overseas. On occasion, USO entertainers visited the area, bringing attractive female performers and other actors, comedians, and singers to the northern camps to entertain the soldiers and construction workers. Word of these and other events was spread along the highway via the *Northwest Newscast,* a newspaper printed especially to bring the international and local news to the camps.

There were many other recreational opportunities. Camp officials and local residents ensured that national celebrations, both Canadian and American, were suitably marked with parties, competitions, music, and other special events. The camps and divisional offices organized their own baseball, basketball, hockey, and bowling leagues where facilities and manpower permitted. Highway rivalries developed as teams travelled to other camps for competitions. In settlements with a sizable civilian population, the locals competed with army and construction teams, adding the spice of competition to their generally friendly relations. Boxing matches always attracted good crowds; skilled fighters travelled up and down the highway staging exhibition matches in front of enthusiastic audiences. At most camps, and particularly in the administrative centre at Whitehorse, trips were organized for those wishing to put their days off to productive use. Buses travelled from Whitehorse to Teslin for a day of sightseeing and fishing, or north to Haines Junction for some time in the local wilderness. In Whitehorse, dances were held almost nightly. Local dance bands worked constantly as the various military and civilian branches took turns sponsoring an active social round. There were occasional problems, particularly if alcohol flowed too freely.

Given the sexual imbalance in the territory, the range of social activities kept the small number of unmarried women in the area very much the centre of attention, and there were several suitably romantic highway marriages. Of course, prostitutes could be found in all highway communities, and venereal disease reached almost epidemic proportions there. The Yukon territorial government gave itself the authority to imprison anyone carrying the infection, a law applied primarily to prostitutes and Native women, but seldom to men. The U.S. authorities also struggled with the problem, offering medical advice, requiring attendance at graphic films on the evils of casual sex, and operating twenty-four-hour prophylactic stations for the men. The warnings and attempted controls did not always work. There were a number of reported rape cases and several convictions for indecent assault. The American authorities provided alternatives for such behaviour and tried to control it in other ways as well. Native villages were placed off-limits to all American personnel, though to little effect. Strongly worded directives circulated through the camps, describing the punishments for rape and sexual assault, and advising highway workers to respect the rights of local residents.

The shortage of white women guaranteed that aboriginal women would be drawn into short-term liaisons with construction workers, often in the context of party drinking. Some, evidently victims of what in those days was called a "line," believed that their relationship would be permanent, only to be disillusioned when the man involved left the territory. The territorial birth rate jumped sharply during the construction years, especially among the aboriginal population.[29]

The territory's racial mix was also enriched by the African American troops used in building the pioneer road. Although American military regulations officially discouraged the use of these troops in northern settings, wartime necessity forced the dispatch of several battalions of black engineers to the Yukon. They were, as one official noted, sent to do the "dirty work" in isolated areas, away from the white population. Local residents were warned not to get too friendly with them, a warning that reinforced existing racial stereotypes. Whitehorse residents were relieved to hear that the black troops were being sent farther up the highway, rather than being stationed in the town to work on airport construction.[30]

The Yukon's First Nations people suffered in a variety of other ways from the arrival of the soldiers and civilian workers. Although the highway gave them improved access to hunting grounds throughout the southern Yukon, it provided others with access to the same resources too. Thus, as already mentioned, the workers competed, for pleasure, for the same game and fish resources that the Native people needed for survival. Although a few First Nations people found some job opportunities, particularly in 1942 and 1943, when their skills as guides and labourers were in demand, it soon became obvious that the wartime projects, like the earlier economic booms, meant lots of work for whites from the outside but few jobs for local aboriginal people. As they had done in the past, they took the short-term and occasionally high-paying jobs when available.

Some Americans disapproved of the high salaries demanded by the Natives. The president of the White Pass and Yukon Route company had little sympathy with such complaints: "In Whitehorse, key to the whole northland, the rate is $7.50 minimum for a 10-hour day, with the Indians getting the same rate ... The [Indians] are among the best workers we ever had. Immediately there was a holler ... that the idea of paying an Indian $7.50 a day was unheard of, immoral, ridiculous, fantastic and all that stuff. Well, we won't have any Jim Crow laws up here. If labour gets $7.50 and labour is Indian, then an Indian gets $7.50."[31] But the Natives also maintained their seasonal movements. Fur harvests remained steady through the first construction years and expanded rapidly thereafter. In 1944–45 and again in 1945–46, Yukon trappers brought in close to $670,000 worth of furs, the highest returns in the first half of the twentieth century.

While the economic impact on the Native people was comparatively light, the same could not be said of the effects on their health. Many of the Yukon First Nations affected by the Alaska Highway had had little earlier contact with non-Natives. Now, suddenly, thousands of strangers had entered their lands, carrying a variety of diseases against which they had little natural protection. Dr J.F. Marchand, stationed at Teslin during the winter of 1942–43, recorded successive attacks of measles, dysentery, jaundice, whooping cough, mumps, and meningitis – all in a single community in one year.[32] Several of these epidemics, especially measles and influenza, swept along the Alaska Highway and cut a deadly swathe through all the native communities in the southern Yukon. Many of the deaths – some of which were never officially recorded but are well remembered in the oral traditions of the affected communities – were of infants and young children, contributing to a horrifying infant mortality rate.

Army and civilian doctors did what they could. Both Canadian and American authorities made their facilities available to the Natives, though there was a short controversy over whether or not American doctors would be permitted to practise medicine on the territory's civilians. On balance, the medical effects were devastating, as C.K. LeCapelain pointed out:

There is no question but what the impact of all the construction in the Southern Yukon and its consequent influx of white people is having a very harmful effect upon the natives, and it is noticeable that the degree of this harm is in direct proportion to the closeness of the association that the natives have with the whites. The new era is here to stay and is and will continue to present many problems ... One of these problems is how to soften the blow upon the natives and ameliorate conditions so as to prevent their complete devastation.[33]

The highway also meant that the southern Yukon peoples came under the scrutiny and influence of the Canadian government. While this brought improved medical service and access to hospitals and government relief, it also resulted in demands that the First Nations send their children to school. The transfer of the RCMP headquarters from Dawson to Whitehorse in 1943–44 had brought greater police attention, and this, combined with increased access to alcohol, had resulted in a dramatic increase in the number of aboriginal people convicted of drinking offences. Although the incidence of serious crime among the indigenous population was low, a number of Native people found themselves before the courts with some regularity, a process that unfortunately helped confirm white stereotypes.

Protests about overhunting in the southwest corner of the territory stimulated an unexpected action. At the urging of C.K. LeCapelain, federal liaison officer, the Canadian government moved quickly to block further development in the land west of the Alaska Highway, and in December 1942, within two weeks of the official opening of the pioneer road, the government set the land aside.[34] The following year the territorial council seconded the federal effort by banning all hunting in the region, including that by Native people. At this, the First Nations people of the area protested, working through the Burwash trader and guide Eugene Jacquot. As a result some revisions were made – a strip of land near the White River was exempted from the freeze – the bulk of the land remained closed to all hunting; although the federal authorities expressed some concern for Native rights, they considered that the land and resources took higher priority. The game sanctuary remained, to become in 1972 Kluane National Park, one of Canada's most impressive wilderness areas and a UNESCO World Heritage Site. For the Natives, displaced from a valued and traditional hunting ground, there were official regrets, some help with muskrat hunting, and the two-edged results of a slowly expanding welfare state.

The building of the Alaska Highway, particularly after Hoge's decision to follow a southern route, caused consternation in Dawson City, whose residents had always pushed for a road that would connect their town with southern Canada, thus ensuring their continued dominance over the territory. But now Whitehorse was booming. And Dawson, already on the skids as a result of the declining gold industry, faced the most serious threat in its history.

Although home to a summer population of around a thousand, Dawson City had little reason for optimism in the early years of the war. The seasonal pattern of the past remained in evidence, forcing Dawson into a cocoon like existence every fall. The city's structures were aging, many of them abandoned, and the community was drained of its life. The presence of a truncated civil service could not offset the dominance of the Yukon Consolidated Gold Corporation. For all of its former glory and its pretenses as capital city, Dawson was really a company town tied to a declining industry.[35]

There was real pain for Dawsonites in watching Whitehorse's spectacular growth and the frenetic activity to the south. As J.E. Gibben noted with some bitterness in 1943, "The people in Dawson and Mayo Districts are receiving no pecuniary benefit from war industries or war projects, and increased taxation has brought about a self-imposed liquor rationing." Many simply surrendered to the new realities and headed south. Workers left the dredges for better prospects along the highway. All through the winter of 1942–43, the exodus continued. Businessmen moved specialized equipment, including the Cascade Laundry dry-cleaning plant, to Whitehorse, where greater markets and handsome boom-town profits awaited. Dawson's already battered armour began to fall away in large chunks. The demands of government work forced key officials to spend long periods of time in the southern Yukon. Some succumbed to the new pressures of business and moved to Whitehorse. Not only did the RCMP relocate, but so did several key federal departments, including the Wartime Prices and Trade Board. Prominent citizens followed suit. George and Martha Black moved to Whitehorse in 1944, as did the Anglican bishop. Dawson, suffering the ignominy of losing government offices – the basis of its claim to territorial prominence – now suffered the pain of watching many of its leading citizens leave forever.

Not everyone gave up hope. Controller George Jeckell resisted all suggestions that he move to Whitehorse or even spend more time there. His reluctance to travel restricted his ability to do his job properly, but his staunch defence of Dawson City encouraged others. The town still had its boosters, and now Jeckell provided it with a rallying cry – Dawson needed a highway of its own. Dawsonites believed – they had to – that Whitehorse would collapse at the end of the war, and they felt that if a connector road was built they could overcome their isolation and be able to serve the entire territory. Jeckell's intransigence ensured that Dawson retained the capital – for now, at least. The seat of government was all it had left, for power and wealth had clearly shifted to Whitehorse.

Whitehorse bore the full weight of changes – both creative and destructive – that accompanied the wartime construction projects. Previously an isolated, seasonal community, tied to the rhythms of river travel and controlled by the White Pass and Yukon Route company, Whitehorse had attracted little attention before the war. Although virtually all goods and people entering the territory had passed through Whitehorse, the travellers had seldom stayed long or thought much of the slow, rough-hewn town on the edge of the Yukon River. Local businesses, with a few exceptions like the still extensive Taylor and Drury operations, had been tied to the rail and steamer system, and there were no expectations of growth. There was copper still in the hills, but Whitehorse residents had long learned not to pin their hopes on the resource.[36]

The town was laid out on the river plain below Miles Canyon and the Whitehorse Rapids, a picturesque setting, flanked on the east by rounded, tree-covered mountains and on the west by high clay hills and a level plateau.

The White Pass and Yukon Route railyards and docks dominated the landscape and provided a focus for the community. Main Street ran perpendicular to the river and boasted a few retail stores, government offices, and hotels. The private homes of civil servants, leading company officials, and businessmen surrounded the business district. The First Nations sporadically occupied their reserve, which lay north of the downtown district. The workers' commitment to the town was little different; many squatted on White Pass and Yukon Route lands in semi-permanent shacks. To all but a few businessmen and citizens, Whitehorse was a way station, a place to earn a few dollars before escaping.

William Hoge and the highway construction roused the town from its slumber. The selection of Whitehorse as the administrative centre for the construction projects made sense, for it had an excellent airfield on the escarpment overlooking the community, it had rail access to the ocean, and it was the base for navigation on the Yukon River. The community was jolted into the twentieth century in June 1942 when more than three thousand soldiers of the U.S. Army Corps of Engineers camped west of the town. While many of these men moved on, shifting to construction camps farther along the highway, others took their place and added to a growing chaos.

As the headquarters for the army and the Public Roads Administration, Whitehorse quickly became a temporary home for thousands of administrators, maintenance workers, soldiers, construction workers, project managers, and support personnel, as well as the site of the Canol refinery and a supply depot for much of the Northwest. A year after construction started on the highway, Whitehorse had some ten thousand people, the vast majority from the United States. It had exploded from a sleepy river depot to a major military and construction complex. That these changes were directed by outsiders was nothing new for a territory used to external control and the instability of a boom-and-bust economy.

Yukoners once more found themselves swamped by foreign nationals, and like the Klondike in 1897–98, Whitehorse was ill equipped to deal with the onslaught. With few houses and only three hotels, the town faced a shortage of bed space. For a while, soldiers and construction workers were housed in tent cities; then civilian contractors, working under the Public Roads Administration, built dozens of barracks, office buildings, and other facilities. The urban landscape of Whitehorse was completely transformed. Local residents participated in the boom; Martin Berrigan built several "log skyscrapers" as rental units in response to an almost unlimited demand. Canadian citizens, denied housing by the U.S. Army's insatiable appetite for land, moved into the rapidly growing squatter settlements of Whiskey and Moccasin flats.

On an individual level, the challenge for Canadians in the Yukon during the Second World War was living with the Yankees – the Americans who (aided by a few Canadians) built the highway, altered the communities, and made the decisions. That this was achieved with surprisingly little strife reflected well on their shared commitment to continental defence and the war effort. However, as one Canadian official complained, "Some of these people do not seem to know that Whitehorse is in Canada and it is high time that proper steps were taken to acquaint them of the fact."[37] The Northwest Service Command headquarters were erected atop the bluff, near the Alaska Highway, and the town began to move up the hill, out of the river valley. A subdivision of "cemesto" family homes in Camp Takhini added to the office and housing complex on the plateau. Unlike the temporary structures built in the lower town, the cemestos were designed for long-term use, though their southern designers made few adaptations for the special needs of the northern environment. The buildings offered only minimal protection from the cold, and residents of both barracks and family homes faced many nights when uninsulated oil pipelines froze, forcing a dependence on wood stoves.[38]

Little was done to protect local residents from the effects of this American reconstruction of their town. Government officials did nothing to stop the spread of squatters' homes onto crown and private land. George Jeckell, who was responsible for the administration of Whitehorse, was indifferent to the town's problems. Believing that the wartime changes would prove temporary, he refused to commit the territory to major expenditures in Whitehorse. In fact, even though Whitehorse was generating sizable revenues at this time, especially through the local liquor store, Jeckell felt no obligation to turn that money back into the community. Instead, he set it aside in a reserve fund for postwar use when, he expected, the *status quo ante bellum* would return. Even when civil servants, transferred to Whitehorse from Dawson, faced astronomical rents, Jeckell remained unmoved and rejected their requests for financial assistance.

The combination of inadequate planning, American military initiative, and limited local control over the transformation of the community had serious implications. Whitehorse's rudimentary sewage and water system could not contend with the massive invasion. Water was delivered by private contractors, while septic fields and pit toilets handled human waste. The U.S. army feared widespread dysentery and built chlorination plants to provide water for its personnel. In the interests of preventing epidemics in the community, the army made its water available to all residents and to local water dealers.

Unbeknownst to Canadian authorities, American plans were underway for the construction of a proper sewer and water system for the community. C.K. LeCapelain wrote to R.A. Gibson, director of lands, parks, and housing: "As far as I know neither you nor the Controller, Yukon Territory, are aware of this proposed work."[39] Their subsequent protests were noted, and there were extensive negotiations on the project, resulting in a mutually agreed plan. But later the Americans abruptly scrapped the plan and proceeded unilaterally with a cheaper, scaled-down version. The system served the army's needs in the downtown area and the homes of a few well-to-do citizens, private businesses, and government offices who, at their own expense, hooked into the system. But many civilian residents and businesses remained without adequate water and sewage facilities. Canadian health officials were far from pleased. One government agent, A.H. Perry, called the townsite "an undeveloped island of cesspits."[40]

A pattern had been set. American activities transformed and disrupted the community, local citizens clamoured for attention to their needs, and George Jeckell and the territorial government ignored them. In 1944, for example, residents angry over the dense dust from construction blanketing the community through the summer petitioned Jeckell for assistance. Nothing could be done, he claimed, because of a lack of oil and the equipment to spread it. The residents' complaints received a more favourable reception in Ottawa, where R.A. Gibson was now director of the Bureau of Northwest Territories and Yukon Affairs. When he learned of the problem, he contacted American officials and secured an offer of oil, free of charge, from the newly opened Canol refinery in town.

The arrogance of some of the American soldiers and construction workers brought about other difficulties. They showed a decided lack of knowledge of the area and an indifference to the diplomatic niceties, a sentiment well summarized in one U.S. soldier's note to his mother: "You know, Mom, the British have got this country now, but don't you worry, we'll soon get it back."[41] The Americans' bravado showed up on a variety of fronts: their disrespect for Canadian authorities, their casual use of Canadian resources, and their lack of attention to the symbols of Canadian sovereignty – at some camps, the Canadian flag was not flown; at others, it was displayed inappropriately. The lack of attention to Canadian sensitivities rankled, although local residents had difficulty complaining, given the almost complete inattention of their own government to such matters.

The Americans, for their part, were not always pleased with Canadian workers and administrators. George Jeckell was viewed as a foot-dragger, and after several unsuccessful attempts at dealing with him, the Americans simply ignored his office. Complaints from local residents, funnelled through civil servants such as LeCapelain, only irritated American officials, who sensed that Canadians were not as keen as they were about the northern projects, even though they stood to reap the lion's share of the benefits. The U.S. ambassador to Canada summarized a general American sentiment when he wrote, "Do not think ... that I am giving the Canadians a clean bill of health and damning the Americans. Canadian construction work is dishearteningly slow, they are short in most modern construction equipment, and their labour is casual and at times dishearteningly apathetic."[42]

The Americans' arrival brought dozens of other changes to Whitehorse.

Little money was spared in providing the soldiers and civilian workers with a full set of recreational facilities to help them survive the long winters in this Canadian outpost with their morale intact. Military and civilian authorities built outdoor hockey rinks and cleared a number of baseball fields. Baseball took root with a vengeance during the war, sparked by intense if friendly rivalries between the army and the "townies"; the community's love affair with the sport outlived the war.

With thousands of potential patrons in town, many on short-term furlough from highway camps, local businessmen seized the opportunity and opened bars (aided by the federal government's decision not to impose wartime liquor rationing in the Yukon), restaurants, and two new theatres. Whitehorse had had only one restaurant in 1941; two years later it could boast ten. One café alone claimed to have served up to nine hundred meals a day during the first year. As well, more rooms were added to schools and the hospital, and the Americans built a small medical facility of their own. Local hotels faced an almost unlimited demand for their rooms. While government regulations prohibited price gouging, there were ways around such rules. Patrons, it seemed, rented the bed, not the room, and had to sleep in shifts, for there was always someone around to take up any empty beds. Barbers and taxi drivers, once marginal and seasonal operators, found a steady supply of customers. So did dry cleaners, laundries, and the local bank, which increased its staff from three to twelve in 1942. Not only in Whitehorse but all along the route, aboriginal women found work as seamstresses or cooks, or by taking in laundry; they also worked to fill an almost inexhaustible demand for Native-made products, especially mukluks, mittens, and coats.

Everyone in Whitehorse seemed to be enjoying the boom. Even though the army provided its own messing facilities and brought in most of its supplies, it still purchased large quantities from local retailers. At the beginning of 1942, according to one report, U.S. government spending in the town quadrupled from one month to the next. But local citizens began to wonder what would happen when the Americans pulled out. After all, the highway was not being completed to civilian standards. Clearly, if it stayed open, it would not be the catalyst for regional economic growth that its promoters had foreseen. Also, the Whitehorse refinery had proved a major disappointment. It had been hoped that the hundreds of workers brought north with their families to work at the refinery would become the backbone of an expanding industrial economy. The decision, taken within months of its opening, to mothball the entire operation was a blow to those looking for a greater measure of stability. Could it be that Whitehorse was about to experience a classic "boom and bust"?

While Yukoners wondered about the possibility of a bust, they got on with the business of living, and in the Yukon of the war years that meant dealing with ten thousand distant cousins camped in their backyard. Although relations between Canadians and Americans were generally peace-able and friendly – as might be expected given the long history of national mixture in the Yukon River valley – many were troubled by the scale and pervasiveness of United States involvement. The Americans made virtually all the decisions and had assumed de facto control of much of the Yukon Territory. J.D. Hickerson of the U.S. Department of State recognized that the scale of American interests created certain problems: "Our relations with Canada are excellent. The only cloud on the horizon is that the extent of our War Department expenditures and activities in western Canada has been so great in connection with the war effort ... that some people feel that we may have, a vested interest there and be reluctant to leave when the war is over. That is of course nonsense but not all Canadians realize it."[43]

While American control made sense from a logistical and administrative perspective, it represented an alarming loss of sovereignty on Canada's part. LeCapelain, in his role as liaison between the U.S. authorities and the feder-al government, travelled extensively throughout the region. Although his re-ports reveal a first-rate understanding of the circumstances and consequences of the wartime projects, he could do little more than observe. With George Jeckell only occasionally venturing out of Dawson City, the territorial inter-ests were not well protected, leaving the Americans to locate the road, place the airfields, construct buildings and facilities, and otherwise make decisions that would shape the future development of the Yukon Territory.

Ottawa, it seemed, was unconcerned about the situation. True, the nation was preoccupied with the pressing challenge of fighting an international war and managing a rapidly expanding domestic economy. But the complete in-difference to the activities of thousands of American nationals in a large seg-ment of the Canadian Northwest was nonetheless astonishing. Historian Donald Creighton, a vigorous critic of the King government's handling of the national war effort, waxed vitriolic in his criticism of the administration of the Alaska Highway:

[The Americans] enjoyed the power of numbers and the authority of command; and the Canadian efforts to regulate their activities, which consisted chiefly in paper commands and exhortations despatched at long range from Ottawa, were singularly ineffectual. The Canadian government showed, in fact, an inexcusable lack of responsibility in its failure to protect one of the nation's greatest assets. No member of the King cabinet ever thought it worth his while to visit the Cana-dian north and really find out what was going on there.[44]

Canada was ultimately jolted into action at the urging of Malcolm Mac-Donald, British high commissioner to Canada. At the request of his govern-ment and an informal group of Ottawa-based "Northern Nationalists," Mac-Donald visited the North in 1942. One of his duties was to stop at Old Crow and extend his thanks, on behalf of the British people, for the donations made by First Nations people there to war relief projects. The high commissioner returned the following year, concerned about continued reports of American liberties in the North and rumours of Yankee designs on the region. Upon his return to Ottawa, MacDonald laid a blunt report on his findings before the Canadian War Cabinet. Canada, he argued, might lose its northern possessions if Americans plans came to fruition:

But certainly many influential American individuals who have had a hand in these developments in the North-West have no serious thought that the interests which they represent shall withdraw. American money, energy and labour have been spent on an immense scale whilst the Canadians have had comparatively little to do with some of the most important undertakings. One can imagine some of these people stirring up quite an unpleasant agitation in Congress circles to force the hands of the Administration, if they feel so disposed.[45]

While there was a certain hysteria (tinged with British self-interest) in MacDonald's rhetoric, there was also a good deal of truth. He drew attention to the limited federal presence in the area – a few officials, with scant resources, scattered throughout an area now host to tens of thousands of Americans, who jokingly called themselves the Army of Occupation. The high commissioner had a solution. He recommended that the federal government immediately appoint a civil servant to represent Canadian interests in the northern defence projects. In May 1943, fully a year after the major construction projects had started and after most of the decisions affecting them had been made, the King government dispatched General W.W. Foster as special commissioner on defence projects in the Northwest. Canada had, once more belatedly, recognized the threat to its ownership of the Northwest.[46]

Based in Edmonton with a small staff, there was little that Foster could actually do. His presence, however, had a salutary influence on the Americans, who now passed most decisions through his office for approval. In a way, it did not matter much. By the end of 1943, work on the Alaska Highway had slowed and construction standards had been relaxed considerably. By the following spring, public revelations from the Truman Commission (which propelled an obscure senator into national prominence in the United States) about grotesque overspending on the Canol pipeline dampened American interest in that project as well, although work continued until the pipeline and refinery were completed. In September 1944 the U.S. government formally asked Canada to take over maintenance responsibility for the Alaska Highway. When a report indicated that the cost of such work would be $6 million for the first two years alone, Ottawa decided that this exceeded the reasonable costs of regaining sovereignty and refused.

By now, however, it was evident that Canada would eventually take over the road. Doubts about American intentions in the North had been laid to rest, if only because the oilfields, pipeline, and refinery had proved such monumental disasters. The federal government would wait out the contract and would take over control of the highway as agreed, six months after the war ended. In the interim, the U.S. government left a small military staff to maintain the highway and airfields. The Public Roads Administration pulled its people out as their work on highway relocation and bridge construction was completed, and it moved them back to the United States. Most major projects were stopped by 1944, and the Americans unilaterally and in violation of international agreements closed down the Haines Lateral, the road connecting Haines, Alaska, and the military highway – a reflection of the changing face of the Pacific War and a grudging admission that the highway did not serve an important military purpose.

The Canadian government now faced a troubling dilemma. Reports from LeCapelain, MacDonald, and others made it clear that the Alaska Highway was neither the road sought by northern residents nor that expected by North Americans. Major expenditures were required to bring the road and bridges up to proper standards. It would not do to criticize the Americans for failing to live up to the initial agreement; they had, after all, built the highway without cost to Canadians. On the other hand, the Canadian government knew it would face much criticism if and when the highway was opened to civilian traffic. That could be prevented during the war years, when civilian traffic was severely limited, but as the end of the confrontations in Europe and Asia neared, it was clear that a decision on the highway was necessary.

The reasons for Canadian reluctance were evident; there was little pleasure in taking over a road that Canada had not wanted and that did not address the economic and social needs of the Northwest. As one civil servant bitterly noted, Canada now had to "build and maintain the kind of road that the United States promised but did not construct." To make matters worse, Canada was put in the uneasy situation of having to buy back its sovereignty in the North. The federal government eventually paid $123,500,000 to the United States for permanent installations along the Alaska Highway, including the highway itself and the staging route. According to Prime Minister King, the payments were essential, for it was "undesirable that any other country should have financial investment in improvements of permanent value such as civil aviation facilities for peacetime use in this country." Wisely, the government refused American requests that Canada purchase the physical assets of the Canol pipeline, already mothballed before the end of the war.[47]

The Yukon had been truly transformed. Native people had been hit with yet another wave of epidemics; the many new graves in First Nations cemeteries at Upper Liard, Teslin, Whitehorse, Champagne, and elsewhere offered mute but poignant testimony to the great personal loss that would always be associated with the highway. Whitehorse was no longer a sleepy river town; instead, it was the most modern and populous community in the North, with the facilities and problems of a city twice its size. Dawson had slipped further down the path towards oblivion, outpaced by its southern rival. The Mayo-Keno mines, for two decades the engine of the territorial economy, had closed down, but the current boom was so great that few commented on the temporary loss. Long isolated from the southern world, the Yukon now found itself astride a potentially important highway and airway and with a new telephone system. Yukoners had long seen the lack of contact with the outside as a major impediment to regional growth. Had the territory's time come once again?

While there was reasonable excitement about the changes, Yukoners, used to the boom-and-bust lifestyle, faced the future with some trepidation. No one knew what would follow the withdrawal of American troops, and the noises emanating from Ottawa about the highway were not encouraging. The closure of the Haines Lateral and of the Whitehorse refinery, once touted as the cornerstone of the city's future, raised doubts about the future of the Alaska Highway itself. Many Yukoners were far from pleased with the highway and the airfields. They had had no say in the location of the facilities, and the traditional corridors of territorial development – from Whitehorse to Mayo and Dawson – had been almost completely ignored.

But the bust never came, at least not for Whitehorse. Under the influence of the Northwest Service Command headquarters and the growing number of federal and territorial offices in town, Whitehorse had taken on a bureaucratic aura. The civilians had brought a measure of stability that it had seldom known in the past, even though the population did drop dramatically from the heights of 1942. In the summer of 1944, Whitehorse still had six thousand residents, many of them temporary. That year, Americans began to pull out in droves as the civilian contractors finished their work and headed south. The Public Roads Administration reduced its northern staff and the U.S. Army moved to cut costs on its expensive northern defence projects.

When word came of the final transfer of the facilities to Canadian authorities, Whitehorse held its collective breath. Would the federal government keep the highway open – and Whitehorse alive? For once, there was little hesitation on Ottawa's part. Hundreds of Canadian army personnel headed north to take over the construction, maintenance, and administrative tasks associated with the Alaska Highway. Whitehorse remained the centre of highway operations and hence retained most of the highway personnel. Five years after the Americans left, Whitehorse still had some five thousand residents – fewer than in the heady days of 1942, but a much larger and more stable population than that of the tiny frontier community of the prewar days.

The legacy of the war would live on in Whitehorse. The community had been pushed up onto the hill, creating an artificial separation between government employees and civilian residents that would last for another three decades. The highway also bypassed the city on the west side, forcing a reorientation of Whitehorse away from the waterfront. A drastically inadequate sewage and water system and large squatters' settlements lingered. So did the dozens of American buildings – barracks, offices, warehouses, and recreation facilities – that filled in much of the lower town and served as the foundation of the military and civilian complexes on the bluff. Within forty years, most of the physical legacy of the war projects would be gone, but the shape of Whitehorse continued to reflect the decisions – largely American ones – made during the Second World War.

The entire Yukon adjusted quickly to the end of the war. Highway communities, some new, some older, became maintenance depots for the Canadian work crews. The airfields did not fare as well. The fields in Fort St John, Fort Nelson, Watson Lake, and Whitehorse were maintained for postwar civilian use, and others were maintained as emergency strips, but some of the airfields, like the one near Aishihik Lake, were mothballed and abandoned. Facilities constructed for the Canol project, including the pipe, transmission stations, and Whitehorse refinery, were dismantled after the war and shipped to Alberta, where they found new life in the Leduc oilfield. Maintenance shops along the route were abandoned, often on only a few days' notice. Bridges were not repaired, and the Canol road was allowed to deteriorate, so much so that the northern section from Ross River to Norman Wells was closed and the southern portion could be used only by heavy trucks equipped with winches to get across the rivers.

The Americans left quickly and with little planning – much the same way as they had arrived. Millions of dollars' worth of equipment and buildings were declared surplus, and attempts were made to sell them off. In Whitehorse, surplus army barracks were bought as private homes, donated to the Whitehorse Baptist Indian School, and otherwise pressed into service by a community that was still short of housing. The Canadian government, which took over many of the buildings and maintenance facilities for its own uses, prevented an extensive sell-off of the American supplies, fearing a total collapse of the northern retail market. Tons of usable materials, everything from heavy equipment to office supplies, were simply dumped, burned, or abandoned. The highway camps, especially along the Canol road, were slowly cannibalized, leaving behind empty buildings, with the windows smashed, and piles of garbage.

One observer, commenting on the Peace River district, described a reaction felt uniformly across the North: "It is difficult to overestimate the dismay and disgust which has greeted recent revelations of waste and destruction in the Peace River. Scattered throughout that district are hundreds of families to whom just one of those blankets would be a Godsend; families that will not buy stoves, coats, blankets, etc. because they cannot afford them. Yet here, before their very eyes, goes on the senseless destruction of the very articles which they need but cannot pay for."[48]

The mounds of smashed and cannibalized bulldozers, rusting equipment, and decaying buildings that now lined the Alaska Highway left a sour taste in the mouths of northerners, a sorry legacy of the enthusiasm, energy, and expenditures of wartime.

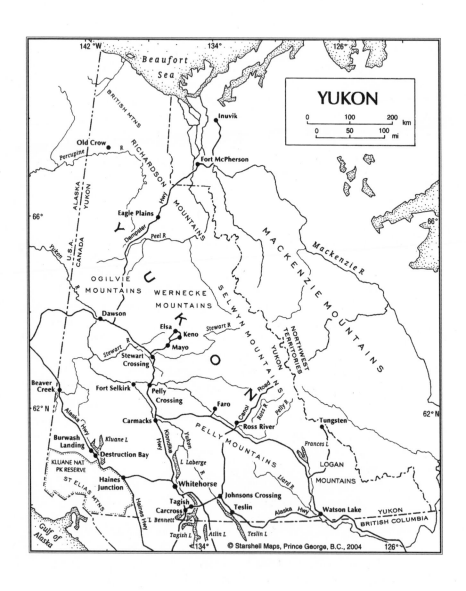

© Starshell Maps, Prince George, B.C., 2004

NINE

The Postwar Yukon

At the beginning of April 1946, after a stay of four years, the last of the American forces left the Yukon, to be replaced as keepers of the Alaska Highway by the Royal Canadian Engineers. The presence of American military and civilian personnel had breathed life into the territory, particularly the Whitehorse region. The Yankees had brought with them boundless energy, a "can-do" spirit, and lots of money – things the Yukon badly needed at the end of the 1930s. Now they were gone, leaving the territory to its Native people, who were still living largely outside the settled communities, and to its small white population. Yukoners said farewell to the Americans with a mixture of sorrow, relief, and apprehension, wondering whether the Canadian government was planning to continue its prewar policy of stinginess towards the North, and whether the bad times were about to return.

Fortunately for the Yukon, there had been two important changes since 1940. The Cold War, which began as soon as the shooting in Europe stopped, guaranteed that the northwest of Canada would have to play a part in continental defence. Thus, some military presence would be necessary in the Yukon. Second, the advent of the welfare state, heralded by the Family Allowance plan of 1945, meant that the bad old days of careful, parsimonious government were over, and a new era of spending, transfer payments, and social assistance of various kinds was about to begin. Within a generation, the era when George Jeckell could rejoice over a $10,000 increase in the federal appropriation for the territory seemed like a bad dream. By the 1960s, the talk was not of a few thousands but many millions.

The Canadian Army was glad to take on the responsibility for the Alaska Highway – not because it was thought to be of much military significance but because it provided good training for the engineers. While the army busied itself with snow removal, grading, culvert replacement, and bridge construction (the latter particularly urgent because of the temporary nature of many of the American bridges), the defence of the region was scaled down. In the early days of the Cold War, Canadian and American military planners shared a common concern about the prospect of a Russian invasion along the Alaska Highway. Steps had to be taken, the military urged, to protect the vulnerable route by means of garrisons at several communities. The government rejected this costly option and instead established a Mobile Striking Force, with the capacity to move armed personnel swiftly into isolated areas. But a series of post-1946 manoeuvres, including Exercise North, Exercise Eagle, and Exercise Sweetbriar, demonstrated that the Mobile Striking Force could not handle the defence requirements of the northern terrain. In subsequent years, military advisers debated the options at great length and reluctantly agreed that there was no cost-effective solution. A token army and air force detachment remained at Whitehorse until the 1960s, but the Canadian government's new-found urge to spend money did not extend to the military, and no systematic attempt was made to mirror the dramatic military buildup underway in Alaska. Except for the highway, the Yukon was returned to the civilians.[1]

With comparatively reliable access to the outside, Yukoners now hoped for economic development, a booming tourist industry, and the beginning of a new era in the territory. The federal government was sympathetic. The Americanization of the Northwest during the war had frightened federal officials out of their lethargy; and Ottawa, led by the Northern Nationalists, a loosely formed group of northern promoters and activists, now aggressively sought to control the North's future. With the support of the government and with public interest in the region kindled by the highway, Yukon boosters hoped that for the first time their dreams for their territory would actually be fulfilled.

The most dramatic changes brought by the war had occurred in Whitehorse. In 1946 it bore only slight resemblance to the small, seasonal company centre of decades past. Whitehorse now had the facilities of a small modern city, with theatres, baseball diamonds, skating rinks, dance halls, a radio station (which continued to operate for a number of years with programs supplied by the U.S. Army), new roads, dozens of new buildings, water and sewage systems, warehouse and maintenance space, and a rapidly growing commercial district.[2]

Residents had worried that the town would collapse when the Americans left. Dawsonites had hoped it would. But the arrival of the Canadian soldiers provided the base for continued prosperity, and there were other favourable omens. After the war, the shift of population to the town continued. The federal government carried on transferring its administrative offices, and by

1950 the public administrator, liquor controller, and sanitary engineer were there, as well as the forestry officer, airways engineer, and chief of the telegraph service. The civil servants still in Dawson City discovered that much of their work had shifted south, forcing prolonged absences from their home offices. Even more offices would have moved had it not been for George Jeckell, who supported Dawson and resisted the shift to Whitehorse, spending as little time there as possible. His replacement in 1948 by John E. Gibben removed a major impediment to the administrative rationalization of the Yukon Territory.[3]

Dawson City, which had watched its remaining power dwindle during the war, had no intention of going down without a fight. Its boosters rallied in a desperate attempt to preserve their community. Led by Jeckell, they presented a simple solution. Whitehorse's claim to territorial pre-eminence rested largely on year-round road access. A road to Dawson City, with connections to the mining camps in the Mayo area, would bring it prosperity as well. But this would cost a great deal of money, and the federal government was not eager to make such a commitment in a losing cause.

Dawson's supporters did not give up easily, for they recognized the importance of such a road to the future of their community, but their cause lost ground steadily. There were even rumours that the territorial capital was to be moved. In 1950 a road north of Whitehorse was completed, but to Mayo rather than Dawson (which had to face the troubling fact that it was now the Yukon's third largest city). When Dawson did finally receive its connection to the Alaska Highway in 1951 via the spectacular "Top of the World" highway, the road went west into Alaska and not south through the Yukon.[4]

The failure to build the road between Dawson and Whitehorse was the writing on the wall for Dawson. In 1951 the axe fell. The federal government announced that the territorial council would be transferred to Whitehorse. Desperate appeals to overturn the decision fell on deaf ears. Robert Winters, minister of resources and development, made it clear that there really was nothing to discuss, that the decision to move the capital was based not on the heritage of the Yukon or on a desire for balanced growth, but on administrative convenience:

Whitehorse has good communications with the rest of Canada and with the United States, including airplane and air mail service six days a week, regular and frequent train, bus and truck connections, and telegraph and telephone service. On the other hand, Dawson has scheduled airplane service three times a week, air mail service twice a week, river boat service during the summer months only, no rail connections with the "outside," no all-weather road connections with the "outside," and no long distance telephone. Whitehorse, as the railhead, is the point through which all incoming supplies are distributed and all outgoing concentrates are shipped. Every person and every article of commerce entering the Territory must pass through Whitehorse. Under these circumstances, the result has inevitably been that most of the problems with which administrative officials have to deal can now be handled much more efficiently from Whitehorse than from Dawson.[5]

The formal transfer of power did not take place immediately, though by this time many administrative offices had already been moved. Construction of a federal government building began in Whitehorse in 1952. The following year, the Yukon's territorial council met in Whitehorse, ending the battle for administrative control of the Yukon Territory.

Dawsonites struggled on, but with limited success, for even the gold-mining sector was in serious trouble. Dawson finally received its road to the south in 1955, when a spur from Stewart Crossing to Dawson opened. This put an end to steamboat travel, and the last boat was pulled out of the Yukon River that same year. Dawson now had its connection to the south, but it no longer had the government offices and status that accompanied the presence of the territorial council. Already devastated by the continued erosion of the gold economy, the once-proud and dynamic city sank into a sad somnolence, which many thought was the inevitable precursor of a slow and lingering death.

Whitehorse, however, also had problems. To the consternation of regional promoters, access to the south via the Alaska Highway did not guarantee prosperity, nor did it immediately usher in the years of growth that many had counted on. Part of the problem lay with the road itself. Poorly sited, unfinished, and without commercial facilities, the Alaska Highway was kept closed to civilian traffic until 1947. The Royal Canadian Engineers lacked the manpower, equipment, and money to upgrade the highway. All they could do was to repair its most severely damaged portions, conduct routine maintenance, and bear the brunt of the criticism about the "rough road north."[6]

As early as 1954, the federal government considered passing responsibility for the highway from the Department of National Defence, which was anxious to be rid of it, to the Department of Public Works, the agency responsible for federal construction projects. The public prodded Ottawa to undertake a major reconstruction of this now vital route. Alaskans seconded the cry, calling for another Canadian-American enterprise to complete the work started during the war. These demands received substantial backing with the release in 1961 of a report by the Batelle Memorial Institute, a private research agency working on Alaska's behalf, which estimated that paving the road would cost some $103 million, money that would be quickly recovered through tourism and expanded economic activity.[7] When a Royal Commission on Government Reorganization recommended that the army be relieved of its highway duties, the federal government finally acted, and on 1 April 1964 it transferred responsibility for the highway to the Department of Public Works.[8]

Public Works was interested in rebuilding the highway rather than supervising its routine maintenance, a job that belonged to provincial and territorial authorities. Even before the transfer, the government gave control of the southernmost 84 miles (135 km) of the road to the B.C. government, and in 1972 the responsibility for maintaining the Yukon portions of the highway went to the Yukon Department of Highways. The remaining sections in British Columbia were still in federal hands. Although the B.C. government had a constitutional responsibility for roads within the province, it steadfastly refused to assume control of these portions of the highway, which were maintained by private contractors.

For Yukoners hoping for the immediate improvement and paving of the Alaska Highway, only disappointment followed. The federal government commissioned its own study of the feasibility of paving the road. The Stanford Research Institute report, issued in 1966, offered a gloomy forecast. Paving the highway could not be justified. The report recommended a limited improvement project, in which the worst portions would be upgraded and paved.[cdvi] The federal government proceeded on this basis, building new bridges, improving major sections of the highway, and continuing negotiations with the B.C. government for final transfer of the provincial sections of the highway.

In 1973 the U.S. government offered to pay for the reconstruction and paving of the Haines Road and portions of the Alaska Highway northwest of Haines Junction. This stretch of highway was lowest on Ottawa's priority list, since most of the traffic in this area was American, but the generous offer could not be ignored. This "Shakwak Project" ran into difficulty in the early 1980s, when key congressional supporters lost their seats in the Reagan sweep, thereby slowing but not stopping construction work. Nevertheless the Haines Road, the poor relation of the Yukon highway system, soon became a paved road of top quality.[10]

Although the highway is now paved from beginning to end, driving it is still something of an adventure, as the northern tourist promoters like to say. One website points out the hazards of travel:

There still are stretches where the highway is narrow and curvy, where it lacks center lines and ample shoulders. Also, watch out for sudden loose-gravel breaks where the pavement has failed or is under repair. Sometimes the gravel gaps are marked with little, red flags; sometimes they aren't. And that asphalt paving can ripple like a roller coaster track in places where "frost heaves" are caused by seasonal freezing and thawing of the ground. Maintenance crews do their best to patch the annual outbreak of frost heaves, but it's a never-ending, high-cost job. Long dry spells can make the gravel portions of the road dusty, and if it's extremely dry, you may have washboard and roughness problems.[11]

The bridges, all new since the war, are of the highest quality. But if it is not the road the Americans left behind, it is also not the highway that northern promoters have longed for since the 1940s. The Alaska Highway, like the Yukon itself, is full of promise only partially fulfilled.

Nonetheless, the highway has become the lifeline of the North, as was demonstrated in 1974, when extremely heavy rains in the Muncho Lake area wiped out more than twenty miles of road surface and undermined several key bridges. The same storm destroyed bridges and broke up portions of the Stewart-Cassiar Road, the only other road access out of the Yukon. Truckers and travellers congregated in Watson Lake, where roadblocks had been set up to prevent people from moving farther down the highway. Congestion at the highway community was intense; people slept in shifts in the hotels, and the restaurants quickly ran out of food. Every available piece of construction equipment in the region was rushed into service, and contractors worked round the clock to reopen the road. Dozens of detours were carved out of the roadside and temporary bridges erected before convoys were permitted to move up and down the highway. When the first convoy of several dozen carloads of people who had been trapped during the storm at Muncho Lake reached Watson Lake, crowds lined the highway to cheer their arrival.

Perhaps the greatest irony of the Alaska Highway is that although the road has been a blessing to Whitehorse, it has had only a minor impact on the economy of the territory. While it has breathed life into the tourist trade (even though a high percentage of the traffic on the highway passes through the Yukon to and from Alaska), it has not provided the stimulus to economic growth that its promoters had counted on. The main reason for this is its location. It does not follow the route that Yukoners wanted; it misses the mid-Yukon corridor, the Mayo mines, and the Dawson area. The areas of the southern Yukon opened by the highway had few exploitable mineral resources and thus did not contribute much to the postwar development of the territory.

Although the Yukon did enjoy considerable postwar growth, the stability and security that its supporters had long sought still escaped it. In the sixty years since the end of the war, the Yukon economy has continued through its boom-and-bust cycles. The immediate postwar period was a time of disappointment, with the highway failing to produce the benefits so long expected. By the mid-1950s, increased federal expenditures in the Yukon had fuelled a boom that brought a new level of prosperity. After a slump in the early 1960s, there was another boom as a result of the opening of new mines and continued government spending. The Yukon seemed to have found a new level, based on a solid core of well-paid federal and territorial employees, long-term mining projects, and continued exploration.

Although the years of prosperity continued throughout the 1970s, the boom came to an abrupt end early in the 1980s, when the closure of all the Yukon's major mines and the collapse of plans for an Alaska Highway natural gas pipeline crippled the territorial economy. Continued federal government expenditures propped up the Yukon economy to a greater degree than the territory's doctrinaire free-enterprisers like to admit, but the confidence built up through the postwar period was badly shaken. The downturn ended in the mid-1980s, giving way to greater stability rather than another boom. The pattern of territorial economic development is still based on the success and failure of Yukon mines, with a safety net of government spending. In the past, this structure harmed the territory; in the present era of government spending and talk of a new commitment to the North, dependence on federal and territorial expenditures has brought a certain level of fiscal stability, if not prosperity.

The territory's economic ebbs and flows did not mean much to the Yukon's aboriginal population until well after the end of the Second World War. Throughout the first half of the twentieth century, the mining sector had provided few opportunities for First Nations people – primarily seasonal, unskilled work as labourers and woodcutters. For a few, there was guiding for big-game hunters; for most, trapping provided what income they required. After 1945, the market for furs and wild game all but collapsed, destroying one of the foundations of their economy. By 1950, new regulations, the registration of traplines, and reduced fur markets had led to a restructuring of the manner in which Native people and other Yukoners viewed and used the natural resources of the territory.[12]

The establishment of the Yukon Fish and Game Association in 1945 reflected a change in attitude towards the environment. Under the leadership of Geoff Bidlake and W.D. MacBride, the association began to lobby for changes in the management of territorial game resources. They advocated the registration of individual traplines, a system that had been adopted more than two decades earlier in British Columbia and was in general use across the country. At their urging, in 1949 a director of game, Them Kjar, was hired to bring trapping practices in line with those in southern Canada. Together they convinced the government to import new species to be hunted, including bison, elk, and mule deer, and to undertake a widespread wolf-kill program. The arrival of American big-game hunters, particularly publicist James Bond and Carson Shade, who introduced fly-in hunting camps – made big-game hunting in the Yukon an international sport. The comparatively unregulated conditions of the past, based on limited demand, harvesting for personal use, and a seeming abundance of game, would no longer be tolerated.[13]

In 1947 the territorial government made substantial amendments to the Yukon Game Ordinance, several of which struck at the heart of Native commercial harvesting practices. From the early days of the Yukon fur trade, First Nations people had sold meat to traders, miners, and townsfolk. In 1947, without warning, the government prohibited the sale of wild game. Controller George Jeckell commented that the change was rooted in squeamishness on the part of white Yukoners: "In past years the white population was small and the amount of game meat sold to the white population by the Indians was insignificant, and this was particularly due to the fact that white people generally do not care to purchase game from Indians because the game they take is not slaughtered carefully and not kept clean and wholesome."[14]

The proposed moves could not have come at a worse time. The long-vital fur trade had entered a prolonged decline shortly after the war, a victim of lost European markets and shifting fashions in North America. Yukon trappers had harvested more than $650,000 worth of pelts in 1945–46. Two years later, their returns fell to $230,000, despite thirty thousand additional pelts being brought to the trading posts. The trade subsequently stayed at this lower level. Many small traders left the industry, and Taylor and Drury closed some of their posts. The changes sapped much of the vitality from the Yukon indigenous economy.[15]

When Kjar drafted the 1949 legislation for trapline registration, he included a $10 annual fee to cover the costs of administration. Aboriginal people around the territory petitioned the government to scrap the fee, arguing that the diminished returns from their traplines made it impossible for them to pay it. But there was no malice behind the decision to require trapline registration; it was intended to forestall conflict between trappers and to guarantee access to the resource for established hunters. In fact, many Native people, faced with competition for areas they had trapped for years, had urged the government to act.

What began as an exercise to ensure the access of Natives and other Yukon veterans to their traplines was quickly turned on its head. Although many First Nations people registered their traplines, over the years a number surrendered or lost their rights. The registration process provided individual ownership of a resource which, for the First Nations people at least, had always been collective property. Now trappers could sell their traplines or could lose their rights through nonuse of the area, in which case someone else could claim it. Five years after registration began, 430 traplines were in use; by 1960, only 190 were, though by 2000 these numbers had increased again, to 400. Although the fur trade had not died, since Native attachment to harvesting sustained it through some bad years, declining markets and the registration system had clearly altered what had long been – a cornerstone of the territorial economy.[16]

The fur trade retained a particular importance in some aboriginal settlements, such as Ross River and Old Crow. In the latter community, the school year was arranged so that children could accompany their families on the annual spring muskrat hunt in the nearby Old Crow flats. Although governments seemed to write it off as a vestige of the distant past, trapping contributed significantly to Native incomes. In the 1970s the emergence of the animal rights movement and international campaigns against trapping once more challenged it. National aboriginal organizations rallied to the defence of the industry which, they pointed out, was essential to the survival of their culture. The threat of protests and boycotts receded in the 1990s, and, today a steady demand for the Yukon's prime furs keeps the trade alive in the territory, where the annual value of fur production between 1998 and 2001 averaged about $300,000. Fourteen species are trapped, with lynx pelts making up half that total.[17]

The fur trade was not the only sector of the Yukon economy to suffer in the postwar years. Declining international markets for gold and falling returns from the Klondike fields continued to plague this once prosperous industry. In 1947 the federal government passed the Emergency Gold Mining Assistance Act, offering production subsidies for companies and individuals willing to sell gold to the Canadian mint.[18] The program was in fact designed for major gold producers in central Canada rather than the dredging companies and the numerous small operators still active in the Yukon. But many of these applied for federal support and kept their mines in operation despite high costs and small returns.

The collapse of the fur trade and decline of the gold-mining sector, once fiercely independent but now tied to government subsidies, signalled the onset of more troubled times for the Yukon. Once again a single company, this time United Keno Hill, propped up the entire regional economy. The company initially worked on the Galena Hill property, but by 1950 it had started development work at the Elsa, Silver King, No Cash, and Calumet properties and was doing exploration on the Ladue, Sadie, Lucky Queen, Porcupine, and King claims. The company experienced many difficulties. Finding and holding a trained workforce proved a constant headache; supplies were difficult to procure and ship; and shortages of mining equipment plagued expansion plans. In June 1949 the processing mill was lost in a fire, forcing a temporary halt to development and exploratory work. But with all available manpower and equipment devoted to rebuilding, United Keno Hill was back in operation by October. The subsequent addition of expanded milling capacity, the construction of a concentrating mill at Keno, the upgrading of transportation facilities, and the expansion of the workforce from 90 men in 1947 to 360 four years later and to 476 in 1955, symbolized the steady growth of this vital cog in the territorial economy.[19]

The handsome returns from the company's Galena Hill property justified the effort and expense. In 1948 the mine produced more than $2.4 million worth of silver and lead, along with small quantities of gold. Company profits mounted steadily through the 1950s as the benefits of the investments in the physical plants began to pay dividends. By the mid-1950s, United Keno Hill's revenues climbed to nearly $10 million, producing a net profit of more than $2 million in 1956.[20]

The effects of the mining activity filtered throughout the territorial economy. High mineral prices in the postwar period fuelled greatly expanded exploration throughout the Yukon. Prospectors, assisted by a skilled band of bush pilots, scoured the creeks and mountainsides with sophisticated equipment. In 1952 mineral production topped $11 million, with silver, lead, and zinc providing most of the returns. There were, of course, failures as well as successes. There had been great hopes that new minable deposits would be found in the Mayo area, but after considerable expenditure the hundreds of claims on Stand-to Mountain, Lynx Dome, and Lime Creek were permitted to lapse. Despite the withdrawal of many prospectors, development or extraction work continued to be done by a number of companies: Ankeno Mines, Bellekeno Mines, Comstock, Keno, Jersey Yukon, Klondike Keno Mines, Mackeno Mines, Mount Keno Mines, Yukeno Mines, and, of course, United Keno Hill Mines.[21]

Returns from the Whitehorse mining district seemed even more encouraging. Three prospectors working for the Yukon Mining Company uncovered a promising nickel deposit on the west side of Kluane Lake in June 1952. The discovery touched off a mini-boom. By December, more than sixteen hundred claims had been staked. Prospectors fanned out in various directions and found additional deposits west of the Donjek River and near the Alaska Highway, generating another 1,247 claims. The Hudson Bay Exploration and Development Company optioned most of the properties and began development work on the claims around Quill Creek. The Yukon Exploration and Development Company began prospecting in the Wheaton River area; Prospectors Airways had started work in the Macmillan River district but later joined the rush to Quill Creek; and the American Smelting and Refining Company sought lead and zinc deposits near Quartz Lake. Independent prospectors, some working under contract to speculative mining companies, pushed the search throughout the White River and Kluane Lake regions.

While most prospecting and exploratory activity focused on lode mining, placer operations remained important. More than eleven hundred placer claims, most of them in the Dawson City area, remained in good standing in 1952. The self-sufficient Yukon Consolidated Gold Corporation ran extensive hydraulic and dredging activities in the Klondike fields. Its power plant on the north fork of the Klondike River supplied all its own power needs, and the surplus went to the town of Dawson. The massive hydraulic operations processed almost 2 million cubic yards (1,670,000 m³) of earth in 1952. Cold-water thawing operations, in which water was run over permafrost, thawed out more than 4,250,000 cubic yards (3,250,000 m³) of material. Yukon Consolidated operated seven dredges during 1952, keeping each in operation for an average of 187 days. The efforts paid off, although not as handsomely as in the past, for the company produced 56,332 ounces of gold and over 12,000 ounces of silver, with a total value of $1,918,000. The mining operation ran from late April to the beginning of December, when the last dredge shut down.

As if to symbolize the declining fortunes of Yukon Consolidated, one of its largest dredges was mothballed in 1952, after more than forty years' service. The machine was later cannibalized to keep the firm's other aging dinosaurs in operation. Although the company was gradually shrinking, it remained one of the territory's largest employers. In May 1952, at the height of the season, the firm had over 450 employees in the field. As had traditionally been the case, many of the seasonal employees left the territory for the winter, and by December only twenty-eight people remained on the company's payroll.

Yukon Consolidated did not have the Klondike field to itself, though it dwarfed its competitors. Yukon Placer Mining Company, Clear Creek Placers, and Yukon Gold Placers ran small dredges or hydraulic operations. Smaller mines, usually one- or two-man operations, kept alive the flavour of gold rush prospecting, though the technology had changed since 1898. R.E. Troburg, working on Bonanza Creek, used a bulldozer and one employee to extract 281 ounces of gold, worth about $10,000. Over on Quartz Creek, R. Hastle and J.E. Lundin, adopting the drifting techniques of the late nineteenth century, worked eight months for a meagre return of 44 ounces of gold. Operators small and large prospected in new areas, retraced miners' paths through old claims, and used new technology in the search for a new Eldorado. The rush to Quill Creek, the persistence of the Klondike placer miners, the conservative professionalism of the United Keno Hill operators, and the fantasies of speculators and foot-slogging prospectors echoed age-old patterns in the Yukon. But with gold prices locked at $35 an ounce, it was clear that even with the government subsidies of the Emergency Gold Mining Assistance Act, placer mining in the Dawson area was rapidly becoming uneconomical.

In the Mayo area, most of the small operators had pulled out, leaving United Keno Hill Mines to dominate the area. Development continued in each of its principal properties as new shafts were cut, mining schedules adjusted to capitalize on rich veins of ore, and exploratory work expanded. The effort paid off, for the company's employees produced 7.3 million ounces of silver, 22 million pounds (9,980,000 kg) of lead, and over 15 million pounds (6,800,000 kg) of zinc. Other lode-mining operations near Mayo slipped into a holding pattern. Most claim holders did only the minimal amount of work required to maintain title to the properties.

The Whitehorse district attracted more activity as prospectors again chased the retreating spring snows into the Kluane, Frances Lake, Sheldon Lake, Quiet Lake, Carmacks, Dezadeash, and Flat River regions. Small operations extracting rich nodes of ore were brought into production, but no large mines started up.

Better days lay ahead for the Yukon mining industry. The modest successes of the 1950s werer replaced by real boom times in the next decade as major new mines came on stream, stimulating a major expansion of the territorial economy. The prospecting activities continued in a variety of directions. Calgary-based Western Minerals struck oil on the Eagle Plains in 1959, sparking short-lived dreams of an oil-rich future.[22] By the 1970s, much attention was focused on the mineral-rich Macmillan Pass area, where promising discoveries held much hope for the future. Although few of these explorations resulted in producing mines (the opening of the Mount Skookum property being a welcome exception), the search continued, pouring millions of dollars annually into the territorial economy.

The search continued because the Yukon still occasionally produced a winner. One mine, even if it lasted only a few years, could produce enough money to make its prospectors rich and pay handsome dividends to its investors. Throughout the 1960s and 1970s, activity centred on the death and rebirth of the Klondike goldfields, the opening of an asbestos mine west of Dawson City at Clinton Creek, renewed development of the Whitehorse copper belt, and, most importantly, the discovery of Canada's largest lead and zinc property in the Ross River area.

In the goldfields, the Yukon Consolidated Gold Corporation had almost run its course by the early 1960s. The dredging and hydraulic equipment was rusting and in ill-repair; as one machine was shut down, its usable parts were cannibalized to keep the others working. Returns had fallen steadily, eroding profits, although dividends continued to be paid until 1965. There was still gold in the ground – a 1965 estimate identified more than $4 million worth of gold at $35 an ounce – but the high operating costs rendered extracting it unprofitable. In November 1966 the last three Yukon Consolidated dredges shut down for the season, and forever. The company sold off what it could, leased out its claims, and wound down its operations. Ironically, it had acted too soon. In 1973 the American decision to let the price of gold float on international markets led to an amazing price surge. Gold-bearing ground that was barely profitable at $35 an ounce was once again rich at more than $600 an ounce. Small operators, most with two or three employees and a bulldozer or two, returned to the creeks in large numbers and pressed the Klondike gold properties into service once more. New extraction techniques, particularly the development of more advanced sluice boxes, allowed miners to go through the old diggings yet again. The Klondike, which had made rich men of the original stampeders and had sustained the large corporate operators for many years, again provided handsome returns to those willing to risk the vagaries of Yukon placer operations.

Early in the century, prospectors had found deposits of asbestos not far from Dawson. The thin stringlike mineral found a market from the 1960s until health concerns in the 1970s and 1980s eliminated many of its uses. In the early 1950s, Conwest Exploration, headed by Fred Connell, had developed the rich Cassiar Asbestos property in northern British Columbia. While that mine was being brought on stream, Connell turned his attentions to reported discoveries on Cassiar Creek, some 30 miles (50 km) from Dawson. When news later surfaced of another strike on nearby Clinton Creek, Connell was immediately interested. In 1965 the Cassiar Asbestos Corporation decided to proceed with mine development. A townsite was quickly built, and two years later the mill opened.[23]

The Clinton Creek property proved expensive to operate, largely because the primary access to the mine was by the Yukon River ferry – there was no bridge, except an ice bridge during the winter. When the river was impassible, supplies and ore had to be transported across the river on a cable skyline. But rich returns from the mine gave the company enough confidence to predict a long life for it. Cassiar Asbestos built a modern, well-equipped company town, complete with a small hospital, a school, recreational facilities, and housing, but when expenses proved unexpectedly high the owners decided to exploit the property, taking out the ore as quickly as possible without worrying about the long-term prospects for the area. Although the Clinton Creek mine had proved highly profitable for Cassiar Asbestos, the returns to the Yukon were negligible, except insofar as they provided an impetus for further exploration. Ten years after the mine opened – and ten years ahead of schedule – the Clinton Creek mine was closed.

There are few things as final as the closing of a company town. Workers had no reason to stay and quickly moved on to other mining communities. Usable equipment, particularly the milling facility, was dismantled and shipped out. Even the houses were shipped out. Auctioned to the highest bidder, most were hauled to Dawson City to replace the town's aging housing stock. By the mid-1980s, Clinton Creek could not even be called a ghost town, for little remained of what had once been a flourishing community, except basement shells where the houses had once stood and a water-filled hole where the company had mined the asbestos.

The Whitehorse mines followed a similar course, though the impact on the community was much less noticeable. The Whitehorse copper belt had been known for years but had attracted only sporadic interest. In 1957 Aubrey Simmons, the Yukon's member of parliament, created New Imperial Mines to bring the Whitehorse properties into production. As always, low prices continued to confound development prospects, and it was not until 1967 that New Imperial started work on an open-pit mine on the Little Chief claim. The company remained in operation only four years. A short-term surge in the price of copper in the early 1970s led to the reorganization of the New Imperial interests into Whitehorse Copper Mines. The new company abandoned the open pits (one of them became the Whitehorse garbage dump) and instead tunnelled into the copper veins. The economic imperative could not, however, be avoided. When copper prices fell again, the always marginal Whitehorse properties had to be abandoned, and in 1981 Whitehorse Copper Mines ceased operations.[24]

The demise of Clinton Creek and Whitehorse Copper received comparatively little attention because of the dominance of another new mine, the Cypress-Anvil property, which was producing zinc and lead at Faro. Like other Yukon mines, this property owed its existence to the persistence of prospectors and investors who had faith in the territory. The story of the Cypress-Anvil property begins with Al Kulan, who had been in the Yukon since 1947, moving about the territory in the hope of striking it rich. Kulan had the special qualities of the determined prospector: "He was a featherweight, as supple as a willow and as strong as a telephone pole. But he was not a scrapper – not belligerent or antagonistic in any way – and avoided arguments and confrontations at any cost. He did everything fast. He made decisions fast; moved toward goals fast; walked fast; ate, and even drank, fast."[25]

Kulan was fixated on the Ross River, and, usually in the company of First Nations guides, he scoured the river valleys and hillsides for signs of minerals. Although he made several promising discoveries, especially on Vangorda Creek, his initial work came to nothing – though he nevertheless found himself embroiled in a series of lawsuits with former partners and employees. Undeterred, Kulan continued his efforts and remained optimistic about the Ross River area.

In the early 1960s, Kulan joined with Dr Aaro Aho to form Dynasty Explorations. Aho was the antithesis of the rough-hewn Kulan. He was sophisticated and well educated, with a PHD from the University of California, and was well connected with the mining industry. Like Kulan, he had extensive Yukon experience and was convinced that the Yukon held major mineral deposits, as yet undiscovered. Dynasty Explorations moved crews into the field to work on the promising properties Kulan had identified. Short of funds to carry on the expensive exploration scheme, Kulan and Aho turned to Cypress Mines, a Los Angeles mining company, for enough money to sustain their development program. It was not like the old days. In 1965 Dynasty Explorations had a full crew of 117 men in the field, along with river barges, two helicopters, and an airstrip. The work cost more than $50,000 a month.

Drilling results exceeded the most optimistic expectations. Kulan and Aho kept the news private for a time, taking advantage of the discovery to stake more claims and secure their hold on the property. When word of the strike leaked out, prospectors from around the territory rushed in, marking out more than seventeen thousand claims in the area in 1966 alone. Additional development only confirmed the scale of the discovery. The Yukon had its first truly world-class mine. Negotiations with two Japanese companies, Mitsui Mining and Smelting and the Toho Zinc Company, resulted in an agreement with Cypress-Anvil, as the new mine was called, to purchase all the concentrates from the mine for a period of eight years. As the confirmed ore reserves expanded, the company signed additional contracts with other smelters, including Cominco's plant at Trail, British Columbia, and firms in Germany, France, and England. Production began in December 1969.[26]

There was much work to be done over and above the mining. A forest fire destroyed the townsite in the middle of construction, forcing a second start on the apartment complexes, dormitories, and houses. Additional facilities, including a small shopping centre, a hotel, and a recreation complex, were added shortly thereafter. Transportation problems also had to be solved. The Cypress-Anvil mine was 220 mile (350 km) by road from Whitehorse, which in turn was 120 mile (190 km) from tidewater. Discussions with the White Pass and Yukon Route company resulted in the construction of an integrated trucking, rail, and shipping system, organized around the Utah shipping yards just south of Whitehorse and a new docking facility in Skagway. Although the new facilities cost the WPYR more than $22 million, the guaranteed work injected new life into the company, which had previously funded exploration and promoted northern mines in the hope of providing greater traffic for its trucking and rail operations.[27]

The mine and community also placed considerable demands on the Yukon power grid. In the early 1970s work began on a controversial project to dam the Aishihik River at Otter Falls (whose likeness had once graced the back of Canada's $5 bills), to provide direct power service to Faro and the mine. The power, it turned out, was not really needed, since the mine drew on regional coal deposits. The project proved extremely costly to Yukon consumers, who paid the cost of the Aishihik dam through their monthly electricity bills.

The federal government provided generous support for the Cypress-Anvil project. According to a 1972 estimate, Ottawa provided more than $28 million in infrastructure support, including the road from Carmacks to Faro and the power line from Whitehorse to the mine site. The government also provided a three-year tax holiday on corporate profits.

There were several of problems during the first year of operation. Although the company had made vague promises to provide work for local First Nations, only a few Native people found temporary work – though, ironically, Natives had played an important role in the initial discovery. There was a major leak of sodium cyanide in 1976. Mine officials did not inform the government as required, and the company was fined $49,000.

By the mid 1970s the Cypress-Anvil mine was the backbone of the Yukon economy. It directly employed more than a thousand workers and provided other benefits throughout the territorial economy. Faro was something of a miners' enclave, isolated from the rest of the Yukon. Most miners were recruited in southern Canada, took their holidays in warmer climates, and stayed in the town for only a few years. They were well looked after in Faro where, thanks to a strong union, wage scales were among the most generous in the Yukon. Other benefits included inexpensive housing, living allowances, and recreational facilities.

But like the Yukon's earlier booms, this one was built on shaky foundations. Despite the public investments in the mine and the seemingly inexhaustible ore body, the Cypress-Anvil mine closed in 1981, the victim of international corporate finance. Cypress-Anvil had been purchased by Hudson's Bay Oil and Gas, which in turn was bought by Dome Petroleum, the darling of the federal government's plan to nationalize the oil industry. To Dome, Cypress-Anvil was a minor component of the larger transaction. When Dome subsequently faced bankruptcy, it lacked the resources to keep Cypress-Anvil afloat during a temporary downturn in the world prices for lead and zinc. When the company attempted a major retrenchment, largely at the workers' expense, the union went on strike. To the dismay of many Yukoners, the Faro mine shut down. The strike proved fortuitous for the company, which had negotiated in a desultory manner, for when the mine closed there was no need to pay severance pay to the striking employees.

Several hundred workers hung on, hoping that government and corporate salvage operations would reopen the mine. Periodic government grants provided short-term work, such as stripping overburden from the ore body to prepare for future mining operations, but the rescue effort seemed to have failed. By 1984 the bustling community, second-largest in the Yukon, had all but closed down. Once home to more than 2,000 people, in 1985 it could claim only 320 residents. By 1996 the population had increased to more than 1,300, but by 1999 it had shrunk to 320. Territorial and federal politicians made every effort to get the mine back in operation, for it had clearly become the one stabilizing force in the vulnerable territorial economy. The White Pass and Yukon Route company was devastated by the closure. The loss of its major customer contributed to the decision in 1981 to close the historic railway between Whitehorse and Skagway. The ripple effect worked its way through the entire economy, forcing hundreds to leave the territory and ushering in the deepest depression in the Yukon since the First World War.

In 1986, after negotiating with several potential operators, federal and territorial officials finally struck a deal with little-known Curragh Resources. The package included generous subsidies, including an agreement to maintain the newly opened Carcross-Skagway road through the winter months, though it had been intended for summer travel only. The historic WPYR railway, one of the territory's leading tourist attractions as well as a useful supply route, remained closed. The mine reopened that year, but under very different labour conditions. Initially a non-union operation, the Curragh mine offered few of the generous bonuses, housing subsidies, or high wages of the earlier Cypress-Anvil operation. From the first, employee turnover was extremely high as the men discovered the high cost of living in an unsubsidized company town. The deal did, however, put the Yukon's largest mine back into operation, providing the basis for a revival of the territorial economy in the mid-1980s.

What remained of Dawson City had been left out of the excitement of the postwar mining booms and had pinned its hopes instead on tourism. In the years before the Second World War, Dawson had done little to develop a tourist trade. The town's most famous site, Robert Service's cabin, had been maintained by a small committee of the local Imperial Order Daughters of the Empire. As the community collapsed further with the expansion of Whitehorse after 1942, even Service's shrine fell on hard times and was taken over by the city government.

Dawson's desperation intensified during the 1950s, when it lost the capital, the sternwheelers were pulled off the Yukon River, and when the dredging operations were all but shut down. Finally, in desperation, the few remaining local boosters turned to tourism. In the early 1950s the community established the Klondike Visitors' Association. The KVA's hopes of success rested in large measure on the writings of a former Dawsonite, Pierre Berton. Although Berton had long since left the Yukon, his magazine articles and in 1957 his popular book *Klondike* did more than any other single factor to resurrect flagging interest in the gold rush legends. This, coupled with a growing interest in the North generally, made Dawson's desperate attempt to save itself more than just a fantasy.

The effort, however, required money. The city kept a few key attractions open – Service's cabin, a museum, and a partially restored Palace Grand Theatre – but these were hardly enough to convince thousands of tourists to undertake the long journey to the northern Yukon. In an era of rapidly expanding dependence on government assistance, it was only a matter of time before the city approached the wellhead of money in Ottawa. The federal government was amenable and in 1962 announced a hastily conceived Dawson City Gold Rush Festival for two years later. There was little local input into the planning, which was dominated by a federally controlled Dawson City Festival Foundation, National Historic Sites, and the National Parks. As part of the undertaking, the government moved an old WPYR steamer, the *Keno*, to Dawson, where it was turned into a museum. The festival drew eighteen thousand tourists – more than twice as many as came to the town in a normal year – but did not stimulate lasting interest. The federal government had invested more than $1.6 million; the visitors spent an estimated $1.9 million. The festival may have failed to revitalize Dawson City completely, but local residents were imbued with hope.[28]

Realizing that the government was willing to fertilize their plans for renewal of the gold rush heritage with cash, Dawson's citizens now organized a more sustained request for federal assistance. The Klondike Visitors' Association sought new means of attracting tourists, such as offering legalized gambling aboard the *Keno* – an idea that initially sent tremors of apprehension through the federal bureaucracy. By the late 1960s, National Historic Sites recognized that an amateur effort would not be enough to save the city's tourist resources, and in 1967 representatives of the Historic Sites and Monuments Board of Canada visited Dawson and made a strong recommendation that the federal government make a major commitment to the preservation of Dawson City.

The establishment of the Klondike National Historic Site was a crucial turning point for Dawson City. Over the next decade, the federal government, working with the Klondike Visitors' Association, poured millions of dollars into Dawson and the surrounding area, restoring old buildings, providing things for tourists to see and do in the town and the goldfields, opening Diamond-Tooth Gertie's as a gambling saloon (in those innocent days it was touted as the only legal gambling casino in Canada), and turning the Palace Grand Theatre into a Klondike repertory theatre. The effort worked, and Dawson gained a new lease on life. Businesses returned to the city, and new hotels, restaurants, and stores opened to cater to a rapidly expanding tourist market.

The revitalization of Dawson City in the 1960s and 1970s was only part, albeit the largest part, of the attempt to capitalize on the territory's tourist potential. In Whitehorse, the federal government moved another steamer, the ss *Klondike,* to a new site and restored it. (The *Casca* and *Whitehorse,*

The ss *Keno,* on display at Dawson City, is one of the last of the wood-burning river steamers (Yukon Government photo [YG]).

When Dawson City was developed as a National Historic Site in the 1960s, a few buildings, such as this old gunshop, were left to moulder as picturesque ruins for tourists to photograph (YA).

the other two remaining sternwheelers in the capital, were later destroyed in a spectacular blaze on the Whitehorse waterfront.) The Anglican Church maintained its Old Log Church in downtown Whitehorse, resisting federal efforts to have the old buildings relocated next to the ss *Klondike*. In the late 1970s the territorial government began to add to the stock of tourist attractions – a sternwheeler at Carcross, decaying for years, was saved at the last minute and preserved as a historic site, only to be destroyed later by fire.

Private investors jumped on the bandwagon. In Whitehorse, the Frantic Follies drew hundreds of visitors each night to its Gay Nineties revue. Boat tours of Miles Canyon allowed travellers to recreate part of the Trail of '98, in much calmer waters than the stampeders had encountered. The efforts reached across the border. Increased cruise ship travel through the Inside Passage inspired Skagway to capitalize on the rapidly growing tourist trade. In a welcome example of Canadian-American cooperation, the historic

An actor recites Robert Service's poetry to an audience of tourists in front of the cabin in which the poet once lived (YG).

Chilkoot Trail was preserved, with guides and facilities placed along the route to assist those desiring to retrace the footsteps of the stampeders.

The promotion of tourism did not stop with the Klondike story. The Yukon's natural wonders, ever more precious in an era of environmental awareness and the rapid loss of wilderness elsewhere in North America, found a ready market, especially in the United States and Germany. Big-game hunters, fishermen, photographers, white-water travellers, hikers, and naturalists were sought out aggressively by the tourism promoters. The Yukon Pavilion at Expo '86 in Vancouver brought together these themes and the days of the Klondike, attracting visitors with the brilliantly colourful entranceway painted by Ted Harrison, the Yukon's most famous artist.[29]

If there is an irony in all this tourist promotion, it is the concentration on the Klondike and the comparative lack of attention to other aspects of Yukon history. The building of the Alaska Highway receives surprisingly little attention; few of the wartime buildings remain in use, and there are few monuments or displays highlighting this equally intense and internationally known side of the Yukon's history. While tourist promotions are market-driven to a certain extent, the Yukon has so far missed the opportunity to overcome the narrow southern image of its history and present a more balanced impression of its past, though there is increasing First Nations and community involvement in changing this approach.

The federal government's investments in the mining sector and the redevelopment of Dawson City represented only the most obvious signs of a massive national commitment to the Yukon Territory, and to the Canadian North generally. In contrast to the earlier years of neglect, the federal gov-

Yukon Quest, a sled dog race from Whitehorse to Fairbanks, was first run in 1984. Sonny Linder, pictured here on the river with his team, was the first winner, completing the course in twelve days (YG).

ernment now offered generous subsidies to the territorial administration and made substantial investments of its own in the Yukon. The new commitment emerged fairly quickly after the Second World War in the form of a new federal Department of Northern Development. In the early 1950s, although the government had maintained the Alaska Highway and provided money for the construction of other new roads in the territory, much of the Yukon remained virtually inaccessible.

The territory's member of parliament, Liberal Aubrey Simmons, argued in favour of more roads, particularly one to the Mackenzie Delta, and eventually he carried the day. Early in 1957, just before the election of John Diefenbaker and the Conservatives, Simmons announced that work on the road would start shortly. The Tory government followed through on the promise. Alvin Hamilton, minister of northern affairs and national resources, supported the plan, declaring, "I visualize making every corner of the Yukon accessible. We can't develop without access. I see a network of trunk roads branching out from Dawson City. The great development possibilities in the northwest corner certainly justify road investments into the Mackenzie River delta area."[30]

Northern roads, unexpectedly, became a major element in the 1958 federal election. In the opening speech of the campaign, Prime Minister Diefenbaker electrified his audience with his plan for northern development: "We intend to start a vast roads program for the Yukon and Northwest Territories which will open up for exploration vast new oil and mineral acres – thirty million acres! We will launch a seventy-five-million-dollar federal-provincial program to build access roads. THIS IS THE VISION … We are fulfilling the visions and dreams of Canada's first prime minister – Sir John A. Macdonald. But Macdonald saw Canada from East to West. I see a new Canada. A CANADA OF THE NORTH!" After the victory, Diefenbaker and Hamilton announced the allocation of $100 million for the northern roads program.

Shortly thereafter, work began on the highway to the Mackenzie Delta. Even as construction was beginning, Hamilton announced that oil had been discovered on Eagle Plains, proof of the value of the access roads. But by 1960, only the first 69 miles (110 km) of the highway had been finished, though winter roads allowed convoys to move supplies farther out onto Eagle Plains. When the energetic Hamilton left his Northern Affairs portfolio, responsibility passed to the more pedestrian Walter Dinsdale. Highway construction slowed and then stopped. Yukoners gained a minor victory in having the highway named after W.J.D. Dempster, the popular old-time RCMP officer who was then in his mid-eighties, but when work on the Eagle Plains oilfield sputtered, federal interest fell even further. The Diefenbaker administration, awash in a sea of political infighting, lost interest in northern development.

There the highway remained for another decade, some 75 miles (120 km) of road heading northeast from Dawson City. The vision of a link to the Mackenzie had been put on hold. Meanwhile, the highway served as an access road for exploration crews and provided hunters with an approach to the massive caribou herds that migrated annually across Eagle Plains. Not until the early 1970s did funding return to what had once been a flagship project for the Canadian government. Much of the renewed interest was based on proposed plans for a pipeline down the Mackenzie River valley. The Canadian Armed Forces built the bridges at Ogilvie and Eagle rivers, another money-saving venture disguised as a northern training exercise. Private contractors worked on the highway under the direction of the Department of Public Works, battling with the environmental and engineering challenges posed by permafrost and arctic weather conditions. Initially slated to cost from $5 to $8 million and to be finished in five years, the Dempster Highway cost nearly $103 million, and was finally opened nineteen years after work started. The initial work cost $55,000 per mile; the last segments of the road, between Rock River and the border between the Yukon and Northwest Territories, cost ten times that.

The government's commitment was not limited to roads and the promotion of tourism. The communications system built by the U.S. Signal Corps during the Second World War had significantly upgraded the Yukon's connections with the rest of Canada. In 1960–61 the existing land-line system was enlarged by the addition of a high-capacity microwave radio system.[31] The Yukon's integration into the broader communications and information networks took much longer. The U.S. Army had left behind the radio station in Whitehorse, which was run on a volunteer basis, and in the early 1970s the Canadian Broadcasting Corporation opened a station in Whitehorse and began broadcasting throughout the territory. The CBC Northern Service offered a variety of national programming, community news, and message services, providing links between Yukon communities and with the rest of the country. The national network was later joined by a private radio station in Whitehorse, CKRW, which offered more contemporary music and was aimed more specifically at the local market.

Television came much later than radio. In Whitehorse, CFWH, one of the many Yukon enterprises owned by the Hougen family, provided an extensive cable system, based on taped programs flown in from outside. Live programs were not available; the landing of Americans on the moon in 1969, for example, was seen in the North on a tape. In the fall of 1972, while much of the rest of the country watched the final game of the Canada-Russia hockey series, Yukoners listened attentively on their radios and then watched the game the next day on a tape flown in by the television station.

That was the year that Canada deployed Anik 1, the first satellite devoted exclusively to domestic communications. The Anik system permitted transmission of live broadcasts from southern Canada, which initially were offered only in the late afternoon and evening. The limited service caused many scheduling problems. For instance, the complaints of those who were not sports fans led to the unexpected cancellation of Friday-night Montreal Expos baseball; but wiser heads soon prevailed, and the Expos took back their weekly slot. The CBC later went to a full-service program, with some special northern programming. In 1986, the weekly program NEDAA began production in Whitehorse under the auspices of Northern Native Broadcasting. This program, like its counterpart *Focus North*, offered a northern insight into contemporary northern issues. Commercial television also expanded in the 1980s. The Cancom system, under the leadership of Rolf Hougen, received a licence from the Canadian Radio and Television Commission in 1981 to beam several southern stations into a large number of communities throughout the Yukon and Northwest Territories.

These services, combined with the generally available satellite programming represented a cultural revolution for the North. In all communities, English- and French-language programming were made available throughout the day, while the American-made programs that dominate the television networks have become part of the cultural baggage of all Yukoners, including Native people in previously isolated hunting villages such as Old Crow. The new technology, though posing a threat to existing cultures, also provides new opportunities. The NEDAA program, CHON-FM (a native-run FM radio station based in Whitehorse), the CBC Northern Service, film work by the Northern Native Broadcasting Company, and a variety of Native language programs on the various media have provided a previously unavailable opportunity for aboriginal people to respond to the intrusion of southern culture.

The renaissance of aboriginal culture through radio and television programming represents one of the most promising signs of the revitalization of Yukon indigenous society. For decades the aboriginal people, the only constant in the territory, faced massive social and economic dislocation; their communities and families still bear the many scars of the difficult transition to the realities of the industrial and administrative revolution that has transformed the Yukon over the past sixty years.

While the standard economic indicators suggest that the Yukon enjoyed reasonable prosperity after 1946, the Native people did not initially share in the new wealth. The new mines were operated by whites with a white workforce, while the roads brought thousands of whites into areas that were previously known almost only to Natives. Their mobile and harvesting lifestyle had coexisted with the advance of the mining frontier and white settlement, but the accommodations of the past no longer worked. The transformation that now occurred had its roots in government programs and coincided with the collapse of the North American fur market. In the early years of the Canadian welfare state, the federal government decided that its poorest citizens, the aboriginal people, should be given special encouragement and assistance as they struggled to adapt to the Canadian mainstream. Business incentive grants, pensions, and welfare programs targeted specifically at Native people expanded rapidly in the 1950s. For the Native people of the Yukon, all but ignored in the previous decades, the new level of intervention brought marked changes in their lifestyles.

Aboriginal people became increasingly reliant on government support payments. The establishment of the Family Allowance in 1945, for example, gave authorities the ability to force regular attendance at public schools; failure to send the children resulted in the quick elimination of the monthly payments, which, though small, were important to people with little cash income. The government's underlying paternalism towards the northern Native people was further reflected in the policy, enforced until the mid-1950s, that the Family Allowance be provided in kind rather than cash, allowing the authorities to determine how the money was spent. Welfare payments, all but ignored by the First Nations before the war, became an increasingly important part of their economy. Before 1944 the government had paid out less than $12,000 in welfare payments each year; by 1954–55 welfare spending on the Yukon's Native people alone reached $90,000, and it rose to more than $200,000 by the mid-1960s.[32]

While subsidies such as old age pensions, welfare, and emergency relief provided a short-term solution, the government's hope was that the aboriginal people could be integrated into the broader economy – on, of course, the dominant society's terms. Loans for aboriginal entrepreneurs, community housing projects, and training programs were provided in the expectation that the First Nations would gain the skills and acquire the values of the modern industrial age. There was little room left in this new economy for traditional harvesting practices and seasonal movements, and as the fur trade declined in importance, the Native people had no choice but to accept government support. Having done so, they were required to follow the instructions of federal administrators.

Government agents were particularly anxious that First Nations children attend school regularly. Families who wanted to maintain their government support payments found that this meant moving to communities where schools were available. While some families resisted the transition, either remaining in the bush or leaving the father behind while the rest of the family moved closer to the school, most reluctantly left the camps for villages. Many students were sent to residential schools – either the Roman Catholic school at Lower Post, British Columbia, or the Anglican school at Carcross (reopened in expanded quarters); or, after 1949, the Baptist school housed in war-surplus buildings in Whitehorse. By 1954, the Department of Indian Affairs could claim that "only a score of school-age children in the entire Yukon Territory were not enrolled in school."[33]

Schooling, as always, proved a mixed blessing. While the children gained new skills, they also discovered a system that was culturally insensitive, offering virtually no support or recognition of Native culture. The residential schoolchildren, sometimes forcibly removed from their parents and kept away for months or years at a time, faced particular difficulties. Cut adrift from their own culture but not readily accepted within the mainstream Yukon society, many of these children left school before graduation only to face grave difficulties in adapting back into their home communities. Both the government and the teachers were aware of the problem and sought more workable techniques. In 1960 Yukon Hall was opened in Whitehorse, replacing the Baptist school. It served as a dormitory for First Nations children, who attended the regular public schools. Similarly, Catholic students were boarded in Catholic dormitories and attended the local Catholic schools. By the late 1960s, all the residential schools had been phased out. Lower Post was closed down, while Carcross operated for a few years as an "alternative" school. As the territorial school system expanded, bringing classrooms closer to the First Nations communities, some of the problem was eliminated.

But the legacy of Yukon First Nations education could not be quickly overcome, and most Natives remained unconvinced of the benefits of the Canadian educational system. Their suspicion rested in large measure on the enormous gap between their lifestyle and the curriculum in the schools, which was based on the British Columbia system. Within the central school program, indigenous cultures and traditions were considered irrelevant – at best, a historical curiosity. Textbooks, problems, and materials were related to a world that few Yukon Natives had experienced. In the past twenty-five years, however, some significant changes have been made. The Yukon Department of Education began to produce its own curriculum materials and used the output of the northern communications companies to add further Yukon content.

The most promising initiative was housed for a number of years in a small facility in Whitehorse Elementary School and is now at the Ayamdigut Campus of Yukon College in Whitehorse. The Yukon Native Languages Centre, founded in 1977 by the Council of Yukon Indians and now under the administration of linguist John Ritter, seeks to preserve Yukon Native languages, several of which face extinction, and to encourage the use of native languages in the classroom. In a number of communities, Native speakers assist teachers in the use of traditional languages and share legends and cultural traditions with the children. As the territorial school system moves to accept Native culture as an important component of the curriculum – for all students, not just those of aboriginal background – it is likely that the aboriginal people's long-standing hostility to formal education will ease.[34]

It was for economic as well as educational reasons that government agents encouraged the Native people to move out of the bush to permanent communities. As one official noted about the Champagne and Aishihik First Nations in 1958, "Some of the younger Indians are being encouraged to locate on the Haines Junction Reserve to improve employment opportunities and to be closer to services." Similar advice was offered to the Ross River band, which was said to have "a welfare problem": "The younger Indians are to be encouraged to move to Upper Liard Bridge permanently and transfer to that Band." Such administrative restructuring of Native society was commonplace after the war.[35]

Aboriginal people accustomed to a harvesting, nomadic lifestyle found the transition to the sedentary life of a government-controlled reserve difficult and stressful. There were, it turned out, few opportunities for them in these communities, and this led to an even greater dependence on government assistance. The difficulties that followed have been well documented: alcoholism and related problems with the law, poor educational attainment, and poverty. The housing provided on the reserves was exceptionally bad, adding to the already serious health problems facing the First Nations. Overriding all of these concerns, however, was the cultural dislocation, reinforced by government agents and a white population that seemed not to value aboriginal culture.

This was evident in federal economic development programs for the First

Nations. While aboriginal harvesting remained (and remains) important, government efforts sought to integrate the aboriginal people into the industrial economy. Through such programs as the Indian Economic Development Fund, Special Agricultural and Rural Development grants, and a myriad of other initiatives, the government offered loans, advice, supervision, and training for Native entrepreneurs, for Native industrial workers, for employers willing to hire Natives, and for villages prepared to undertake community development projects. The individualism required for such capitalist ventures, however, ran counter to the cooperative ethos embedded in First Nations culture. While there were a few success stories, including the construction company started by the Champagne and Aishihik First Nations, most of the government-funded businesses did not prosper. Affirmative action programs and government-funded Native organizations provided many new jobs but carried the danger of creating an internal elite within the Yukon aboriginal society: a small number of well-paid professionals set against the larger, comparatively impoverished aboriginal population. In the past few years, the reason for the repeated failures has finally struck home, leading to greater attention to Native harvesting and alternative methods of First Nations economic development.[36]

The economic and social turmoil of the postwar period struck at the very heart of indigenous culture. Pulled into highway communities, forced into a culturally insensitive education system, and encouraged to adapt to an economic system that offered few prospects, many of the Yukon's Native people sank into despair, a dislocated and colonized people. Whites often reacted with disapproval (though occasionally with concern) to the visible signs of the despair: the startlingly impoverished villages, drunken people on the streets of Whitehorse, Natives outside grocery stores discounting their welfare chits for cash, and a surfeit of indigenous names on the court docket. But such critics were slow to appreciate the deep cultural loss that had attended the collapse of the harvesting economy and the far-reaching effects of the modernization of the Yukon.

Traditional aboriginal leaders, raised in the bush, often lacked the skills necessary for the bureaucratic age. The new communities, some inhabited by people from several bands, came under the official control of elected band councils, but in fact, government agents made most of the decisions, leaving the councils to carry the word to the community. Native people became increasingly suspicious of these officials, whom they saw as apprehending their children and sending them off to distant boarding schools, forcing elderly people into hospitals, and making most of the important decisions. The agents, for their part, struggled with the obligations of their jobs, and often suffered in silence with their Native clients, though a few made their protests public. But they persevered in their tasks, convinced that the government's plan was in the Natives' long-term interests.

It would fall to these Native people themselves to force greater awareness of their condition. In the mid-1960s, a number of prominent First Nations leaders began to discuss the need for a territorywide aboriginal organization. Led by the quiet eloquence of Elijah Smith, they formed the Yukon Native Brotherhood, determined to end the "welfare thinking of Indian Affairs and our people," as Smith put it. The sense of shared grievance, often heightened by a common experience in residential school, drew the various First Nations to the Yukon Native Brotherhood and turned the organization into an influential territorial force. The Native people did not stand alone. The Christian churches had, in the main, overcome their traditional paternalism and now declared their intention to support the aboriginal people's search for social justice, and many white individuals offered their assistance to the movement.[37]

The Yukon First Nations had an ace in the hole. They had never been taken under treaty, contrary to the Canadian government's often-stated commitment to the terms of the Royal Proclamation of 1763, which required that a treaty be signed before aboriginal lands were occupied. The growing confidence and radicalism of the Yukon Native Brotherhood culminated in the 1973 publication of *Together Today for Our Children Tomorrow*, the first salvo in the Yukon land claims process.[38] The thoughtful, provocative, and wide-ranging document called for the transfer of substantial tracts of land to the Native people, cash payments to compensate for previous losses, resource revenues, sweeping education reforms, and other benefits. Perhaps recognizing the government's legal vulnerability on the question of Yukon land claims, Prime Minister Pierre Trudeau agreed to negotiate the brotherhood's land claim – the first comprehensive land claim accepted for negotiation in Canada.[39]

Many white Yukoners responded with bitterness and fear to this proposal and wondered aloud if the federal government would adequately protect their rights. The declaration of Native intentions injected an element of uncertainty into the territorial economic climate and placed some major projects in doubt. In the pro-development atmosphere of the 1970s, such interference with the "natural" process of regional economic expansion seemed perverse to some people. The territorial government, controlled by the Conservative Party, favoured the pro-business position, particularly when the First Nations combined a demand for greater self-government with their land claim. The territorial government went one step further, demanding that its outstanding claim for control of natural resources be settled before the Natives' claim was addressed.[40]

Settling the claim has proved difficult. A tentative agreement was reached among the Council of Yukon Indians (which in 1973 combined the Yukon Native Brotherhood and the Yukon Association of Non-Status Indians), only to be rejected by the communities when a ratification vote was taken.

Representatives returned to the bargaining table – the Native work being funded out of advance payments from the eventual settlement – and in 1984 it seemed that the negotiations would have a favourable conclusion. The federal Liberal government, facing an election, reached an agreement in principle with the Council of Yukon Indians in early summer, leaving the rest of the year for final negotiations and ratification. But the Conservative sweep of September 1984 quickly altered the equation. Although ten of the fourteen Yukon First Nations accepted the deal, the federal government pulled out of subsequent discussions.

Negotiations continued, though the parameters for discussion seemed to shift continually. The Yukon First Nations – only too aware of the problems in Alaska, where the Natives had accepted a deal they later regretted – battled on, determined to achieve a fair and lasting settlement of their aboriginal entitlement. In May 1993 the Council of Yukon Indians signed an Umbrella Final Agreement with the government; this was a framework under which the fourteen First Nations of the Yukon would conclude final land claims settlement agreements.[41] Four First Nations immediately did so: the Vuntut Gwitch'in, the Nacho Nyak Dun, the Champagne and Aishihik, and the Teslin Tlingit. The other ten continued to negotiate, and although it is risky to make predictions in such matters, perhaps by the time this book emerges from the press, all of the settlements will have been successfully negotiated.

There was another aboriginal land claim that affected the Yukon. This was at its northernmost point. Although by the 1970s the Inuit of the Western Arctic no longer occupied their traditional lands on the Yukon's north slope, they had traditional claims to it. The Inuvialuit (Inuit of the Western Arctic-Mackenzie Delta region), who had organized as the Committee for Original People's Entitlement, submitted a comprehensive land claim to the federal government in 1976. An agreement in principle was signed in 1978 and a final agreement signed and ratified in 1984.[42] Part of the settlement lands which the Inuvialuit retained under this agreement are in the far northern Yukon.

The politicization of the Yukon's aboriginal people has had its effects. The government can no longer ignore their many pressing needs. New housing projects are being undertaken on reserves around the territory. Even Old Crow, the Yukon's most northerly village, has its own modern "suburb." The change is particularly noticeable in Whitehorse. The First Nations reserve, relocated several times, sat for many years next to the industrial area, one of the most unattractive locations in the community. When a planned housing development atop the bluff surrounding Whitehorse fell through, the aboriginal people petitioned for the right to move their reserve there. After lengthy negotiations, the proposal was accepted. New houses were built, and the reserve was moved to its new site – chosen this time by the inhabitants instead of the authorities, and in one of the best locations in the community. Some residents subsequently expressed a desire to return to the old reserve. The change can also be seen in the growing integration of aboriginal and white segments of the Yukon community. Once firmly divided, especially in the residential sphere, the communities are now growing together. Riverdale, across the river from downtown Whitehorse and long a white preserve, now has a growing Native population, a sign of one of the most important social shifts in the Yukon.

The painful and complex process of modernization in the North is further illustrated by the dispute over the Whitehorse squatters. Squatters had set up temporary but highly visible shacks in Whiskey and Moccasin Flats during the Second World War, responding to the acute shortage of housing in the area. Government officials, particularly federal ones, recoiled at the informality and illegality of these settlements, which they considered a blight on the new Whitehorse. To them, the squatters were an affront to Whitehorse's status as a territorial capital. Contrary to official perceptions, however, the squatters were not all ne'er-do-wells (the "colourful five percent" of local folklore). Most were gainfully employed, but the tightly controlled Whitehorse land market kept them from building their own homes. The development of Riverdale and Porter Creek in the 1960s gave an exit to some, but many remained. Whitehorse City Council, though reluctant to take action, was under pressure from the federal government, and it offered these remaining residents a deal. Their homes would be moved outside the city limits – some ten miles south of town after the city had expanded its boundaries – where they would be freed from taxes. The flats were cleared out in the early 1970s, and Whiskey Flats, which sat in front of the handsome new Government Administration Building, was developed into an attractive park by the local Rotary Club.[43]

Although Yukon society in the 1980s changed on a variety of other fronts, the dominance of Whitehorse continued. In 2001, more than 22,000 of the Yukon's 30,000 people lived in the community. The political, administrative, economic, and cultural centre, Whitehorse controled much of the life of the Yukon, and it increasingly showed signs of its growing maturity. Most of the wartime buildings were gone by then, replaced by impressive and expensive public facilities, a trend begun in the 1950s when the hospital and the high school were built across the river from downtown. Since that time, the city has been modernized considerably, with a new territorial government building, a new justice building, and numerous other developments: the Qwanlin Mall (the city's commercial centre), Rolf Hougen's sprawling retail complex along Main Street, new recreation facilities around the city, a territorial jail in Camp Takhini, and suburban developments in Porter Creek and Wolf Creek, as well as a major recreational complex at the top of Two Mile Hill. As well, a new campus had been constructed for Yukon College. Initially

More than 22,000 of the Yukon's 30,000 people now live in Whitehorse. The park in the foreground was once Whiskey Flats, home to some of the territory's "colourful five per cent," until they were removed in a campaign of civic beautification (YG).

housed in the Whitehorse Vocational School, the college offered a wide range of vocational and academic courses, including an expanded university transfer program with a specialization in northern studies. By 1990 Whitehorse had facilities and conveniences that few towns its size anywhere in Canada could match, a mark of its position as territorial capital and a reflection of the generous government spending over the previous two decades.

The Yukon's other communities did not develop as rapidly. Dawson City remained a seasonal centre, crowded in the summer with tourists and with students who came north to work, and shrinking to its core in the winter months. Several of the key businesses, including some of the hotels and the placer operations, closed down for the winter, adding to the sense of isolation. Most of the smaller communities were built on a similarly seasonal foundation, dependent on tourist traffic along the Alaska Highway or summer mineral exploration. Their permanence rested in large measure on the stable Native population and the few regular, mostly government, jobs based in the community.

The mining communities had a different history in this period. During the days of the Cypress-Anvil mine, Faro had a measure of stability, but when the mine closed, most workers left the territory in search of new opportunities. The reopened mine, with its less generous terms of employment, had trouble keeping its workers, adding to the transient nature of the community. Faro and Clinton Creek were, perhaps, the last of the Yukon's company towns. Plans for new mines in the territory's north called for workers to be based in existing communities, possibly Whitehorse (but just as likely to be Edmonton or Vancouver) and flown in and out on rotation.

The sizable emigration of about three thousand people during the 1981–85 depression was only the most visible sign of a deeply entrenched social pattern. Most of those who came north to work in the mines, government offices, and private businesses stayed only a few years before moving south again. This pattern began to change only in the latter half of the 1970s, a welcome trend that continued over the next decade. The gradually increasing social stability had an important commercial dimension. In years past, much of the Yukon's wealth was exported south, often by business people who lived outside during the winter. While this pattern was not broken entirely, there were noticeable signs of change. Men such as Rolf Hougen, whose investments blanket the Yukon, have stayed in the North, reinvesting their profits in the region. Hougen's family started a retail business on Whitehorse's Main Street, an outlet he used over the years as the cornerstone of holdings that grew to include a radio and television station, a car dealership, real estate, and other ventures.

Another example of a businessman who stayed on in the North is Con Lattin, who arrived in the Yukon after the war and lived for a time in Whiskey Flats. Lattin and his family first invested in a pop- and milk-bottling plant. The milk-processing business collapsed when milk trucked in from the south cornered the market, and the pop-bottling enterprise ended with a fire that destroyed the plant. But the company remained in business, eventually expanding into every corner of the territory and diversifying in other service ventures. These people, much like Taylor and Drury in an earlier era, held promise for the future of a society struggling for stability. The roots of a self-sustaining community rested in this type of commitment, one that has long been missing in the Yukon Territory.

On the political level, the elected territorial council continued to provide an increasing measure of representative government. Two additional members were added to the council in 1951, making a total of five elected members. Two years later, the council received the authority to borrow money, subject to a federal veto. In the main, however, the territory remained under the control of a commissioner, who was appointed by Ottawa and answered to no territorial authorities. As federal investment in the Yukon escalated, the commissioner's status likewise improved. No longer an administrator, the commissioner became a political force, having a great deal to do with the territory's direction.

The Yukon went through three commissioners from the mid-1950s to the end of the 1960s. Frederick Collins was an outsider, well connected in Ottawa and an able administrator. The government appointed Gordon Cameron to succeed him. Cameron, as a Yukoner, was expected to quiet the growing territorial demands for greater local autonomy, but he grew frustrated when he found himself trapped between the wishes of the territorial council and the demands of his federal superiors. As he reportedly commented on many occasions, "You can't drive a team of horses with reins 4,000 miles long. By the time you give the signal, you've missed the turn."[44]

Led by Erik Nielsen, who served as the Yukon's member of parliament for more than a quarter of a century, territorial politicians demanded greater local control and freedom from the old colonial structures. As one territorial councillor commented in 1958, "As the voice of the Yukon's population, we have a mandate, I believe, to push with all the aggressiveness at our command to improve the local scene and make the Yukon an attractive place for people to live and prosper. The mandate includes laying of the foundations for the day of responsible government – a day which may not be so far distant."[45] Erik Nielsen was more blunt: "There is a rising tide of resentment in both Territories against the continuing situation whereby people living in the Territories have no direct control over the development of their respective territories ... We believe that we in the Territories exist in a state of vassalage ... ignored in all high-level deliberations."[46] The protests culminated in 1966 with the demand that the Yukon be granted provincial status.

The lack of control, and the fact that the federal government continued to make major decisions without involving territorial politicians, forced elected officials and their public allies into extreme, often radical positions. The selection in 1966 of a new commissioner, the well-respected local businessman James Smith, was intended to smooth the waters, but major decisions, including the contract with Cypress-Anvil, were made without consulting territorial councillors, and like Cameron, Smith found himself taking the heat for federal actions. Nonetheless, he handled the job with tact and aplomb; no one doubted his commitment to the Yukon and his desire to see the territory move towards political maturity.

During Smith's tenure, the balance of power began to tip towards the territorial council. Always a forum for colourful debate, the council, which now had sixteen elected members, proved itself capable of serious work. In 1969 the federal government established an executive council, consisting of the commissioner, appointed officials, and several members of the elected council, who were empowered to handle the routine business of the government.

Another eight years passed before elected members secured a majority of the seats on the executive council, thus gaining some measure of responsible government for the Yukon.[47]

The concerted campaign for local autonomy obscured, at least in part, the very different views on the future of the Yukon. The business community, whose political interests were well represented by Nielsen, sought territorial control of resources and a pro-development approach to government. Native people (who gained representation on the territorial council by the drafting of electoral boundaries that created several largely First Nations constituencies) and some white sympathizers had a different view, which favoured Native rights, environmental concerns, and a more cautious development program. Dislodging the territorial Conservatives would prove a difficult challenge, although the opposing forces came close on a few occasions. In the federal election of 1972, for example, the Liberal candidate nearly defeated Nielsen.

It was the Conservatives who decided that party distinctions should be brought to the territorial council. In the 1978 territorial election, Chris Pearson's Conservative caucus won eleven of the sixteen seats. As government leader, Pearson selected the executive council from within his caucus, marking a watershed in territorial politics. Tory power gathered steam. In the federal election of 1979, the Conservatives squeaked into office; Nielsen was named minister of public works, a crucial post in view of the importance of highway construction and government investment in the Yukon. The federal government acted quickly to reduce the powers of the commissioner further, granting greater autonomy to local officials. Not all were pleased with the change. Commissioner Ione Christensen resigned over the reduction in her role. As the council became more powerful, the commissioner became less so and by the mid-1980s the position was largely ceremonial.

Promising signs showed up on other fronts as well. The election of Joe Clark and the Conservatives federally seemed particularly fortuitous. As early as 1976, Clark had announced his determination to grant the Yukon Territory full provincial status. To his surprise, he discovered that Yukoners were not particularly pleased with the proposal. Serious critics of the proposition worried about the possible cost to Yukoners and wondered whether the emphasis on political reform might be better expended on economic and social improvements. As one commentator noted, "To talk about provincehood under such circumstances seems to be unrealistic and even dangerous, because someone might just say yes."[48]

The election of Brian Mulroney's Conservative government in 1984 – and Nielsen's elevation to the position of deputy prime minister – seemed to hold considerable promise for the territory. But Nielsen, near retirement and distracted by the many problems of the early Mulroney years, put little public effort into the Yukon political campaigns. Provincial status remained on hold, replaced by more pressing concerns, including a prolonged debate over the high charges and massive debt of the Northern Canada Power Commission.

The most immediate of these concerns, which held the Yukon's attention for much of the late 1970s, revolved around proposed pipeline developments. In the early 1970s the Arctic Gas consortium came forward with plans for a pipeline to deliver Alaskan natural gas down a Mackenzie River corridor. Facing opposition from Native and environmental organizations, the federal government agreed to place the matter before a royal commission chaired by Judge Thomas Berger, a former New Democratic Party politician whose support of aboriginal rights and concern about the environment were well known. Berger launched a high-profile inquiry that visited the affected communities in the Northwest Territories and the Yukon and brought the concerns of northern Native people before the Canadian people in a way that no other forum has done before or since.[49]

The Berger Commission recommended that the Mackenzie Valley pipeline project be delayed, and it called the government's attention to the pressing need to settle Native land claims and protect the environment. It also suggested alternative routes, including a proposal brought forward by the Foothills Pipe Lines Company of Bob Blair. Blair, the upstart in the pipeline wars, had proved surprisingly persuasive, and it appeared that his project would carry the day. The federal government established another investigative commission, this time under the leadership of Kenneth Lysyk, from the University of British Columbia's Faculty of Law, with Yukon representatives Willard Phelps and Edith Bohmer, to examine the proposal. The Alaska Highway Pipeline Inquiry report, issued in 1977, called for careful attention to the needs of the Yukon's aboriginal people and to the social, economic, and environmental changes that would accompany the massive project.[50]

Despite these cautions, the government was determined to proceed, and the Yukon braced for another construction boom, one that promised to match the building of the Alaska Highway in intensity. Yukon businesses expanded operations in anticipation. The city of Whitehorse opened new lots and a new subdivision (now the First Nations reserve) in expectation of a building boom. Just as excitement peaked, Blair's dream began to unravel. Declining oil and gas prices, combined with reduced demand in the United States, scuttled the project. Although the plans remain in place and there are still hopes that the project will be revived, the much-awaited construction explosion proved illusory.

The collapse of the pipeline project, combined with the depression of the early 1980s, raised serious questions about the viability of the Yukon's economy. Government expenditures made up a strikingly high percentage of the territorial economy, particularly with the Faro mine shut down. The demise of the mining sector and the pipeline project also called into question the territorial Conservative Party's dependence on development as the basis for the regional economy. Chris Pearson resigned the government leader's chair in 1985 and assumed a patronage appointment as Canada's representative in Dallas, Texas. He was replaced by Willard Phelps, a man with deep Yukon roots but wedded to the standard Tory model of regional development.

Less than three months after his selection, Phelps faced his first major test. To the surprise of many, the May 1985 election saw the election of a New Democratic Party minority government, led by Tony Penikett. The NDP had gained eight seats – half of those available – in the exceptionally close campaign, while Phelps's Tories fell to only six. The Liberals, with the remaining two seats, held the balance of power. Sam Johnston of Teslin was appointed speaker, the first Native in Canada to hold such a post. The Liberals supported the government initially, but then their leader Roger Coles was charged and found guilty of possession of cocaine, and a February 1987 by-election in the Tatchun constituency returned an NDP member, solidifying the government's hold on office.

The new government faced no shortage of challenges, the most serious of which was attending to the collapsing territorial economy. Penikett and the government moved quickly to reassure the business community that their socialist leanings would not bring startling changes in government policy. The successful reopening of the Faro mine provided substantial evidence that the government was not opposed to development. The government also paid particular attention to the concerns of Native people and the outlying communities. Perhaps surprisingly, however, the sizable Native representation in the governing party and the council did not quickly translate into a major political power block. Perhaps the NDP's greatest success lay in the revitalization of the territorial bureaucracy. The former Conservative government, staunch defenders of the individualistic, growth-oriented frontier ethic, had given the civil servants little latitude to propose new programs. Under the NDP, initiative and innovation from civil servants was clearly welcomed, breathing new life into this large and important sector of Yukon society.

Evidence of the new spirit of innovation was the establishment of the Yukon 2000 process in the spring of 1986. The government invited all Yukoners to participate in a lengthy territorial economic planning process, which included extensive research and numerous opportunities for community consultation. Yukon 2000 centred on a series of public forums – in Faro and Whitehorse in 1986 and Dawson in 1987 – in which representatives from all sectors of Yukon society and economy debated the region's future. Although the process produced few new ideas, it did reveal a strong consensus on the need for economic diversification and measures to ensure economic equality and social stability within the territory.

In 1986 Erik Nielsen announced his resignation from the House of Commons.[51] For the first time in a quarter-century, the federal Yukon seat was truly open. The NDP put its considerable resources and expertise into the campaign of Audrey McLaughlin and won a narrow victory over the popular Whitehorse mayor Don Brannigan, the Liberal candidate. The Conservatives finished third. The success of the NDP campaign rested, at least in part, on the strong opposition of McLaughlin and the Yukon government to an announced constitutional deal involving the federal government and the provinces.

In the spring of 1987, Prime Minister Brian Mulroney and the ten provincial premiers emerged from a marathon meeting at a resort at Meech Lake in Quebec to announce the signing of a constitutional accord. Most political leaders rushed to support the deal, which brought Quebec into the constitution and expanded provincial influence over Senate and judicial appointments and future constitutional change. To their dismay, Yukoners discovered that no one had stood up for northern concerns. The Yukon government would have no say in the new appointment processes, nor would it be able to negotiate solely with the federal government on future provincial status, as had all other late entries into Confederation. Under the terms of the proposed accord, such changes would be subject to approval by the federal government and the ten provincial premiers, a level of unanimity seldom achieved in Canada.

It was a constitutional slap in the face of the most egregious kind. The governments of the Yukon and the Northwest Territories protested the provisions in the strongest terms. Tony Penikett spoke out loudly against the deal, as did Audrey McLaughlin, who broke ranks with her national party over the issue. The Yukon government went even further, challenging the constitutional deal in the courts. Ironically, the campaign against the Meech Lake Accord drew Yukoners together, providing the kind of common cause for protest that so often forms the basis of a regional identity. As such, it had the potential to contribute to the development of political and social stability in a region not noted for either.

TEN

Rebuilding the Modern Yukon

When we wrote the first edition of *Land of the Midnight Sun* in 1987–88, the future of the Yukon Territory appeared highly uncertain. The Meech Lake Accord threatened to marginalize the territory constitutionally. Indigenous land claims seemed no closer to resolution than they had been a decade before. The territory's economic base was no firmer than it had ever been; the gradual improvements associated with the intense summertime tourist season provided a poor replacement for a stable mining industry. The crucial Faro mine, which was for much of the time the Yukon's only operating mine, opened, closed, opened again, and seemed to be trapped in a cycle of federal subsidies and territorial bailouts. Mineral production in the Yukon fluctuated wildly. In 1991 it was nearly $500 million, in 1994 barely one-tenth of that, in 1996 about $400 million, in 1999 back to $90 million, and so on.[1] As had been the case throughout the entire twentieth century, transiency remained the defining characteristic of the non-aboriginal population, with workers migrating north for summer jobs or for short-lived territorial experiences.

Although some things have changed in the seventeen years since this book was written, many elements of territorial life remain much the same. The hoped-for rebirth of the Yukon – which boosters promised would emerge around a revitalized mining sector, expanded tourism, a pipeline to Alaska, and the resolution of aboriginal land claims, – has materialized only in part, nor did the NDP administration's much-touted effort at economic diversification prove very successful. The territorial economy languishes, propped up by substantial federal transfers, struggling to find a twenty-first-century Bonanza Creek. The territory's population, of whom about one-third are indigenous, has actually declined, from 31,166 in 1999 to 30,273 in 2001. As before, the majority (22,500) lived in Whitehorse, which claimed nearly three-quarters of the territorial total. The next biggest communities – Dawson City (1,800) and Watson Lake (1,500) – are less than one-tenth of the size of the capital. These figures mask several key realities: that non-aboriginal people continue to pass through the Yukon with considerable rapidity; that seasonal migration remains a central element in northern life; and that aboriginal people continue to shift from the smaller centres to the Yukon capital.

We ended the first edition of this book with the following comment: "Meech Lake reveals the Yukon's continuing vulnerability to federal politics and southern Canadian priorities. Once more the Yukon has been sacrificed to a greater Canadian ambition. It now seems that the Yukon Territory could well be doomed to the status of a permanent colony, denied even the ambition of constitutional evolution that sits at the base of the Canadian political tradition." But making such political predictions is a tricky game. The Meech Lake Accord, far from being a serious blow to the Yukon, ended in farce, with a single member of the Manitoba legislature and then the Government of Newfoundland and Labrador exercising a veto over it. Canada then entered a period of near crisis, when Jean Chrétien's ineptitude and his unpopularity in Quebec brought the sovereigntists to within a few thousand votes of a victory in a referendum on separation. Canadians subsequently tired of constitutional battles, so much so that the Parti Québécois lost control of the Quebec legislature in 2003 in an election that paid no attention to the separatist or any other constitutional issue. Yukoners remained upset with the manner in which they were ignored in the Meech Lake process, but they too seemed to lose a sense of urgency on this matter.

Tony Penikett, government leader in the Yukon from 1985 to 1992, had been at the forefront of the national political struggles over Meech Lake, and he continued to push for greater local control over territorial affairs. His replacement as NDP leader, Piers McDonald (Yukon premier from 1996 to 2002), continued the process and lobbied hard for a continued devolution of power to the Yukon government. To the surprise of many in the North, the federal government under Prime Minister Chrétien agreed. Over a decade, discussions continued on the best means of strengthening responsible government and ensuring the Yukon government of a greater say in regional affairs. The pattern of devolution of federal responsibilities, begun in the 1960s, continued with greater urgency, as did the redrafting of the Yukon Act. The latter, the first major rewriting of the legislation, was particularly important, for it confirmed the fact that the role of the Yukon commissioner was purely ceremonial, like that of provincial lieutenant-governors, and it thus entrenched the authority of the elected representatives. The passage of Bill C-39 (the Yukon Act) on 27 March 2002 represented a significant watershed in territorial development. With the formal transfer of personnel on 1 April 2003, the Government of Yukon assumed full responsibility for the management of land, resources, water, forests, and environmental matters, thus gaining what are arguably the most important rights of regional governance.

As the Yukon worked its way towards greater political autonomy, it did so through a period of electoral transition and political flux. Tony Penikett had set a new standard for national engagement and territorial leadership. Under his premiership, the government became more active, particularly on economic and aboriginal matters. Repeated efforts to stimulate the economy failed, however, and the government was sharply criticized for its lack of success. In 1992 Penikett lost his majority, and he left the territory shortly thereafter, working for the NDP government in British Columbia before relocating to Saskatchewan. He was succeeded by John Ostashek (known locally as Johnny O) and the right of centre Yukon Party, which took a less interventionist approach to government and counted on the private sector to renew the territorial economy. Ostashek in turn was defeated by Piers McDonald of the NDP, who held office until early 2000. McDonald ran a careful and cautious administration, focusing on economic diversification and the completion of First Nations land claims. He and his party ran up against the standard challenges of a long-serving government, the continued stagnation of the territorial economy, and a particularly heated debate about the development of public lands in Whitehorse.

In 2000 the NDP lost a close election to Pat Duncan and the Liberal Party (ten Liberals, six NDP, and one Yukon Party seat), but Duncan's term in office proved short-lived. She had trouble with her caucus, removing several cabinet ministers and seeing them cross the floor to sit as independents. Now running a minority government, she persisted with a strong legislative program until she called an election for November 2002. Although the territorial sentiment appeared to be running against Duncan and the Liberals, few anticipated the magnitude of the shift. Dennis Fentie and the Yukon Party secured over 40 per cent of the vote and twelve of the eighteen seats. The NDP became the official opposition, taking five seats under its new leader, Todd Hardy, and leaving a solitary seat, held by the ex-premier, for the Liberals. The Liberals actually won more of the popular vote than the NDP, but their support was more widely scattered.

On the national political stage, the Yukon's federal representatives had managed to raise the profile of the territory, beginning with Erik Nielsen in the 1960s, who two decades later served as deputy prime minister in the Mulroney government before retiring to a sinecure at the Canadian Transportation Agency. His replacement in the 1987 by-election, Audrey McLaughlin of the NDP, had come north from Ontario in 1979 to start a new life. She became chair of the NDP caucus in 1988 and the following year contested the national party leadership. After a tense struggle, capped by a dramatic convention in Winnipeg, McLaughlin was selected as the first woman to lead a national political party. The NDP did not, however, fare well during her term in office. Whether this was because of her failings as a leader or because the party had run out of palatable ideas is for the political scientists to judge. Although she retained her seat, the NDP was reduced to a nine-seat rump in the 1993 sweep by Jean Chrétien and the Liberals. McLaughlin stepped down in 1995 and left the House of Commons. In 1997 she was replaced as the Yukon's member by Louise Hardy, who lost the seat to Larry Bagnell of the Liberal Party in 2000.

On the surface, it appears that the Yukon has oscillated wildly on the political spectrum, electing left (Penikett, NDP), right (Ostachek, Yukon party), left (McDonald, NDP), centre (Duncan, Liberal), and right (Fentie, Yukon Party) territorial governments in the space of only a few years, and right (Neilsen, Conservative), left (McLaughlin and Hardy, NDP), and centre (Bagnell, Liberal) members at the national level. These elections do not, however, necessarily represent dramatic shifts of political feeling in the Yukon, for unlike the situation at the national and provincial levels, the politics of smallness play a major role in determining the outcome of territorial elections. Constituencies are very small, and a handful of voters, swayed by a single issue, can easily determine the outcome of an election, which can take on the character of a municipal election more than a provincial one. This was the way that Piers McDonald lost not only the premiership but also his seat.

There is also a fair amount of political shifting within territorial politics. Pat Duncan, for example, once worked as constituency assistant for the Conservative MP Erik Nielsen. Denis Fentie had been elected for the NDP before becoming a member of the Yukon Party. But whatever the party label, the problems of governing were always the same. In office, each of the administrations faced similar agendas and realities, including limited fiscal flexibility, demands for immediate economic action, and unrealized (and unrealistic) expectations, some fuelled by the leaders' pronouncements. All parties shared a commitment to expanding the territorial economic base, although the plans for doing so were generally vague. Eventually, a grudging consensus began to emerge that the Yukon's economic woes were deeply entrenched and unlikely to see a quick solution.

One issue dominated territorial public life in this period: the resolution of aboriginal land claims in the Yukon. Significantly, all political parties in the Yukon declared themselves in favour of resolving the claims, though the Yukon Party did so later and more reluctantly than the others. The Yukon Party's current platform, for example, highlights the importance of completing land claims negotiations and speaks, more generally, to

formalizing government to government relationships with Yukon First Nations based on mutual respect, consultation, cooperation, and benefit for the better operation of all governments in the territory with the objective of reducing barriers and providing more cost-effective services to all Yukon citizens [and] working with Yukon First Nations to make them full partners in the economic development of the territory to the mutual benefit of all Yukoners to avoid litigation and to create a positive, "united-front" investment climate that will encourage responsible economic development in the territory.[2]

There is no greater sign of the fundamental transformation of territorial politics than the centrality given to the resolution of land claims and the greater attention given to indigenous issues more generally. Yukon land claims negotiations began in 1973 and appeared to drag on interminably after that. After fifteen years, an umbrella final agreement, which provided a territorywide basis for the establishment of land entitlements, financial compensation, self-government powers, and aboriginal representation on government boards and commissions, was concluded in 1988. On 29 May 1993 the Council for Yukon First Nations, the Government of Canada, and the Government of Yukon officially signed the Final Agreement, which to be literally final then had to be ratified by all of the First Nations communities. The agreement was substantial. Yukon First Nations received more than 10,000 square miles (25,900 km²), representing 8.5 per cent of the Yukon. They secured mineral and oil and gas rights to 16,000 square miles (41,000 km²), more than half of their total land entitlement. In addition, the settlement involved over $242 million (1989 dollars) in a cash settlement and a variety of agreements on resource and harvesting rights, heritage and culture, and various administrative matters. As of 1993, four Yukon First Nations (Vuntut Gwich'in, Champagne and Aishihik, Teslin Tlingit, and Nacho Nyuk Dun) had reached final settlements. By 2003, a total of four more First Nations had signed (Selkirk, Little Salmon/Carmacks, Ta'an Kwäch'än, and Tron'dëk Hwëch'in, formerly known as the Dawson Nation), and most of the other First Nations were nearing agreements and ratification of the accords. In addition to the general settlement, each First Nation negotiated a self-government agreement with the federal and territorial governments, outlining the precise administrative duties and responsibilities that would be absorbed by the First Nation.

Thirty years after the land claims process officially began, the process is substantially implemented and fully embedded in the political culture of the Yukon Territory. While the benefits have yet to work their way fully through the territory, a number of initiatives have been undertaken, such as the development of aboriginal capacity through training programs at Yukon College, and the inclusion of native people on all major consultative and administrative committees in the territory. It can be argued, however, that the treaty process has exhausted the territory as much as it has energized it. For a generation, a large portion of the political and administrative talent at the

Carcross (population 400), where the White Pass and Yukon Railway crosses on a swing bridge between Lakes Bennett and Nares. The old railway station has been converted into a museum and gift shop (YG).

territorial and aboriginal level in the Yukon has been devoted to this issue, and it is inevitable that time will be required to shift from the negotiating mode of the past to the implementation and development ethos required for the future. At the same time, native and non-Native governments have managed to achieve what many believed impossible: a reasonable, sustainable political accommodation between First Nations and other Yukoners and Canadians. In the process, they have provided a foundation that will ensure that the future will look very different from the past.

If the resolution of aboriginal land claims symbolizes the unfinished business of the past generation, the recent opening of the Walmart in Whitehorse speaks volumes about the changing character of the territory. There is nothing "northern" about this Walmart; it looks and feels every bit like every standard outlet of the world's largest retailer. There is a small McDonald's restaurant tucked into one corner, the ever-cheerful greeters, and the heavily discounted prices that have quickly attracted Yukon consumers. The store did not arrive without controversy. In town after town across North America (and increasingly, internationally as well), local retailers have fought against the intrusion of megastores of the Walmart variety, which have been blamed for ruining small town business districts and having a major impact on commercial activity (though in towns such as Prince George, the effect has been on businesses in other regional towns – the Walmart store acts as a magnet). According to critics, the NDP government, under Piers McDonald, and the Whitehorse City Council made significant concessions to attract the mall developer, Argus Properties of Kelowna, and then to attract Walmart. The politicians underestimated the protests that would follow.

A group of Whitehorse residents fought back through 2000. Downtown businesses, fearing the shift in business activity to the site, challenged the government's decisions in court but failed to block the plan. Local residents, led by Yukon College instructor Norm Easton, established an action committee, Citizens for Responsible Planning and Development, which quickly gathered hundreds of members. Their "Folk the Mall" campaign attracted considerable attention – community members tackling ubiquitous big-box retailers makes for great press – but they failed to sway the authorities or the companies involved. Murray Lundberg, a regular commentator on northern affairs, said of the affair: "I moved to the Yukon because I love the feel of it. Unfortunately, there are still a lot of people here who obviously wish they were somewhere else (Mayor [Kathy] Watson being on top of my list in that category). The result is that we get bizarre projects that attempt to make Whitehorse look like Calgary or Vancouver. I am strongly opposed to the mall, and will do anything I can to stop construction, and to make it possible for members of Council who voted for the project to finalize their commitments in Whitehorse so that they can move to whichever city it is they would really like to be in."[3]

In the end, however, "low low" prices trumped the Yukoners' sense of exceptionalism, and Walmart and its local supporters carried the day, though only after many town hall meetings, protests, and an extensive letter-writing campaign. The new store opened late in 2001, promising to hire some 150 people (about 100 full-time). Local retailers, particularly those along Fourth Avenue and Main Street, braced for a crisis, but it did not hit. Walmart attracted many shoppers and appears to have had the same kind of impact on Whitehorse that it has had on hundreds of other communities – a shifting of shopping patterns in the consumers' favour, the slow erosion of the viability of independent stores, and the creation of a more competitive commercial environment for other chain or major stores (which in Whitehorse consists of Canadian Tire and the long-established Hougen's companies).

There were further ironic twists to the Walmart development, which expanded to include a sixplex theatre (Whitehorse previously had two double theatres) and other facilities. The big-box store has had a long-standing policy of permitting owners of recreational vehicles to park overnight in the parking lot without charge, both as a service to travellers and as a means of attracting their business. In major centres, this concession is a relatively minor matter. But not in Whitehorse. In 2002, in particular, Whitehorse-area parks for recreational vehicles protested Walmart's practice, arguing that it drew customers away from their operations and cut heavily into their returns during the short summer tourist season. Walmart relented somewhat, promising to limit the number of vehicles permitted to stay each evening – though the vigilant park owners pointed out the following year that the store was not honouring the deal and that they continued to lose business. Walmart and others in the community argued back that the availability of free parking kept travellers – and shoppers – in town who otherwise would have kept moving up the highway. The mayor, Ernie Bourassa, contemplated a ban on recreational vehicle parking in such spaces.

The Walmart development is but one sign of the continued transformation of Whitehorse and the Yukon. The territory is slowly losing its unique northern character, replacing it with the popular culture, mass-market commercial and entertainment environment that is the norm across the continent. A huge gap remains between Whitehorse and the outlying communities, of course, for there is no Walmart in Ross River. Most of the towns and villages are tiny and are highly seasonal economically, suffering continual outmigration to the capital city. People from the other communities travel to Whitehorse regularly for shopping and social opportunities, thereby reinforcing the power of the territory's largest centre. Many Whitehorse residents, – in the Walmart debate and subsequently – have complained about the transition, which is resulting in the introduction of a chain-store culture and mass-market reality in a community long known for its distinctiveness and northern character. Many others welcome the transition and the lower prices and opportunities that have accompanied the change.

The domination of Whitehorse in the territory – unique in Canada, for in no other province or territory does the capital city make up such a large percentage of the population – seems likely to continue and even to increase. The development of new facilities began in the 1980s and 1990s with the construction of the new territorial government building, a refurbished federal government centre, Yukon College's dramatic new campus, an impressive justice building, and the first phase of a major recreational complex. Along with this came the expansion of housing, the construction of several new schools, and the expansion of the multiplex in anticipation of the Canada Winter Games in 2007 (which attracted a $20 million grant from the federal government for the building of sports facilities), and of course Walmart. With the settlement of most of the Yukon's First Nations land claims, aboriginal groups now have investment capital. Kwanlin Dun, the local First Nation, has been seeking to develop a waterfront site for several years (the first attempt collapsed in a messy legal challenge) and will clearly be a major player in the community in the years to come.

Development proceeds much more slowly in the outlying communities. The continued importance of the Alaska cruise industry has resulted in up-

Teslin, population 450, is a mainly aboriginal community. It lies 106 miles (170 km) southeast of Whitehorse and is home to the Tlingit Nation. The bridge at Teslin is the longest on the Alaska Highway (YG).

grades along the Carcross-Whitehorse-Dawson corridor, though several of the largest hotels still close for the winter season. Haines Junction has grown in reaction to the continuing promotion of Kluane National Park. Faro, in contrast, is hanging on by its fingertips, mostly because the mine has not re-opened. Even there, however, 1997 saw the opening of a new town hall and the Campbell Region Interpretive Centre. The revitalization of predominant-ly aboriginal communities continues apace through the construction of im-proved band and recreational facilities, a steady expansion of housing, and improvements to sewer and water systems. These developments, combined with the gradual reconstruction of territorial highways, have given the terri-tory a more contemporary, updated appearance. There are now very few buildings remaining from the Second World War era, and only a handful of prewar facilities. The territory looks static, secure rather than prosperous, though even a cursory examination reveals that almost all of the newer build-ings are public sector. The hand of private business is only occasionally in ev-idence throughout the territory, as might be expected in a region where 5,000 people work for the federal, territorial, and municipal governments.

Until the Second World War, the Yukon's transportation was oriented to the railway from Skagway and the Yukon River steamboats. It is now centred on the Alaska Highway, seen here running through the small community of Carmacks (YG).

In the first years of the twenty-first century, the prospect of mega project-driven prosperity surfaced yet again, when the much-postponed Alaska Highway natural gas pipeline re-emerged as a serious possibility. As before, the pipeline through the Yukon competed with two other routes, one down the Mackenzie River valley and the other paralleling the Alyeska oil line from Prudhoe Bay to Valdez, Alaska. Pat Duncan, who was Yukon premier at the time, pushed hard for the Yukon route in the midst of a continentwide rush to secure additional energy supplies in the wake of further conflict in the Middle East. By 2003, however, it appeared that the Yukon had lost to the Mackenzie route. In a striking reversal from the mid-1970s, when aboriginal protests killed the possibility of constructing a pipeline through the Northwest Territories, the First Nations leaders there were eager to join with southern businesses and northern governments in striking a deal that guaranteed substantial indigenous ownership and would see the project proceeding expeditiously.

The next Yukon premier, Dennis Fente, applauded the agreement, reminding Yukoners of two key elements. First, an interterritorial energy accord with the Northwest Territories had assured that the Yukon and NWT would share the benefits of whichever pipeline was built, thus lessening the rivalry and ensuring that the two western territories would share in construction-drive prosperity. Secondly, Fente remained confident that the Alaska Highway project would be built eventually, given the growing North American demand for natural gas and the fact that the Mackenzie pipeline could not deliver product from the Alaskan north-slope gas fields. But for the time being, the pipeline, like earlier visions of megaproject economic salvation, remains in the future, still only a vision of resource-based prosperity.

Over the past decade, the Yukon has become increasingly active in international affairs. Some of the global engagement originates with the territory's automatic participation in national initiatives, such as Prime Minister Chrétien's highly publicized Team Canada trade missions. Yukon College – particularly through its long-serving president Sally Webber and the late Aron Senkpiel, dean of arts and science – played a critical role in the establishment of the University of the Arctic, a consortium of fifty-nine universities and colleges from nine countries. In 2003 Dawson City mayor Glen Everitt and adminstrative officer Scott Coulson played important roles in the establishment of the bilateral Association of Circumpolar Municipalities with counterparts from Russia. These initiatives have built upon the foundation set by involvement in the Arctic Games and the growing number of political and economic activities associated with the burgeoning interest in circumpolar cooperation. The emergence of the Yukon as a significant player in northern international engagement – punching well above its weight in circumpolar affairs – has helped shed the often parochial perspective of an isolated territory and is creating an internationally confident and savvy political and administrative culture in the region.

The Yukon in 2005 is in several ways a considerably different place than it was in 1988, when the first edition of *Land of the Midnight Sun* appeared. Yet little of the change shows on the surface. The resource sector of the economy remains largely moribund, and the hope of a quick return to a mining-based period of growth is unfulfilled. The demography and settled landscapes of the Yukon are much the same, and there is little reason to expect a dramatic shift. But other, fundamentally important developments have occurred. With devolution and the redrafting of the Yukon Act, the territory has a far greater measure of control over resources, spending, and policy-making than at any time in its history. Politically, the Yukon has continued to play a significant role on the national stage, including at premiers' conferences. For a jurisdiction of slightly more than 30,000 people, the territory continues to attract a fair bit of national attention.

In no area, has the transformation been as profound and important as in the role of the aboriginal people. In 1988 Yukon aboriginal leaders were in

Kluane National Park in the Yukon's southwest corner contains spectacular icefields as well as Mount Logan, at 19,850 feet (6,050 m) the highest peak in Canada (YG).

the midst of a seemingly endless process of negotiations and politicking. By the mid-1990s the first settlements had been achieved, and by 2003 most of the Yukon First Nations had signed treaties. The money that came from these agreements was welcome (though a fair portion went to paying off debts accumulated during the negotiations), but in the long run it will be the changing power relationships that will be the most important. The Yukon land claims settlements establish First Nations peoples, communities, and organizations as pivotal players in the territorial political order. Evidence of the impact is now abundant, with aboriginal representation guaranteed on dozens of boards and commissions, and with indigenous input assured on major resource, cultural, and environmental decisions.

The full meaning of the transition can be seen elsewhere. Yukon society is slowly being recrafted, this time with aboriginal people in a more central and equal role. Although tensions are still in evidence, relations between Native and non-Native people appear to be improving. Many non-Native Yukoners take on active interest in indigenous cultures, art, and knowledge.

Miles Canyon, once a dreaded obstacle to those who tried to go through it with flimsy craft in 1898, was tamed when a hydro-electric dam backed up the waters of the Yukon River, making it safer for pleasure boaters (YG)

Northern Native Broadcasting Yukon, a First Nations–controlled media outlet, provides radio and television coverage from a Native perspective, and the CBC North outlet in Whitehorse pays ample attention to aboriginal issues. In the 1970s, aboriginal and non-aboriginal residence patterns rarely overlapped; today, there is much more social mixing throughout the territory. As in the rest of the country, there are elements of concern in the process. Aboriginal women have been marrying outside their communities at a fairly rapid pace, creating a demographic imbalance. Commercial joint ventures are more common, solid political connections can be seen in all political parties, and the celebration and recognition of indigenous culture continues to grow. The appointment of Judy Gingell, a member of the Crow Clan of the Tagish Nation, as commissioner of the Yukon in 1995 and the fact that Native people have served as speaker of the legislature and now routinely serve as cabinet ministers suggests that a great deal has changed. While little of this transition attracts external comment, it is of fundamental importance to the people of the Yukon. The territory is emerging as a balanced, multicultural environment in which substantial respect for aboriginal people is gradually replacing the distrust and misunderstanding of the past.

However, if gradual shifts are underway in the Yukon, significant transitions are occurring on the national stage as well. Put simply, the Yukon and the North generally are losing their iconic status. For generations, the "true North" has held an almost mythical place in the Canadian mind, based on a fascination with Arctic exploration and the omnipresence of the North in fantasies about national prosperity and future population growth. These visions are receding, and even the development of northern oil fields and the discovery of diamonds in the Northwest Territories have not been sufficient to rekindle the dream of a country sustained and enriched by its northern resources. Instead, Canadian politicians speak of a national innovation agenda and invest the billions formerly spent on rural and northern infrastructure on research parks, basic sciences, and technology-based initiatives. While there are occasional references to the North – through such things as vague promises to extend the benefits of the Internet throughout the country to ensure that no region is locked out of the digital age – the reality is that the nation's dreams have turned away from the North. John Diefenbaker's "northern vision" of the late 1950s was a long time ago, both in time and in attitude.

The transition can be seen in other ways. Over the past thirty years, Canada has been enriched through the immigration of hundreds of thousands of new Canadians, most of whom, rather than coming from Europe and the United States, are from East and South Asia, the Caribbean, and Africa. These new Canadians have concentrated in a handful of major cities and have emerged in recent years as a potent cultural and political force. In a change that has been little noticed, this emerging political group has started to change the Canadian policy landscape. Unlike so many earlier European immigrants, they are not connected with the history of the North or the process of disempowering Aboriginal people. Their agenda focuses on urban challenges, the need for real multicultural programs and services, and the desire to engage Canada more effectively in global affairs. These political priorities place little emphasis on the issues of northern development, aboriginal affairs, or the redressing of historical injustices. And when the Yukon's population is but a tiny fraction of the size of the Italian, Portuguese, and Chinese populations in Toronto, or the Haitian community in Montreal, or the East Indian and Chinese people in Vancouver, it is easy to understand how the North is slipping down – and potentially off – the national political agenda.

We ended the first edition on a somewhat gloomy and argumentative note, suggesting that the national preoccupation with constitutional change had provided striking evidence of the Yukon's marginal place within Confederation. We saw this as evidence that the Yukon had to struggle to secure southern attention and the resources and authority necessary to control its destiny. Our pessimism seems to have been misplaced in this regard, since parts of this political agenda have been secured, principally through devolution and the redrafting of the Yukon Act. The territorial government now has considerable levers of power at its disposal. At the same time, the continued negotiation of First Nations agreements has resulted in the diversification of political authority in the territory, ensuring aboriginal people a greater role in the evolution of the Yukon. But the Yukon has not yet found its feet, and the future remains uncertain. The territory continues to depend, more heavily than most people in the North like to acknowledge, on federal transfers. The vulnerability that has plagued the Northwest since the Klondike gold rush remains very much in evidence.

One must, however, reflect on the positive and constructive changes that have occurred in the Yukon. The re-empowerment of aboriginal people provides a foundation for cultural partnership that is unmatched in Canada, and there is substantial evidence that this potential is being realized. Major territorial debates about the balance between resource development and environmental protection have made it clear that future mineral, water, oil and gas, and tourism activity will have to take local environmental sensitivities into account. There will be, it seems clear, no tradeoff between short-term economic gains and serious ecological consequences. As well, an effort is being made to develop a new portrait of the Yukon for outsiders, one that incorporates the Klondike gold rush and the building of the Alaska Highway into a more comprehensive image of a land long and creatively occupied by indigenous people. Perhaps most important, the perspective of Yukoners has shifted from the short-term opportunities that attracted so much attention in the past to a belief in long-term possibilities and challenges. Aboriginal and non-aboriginal alike are focusing on the land of the future, their land, shared and jointly occupied, developed and stewarded in a manner that is sustainable, achievable, and in the communities' collective self-interest. A new Yukon has emerged in the past quarter-century, one that demonstrates greater commitment to the land, its people, and their future. The territory is becoming a place in which to make a living, not simply a place to make a killing. The North will be the better for the transformation.

NOTES

CHAPTER ONE

1 On the subject of Canadian thinkers and the North, see Morton, "The North in Canadian History," Hamelin, *Canadian Nordicity: It's Your North Too,* and Coates and Morrison, "Northern Visions: Recent Writing in Northern Canadian History." On the nationalistic rhetoric of Canadian nordicity, see Berger, "The True North Strong and Free." On the history of the Canadian North, see Coates, *Canada's Colonies: A History of the Yukon and Northwest Territories,* and Morrison *True North: The Yukon and Northwest Territories.*

2 See Berger, *Northern Frontier/Northern Homeland,* and Page, *Northern Development: The Canadian Dilemma.*

3 Coutts, *Yukon Places and Names,* deals with the question of place names, although the historical materials are not always reliable.

4 The following section draws heavily on Fagan, *The Great Journey: the Peopling of Ancient America,* and McClellan, *Part of the Land, Part of the Water: A History of the Yukon Indians,* 44–62.

5 McClellan, *Part of the Land,* 4–5.

6 There is a vast anthropological and ethnographic literature on the aboriginal inhabitants of the Yukon River basin. Among the best sources are McClellan, *Part of the Land;* Helm, ed., *Subarctic Indians;* Osgood, *Contributions to the Ethnography of the Kutchin* and *The Han Indians;* Honigmann, *The Kaska Indians;* McClellan, My *Old People Say: An Ethnographic Survey of Southern Yukon Territory;* and Van Stone, *Athapaskan Adaptations: Hunters and Fishermen of the Subarctic Forests.* The following description draws on these sources, among others.

7 A fine history of the early Inuit is McGhee's *Ancient People of the Arctic.*

8 Anglican Church of Canada, General Synod Archives, M56-2, series C-23, Canham Papers, T.H. Canham, "Untitled Comments on the Indians of the Far North."

CHAPTER TWO

1 Wright, *Prelude to Bonanza: The Discovery and Exploration of the Yukon*, 1–58; Mackenzie, *Voyages from Montreal ... in the Years 1789 and 1793*, p. 54.

2 Karamanski, *Fur Trade and Exploration: Opening the Far Northwest, 1821–1852*, 3–38.

3 Newman, *Caesars of the Wilderness.*

4 Johnson, "Baron Wrangel and the Russian-American Company."

5 Johnson, "Baron Wrangel"; Coates, "Furs along the Yukon: Hudson's Bay Company-Native Trade in the Yukon River Basin, 1830–1893," 25–56.

6 Coates, "Furs along the Yukon"; Karamanski, *Fur Trade and Exploration*, ch. 5.

7 Hudson's Bay Company Archives (HBCA), D4/24, fol. 5, Simpson to McPherson, 28 February 1838.

8 For a sympathetic portrayal of Robert Campbell, see Wright, *Prelude to Bonanza*, and Wilson, *Campbell of the Yukon*. For a more critical analysis of his career, see Coates, "Furs along the Yukon."

9 HBCA, D5/15, fol. 47, Governor and Committee to Governor and Council, 1 June 1838.

10 Simpson, *Narrative of the Discoveries on the North Coast of America*, HBCA, D5/14, fol. 326, P.W. Dease and T. Simpson to Governor Simpson, 5 September 1837. Also Coates, "The Commerce of Discovery: The Hudson's Bay Company and the Simpson and Dease Expeditions," unpublished paper (author's collection).

11 Coates, "Furs along the Yukon, 46–8;" Karamanski, *Fur Trade and Exploration*, 161–9.

12 HBCA, D5/14, fol. 212–15, Bell to Simpson, 1 August 1845.

13 Karamanski, *Fur Trade and Exploration*, 214–44.

14 HBCA, D5/5 fol. 3266, Campbell to Simpson, 30 September 1840.

15 Karamanski, *Fur Trade and Exploration*, 210–14.

16 Coates, "Furs along the Yukon," 67–90.

17 Karamanski, *Fur Trade and Exploration*, 244–55.

18 HBCA, D4/71, fol. 241, Simpson to Campbell, 20 June 1850.

19 HBCA, B200/b/22, fol. 15, Murray to McPherson, 20 November 1847;

HBCA, B240/a/1, fol. 45, Youcon Journal, 27 November 1847. See also Murray, *Journal of the Yukon 1847–1848.*

20 For the Hudson's Bay Company's side of this story, see Coates, "Protecting the Monopoly: The Hudson's Bay Company and Scientific Knowledge of the Yukon Valley," 312. For the Russian perspective, see Arndt, "Russian-American Company Trade on the Middle Yukon River, 1839–1867," unpublished paper (author's collection).

21 Coates, "Furs along the Yukon," 67-84. For a more favourable portrait, based largely on Campbell's memoirs, see Karamanski, *Fur Trade and Exposition,* ch. 8 and 9.

22 HBCA, D5/20, fol. 510, McPherson to Simpson, 23 November 1847; HBCA, D5/21, fol. 341, McPherson to Simpson, 1 March 1848.

23 This encounter can be followed in greater detail in Wright, *Prelude to Bonanza,* 70-77. The Tlingit trade with the interior is documented in Ostenstat, "The Impact of the Fur Trade on the Tlingit during the Late Eighteenth and Nineteenth Centuries."

24 Campbell, *Two Journals of Robert Campbell, 1808 to 1853.* The accounts by Wright and Karamanski draw rather uncritically on these memoirs.

25 HBCA, D4/37, fol. 183, Simpson to Campbell, 12 June 1848.

26 HBCA, D5/34, fol. 71, Anderson to Simpson, 10 July 1852.

27 National Archives of Canada (NA) MG19, A25, Pelly Banks Journal.

28 Hammond, "Any Ordinary Degree of System: The Columbia Department and the Harvesting of Wildlife, 1825–1849."

29 The following analysis of the Hudson's Bay Company's trade can be followed in Coates, "Furs along the Yukon" (MA thesis), and in shortened form in Coates, "Furs along the Yukon: Hudson's Bay Company-Native Trade in the Yukon River Basin, 1840–1893"(*BC Studies,* no. 55), 50–78. See also Krech, "The Eastern Kutchin and the Fur Trade, 1800–1860," 213–35.

30 Arndt, "Russian-American Company Trade," unpublished paper (author's collection).

31 Ibid.

32 Stuck, *Voyages on the Yukon and Its Tributaries,* 136-7.

33 Krech, "On the Aboriginal Population of the Kutchin," 89–104, and "Throwing Bad Medicine: Sorcery, Disease, and the Fur Trade among the Kutchin and Other Northern Athapaskans."

34 HBCA, B200/b/36, fol. 58. McDougall to Hardisty, 5 July 1866.

35 Kirkby, "A Journey to the Youcon, Russian America," 416–20.

36 Peake, "Fur Traders and Missionaries: Some Reflections on Attitudes of the H.B.C. towards Missionary Work among the Indians," 77–93.

37 Peake, "Robert McDonald (1829–1913): The Great Unknown Missionary of the Northwest," 54–72.

38 On the Anglican Church generally, see Boon, *The Anglican Church from the Bay to the Rockies.* For a hagiographic portrait of Bompas, see Cody, *An Apostle of the North.* See also the new edition of Cody's book published by the University of Alberta Press (2003) with a critical introduction by K.S. Coates and W.R. Morrison. On the difficulties of recruiting for the North, see Coates, "Send Only Those Who Rise a Peg: The Recruitment and Use of Anglican Missionaries in the Yukon, 1858–1932," 3–18.

39 On Kennicott, see James, *The First Scientific Exploration of Alaska, and the Purchase of Alaska I.*

40 This analysis of Kennicott's Yukon career can be followed in Coates, "The Kennicott Network: Robert Kennicott and the Far Northwest," 25–33.

41 Wright, *Prelude to Bonanza,* ch. 4; Webb, *The Last Frontier: A History of the Yukon Basin of Canada and Alaska,* ch. 3. See also two very good memoirs: Dall, *Alaska and Its Resources,* and Whymper, *Travel and Adventure in the Territory of Alaska.*

42 Coates, "Protecting the Monopoly."

43 Coates, "Furs along the Yukon," 123–52 (MA thesis).

44 For Raymond's report on this exercise, see United States, *Compilation of Narratives of Explorations in Alaska.*

45 Coates, "Furs along the Yukon" (MA thesis).

CHAPTER THREE

1 Coates, "Furs along the Yukon" (*B.C. Studies,* no. 55).

2 Sealey, "The History of the Hudson's Bay Company, 1870–1910."

3 Hudson's Bay Company Archives (HBCA), B200/b/40, fol. 65-7, McDougall to Hardisty, 4 November 1872.

4 HBCA, B200/b/40, fol. 68. Hardisty to Smith.

5 HBCA, B200/b/37, fol. 255, Hardisty to Council, 2 August 1870.

6 Coates, "Furs along the Yukon" (MA thesis).

7 McConnell, "Report of an exploration in the Yukon and Mackenzie Basins, N.W.T. ," *Canadian Geological Survey Annual Report, 1888–1889.* On the history of the Geological Survey, see Morris Zaslow, *Reading the Rocks: The Story of the Geological Survey of Canada, 1842–1872.*

8 Turner, "The Boundary North of Fort Yukon."

9 HBCA, B200/b/43, fol. 755, Camsell to Chipman, 30 March 1892.

10 The following section draws on Webb, *The Last Frontier: A History of the Yukon Basin of Canada and Alaska,* ch. 3.

11 Hunt, *North of '53: The Wild Days of the Alaska-Yukon Mining Frontier, 1870–1914.*

12 On the history of the Yukon before the gold rush, see Wright, *Prelude to Bonanza*.

13 Ogilvie, *Early Days on the Yukon and the Story of Its Gold Finds*, 85–87.

14 McQuesten, *Recollections of Leroy N. McQuesten*, 3.

15 Ibid., 7.

16 Ibid., 4–7.

17 Cooke and Holland, *The Exploration of Northern Canada, 500 to 1920: A Chronology*, 228. For a description of Tlingit attempts to control the passes, see Ostenstat, "The Impact of the Fur Trade on the Tlingit during the Late Eighteenth and Nineteenth Centuries."

18 Goodrich, "History and Conditions of the Yukon Gold District to 1897," 103–33.

19 Pierce, *Thirteen Years of Travel and Exploration in Alaska, 1877–1889*, quoted in Webb, *The Last Frontier*, 78.

20 Webb, *The Last Frontier*, 78.

21 Coates, "Furs along the Yukon" (MA thesis).

22 "Report of Inspector Constantine, 20 January 1896, "*Report of the North-West Mounted Police, 1896*.

23 National Archives of Canada (NA), Department of Indian Affairs Papers, RG10, vol. 3962, file 147,654-1, part 2, W.C. Bompas to Indian Commissioner, 5 September 1896.

24 NA, Ogilvie papers, MG20, B22, W.C. Bompas to Lieutenant Governor, 3 December 1891.

25 Coates, "Best Left as Indians: Indian-White Relations in the Yukon Territory, 1840–1950."

26 HBCA, B200/b/43, fol. 698, Camsell to Wrigley, 25 March 1891; B200/b/43, fol. 719, Camsell to Chipman, 11 September 1891.

27 Stuart and Gould, "Permafrost Gold: A Treatise on Early Klondike Mining: History, Methods, and Technology."

28 Webb, *The Last Frontier*, 82.

29 Gates, *Gold at Fortymile Creek: Early Days in the Yukon*.

30 Webb, *The Last Frontier*, 85.

31 The term *creole* was used in Alaska to describe people of mixed Russian and Native parentage.

32 Goodrich, "History and Conditions of the Yukon Gold District to 1897," 332.

33 Berton, *Klondike: The Last Great Gold Rush*, 17.

34 Ibid.

35 This discussion of mining society is indebted to the work of Thomas Stone, especially his "Atomistic Order and Frontier Violence: Miners and Whalemen in the Nineteenth Century Yukon," "Flux and Authority in a Subarctic Society: The Yukon Miners in the Nineteenth Century," and "The Mounties as Vigilantes: Perceptions of Community and the Transformation of Law in the Yukon, 1885–1897."

36 Stone, "Atomistic Order," 328–29.

37 This account is taken from Stone, "Flux and Authority," 204–6.

38 Goodrich, "History and Conditions of the Yukon Gold District to 1897," 127, quoted in Stone, "The Mounties as Vigilantes," 87.

39 Colson, *Tradition and Contract: The Problem of Order*, 54.

40 Brody, *The Living Arctic*.

41 William Ogilvie told the story in *Early Days on the Yukon*, ch. 3, but called Leslie "the Discoverer," perhaps to avoid a libel suit.

42 Stone, "Atomistic Order," 332.

43 McGrath, *Gunfighters, Highwaymen, and Vigilantes*, discusses violence on the American mining frontier.

44 Stone, "The Mounties as Vigilantes," 93.

45 Frederick Schwatka, *A Summer in Alaska*, 83–4, quoted in Wright, *Prelude to Bonanza*, 144.

46 Dawson's *Report on an Exploration in the Yukon District, n.w.t. and Adjacent Northern Portion of British Columbia, 1887* gives his account of the trip. Ogilvie's version is in *Early Days on the Yukon*. On the Canadian Geological Survey, see Zaslow, *Reading the Rocks*.

47 Dawson, *Report,* 33, quoted in Wright, *Prelude to Bonanza*, 180.

48 Tagish Lake, for example, had been named Bove Lake by Schwatka, after an Italian naval officer. Dawson reinstated the original name.

49 See Minter, *The White Pass: Gateway to the Klondike*.

50 Quoted in Wright, *Prelude to Bonanza*, 191.

51 Ogilvie, *Early Days on the Yukon*, 139.

52 McConnell, "Extracts Relating to the Yukon District ..." in Dawson, *Report*, quoted in Wright, *Prelude to Bonanza*, 203.

53 Ibid., 232–3.

54 Ogilvie, *Early Days on the Yukon*, 143.

55 He died the next year, 1892, age forty-three, of an overdose of laudanum taken to treat stomach ulcers (Webb, *The Last Frontier*, 118).

56 Coates, *The Northern Yukon*, 42.

57 Coates, "Send Only Those Who Rise a Peg."

58 Quoted in Coates, "Send Only Those Who Rise a Peg."

59 Wesbrook, "A Venture into Ethnohistory: The Journals of V.C. Sim."

60 Quoted in Coates, "Send Only Those Who Rise a Peg."

61 Archer, *A Heroine of the North*, 132. See also Cody, *An Apostle of the North*, and the 2003 edition of his book with a critical essay on the missionary enterprise.

62 Gartrell, "The Work of the Churches in the Yukon During the Era of the Klondike Gold Rush," quoted in Wright, *Prelude to Bonanza*, 255. The letter is found originally in NA, Constantine Papers, MG30, E55, vol. 3.

63 NA, RG10, vol. 3906, file 105,378, Bompas to Minister of the Interior, 5 June 1894.

64 Coates, "Asking for All Sorts of Favours."

65 A copy of this is in NA, Constantine Papers, MG30, E55, vol. 3.
66 He later rose to the rank of superintendent and died while on sick leave in 1912. See Stewart, *Sam Steele: Lion of the Frontier*.
67 *Report of the North-West Mounted Police, 1894*, C, 81.
68 *Report of the North-West Mounted Police, 1895*, 7.
69 *Report of the North-West Mounted Police, 1894*, C, 77.
70 *Report of the North-West Mounted Police, 1894*, C, 78.
71 NA, RCMP Papers, Commissioner's Office, RG18, B2, vol. 2182.
72 Brown, "The Evolution of Law and Government in the Yukon Territory," 198. The districts of Franklin, Ungava, and Mackenzie were created at the same time.
73 Hayne and Taylor, *The Pioneers of the Klondyke*.
74 The incident is recounted in Constantine's report to Frederick White, comptroller of the NWMP, 13 July 1896, in NA, RCMP Papers, RG18 A1, Comptroller's Correspondence, vol. 123.
75 Hunt, *Distant Justice: Policing the Alaska Frontier*, shows the evolution of law and order west of the 141st meridian.

CHAPTER FOUR

1 Innis, *Settlement and the Mining Frontier*; Hunt, *North of '53: The Wild Days of the Alaska-Yukon Mining Frontier, 1870–1914*.
2 Malcolm, *The Canadians*, 342–45, tells the story.
3 He became known to the world as Tagish Charlie, or Charley.
4 Wright, *Prelude to Bonanza* (Whitehorse: Arctic Star Printing, 1980), 247–90.
5 Berton, *Klondike*, 44.
6 Wright, *Prelude to Bonanza*, 295.
7 This discussion is drawn from Webb, *The Last Frontier*, Berton, *Klondike*, Zaslow, *The Opening of the Canadian North, 1870–1914*, and Guest, "A History of Dawson City, Yukon Territory."
8 Berton, *Klondike*, 73–4.
9 MacDonald, "Seattle, Vancouver, and the Klondike."
10 MacGregor, *The Klondike Rush through Edmonton, 1897–1898*, Coates, *The Northern Yukon: A History*.
11 Steele, *Forty Years in Canada*, 296.
12 Friesen, *The Chilkoot Pass*. On the trail's history, see Neufeld, *Chilkoot Trail*.
13 Steele, *Forty Years in Canada*, 296.
14 Black, *My Ninety Years*, 30.
15 Ibid.
16 Green, *The Boundary Hunters*. See also Classen, *Thrust and Counterthrust: The Genesis of the Canada-United States Boundary*.
17 Quoted in Berton, *Klondike*, 143–4.

18 Bennett, *Yukon Transportation: A History*, 24–58.

19 Steele, *Forty Years*.

20 Morrison, *Showing the Flag*, recounts the history of the police force during the gold rush.

21 Quoted in Morrison, *Showing the Flag*, 37.

22 *Report of the North-West Mounted Police, 1897*.

23 Quoted in Morrison, *Showing the Flag*, 40.

24 See Disher, "The Long March of the Yukon Field Force," and Greenhous, *Guarding the Goldfields*.

25 Zaslow, "The Yukon: Northern Development in a Canadian American Context."

26 Quoted in Disher, "The Long March of the Yukon Field Force." On the expedition, see Greenhous, *Guarding the Goldfields*.

27 His reminiscences are in "Klondike Memories," *Beaver*, March, June, September 1951; see also Bostock, "Prospecting on Russell Creek."

28 Guest, *A History of Dawson City*; *See also* Guest, *A Socioeconomic History of the Klondike Gold Fields, 1896–1966*.

29 The Yukon had been made a district of the North-West Territories in 1895.

30 Hall, *Clifford Sifton*. See also Thomas, *The Struggle for Responsible Government in the Northwest Territories*.

31 Several of these cases are analysed in Coates and Morrison, *Strange Things Done: Murder in Yukon History*.

32 Berton, *Klondike*, 308.

33 On dance halls and gender in Dawson City, see Kelcey, *Alone in Silence*, and Porsild, *Gamblers and Dreamers*.

34 The following section is drawn from Booth, "Gold Rush Theatres of the Klondike."

35 Franks, "How the Sabbath Came to the Yukon."

36 Guest, *A History of Dawson City*.

37 Karp, "The Writing of Dan McGrew."

38 Morrison, "Policing the Boom Town." On the subject of more serious crime, see Coates and Morrison, *Strange Things Done*.

39 Steele, *Forty Years in Canada*, 327.

40 Stone, "The Mounties as Vigilantes."

41 Hall, *Clifford Sifton*, vol. 1, ch. 7.

42 The activities of the Yukon First Nations during the gold rush are examined in Coates, *Best Left as Indians: Native-White Relations in the Yukon Territory, 1840–1973*.

43 Coates, "Best Left as Indians: The Federal Government and the Indians of the Yukon Territory, 1894–1950."

44 For a general description of the impact of the gold rush on the subarctic Native people, see Kehoe, *North American Indians: A Comprehensive Account*. See also Helm, ed., *Handbook of North American Indians*, vol. 6: *Subarctic*.

45 Gartrell, "The Work of the Churches in the Yukon during the Era of the Klondike Gold Rush."

46 NA, RG10, vol. 4001, file 207,418, Congdon to Pedley, 28 May 1903. On this general theme, see Coates, "Asking for All Sorts of Favours."

47 The best study of the railway is Minter, *White Pass*. See also, Bennett, *Yukon Transportation*.

48 Korischil, "Whitehorse: The Company Town, 1899–1945," unpublished paper (author's collection).

49 Hall, *Clifford Sifton*, 1: 189. See also Green, *The Gold Hustlers*.

CHAPTER FIVE

1 Usher, "The Canadian Western Arctic: A Century of Change."

2 Quoted in Francis, *The Discovery of the North*, 72.

3 Ibid., 96.

4 Bruemmer, "Herschel, the Big Town," 26.

5 Francis, *Discovery of the North*, 117.

6 Alexander Simpson, *The Life and Travels of Thomas Simpson, the Arctic Discoverer*. See also Barr, *From Barrow to Boothia: The Arctic Journal of Chief Factor Peter Warren Dease, 1836–1839*; and Thomas Simpson, *Narrative of the Discoveries on the North Coast of America*.

7 On the northern whaling industry, see Francis, *Arctic Chase*.

8 Bockstoce, *Steam Whaling in the Western Arctic*, 36. Bockstoce is the best source on the history of whaling in this area.

9 Bruemmer, "Herschel, the Big Town," 28.

10 Quoted in Bockstoce, *Steam Whaling in the Western Arctic*, 39. Bodfish was later master of the *Beluga*.

11 Ibid., 40.

12 Ibid.

13 Ibid.

14 See http://www.phoons.com/maryhume.html and http://www.shpo.state.or.us/databases/nr/curry/curry08.html (both accessed February 2004).

15 There were only thirteen ships there that year, and since there were not a hundred men on each ship (the average crew was closer to thirty), this total is either inaccurate or includes all the Inuit employees of the whalers as well as those Inuit who simply lived on the island.

16 Bruemmer, "Herschel, the Big Town," 28.

17 National Archives of Canada (NA), RCMP Papers, RG18, Comptroller's Correspondence, vol. 309, Inspector D.M. Howard's report, August 1906.

18 On the economics of the whaling industry, see Bockstoce, *Steam Whaling in the Western Arctic*, and Francis, *Arctic Chase*, ch. 2.

19 Stone, "Atomistic Order and Frontier Violence"; also Bockstoce, *Steam Whaling*, 43.

20 Stone, "Atomistic Order and Frontier Violence."

21 Ibid., quoting from Bodfish, *Chasing the Bowhead*, 159–60.

22 Stone, "Atomistic Order and Frontier Violence."

23 Bockstoce, *Steam Whaling in the Western Arctic*, 46.

24 Stevenson, "Whaler's Wait," quoted in Stone, "Whalers and Missionaries at Herschel Island."

25 Jenness, *Eskimo Administration II: Canada* , 14.

26 Bodfish, *Chasing the Bowhead*, quoted in Usher, "Canadian Western Arctic: A Century of Change," 174.

27 Peake, *The Bishop Who Ate His Boots*. He boiled them and drank the broth.

28 Quoted in Stone, "Whalers and Missionaries at Herschel Island."

29 Ibid.

30 Bruemmer, "Herschel, the Big Island," 33.

31 NA, Constantine Papers, MG30, E55, vol. 3, file 4, Fitzgerald to Commanding Officer, G Division, 6 September 1903.

32 Maurice Metayer, trans., *I, Nuligak*, 29.

33 Quoted in Morrison, *Showing the Flag*, 74.

34 Quoted in Stone, "Whalers and Missionaries at Herschel Island."

35 Quoted in Bruemmer, "Herschel, the Big Island," 26.

36 Quoted in Morrison, *Showing the Flag*, 75.

37 Quoted in Bockstoce, *Steam Whaling in the Western Arctic*, 43.

38 *R.N.W.M.P. Report*, 1908, K, 140.

39 NA, RCMP Papers, RG18, Comptroller's Correspondence, vol. 293, J.A. Smart memo, n.d. (probably summer 1903).

40 See Morrison, *Showing the Flag*, ch. 6.

41 Provincial Archives of Manitoba (PAM), Ecclesiastical Province of Rupertsland, MG7, A1, box N, no. 4003, C. E. Whittaker, "Memoranda," July 1907. See also North, *The Lost Patrol*.

42 The episode is discussed in Morrison, *Showing the Flag*, ch. 10.

43 Usher, *Fur Trade Posts of the Northwest Territories 1870–1970*; Coates, *The Northern Yukon: A History*, Manuscript Report.

44 Quoted in Bruemmer, "Herschel, the Big Island," 34.

45 Amundsen, *The North West Passage*.

46 Diubaldo, "Wrangling over Wrangel Island."

47 The best biography of the explorer is Diubaldo, *Stefansson and the Canadian Arctic*. See also Hunt, *Stef: A Biography of Vilhjalmur Stefansson, Canadian Arctic Explorer*.

48 NA, RCMP Papers, RG18, Comptroller's Correspondence, vol. 353.

49 NA, Department of Mines, RG45, vol. 67, file 4078, Acting Chief, Biological Division, Victoria Memorial Museum, to Camsell, 4 January 1912.

50 NA, Chipman Papers, MG30, "Diary of Canadian Arctic Expedition," entry for 4 April 1914.

51 NA, RCMP Papers, RG18, Comptroller's Correspondence, vol. 353.
52 His autobiography is Larsen, *The Big Ship*.
53 For a discussion of the case, see Morrison, *Showing the Flag*, ch. 10, and Coates and Morrison, *Strange Things Done*. For a similar case, see Moyles, *British Law and Arctic Men*.
54 Hudson's Bay Company Archives (HBCA), B434/a/1, Shingle Point Journal, 1937–38; B419/a/104, Herschel Island Journals.
55 NA, Northern Administration Branch, RG85, vol. 792, file 6271, extract from the report of M. Meikle, 30 July 1937.
56 Margaret Alstrom, "Draft History of Yukon Education," unpublished manuscript, ch. 8, "Native Education: Residential Schools, 1906–1940" (author's collection).
57 NA, Chipman Papers, MG30, B66, Diary no. 2, entry for 27 April 1914.
58 NA, Osborne Papers, MG30, D66, Stringer to Osborne, 14 March 1927.
59 Tanner, "The Structure of Fur Trade Relations," 21.
60 NA, Northern Administration Branch, RG85, vol. 792, file 6271, Finnie to Gibson, 2 January 1929.
61 On this subject, see the excellent study by Robert Page, *Northern Development: The Canadian Dilemma*.
62 On the controversy over the future of the region, see Thomas Berger, *Northern Frontier, Northern Homeland*, and Cohen, *Mackenzie Basin Impact Study Final Report*.
62 The U.S. government abandoned this idea, but President George W. Bush revived the plan at the end of the century.

CHAPTER SIX

1 McCandless, *Yukon Wildlife: A Social History*, 108–9.
2 Guest, *A History of Dawson City, Yukon Territory, 1896–1920*."
3 Ibid., 67.
4 Webb, *The Last Frontier*, 201-202.
5 Guest, "A History of Dawson City," 103.
6 Guest, "A History of Dawson City." See also Zaslow, *The Opening of the Canadian North, 1870–1914*, 124–46, for an analysis of the decline of Dawson City. For a comparison with British Columbia, see Clark, "The Gold Rush Society of British Columbia and the Yukon."
7 Zaslow, *The Opening of the Canadian North, 1870–1914*, 137.
8 Guest, "A History of Dawson City," 246.
9 Ibid., 245–58.
10 Ibid., 291.
11 Laura Berton, *I Married the Klondike*, 44–5.
12 Ibid., 52.
13 Ibid., 46–8.

14 Peake, *The Bishop Who Ate His Boots*, 142. On the relationship between the Native people and the white population, see Coates, *Best Left as Indians*.

15 Laura Berton, *I Married the Klondike*, 63.

16 David Morrison, *The Politics of the Yukon Territory, 1898–1909*.

17 Berton, *I Married the Klondike*, 59–61.

18 Ibid., 68–72.

19 Rea, *The Political Economy of the Canadian North*, 99.

20 For a thorough analysis of Sifton's activities relating to the Yukon, see Hall, *Clifford Sifton*.

21 The advance of the dredging mining sector is ably traced in Green, *The Gold Hustlers*.

22 Hall, *Clifford Sifton*, 2: 133.

23 Green, *The Gold Hustlers*, 62.

24 Hall, *Clifford Sifton*, 2: 139.

25 Green, *The Gold Hustlers*, 71. The word is actually "simoom," a hot desert wind.

26 Quoted in Green, *The Gold Hustlers*, 91–2. "Skookum" is a west coast First Nations word meaning strong or splendid.

27 This survey of Boyle's career is drawn from Green, *The Gold Hustlers*, and from two biographies of the man: Rodney, *Joe Boyle: King of the Klondike*, and Taylor, *The Sourdough and the Queen*.

28 Rea, *The Political Economy of the Canadian North*, 105.

29 Coutts, *Yukon Places and Names*, 162.

30 Morritt, *Land of the Fireweed*, 153–4.

31 Coates, *The Northern Yukon: A History*, 129.

32 Diane Johnston, "Carrying the Yukon: Silver-Lead Mining in the Mayo District, 1919–1942," unpublished paper (author's collection).

33 Zaslow, *The Opening of the Canadian North*, 121; Paul Korischil, "Whitehorse: The Company Town, 1899-1945," unpublished paper (author's collection).

34 Riggs, "Running the Alaska Boundary," 42.

35 Quoted in McCandless, *Yukon Wildlife: A Social History*, 105.

36 McCandless, *Yukon Wildlife: A Social History*, 112–14.

37 This analysis of the development of Yukon transportation is drawn from Bennett, *Yukon Transportation: A History*. See also Minter, *The White Pass*.

38 This theme is explored in Coates and Morrison, *The Sinking of the Princess Sophia*.

39 Korischil, "Whitehorse: The Company Town."

40 Bennett, *Yukon Transportation: A History*, 77.

41 Ibid., 77.

42 Thomas, *The Struggle for Responsible Government in the Northwest*

Territories, 1870–97, 208; David Morrison, *The Politics of the Yukon Territory*, 23.

43 W.R. Morrison, *Showing the Flag*. See also Coates, *The Northern Yukon: A History*.

44 Coates, "Send Only Those Who Rise a Peg," 10.

45 Peake, *The Bishop Who Ate His Boots*.

46 Zaslow, *The Opening of the Canadian North*, 128–9; George Gartrell, "The Work of the Churches in the Yukon During the Era of the Klondike Gold Rush."

47 Swanson, *The Days of My Sojourning*, 36.

48 Coates, "Send Only Those Who Rise a Peg," 12.

49 Quoted in Coates, "A Very Imperfect Means of Education," 132–49.

50 GAnglican Church of Canada (ACC), General Synod Archives, M75-103, Series 2-14, MSCC, Frank Oliver to ACC, 28 January 1908.

51 Coates, "Betwixt and Between," 27–47.

52 Charles Maier, "Responsible Government and Federal Administrators in Yukon, 1898–1913," unpublished paper (author's collection).

53 Guest, "The Incorporation and Disincorporation of Dawson City," unpublished paper (author's collection). See also Guest, "A History of Dawson City."

54 The administration of justice, as reflected in the major capital murder cases of this period, is discussed in Coates and Morrison *Strange Things Done*.

55 The political battles described in the following paragraphs are best followed in David Morrison, *The Politics of the Yukon Territory*, and Hall, *Clifford Sifton*. The latter is particularly good on relations between the national Liberal government and local Liberal politicians. See also Laura Berton, *I Married the Klondike*, and Black, *My Seventy Years*.

56 Laura Berton, *I Married the Klondike*, 108.

57 David Morrison, *The Politics of the Yukon Territory*, 94.

58 Laura Berton, *I Married the Klondike*, 128.

59 Black, *My Seventy Years*, 255.

60 Yukon Archives, IODE Records, Acc. 82/463, fol. 717; Yukon Record Group One, vol. 44, file 29461.

61 The total number of volunteers from the Yukon during the war was 2,327 – one-third of its population. This remarkable figure was more than three times the next highest rate (Manitoba, at 9.8%). It was partly due to the dominance of single males in the territory's population but is dramatic proof of the Yukon's enthusiasm for the war.

62 Black, *My Seventy Years*, 238.

63 Green, *The Gold Hustlers*, ch. 9. See also the biographies of Boyle by Rodney and Taylor, cited above.

64 *Dawson News,* 12 October 1914.

65 Black, *My Ninety Years,* 106.

66 *Dawson News,* 23 June 1916.

67 *Whitehorse Star* and *Dawson News,* May to September 1916, carry the details and rhetoric of the debate.

68 Laura Berton, *I Married the Klondike,* 96.

69 See Coates and Morrison, *The Sinking of the Princess Sophia,* for an examination of this episode.

70 Thomas, *The Struggle for Responsible Government in the Northwest Territories,* ch. 10, "Reflections on Territorial Government."

CHAPTER SEVEN

1 Rea, *The Political Economy of the Canadian North.* See, in particular, the statistical material assembled in the tables at the end of the book.

2 The following discussion of the Keno area mines relies heavily on Diane Johnston, "Carrying the Yukon: Silver-Lead Mining in the Mayo District, 1919–1942," unpublished paper (author's collection).

3 Bennett, *Yukon Transportation: A History,* 96–104.

4 Rea, *The Political Economy of the Canadian North,* 394–5.

5 The evolution of gold-mining activity in the Yukon can be followed in Green, *The Gold Hustlers.*

6 Ibid., 238 and *passim.*

7 Ibid., 263.

8 The fur trade is analysed in McCandless, *Yukon Wildlife: A Social History,* 103–36, and Coates, "Best Left as Indians: Native-White Relations in the Yukon Territory, 1840–1950," 92–125.

9 Quoted in McCandless, *Yukon Wildlife: A Social History,* 121.

10 For an anthropological analysis of the twentieth-century trading system, see Tanner, "The Structure of Fur Trade Relations."

11 The nature of social relations in the fur trade districts is examined in Coates, "Best Left as Indians."

12 On big-game hunting, see McCandless, *Yukon Wildlife: A Social History,* 42–63. There are a number of memoirs written by big-game hunters, including Armstrong, *After Big Game in the Upper Yukon,* Auer, *Camp Fires in the Yukon,* and Martindale, *Hunting in the Upper Yukon.*

13 Quoted in McCandless, *Yukon Wildlife: A Social History,* 60.

14 On railroads in the territory, see Bennett, *Yukon Transportation: A History,* 24–50.

15 Laura Berton, *I Married the Klondike,* 154.

16 Bennett, *Yukon Transportation: A History,* 110.

17 A second firm, with the same name, lost all three of its planes in less than six months and had to close down.

18 Livermore, "Percy DeWolfe: Iron Man of the Yukon," 16–20.
19 Laura Berton, *I Married the Klondike*, 145. For another perspective on life in the Dawson area in the 1920s, see Pierre Berton, *Starting Out, 1920–1947*.
20 Berton, *I Married the Klondike*, 151.
21 Paul Korischil, "Whitehorse: The Company Town, 1899–1945," unpublished paper (author's collection).
22 Laura Berton, *I Married the Klondike*, 135–6.
23 There is some excellent material available on the Yukon First Nations in this period. See McClellan, *Part of the Land, Part of the River*. For ethnographic material on the Yukon peoples, see Osgood, *The Han Indians*, and *Contributions to the Ethnography of the Kutchin*; and McClellan, *My Old People Say*. For a historical analysis of this period, see Coates, *Best Left as Indians*.
24 Yukon Archives (YA), Anglican Church Records, Fort Yukon file, Grafton Burke to John Hawksley, 21 May 1926.
25 Laura Berton, *I Married the Klondike*, 169.
26 The government's involvement with this is described in Coates, "Best Left as Indians: The Federal Government and the Indians of the Yukon, 1894-1950."
27 Coates, "Send Only Those Who Rise a Peg."
28 Peake, *The Bishop Who Ate His Boots* ; Boon, *The Anglican Church from the Bay to the Rockies*.
29 Coates, "Betwixt and Between."
30 YA, Anglican Church Records, McCullum file, Wood to Stringer, 14 April 1926.
31 YA, Anglican Church Records, Carmacks-Little Salmon file, Report of Missionary Work carried on from 23 May to 31 August 1934, in and about Carmacks.
32 Peake, *The Bishop Who Ate His Boots*, 108–9.
33 NA, Department of Indian Affairs Records, RG10, file 941-1, pt. 1, Bishop Geddes to Dr H.W. McGill, 27 January 1943.
34 YA, Anglican Church Records, St Agnes Hostel file, Extract from *Mayo-Keno Bulletin*, 8 September 1925.
35 This section draws on Coates, *Best Left as Indians*.
36 YA, Yukon Record Group 1, series 3, vol. 8, file 12-15, Camsell to Gibson, 14 September 1935.
37 Rea, *The Political Economy of the Canadian North*, 314–18.
38 Black, *My Seventy Years*. On the later part of her life, see Black, *My Ninety Years*.
39 Lotz, *Northern Realities*, 80. On the pattern of government development, see also Richard Stuart, "Undeveloping the Yukon, 1840–1940," unpublished paper (author's collection).
40 Stuart, "Duff Pattullo and the Yukon Schools Question of 1937."
41 Lotz, *Northern Realities*, 79.

CHAPTER EIGHT

1 Green, *The Gold Hustlers*, 286.
2 Stuart, "The Impact of the Alaska Highway on Dawson City," 195.
3 Diane Johnston, "Carrying the Yukon: Silver-Lead Mining in the Mayo District, 1919-1942," unpublished paper (author's collection).
4 David Remley, "The Latent Fear: Canadian-American Relations and Early Proposals for a Highway to Alaska," and Robin Fisher, "T.D. Pattullo and the British Columbia to Alaska Highway," in Coates, *The Alaska Highway*, offer different perspectives on this issue. See also Remley, *The Crooked Road*, and Fisher, *Duff Pattullo of British Columbia*. On the social and labour history of the highway, see Coates and Morrison, *The Alaska Highway in World War II: The U.S. Army of Occupation in Canada's Northwest*.
5 This debate can be followed in Edmonton Municipal Archives (EMA), RG11, class 90, files 28–32.
6 D.W. Thomson, "Surveying the Line: The Canadian Participation," in Coates, *The Alaska Highway*.
7 M.V. Bezeau, "The Realities of Strategic Planning: The Decision to Build the Alaska Highway," in Coates, *The Alaska Highway*, 33.
8 Ibid., 32.
9 EMA, RG11, class 90, file 32, Report of Halvor Halvorson, President, United States-Canada-Alaska Prairie Highway Association, 23 October 1942.
10 John Greenwood, "General Bill Hoge and the Alaska Highway," and D.W. Thomson, "Surveying the Line," in Coates, *The Alaska Highway*.
11 D.W. Thomson, "Surveying the Line," in Coates, *The Alaska Highway*, 78–9.
12 Cook died shortly afterwards, crashing his plane on a Whitehorse street.
13 United States National Archives (USNA), RG59, file 842-154, Lewis Clark to U.S. Secretary of State, 14 March 1942.
14 Greenwood, "General Bill Hoge," in Coates, *The Alaska Highway*, 49.
15 Heath Twichell, "Cut, Fill and Straighten: The Role of the Public Roads Administration in the Building of the Alaska Highway," in Coates, *The Alaska Highway*.
16 Richard Diubaldo, "The Alaska Highway in Canada-United States Relations," in Coates, *The Alaska Highway*.
17 Ibid. See also Diubaldo, "The Canol Project in Canadian-American Relations," 178–95.
18 NA, Northern Administration Branch, RG85, vol. 1160, file 331-2/200-1, memorandum, December 1942.
19 U.S. Army Corps of Engineers, Historical Division, Acc. 72-A-3173, box 15, file 50-19, Rogers to Black, 20 May 1942.

20 NA, Department of Labour, RG27, vol. 676, file 6-5-75-3, Moore to Mitchell, 4 July 1944.

21 On the subject of labour on the highway, see Coates and Morrison, *Working the North: Labor and the Northwest Defense Projects, 1942–1945.*

22 NA, RG27, vol. 676, file 6-5-75-1, memorandum, Cabinet War Committee, 5 March 1943.

23 These were buildings of corrugated metal laid over semicircular steel ribs. The basic model was 20 feet wide by 48 feet long (6 x 15 m), but they came in several sizes. They were first produced at Quonset, Rhode Island.

24 NA, Northern Administration Branch, RG85, vol. 944, file 12743, Part 1, R.A. Gibson memorandum, 27 May 1943.

25 USNA, RG59, file 842-154, Moffat to Hickerson, 29 July 1942.

26 NA, Northern Administration Branch, RG85, vol. 944, file 12743, part c, Phillips to RCMP, 17 August 1944.

27 McCandless, in *Yukon Wildlife: A Social History*, ch. 4, argues that the harmful effects on the wildlife have been exaggerated.

28 Yukon Archives (YA), Yukon Record Group 1, series 3, vol. 10, file 12-20B, Gibson to Hoffmaster, 23 January 1943.

29 See the statistics in Coates, "The Indians of the Southern Yukon and the Construction of the Alaska Highway, 1942–1950, in Coates, *The Alaska Highway,* 151–71.

30 On the subject of black troops, see Lee, *The United States Army in World War II*, and Buchanan, *Black Americans in World War II.*

31 "Money Makes Indian Squaws Fashion Leaders," *Edmonton Journal,* 12 July 1941. See also Coates, "The Indians of the Southern Yukon and the Construction of the Alaska Highway, 1942–1950," in Coates, *The Alaska Highway.*

32 J.F. Marchand, "Tribal Epidemics in Yukon," 1019–20.

33 NA, Yukon Government Records, RG91, vol. 9, file 1490, pt. J, LeCapelain to R.A. Gibson, 17 July 1943.

34 McCandless, *Yukon Wildlife: A Social History*, 79.

35 This section on Dawson City, including the quotations, is drawn from Stuart, "The Impact of the Alaska Highway on Dawson City," in Coates, *The Alaska Highway.*

36 The impact of the construction phase on Whitehorse is described in Coates and Powell, "Whitehorse and the Building of the Alaska Highway."

37 NA, Northern Administration Branch, RG85, vol. 1160, file 331-2/200-1, memorandum, December 1942.

38 Merritt, *Land of the Fireweed*, details the postwar problems with these buildings.

39 NA, Northern Administration Branch, RG85, vol. 1160, file 331-2/200-1, LeCapelain to Gibson, 13 March 1943.

40 See Dwight Oland, "The Army Medical Department and the Construction of the Alaska Highway," in Coates, *The Alaska Highway*.

41 "Alaskan Highway: An Engineering Epic," *National Geographic*, February 1943.

42 NA, RG338, box 1, NWSC092, Foreign Affairs and Relations, Pierrepont Moffat, American minister to Canada, to J.D. Hickerson, 23 October 1943.

43 USNA, RG59, file 711.42/255, J.D. Hickerson, Department of State, memorandum, 20 May 1943.

44 Creighton, *The Forked Road: Canada, 1939–1957*, 73–4. Creighton was wrong (not the only mistake in a flawed book), for Ian Mackenzie, B.C. member of the cabinet, attended the opening ceremonies. See Robin Fisher, "T.D. Pattullo and the British Columbia to Alaska Highway," in Coates, *The Alaska Highway*, 9.

45 Curtis Nordman, "The Army of Occupation: Malcolm MacDonald and U.S. Military Involvement in the Canadian Northwest," and "Appendix: Note on Development in North-Western Canada, by Malcolm MacDonald," in Coates, *The Alaska Highway*, 83–101.

46 On the question of northern sovereignty, see Grant, *Sovereignty or Security? Government Policy in the Canadian North, 1936–1950*.

47 Diubaldo, "The Alaska Highway in Canada–United States Relations," in Coates, *The Alaska Highway*.

48 NA, Special Commissioner on Northern Defence Projects, RG36/7, vol. 36, file 11-16, T.M. Dauphine to W.L. Mackenzie King, Prime Minister, 12 July 1944.

CHAPTER NINE

1 Stephen Harris, "Really a Defile Throughout Its Length: The Defence of the Alaska Highway in Peacetime," in Coates, *The Alaska Highway*.

2 For a good description of Whitehorse after the war, see Morritt, *Land of the Fireweed*.

3 Richard Stuart, "The Impact of the Alaska Highway on Dawson City," in Coates, *The Alaska Highway*. On Whitehorse, see Coates and Powell, "Whitehorse and the Building of the Alaska Highway, 1942–1946."

4 Stuart, "The Impact of the Alaska Highway on Dawson City."

5 *Dawson News*, 22 March 1951, quoted in Stuart.

6 Remley, *The Crooked Road*.

7 Batelle Memorial Institute, *An Integrated Transport System to Encourage Economic Development of Northwest North America*. The report was released to the public early in 1961.

8 Coates, "The Civilian Highway: Public Works Canada and the Alaska

Highway, 1964–83," in Coates, *The Alaska Highway.*

9 Stanford Research Institute, *Improvement Program for the Alaska Highway: An Analysis of Economic Benefits.*

10 Coates, "The Civilian Highway."

11 http://www.outwestnewspaper.com/akhwy.html (accessed October 2003).

12 This issue is examined in Julie Cruikshank, "The Gravel Magnet: Some Social Impacts of the Alaska Highway on Yukon Indians," in Coates, *The Alaska Highway.*

13 McCandless, *Yukon Wildlife: A Social History.*

14 Yukon Archives (YA), series 3, vol. 10, file 12-20c, Jeckell to Gibson, 13 January 1944.

15 Rea, *The Political Economy of the Canadian North.*

16 Tanner, *Trappers, Hunters, and Fishermen.*

17 One of the best statements on the continued importance of harvesting is Ross River Indian Band, *So That the Future Will Be Ours.* See also Duerden, *Teslin: The Indian Village and Community Economy.* For the contemporary situation, see http://www.environmentyukon.gov.yk.ca/hunting/trapping.shtml (accessed October 2003).

18 Pierre Lasserre, "L'aide aux mines d'or ou les silences du fantôme de Bretton Woods," 446–57.

19 Rae, *The Political Economy of the Canadian North,* offers a good survey of mining activity in the 1950s.

20 Debicki, *Yukon Mineral Industry, 1941 to 1959.*

21 The following is drawn from Debicki, *Yukon Mineral Industry,* Griffen, *Cashing In,* and Rea, *The Political Economy of Northern Development.*

22 Campbell, "The Search for Oil in the Yukon Territory."

23 Griffen, *Cashing In,* recounts this process. There is an excellent account of the rise of Cassiar and Clinton Creek at www.cassiar.ca/cassiar/cassiar.htm (accessed October 2003).

24 See Rea, *The Political Economy of Northern Development.*

25 Griffen, *Cashing In.*

26 MacPherson, "The Cypress-Anvil Mine."

27 The postwar development of the White Pass and Yukon Route is discussed in Bennett, *Yukon Transportation,* 145–6.

28 A good account of this exercise is provided in Lotz, *Northern Realities.*

29 Tueli, "Studied Naivete: The Art of Ted Harrison," *Northern Review* 1, no. 1 (1988).

30 William G. MacLeod, "The Dempster Highway," in Peterson and Wright, *Northern Transitions,* vol. 1.

31 R.A.C. Caldwell, "Communications to – and for – the North," *North,* Sept./Oct. 1964), 1–8.

32 Coates, "Best Left as Indians: The Federal Government and the Indians of the Yukon Territory, 1894–1950."

33 Coates, "A Very Imperfect Means of Education." In 1988 Northern Native Broadcasting produced *The Mission School Syndrome*, a harrowing account of the residential school system in the Yukon.

34 Ronald Wright, "Beyond Words," *Saturday Night*, April 1988, 38–46. On the Yukon Native Languages Centre, see www.yukoncollege.yk.ca/ynlc/About.html (accessed October 2003).

35 Coates, "Upsetting the Rhythms."

36 "Participation of Indians in the Economy." Discussion Paper prepared for the Yukon 2000 Whitehorse Fall Conference, 1986.

37 Hendry, *Beyond Traplines*. See also McCullum, *This Land Is Not for Sale*.

38 Yukon Native Brotherhood, *Together Today for Our Children Tomorrow*.

39 Morrison, *A Survey of the History and Claims of the Native Peoples of Northern Canada*.

40 The best review of northern politics in this era is Dacks, *A Choice of Futures*.

41 The Yukon's fourteen First Nations are as follows: Carcross/Tagish; Champagne and Aishihik; Tron'dëk Hwech'in; Kluane' Kwanlin Dun; Liard; Little Salmon/Carmacks; Nacho Nyak Dun; Ross River Dena; Selkirk; Ta'an Kwäch'an; Teslin Tlingit; Vuntut Gwich'in; and White River.

42 On the Inuvialuit, see Ishmael Alunik et al., *Across Time and Tundra*.

43 Lotz, *The People Outside*, 114–28.

44 Lotz, *Northern Realities*, 87.

45 Zaslow, "Recent Constitutional Developments in the North," 167–80.

46 Lotz, *Northern Realities*, 93.

47 Dacks, *A Choice of Futures*.

48 Anthony Alexander, "On Provincehood," *Whitehorse Star*, 7 February 1976.

49 Page, *Northern Development*.

50 Lysyk, Bohmer, and Phelps, *Alaska Highway Pipeline Inquiry*.

51 His autobiography, *The House Is Not a Home*, gives full evidence of his rebarbative personality.

CHAPTER TEN

1 These figures are taken from the Yukon Government, Executive Council Office, Bureau of Statistics, *Yukon Annual Statistical Review 2001*.

2 http://yukonparty.com/platform.html (accessed June 2003)

3 Murray Lundberg, "Killing a Northern Town," http://www.explorenorth.com/library/weekly/aa031200a.htm (accessed June 2003).

BIBLIOGRAPHY

PRIMARY SOURCES

Anglican Church of Canada, General Synod Archives (ACCC)
Edmonton Municipal Archives (EMA)
Hudson's Bay Company Archives (HBCA)
National Archives of Canada (NA)
Provincial Archives of Manitoba (PAM)
United States National Archives (USNA)
Yukon Archives (YA)

SECONDARY SOURCES

Alunik, Ishmael, et al. *Across Time and Tundra: The Inuvialuit of the Western Arctic*. Vancouver: Raincoast Books, 2003
Amundsen, Roald. *The North West Passage*. London: Constable, 1908
Archer, A.S. *A Heroine of the North: Memoirs of Charlotte Selina Bompas*. London: Macmillan, 1929
Armstrong, Nevill A.D. *After Big Game in the Upper Yukon*. London: John Long, 1937
Arndt, Katherine Louise. "Dynamics of the Fur Trade on the Middle Yukon River, Alaska, 1839 to 1868." PHD dissertation, University of Alaska Fairbanks, 1996.
Auer, H.A. *Camp Fires in the Yukon*. Cincinatti: Stewart and Kidd, 1916
Backhouse, Frances. *Women of the Klondike*. Vancouver: Whitecap, 1995.
Baker, D.C., and W.R. Morrison. "The Development of Property Rights on the Canadian and American Mining Frontiers." *American Review of Canadian Studies* 29, no. 3 (1999)

Barr, William. *From Barrow to Boothia: The Arctic Journal of Chief Factor Peter Warren Dease, 1836–1839*. Montreal: McGill-Queen's University Press, 2002

Batelle Memorial Institute. *An Integrated Transport System to Encourage Economic Development of Northwest America*. Columbus, Ohio: BMI, 1937

Bennett, Gordon. *Yukon Transportation: A History*. Canadian Historic Sites: Occasional Papers in Archaeology and History, no. 19. Ottawa: National Historic Parks, 1978

Berger, Carl. "The True North Strong and Free." In *Nationalism in Canada*, ed. Peter Russell. Toronto: McGraw-Hill, 1966

Berger, Thomas. *Northern Frontier/Northern Homeland*. Report of the Mackenzie Valley Pipeline Inquiry. Vol. 1. Ottawa: Department of Supply and Services, 1977

Berton, Laura. *I Married the Klondike*. Toronto: Little, Brown, 1954

Berton, Pierre. *Klondike: The Last Great Gold Rush*. Toronto: McClelland and Stewart, 1972

– *Starting Out, 1920–1947*. Toronto: McClelland and Stewart, 1987

Black, Martha. *My Ninety Years*. Anchorage: Alaska Northwest Publishing, 1976

– *My Seventy Years*. London: Thomas Nelson, 1938

Bockstoce, John R. *Steam Whaling in the Western Arctic*. New Bedford, Mass.: Old Dartmouth Historical Society, 1977

Bodfish, H.H. *Chasing the Bowhead*. Cambridge, Mass.: Harvard University Press, 1936

Boon, T.C.B. *The Anglican Church from the Bay to the Rockies*. Toronto: Ryerson Press, 1962

Booth, Michael R. "Gold Rush Theatres of the Klondike." *Beaver*, Spring 1962

Bostock, H.S. "Prospecting on Russell Creek." *North*, Nov./Dec. 1970

Brody, Hugh. *The Living Arctic*. Vancouver: Douglas & McIntyre, 1987

Brown, J.N.E. "The Evolution of Law and Government in the Yukon Territory." In *Municipal Government in Canada*, ed. S.M. Wickett. Toronto: University of Toronto Press, 1907

Bruemmer, Fred. "Herschel, the Big Town." *Beaver*, Winter 1980.

Buchanan, A. Russell. *Black Americans in World War II*. New York: Oxford University Press, 1977

Burley, David V., and Michael H. Will. "The Beer That Made Klondike Famous and Milwaukee Jealous: The O'Brien Brewing and Malting Company Site, Klondike City, Yukon." *Journal of the Society for Industrial Archeology* 26, no. 1 (2000)

Burns, Jane. "Abandoned Buildings, Living Communities: Local Resistance to Preservation in Dawson City, Yukon." *Ethnologies* 21, no. 1 (1999)

Cameron, Kirk, and Graham White. *Northern Governments in Transition: Political and Constitutional Development in the Yukon, Nunavut, and the Western Northwest Territories*. Montreal: Institute for Research on Public Policy, 1995

Campbell, Robert. *Two Journals of Robert Campbell, 1808 to 1853*. Seattle: John W. Todd, Jr, 1951

Campbell, Walter. "The Search for Oil in the Yukon Territory." *Canadian Geographical Journal*, October 1961

Chaput, Don. "Striking it Rich." *American History* 33, no. 1 (1998)

Clark, S.D. "The Gold Rush Society of British Columbia and the Yukon." In *The Developing Canadian Community*. Toronto: University of Toronto Press, 1970

Classen, H.G. *Thrust and Counterthrust: The Genesis of the Canadian–United Statres Boundery*. Toronto: Longmans, 1965

Coates, K.S. "Asking for All Sorts of Favours: The Anglican Church, the Federal Government and the Natives of the Yukon Territory, 1891–1909." In *The Anglican Church and the World of Western Canada 1820–1970*. Proceedings of the conference The Role of the Anglican Church in Western Canadian History, February 1987

– "Best Left as Indians: Indian-White Relations in the Yukon Territory, 1840–1950." PHD thesis, University of British Columbia, 1984

– "Best Left as Indians: The Federal Government and the Indians of the Yukon Territory, 1894–1950." *Out of the Background: Readings in Native History*, ed. Robin Fisher and K.S. Coates. Toronto: Copp Clark Pitman, 1988

– *Best Left as Indians: Native-White Relations in the Yukon Territory, 1840–1973*. Montreal: McGill-Queen's University Press, 1991

– "Betwixt and Between: The Anglican Church and the Children of Carcross (Choutla) Residential School, 1911–1955." *BC Studies* 62 (Winter 1984–85): 27–47

– *Canada's Colonies: A History of the Yukon and Northwest Territories*. Toronto: James Lorimer, 1985

– "Furs along the Yukon: Hudson's Bay Company–Native Trade in the Yukon River Basin, 1830–1893." MA thesis, University of Manitoba, 1979

– "Furs along the Yukon: Hudson's Bay Company–Native Trade in the Yukon River Basin, 1840–1893." *BC Studies* 55 (Autumn 1982): 50–78

– "The Kennicott Network: Robert Kennicott and the Far Northwest." Yukon Museums and Historical Association *Proceedings, 1982* (1983)

– *The Northern Yukon: A History*. Manuscript Report Series 403. Winnipeg: Parks Canada, 1979

– "On the Outside in Their Homeland: Native People and the Evolution of the Yukon Economy." *Northern Review*, Summer 1988

- "Protecting the Monopoly: The Hudson's Bay Company and Contemporary Knowledge of the Far Northwest, 1830–1893." Yukon Museums and Historical Association, *Proceedings of the Fall Meeting, 1983*, no. 2 (1984)
- "Protecting the Monopoly: The Hudson's Bay Company and Scientific Knowledge of the Yukon Valley." Yukon Museums and Historical Association *Proceedings, 1982* (1983)
- "Send Only Those Who Rise a Peg: The Recruitment and Use of Anglican Missionaries in the Yukon, 1858–1932." *Journal of the Canadian Church Historical Society*, Summer 1986, 3–18
- "Upsetting the Rhythms: The Federal Government and Native Communities in Yukon Territory, 1945 to 1973." In *Northern Communities: The Prospects for Empowerment*, ed. Gurston Dacks and K.S. Coates. Edmonton: Boreal Institute, 1988
- "A Very Imperfect Means of Education: Indian Day Schools in the Yukon Territory, 1890–1955." In *Indian Education in Canada*, Vol. I: *The Legacy*, ed. by Jean Barman, Y. Hebert, and D. McCaskill. Vancouver: University of British Columbia Press, 1986
Coates, K.S., ed. *The Alaska Highway: Papers of the Fortieth Anniversary Symposium*. Vancouver: University of British Columbia Press, 1985
Coates, K.S., and W.R. Morrison. "The Alaska Highway: Defending the Far North-West." *Journal of the West*, October 1993
- *The Alaska Highway in World War II: The U.S. Army of Occupation in Canada's Northwest*, Norman, Okla.: University of Oklahoma Press, 1992
- "The American Rampant: Reflections on the Impact of the U.S. Armed Forces Overseas during World War II." *Journal of World History* 2, no. 2 (1991)
- "Controlling the Army of Occupation: Legal Processes and the Northwest Defence Projects, 1942–1946." In *Law for the Elephant, Law for the Beaver: Essays in the Legal History of the North American West*. Regina: Canadian Plains Research Centre, 1992
- "A Drunken Impulse: Aboriginal Justice Confronts Canadian Law." *Western Historical Quarterly* 27, no. 4 (1996)
- "The Federal Government and Urban Development in the North after World War II: Whitehorse and Dawson City, Yukon Territory." *BC Studies*, Winter 1994–95
- "Native People and the Alaska Highway." In *Consuming Canada: Readings in Environmental History*, ed. Chad and Pam Gaffield. Toronto: Copp Clark, 1995
- "Northern Visions: Recent Writing in Northern Canadian History." *Manitoba History*, (Fall 1985)
- *The Sinking of the* Princess Sophia: *Taking the North Down with Her.* Toronto: Oxford University Press, 1990

– "So Far from Power: The Politics of the Yukon Territory." In *The Provincial State: Politics in Canada's Provinces and Territories*, ed. K. Brownsey and M. Howlet, Toronto: Copp Clark Pitman, 1992

– "Soldier-Workers: The U.S. Army Corps of Engineers and the Northwest Defence Projects, 1942–1946." *Pacific Historical Review*, Fall 1993

– *Strange Things Done: Murder in Yukon History*. Montreal: McGill-Queen's University Press, 2004

– "'To Make These Tribes Understand': The Trial of Alikomiak and Tatamigana." *Arctic* 51, no. 3 (Sept. 1998)

– "Towards a Methodology of Disasters: the Case of the *Princess Sophia*." In *Digging into Popular Culture: Theories and Methodologies in Archaeology, Anthropology and Other Fields*, ed. Ray Browne et al. Bowling Green, Ohio: Popular Press, 1991

– "Transiency in the Far Northwest: The Passengers of the *Princess Sophia*." In *Interpreting the North: Selected Readings*, ed. K.S. Coates and W.R. Morrison. Toronto: Copp Clark, 1989

– "War Comes to the Yukon." *Beaver*, Oct./Nov. 1989.

– "Wartime Boom Town: Fort St John during World War II." *Journal of the West*, October, 1997

– *Working the North: Labor and the Northwest Defense Projects, 1942–1945*. Fairbanks: University of Alaska Press, 1994

– "Writing the North: An Analysis of Contemporary Writing on Northern Regions." *Essays on Canadian Writing* 59 (Fall 1996)

– "The Yukon at War." *Beaver* 69, no. 5 (1989)

Coates, K.S., and Judith Powell. *The Modern North: People, Politics, and the Rejection of Colonialism*. Toronto: James Lorimer, 1989

– "Whitehorse and the Building of the Alaska Highway, 1942-1946." *Alaska History* 4, no. 1 (1989)

Coates, K.S., D. McCrady, and W.R. Morrison. "Integration and Reintegration in the Yukon River Basin: The History of the Yukon/Alaska Boundary." *Locus* 5, no. 1 (Fall 1992)

Cody, H.A. *An Apostle of the North: Memoirs of the Right Reverend William Carpenter Bompas, DD*. New York: E.P. Dutton, 1908. New edn, Edmonton: University of Alberta Press, 2003

Cohen, S.J. *Mackenzie Basin Impact Study Final Report: Summary of Results*. Ottawa: Environment Canada, 1997

Cohn, Steven Mitchell. "Competing Claims, Uncertain Sovereignties: Resource Conflict and Evolving Tripartite Federalism in Yukon Territory, Canada." PHD dissertation, University of California, Berkeley, 2001

Colson, E. *Tradition and Contract: The Problem of Order*. Chicago: Aldine Publishing, 1974

Cooke, Alan, and Clive Holland. *The Exploration of Northern Canada, 500 to 1920: A Chronology*. Toronto: Arctic History Press, 1978

Coutts, R. *Yukon Places and Names*. Sidney, BC: Gray's Publishing, 1980

Creighton, Donald. *The Forked Road: Canada, 1939–1957*. Toronto: McClelland and Stewart, 1976

Cruikshank, Julie. "Images of Society in Klondike Gold Rush Narratives: Skookum Jim and the Discovery of Gold." *Ethnohistory* 39, no. 1 (1992)

– *Life Lived Like a Story: Life Stories of Three Yukon Native Elders*. Vancouver: University of British Columbia Press, 1990

– *The Social Life of Stories: Narrative and Knowledge in the Yukon Territory*. Lincoln: University of Nebraska Press, 1998

Dacks, Gurston. *A Choice of Futures*. Toronto: Methuen, 1981

– ed. *Devolution and Constitutional Development in the Canadian North*. Ottawa: Carleton University Press, 1990

Dacks, Gurston, and K.S. Coates, eds. *Northern Communities: The Prospects for Empowerment*. Edmonton: Boreal Institute, 1988

Dall, William. *Alaska and Its Resources*. Boston: Lee and Chepard, 1870

Dawson, G.M. *Report on an Exploration in the Yukon District, N.W.T., and Adjacent Northern Portion of British Columbia, 1887*. Ottawa: King's Printer, 1888

Debicki, R.L. *Yukon Mineral Industry, 1941 to 1959*. Ottawa: Department of Indian and Northern Affairs, 1982

Disher, A.L. "The Long March of the Yukon Field Force." *Beaver*, Autumn 1962

Diubaldo, R.J. "The Canol Project in Canadian-American Relations." Canadian Historical Association, *Historical Papers, 1977*

– *Stefansson and the Canadian Arctic*. Montreal: McGill-Queen's University Press, 1978

– "Wrangling over Wrangel Island." *Canadian Historical Review* 68, no. 3 (1967)

Dobrowolsky, Helene, and Rob Ingram. *Edge of the River, Heart of the City: A History of the Whitehorse Waterfront*. Whitehorse: Lost Moose, 1994

Ducker, James H. "Gold Rushers North: A Census Study of the Yukon and Alaskan Gold Rushes, 1896–1900. *Pacific Northwest Quarterly* 85, no. 3 (1994)

Duerden, Frank. *The Development and Structure of the Settlement System in the Yukon*. Whitehorse: Government of Yukon, 1981

– *Teslin: The Indian Village and Community Economy*. Toronto: Ryerson, 1989

Duncan, Allen. *Medicine, Madams, and Mounties: Stories of a Yukon Doctor, 1933–1947*. Vancouver: Raincoast Books, 1989

Fagan, Brian M. *The Great Journey: The Peopling of Ancient America*. New York: Thames and Hudson, 1987

Fisher, Robin. *Duff Pattullo of British Columbia*. Toronto: University of Toronto Press, 1991

– "T.D. Pattullo and the North: The Significance of the Periphery in British Columbia Politics." *Pacific Northwest Quarterly* 81, no. 3 (1990)

Francis, Daniel. *Arctic Chase*. St John's: Breakwater Books, 1984

– *The Discovery of the North*. Edmonton: Hurtig, 1986

Franks, C.E.S. "How the Sabbath Came to the Yukon." *Canadian Public Administration* 10 (March 1967)

Friesen, Richard J. *The Chilkoot Pass: A History of the Great Gold Rush of 1898*. Manuscript Report no. 276. Ottawa: Parks Canada, 1978

Gartrell, G.E. "The Work of the Churches in the Yukon during the Era of the Klondike Gold Rush." MA thesis, University of Western Ontario, 1970

Gates, Michael. *Gold at Fortymile Creek: Early Days in the Yukon*. Vancouver: University of British Columbia Press, 1994

Geller, Peter. "Northern Exposures: Photographic and Filmic Representations of the Canadian North, 1920–1945." PHD dissertation, Carleton University, 1995

– "Visions of a Northern Nation: Richard Finnie's Views of Natives and Development in Canada's 'Last Frontier.'" *Film History* (Australia), 8, no. 1 (1996)

Goodrich, H.B. "History and Conditions of the Yukon Gold District to 1897." In *Geology of the Yukon Gold District, Alaska: Eighteenth Annual Report of the United States Geological Survey to the Secretary of the Interior, 1896–7*. Part 3, ed. J.E. Spurr. Washington, DC: Government Printing Office, 1898

Grant, Shelagh. *Sovereignty or Security? Government Policy in the Canadian North, 1936–1950*. Vancouver: University of British Columbia Press, 1988

Green, Lewis. *The Boundary Hunters*. Vancouver: University of British Columbia Press, 1982

– *The Gold Hustlers*. Vancouver: J.J. Douglas, 1972

Greenhous, Brereton. *Guarding the Goldfields*. Toronto: Dundurn Press, 1987

Griffen, Jane. *Cashing In*. Whitehorse: Word Pro, 1980

Guest, H. *A History of Dawson City, Yukon Territory, 1896–1920*, Microfiche Report Series, no. 7. Ottawa: Parks Canada, 1983

– *A Socioeconomic History of the Klondike Gold Fields, 1896–1966*. Microfiche Report Series, no. 181. Ottawa: Parks Canada, 1985

Hall, David. *Clifford Sifton*. 2 vols. Vancouver: University of British Columbia Press, 1982 and 1985

Hamelin, L.-E. *Canadian Nordicity: It's Your North Too*. Trans. by W. Barr. Montreal: Harvest House, 1978

Hammond, Lorne. "Any Ordinary Degree of System: The Columbia Department and the Harvesting of Wildlife, 1825–1849." MA thesis, University of Victoria, 1988

Haycox, Stephen. "Fenced In: Cross-border Perspectives in Alaska History." *Columbia* 12, no. 3 (1998)

Hayne, M.H.E., and H.W. Taylor, *The Pioneers of the Klondyke*. London: Sampson Low, Marston, 1897

Heine, Michael K., and Kevin B. Wamsley. "'Kickfest at Dawson City': Native Peoples and the Sports of the Klondike Gold Rush." *Sports History Review* 27, no. 1 (1996)

Helm, June, ed. *Handbook of North American Indians*, Vol. 6: *Subarctic*. Washington: Smithsonian Institution, 1981

Hendry, Charles. *Beyond Traplines*. Toronto: Ryerson Press, 1969

Honigmann, John. *The Kaska Indians*. New Haven: Yale University Press, 1954; and Whitehorse: Yukon Native Brotherhood, 1973

Hunt, William R. *Distant Justice: Policing the Alaska Frontier*. Norman: University of Oklahoma Press, 1987

– *North of '53: The Wild Days of the Alaska-Yukon Mining Frontier, 1870–1914*. New York: Macmillan, 1974

– *The Opening of the Canadian North, 1870–1914*. Toronto: McClelland and Stewart, 1971

– *Stef: A Biography of Vilhjalmur Stefansson, Canadian Arctic Explorer*. Vancouver: University of British Columbia Press, 1986

Innis, H.A. *Mining Settlement and Mining Frontier*. Toronto: Macmillan, 1936

James, James G. *The First Scientific Exploration of Alaska, and the Purchase of Alaska*. Evanston: Northwestern University Press, 1942

Jenness, Diamond. *Eskimo Administration II: Canada*. Montreal: Arctic Institute of North America, 1964

Johnson, Stephen. "Baron Wrangel and the Russian-American Company." PHD thesis, University of Manitoba, 1978

Karamanski, Theodore. *Fur Trade and Exploration: Opening the Far Northwest, 1821–1852*. Vancouver: University of British Columbia Press, 1983

Karp, Lawrence E. "The Writing of Dan McGrew." *North*, Sep./Oct. 1974

Kehoe, Alice. *North American Indians: A Comprehensive Account*. Englewood Cliffs: Prentice-Hall, 1981

Kelcey, Barbara. *Alone in Silence: European Women in the Canadian North before 1940*. Montreal: McGill-Queen's University Press, 2001

– "What to Wear to the Klondike: Outfitting Women for the Gold Rush." *Material History Review* 37 (1993)

Kirkby, W.W. "A Journey to the Youcon, Russian America. "*Annual Report, 1864*, 416–20. Washington, DC: Smithsonian Institution, 1865

Koroscil, Paul. "The Historical Development of Whitehorse." *American Review of Canadian Studies* 18, no. 3 (1988)

Krech, Shepherd, III. "The Eastern Kutchin and the Fur Trade, 1800–1860," *Ethnohistory* 23 (Summer 1976): 213–35
– "On the Aboriginal Population of the Kutchin," *Arctic Anthropology* 15 (1978): 89–104
– "Throwing Bad Medicine: Sorcery, Disease, and the Fur Trade among the Kutchin and Other Northern Athapaskans." In *Indians, Animals, and the Fur Trade*, ed. Krech. Athens: University of Georgia, 1982
Larsen, Henry. *The Big Ship*. Toronto: McClelland and Stewart, 1967
Lasserre, Pierre, "L'aide aux mines d'or ou les silences du fantôme de Bretton Woods." *Canadian Public Policy* 9, no. 4 (1983): 446–57
Lee, Ulysses. *The United States Army in World War II: The Employment of Negro Troops*. Washington, DC, 1966
Livermore, Carol. "Percy DeWolfe: Iron Man of the Yukon." *Beaver*, Autumn 1977
Lotz, Jim. *Northern Realities: The Future of Northern Development in Canada*. Toronto: New Press, 1972
– *The People Outside: Studies of Squatters, Shack Town, and Shanty Residents and Other Dwellings on the Fringe of Canada*. Ottawa: Saint Paul University, 1971
Lysyk, Kenneth, E . Bohmer, and W. Phelps, *Alaska Highway Pipeline Inquiry*. Ottawa: Supply and Services, 1977
McCandless, Robert. *Yukon Wildlife: A Social History*. Edmonton: University of Alberta Press, 1985
McClellan, Catherine. *My Old People Say: An Ethnographic Survey of Southern Yukon Territory*. Ottawa: National Museums of Canada, 1975
– *Part of the Land, Part of the Water: A History of the Yukon Indians*. Vancouver: Douglas & McIntyre, 1987.
McConnell, R.G. "Report of an Exploration in the Yukon and Mackenzie Basins, N.W.T." *Canadian Geological Survey Annual Report, 1888–1889*. Ottawa: King's Printer, 1890
McCullum, Hugh, and Karmel McCullum. *This Land Is Not for Sale*. Toronto: Anglican Book Centre, 1975
MacDonald, Cheryl. "From Founding to Frontier: The VON in the Klondike." *Beaver* 77, no. 5 (1997)
MacDonald, Norbert. "Seattle, Vancouver, and the Klondike." *Canadian Historical Review* 49, no. 3 (Sept. 1968)
McGhee, Robert. *Ancient People of the Arctic*. Vancouver: University of British Columbia Press, 1996
McGrath, Roger D. *Gunfighters, Highwaymen, and Vigilantes: Violence on the Frontier*. Berkeley: University of Calfornia Press, 1984
MacGregor, J.G. *The Klondike Rush through Edmonton, 1897–1898*. Toronto: McClelland and Stewart, 1970

Mackenzie, Alexander. *Voyages from Montreal, on the River St. Lawrence, through the Continent of North America to the Frozen and Pacific Ocean in the Years 1789 and 1793*. London: Noble, 1801

MacPherson, Janet. "The Cypress-Anvil Mine." In *Northern Transitions*, vol. 1, ed. E. Peterson and Janet Wright. Ottawa: Canadian Arctic Resources Committee, 1978

McQuesten, L.N. *Recollections of Leroy N. McQuesten*. Whitehorse: Yukon Archives, Coutts Collection, Pamphlets 1952–53

Malcolm, Andrew H. *The Canadians*. Toronto: Fitzhenry & Whiteside, 1985

Marchand, J.F. "Tribal Epidemics in Yukon." *Journal of the American Medical Association*, 123 (1943)

Martindale, Thomas. *Huntng in the Upper Yukon*. Philadelphia: George W. Jacobs, 1913

Mayer, Melanie. *Klondike Women: True Tales of the 1897–98 Gold Rush*. Akron: Ohio University Press, 1989

Metayer, Maurice, trans. *I, Nuligak*. New York: Pocket Books, 1971

Millman, Thomas R. "Bishop Henry Marsh and His Forebears." *Journal of the Canadian Church Historical Society* 38, no. 2 (1996)

Minter, Roy. *The White Pass: Gateway to the Klondike*. Toronto: McClelland and Stewart, 1987

Mishler, Craig. "Missionaries in Collision: Anglicans and Oblates among the Gwich'in, 1861–65." *Arctic* 43, no. 2 (1993)

Morgan, Lael. *Good Time Girls of the Alaska-Yukon Gold Rush*. Fairbanks: Epicenter, 1998

Morrison, David. *The Politics of the Yukon Territory, 1898–1906*. Toronto: University of Toronto Press, 1968

Morrison, William R. "Eagle over the Arctic: Americans in the Canadian North, 1867–1985." In *Interpreting the North: Selected Readings*, ed. K.S. Coates and W.R. Morrison. Toronto: Copp Clark, 1989

– "Imposing the British Way: The Mounted Police and the Klondike Gold Rush." In *Policing the Empire: Government, Authority and Control, 1830–1940*, ed. D. Killingray. Manchester: University of Manchester Press, 1991

– "Policing the Boom Town: The Mounted Police as a Social Force on the Gold Rush Frontier, 1895–1905." *Northern Review*, Winter 1990

– *Showing the Flag: The Mounted Police and Canadian Sovereignty in the North, 1894–1925*. Vancouver: University of British Columbia Press, 1985

– *A Survey of the History and Claims of the Native Peoples of Northern Canada*. Ottawa: Treaties and Historical Research Centre, Department of Indian and Northern Affairs, 1984

– *True North: The Yukon and Northwest Territories*. Toronto: Oxford University Press, 1998

Morritt, Hope. *Land of the Fireweed: A Young Woman's Story of the Alaska Highway Construction Days.* Anchorage: Alaska Northwest Publishing, 1985

Morton, W.L. "The North in Canadian History." In *Contexts of Canada's Past,* ed. A.B. McKillop. Ottawa: Carleton University Press, 1980

Moyles, R.G. *British Law and Arctic Men.* Saskatoon: Western Producer Prairie Books, 1979

Murray, Alexander Hunter. *Journal of the Yukon 1847–1848,* ed. L.J. Burpee. Publications of the Canadian Archives no. 4. Ottawa: Government Printing Bureau, 1916

Murray, Jeffrey S. "Mapping Klondike Gold: More Than Fools' Gold Fooled Klondike Prospectors." *Rotunda* 22, no. 2 (1989)

Nadasdy, Paul Eric. "Hunters and Bureaucrats: Power, Knowledge, and the Restructuring of Aboriginal-State Relations in the Southwest Yukon, Canada." PHD dissertation, Johns Hopkins University, 2001

Neufeld, David. "Commemorating the Cold War in Canada: Considering the DEW Line." *Public Historian* 20, no. 1(1998)

– "Revolution and Residential Schools in the Yukon: Meeting on a Mennonite-Han Frontier in Yukon." *Journal of Mennonite Studies* 19 (2001)

Neufeld, David, and Frank Norris. *Chilkoot Trail: Heritage Route to the Klondike.* Whitehorse: Lost Moose, 1996

Newman, Peter C. *Caesars of the Wilderness.* Toronto: Penguin, 1987

Nielsen, Erik. *The House Is Not a Home.* Toronto: Macmillan, 1989

Norris, Frank. "Skagway, the White Pass Railroad, and the Struggle to Build the Klondike Highway." *Alaska History* 15, no. 1 (2000)

North, Dick. *The Lost Patrol.* Anchorage, Alaska: Northwest Publishing, 1978

North-West Mounted Police. *Report of the North-West Mounted Police.* Annual reports. Ottawa: King's Printer, 1894–98

Ogilvie, William. *Early Days on the Yukon and the Story of Its Gold Finds.* Ottawa: Thorburn and Abbott, 1913

Osgood, C. *The Han Indians.* New Haven: Yale University Press, 1954

– *Contributions to the Ethnography of the Kutchin.* New Haven: Yale University Press, 1970

Ostenstat, William. "The Impact of the Fur Trade on the Tlingit during the Late Eighteenth and Nineteenth Centuries." MA thesis, University of Manitoba, 1976

Ostrogorsky, Michael. "Women Were Everywhere: Female Stampeders to the Klondike and Alaska." *Columbia* 8, no. 1 (1994)

Page, Robert. *Northern Development: The Canadian Dilemma.* Toronto: McClelland and Stewart, 1986

Peake, F.A. *The Bishop Who Ate His Boots: A Biography of Isaac O. Stringer.* Don Mills: Anglican Church of Canada, 1966

– "Fur Traders and Missionaries: Some Reflections on Attitudes of the
H.B.C. towards Missionary Work among the Indians." *Western Canadi-
an Journal of Anthropology* 3, no. 1 (1977): 77–93
– "Robert McDonald (1829–1913): The Great Unknown Missionary of
the Northwest." *Journal of the Canadian Church Historical Society* 17,
no. 3 (1975): 54–72
Peterson, E., and Janet Wright, *Northern Transitions*. Vol. 1. Ottawa:
Canadian Arctic Resources Committee, 1978
Pierce, W.H. *Thirteen Years of Travel and Exploration in Alaska,
1877–1889*. Anchorage: Alaska Northwest Publishing, 1977
Porsild, Charlene. "Culture, Class, and Community: New Perspectives
on the Klondike Gold Rush, 1895–1905." PHD dissertation: Carleton
University, 1994
– *Gamblers and Dreamers: Women, Men, and Community in the
Klondike*. Vancouver: University of British Columbia Press, 1998
– "Klondike Family Life." *BC Studies* 123 (1999)
– "Mining the Rush: Recent Publications Relating to the Klondike Gold
Rush." *BC Studies* 128 (2000–1)
Rea, Kenneth J. *The Political Economy of Northern Development*. Science
Council of Canada Background Study no. 36. Ottawa: Science Council
of Canada, 1976
– *The Political Economy of the Canadian North*. Toronto: University
of Toronto Press, 1968
Remley, David. *The Crooked Road: The Story of the Alaska Highway*.
Toronto: McGraw-Hill, 1976
Riggs, Thomas. "Running the Alaska Boundary." *Beaver*, Sept. 1945
Robertson, Gordon. *Northern Provinces: A Mistaken Goal?* Ottawa:
Institute of Public Policy Research, 1986
Rodney, William. *Joe Boyle: King of the Klondike*. Toronto: McGraw-Hill
Ryerson, 1974
Ross River Indian Band. *So That the Future Will Be Ours*. Ross River:
Ross River Indian Band, 1984
Royal North-West Mounted Police Report, 1908. Ottawa: King's Printer,
1909
Rutherdale, Myra. "New Approaches to the Klondike Gold Rush: A
Review Essay." *BC Studies* 121 (1999)
– "Revisiting Colonization through Gender: Anglican Missionary Women
in the Pacific Northwest and the Arctic, 1860-1945." *BC Studies* 104
(1994–95)
Ryley, Bay. *Gold Diggers of the Klondike: Prostitution in Dawson City,
Yukon*. Winnipeg: Shillingford, 1997
Saku, James C., et al. "Towards and Institutional Understanding of Com-
prehensive Land Claims Agreements in Canada." *Etudes/Inuit/Studies*
22, no. 1 (1998)

Sealey, G. "The History of the Hudson's Bay Company, 1870–1910."
    MA thesis, University of Western Ontario, 1967
Simpson, Alexander. *The Life and Travels of Thomas Simpson, the Arctic
    Discoverer.* London: Richard Bentley, 1845
Simpson, Thomas. *Narrative of the Discoveries on the North Coast of
    America.* London: Richard Bentley, 1843
Smyth, Steven. "Colonialism and Language in Canada's North: A Yukon
    Case Study." *Arctic* 49, no. 2 (1996)
– "The Constitutional Context of Aboriginal and Colonial Government in the
    Yukon Territory." *Polar Record* 29 (1993)
– "The Constitutional Status of Yukon Territory." *Polar Record* 26 (1990)
– "The Quest for Provincial Status in Yukon Territory." *Polar Record* 28 (1992)
Stanford Research Institute. *Improvement Program for the Alaska Highway:
    An Analysis of Economic Benefits.* Ottawa: Queen's Printer, 1966
Steele, S.B. *Forty Years in Canada.* London: Jenkins, 1915
Stewart, R. *Sam Steele: Lion of the Frontier.* Toronto: Doubleday, 1979
Stone, Thomas. "Atomistic Order and Frontier Violence: Miners and
    Whalemen in the Nineteenth Century Yukon." *Ethnology* 22 (Oct. 1983)
– "Flux and Authority in a Subarctic Society: The Yukon Miners in the
    Nineteenth Century." *Ethnohistory* 30, no. 4 (1983)
– *Miners' Justice: Migration, Law and Order on the Alaska-Yukon Frontier,
    1873–1892.* New York: Peter Lang, 1989
– "The Mounties as Vigilantes: Perceptions of Community and the Transfor-
    mation of Law in the Yukon, 1885–1897." *Law and Society Review* 14,
    no. 1 (Fall 1979)
– Whalers and Missionaries at Herschel Island." *Ethnohistory* 28 (Spring 1981)
Stuart, Richard. "Duff Pattullo and the Yukon Schools Question of 1937
    Canadian Historical Review 64, no. 1 (1983): 25–44
– "The Impact of the Alaska Highway on Dawson City." In *The Alaska
    Highway: Papers of the Fortieth Anniversary Symposium,* ed. K.S. Coates.
    Vancouver: University of British Columbia Press, 1985
Stuart, R., and J. Gould. *Permafrost Gold: A Treatise on Early Klondike
    Mining: History, Methods, and Technology.* Microfiche. Ottawa: Parks
    Canada, 1983
Stuck, Hudson. *Voyages on the Yukon and Its Tributaries.* New York:
    Scribner's Sons, 1917
Swanson, Cecil. *The Days of My Sojourning.* Calgary: Glenbow-Alberta
    Institute, 1979
Tanner, Adrian. "The Structure of Fur Trade Relations." MA thesis,
    University of British Columbia, 1965
– "The Structure of the Fur Trade." PHD thesis, University of British
    Columbia, 1966
– *Trappers, Hunters and Fishermen.* Ottawa: Department of Northern Affairs
    and Natural Resources, 1966

Taylor, Leonard. *The Sourdough and the Queen.* Toronto: Methuen, 1983

Thomas, Lewis. *The Struggle for Responsible Government in the Northwest Territories, 1870–97.* 2nd edn. Toronto: University of Toronto Press, 1970

Tueli, Nick. "Studied Naivete: The Art of Ted Harrison." *Northern Review* 1, no. 1 (1988)

Turner, J.H. "The Boundary North of Fort Yukon. " Part 2 of "The Alaska Boundary Survey." *National Geographic* 4 (Feb. 1893)

United States. *Compilation of Narratives of Explorations in Alaska.* Washington: Government Printing Office, 1900

Usher, Peter J. "Canadian Western Arctic: A Century of Change." *Anthropologica* 13, no. 1–2 (1971): 169–83

– *Fur Trade Posts of the Northwest Territories 1870–1970.* Ottawa: Department of Indian Affairs and Northern Development, 1971

Van Stone, James. *Athapaskan Adaptations: Hunters and Fishermen of the Subarctic Forests.* Chicago: Aldine, 1975

Webb, Melody. *The Last Frontier: A History of the Yukon Basin of Canada and Alaska.* Albuquerque: University of New Mexico Press, 1985

Wesbrook, M. "A Venture into Ethnohistory: The journals of V.C. Sim." *Polar Notes* 9 (1969)

Whymper, Frederick. *Travel and Adventure in the Territory of Alaska.* Ann Arbor: University Microfilms, 1966

Williams, David R. "The Invasion of the Yukon." *Beaver* 78, no. 3 (1998)

Wilson, Clifford. *Campbell of the Yukon.* Toronto: Macmillan, 1970

Wright, A.A. *Prelude to Bonanza: The Discovery and Exploration of the Yukon.* Whitehorse: Arctic Star Printing, 1980

Yukon Native Brotherhood, *Together Today for Our Children Tomorrow.* Whitehorse: Yukon Native Brotherhood, 1973

Zaslow, Morris. *The Opening of the Canadian North, 1870–1914.* Toronto: McClelland and Stewart, 1971

– *Reading the Rocks: The Story of the Geological Survey of Canada, 1842–1872.* Toronto: Macmillan, 1975

–"Recent Constitutional Developments in the North." *Canadian Public Administration* 10 (June 1967): 167–80

– "The Yukon: Northern Development in a Canadian American Context." In *Regionalism in the Canadian Community, 1867–1967*, ed. Mason Wade. Toronto, 1969

INDEX

Aho, Aaro, 276–7

air transport, 205–7; first airmail flight, 206

Aishihik, 6, 9. *See also* Champagne and Aishihik First Nation

Aishihik dam, 277

Aitken, Thomas, 166

Aklavik, 144–5

Alaska Commercial Company, 48, 50

Alaska Highway, 9; after World War II, 266–8, 282–3; and Canadian Army, 263–4; Canadian takeover, 258–60; and environment, 246–8; first phase of construction, 230–7; impact on Yukon, 241–2; impact on White Pass and Yukon Railway, 242–3; legacy, 260–1; military-civilian relations, 245–6, 248–9, 253–5; planning for, 225–30; second phase of construction, 238–41; transferred to Public Works, 267; turnover to Canadians, 258–9, 263; wage rates, 242–4; workers' morale, 246–9. *See also* Yukon First Nations

Alaska Highway gas pipeline, 269, 297, 309–10

Alaska Railroad, 203

Alaska Steamship Company, 202

Alexander, Capt., 167, 187

Alikomiak, 144

all-Canadian rail link to Yukon, 114–15

Alsek River, 11

Alyeska pipeline, 309

American Yukon Navigation Company, 170, 203

Amundsen, Roald, 134, 141

Amur River, 37

Anderson, James, 25–7

Anderson, R.M, 141

Anglican Church. *See* missionary activity

Armstrong, Neville A.D., 102

asbestos mining, 275

Ashcroft, BC, 87

Athapaskan people. *See* Dene

Atlas Mining, 167

Atlin, BC, 117, 149–50, 187, 202

Attu, Alaska, 228

Austin, Shorty, 200

automobiles, introduced to the Yukon, 172